NEW EDITION

MY WAY WITH
FOOD

A PRACTICAL GUIDE TO COOKING

Much have I learned from my teachers,
More from my colleagues, but most
from my students – *Talmud*

To Issie, with love

NEW EDITION

MY WAY WITH FOOD

A PRACTICAL GUIDE TO COOKING

PAMELA SHIPPEL

ACKNOWLEDGEMENTS

I would like to thank Pick 'n Pay, who entrusted me with setting up and developing the Pantry Pride School of Cooking in 1982. Their constant support and encouragement, as well as the faith they have placed in me enabled the school to become the force in is in the South African food world.

To Leslie Mckenzie, who discovered our common passion for cooking, talking about it and sharing it.

Some of the recipes in this book were developed by my teaching team: Renera Colussi, Rhona van der Mewe, Michelle Adelhelm and chef Guiseppe Massolini. Their sharing, camaraderie and constructive criticism have turned the school into a stimulating environment with an atmosphere of creativity – something I hope this book will reflect. I am very grateful for their contributions, help and support.

Most of all, my thanks go to all the South Africans who share my love for good food and creative cooking. By sharing their problems, solutions, cooking hints and ideas, cooking will remain for me an ever changing, exciting adventure.

Published by Spearhead
An imprint of New Africa Books (Pty) Ltd.
99 Garfield Road
Claremont 7700
South Africa

(021) 674 4136
www.newafricabooks.co.za

Copyright © text Pamela Shippel, 2005
Copyright published work © Spearhead, 2005
Copyright photographs © New Africa Books, 2005

All rights reserved. No part of this publication may be reproduced or transmitted in any form or by any means without prior written permission from the publisher.

First edition 1994 Don Nelson Publishers
Second edition, Spearhead 2005

ISBN: 0-86486-579-1

Proofreading by Dianne McAdorey
Layout and design by Fresh Identity
Cover design by Nic Jooste, Comet Design
Photography and food styling by C&D Photography
Printing and binding by Shumani Printers

CONTENTS

FOREWORD by Phillippa Cheifitz vi

INTRODUCTION vii

SO WHAT'S NEW? 1

MEASURING 3

STARTERS AND SALADS 7

SOUPS 32

FISH 43

MEAT 60

POULTRY 85

VERSATILE MAIN COURSES 113
    Vegetarian 114
    Egg and Cheese 117
    Rice 119
    Pasta 121

VEGETABLE SIDE DISHES 130

SAVOURY SAUCES 144

DESSERTS 154

THIS AND THAT 177
    Drinks 180
    Pickles and Chutney 181
    Sweets 182
    Odds and ends 184

BAKING 187
    Questions and answers 187
    Quickmix 189
    Cakes 201
    Gateaux and other treats 210
    Biscuits 212
    Pastry – sweet and savoury 220

PROBLEM FREE YEAST BAKING 233

INDEX 246

FOREWORD

Passion is the name of the game when it comes to food. And Pamela Shippel is certainly not lacking it. But even more important is integrity. That's where Pamela scores. Pamela knows about real food, and how to cook using the best of fresh, seasonal ingredients. Not only is she creative in the kitchen, but she is a superb teacher. Her years running the popular Pick 'n Pay Cooking School earned her this reputation. She not only gives delicious recipes, but shares her practical techniques and tips to make sure that you will have the same success in your own kitchen.

My Way With Food contains all the favourites that you need for an impressive repetorire – the best wholewheat bread, perfect muffins, an excellent cheesecake. But between the familiar, are gems to discover, fabulous examples of Pamela's love of Middle Eastern Food, strengthened by her stay in Israel. In Israel she became a renowned caterer, skilfully organising functions for diplomats and special celebrations. Today she runs the tea room at Kirstenbosch Gardens with all the care and attention that she devotes to every one of her notable ventures. *My Way with Food* was a bestseller first time around, and undoubtedly this new edition will enjoy the same response.

Phillippa Cheifitz

Author, magazine editor and food writer

INTRODUCTION

Food is the very first pleasure we experience. The preparation of food is an act of love – the sharing of it with family and friends, its consumption. The main ingredients for successful cooking are enthusiasm, perseverance, a spirit of adventure and the anticipation of joy. These ingredients are essential to every recipe. It reminds me of the lady who phoned me after injuring her right hand and asked for a left-handed chicken recipe!

My philosophy on cooking is that there is no such thing as a flop ... only an unexpected end result. Some of my best creations have come about unexpectedly, not the least of them the recipe that won me the Argus Cook of the Year award in 1980! It is like wearing a negligee to the opera – you are the only one who knows it is a nightie and if you have the confidence to carry it off, you may as well be wearing an original!

A recipe is not an exercise in painting by numbers. It offers scant outlines for you to fill in the colour and tone. Use them as guides to create your own originals.

How to use this book

My experience as a teacher and answering thousands of cooking queries have helped me identify common problems experienced in cooking and baking. It has helped me discover the methods and techniques behind the mysteries in cooking and to develop a simple practical road to success. I have tried to deal with them by explaining how and why things happen, so that by understanding the cause, you can control the effect.

These explanations are at the beginning of each chapter and to get the most out of this book, it is important that you read the introduction to each chapter before using the recipes.

Quantities in cooking are very flexible, but in baking, accuracy in measuring is critical!

Remember when adding seasoning to a recipe there is an unwritten approximate sign before each ingredient. Tastes differ, so season according to your own.

Tip

If a dish needs something and you are not quite sure what it is, add a squeeze of fresh lemon juice – it is a natural flavour enhancer and means that less salt is needed.

The majority of problems are relating to baking, so I have dedicated a large portion of this book to the art of baking.

Altitude has a major effect on baking but not on cooking. I have tested all the baking recipes both at sea level in Cape Town and in Johannesburg at an altitude of 1760 metres (7 000 feet). Adjustments allowing for this are supplied.

SO WHAT'S NEW?

Judging from the many comments I have received over the years, *My Way With Food* has found its way from the kitchen to the bedside table, the coffee table and the classroom, and into the hearts of my readers. So what's new in this edition? The explosion of interest in cooking has made many exotic cuisines from around the world very popular. In addition to the traditional and essential favourites, you will find recipes from Cajun and Mexican to Chinese, Mediterranean and Middle Eastern to European. These dishes are now very easy to prepare with the availability of ingredients.

Ingredients

I have removed ingredients that are no longer available and changed the name of certain ingredients where necessary. With the worldwide cookery explosion, we now have even more exciting ingredients to cook with. There are plenty of fresh herbs available, so try to use these whenever you can. There's a simple principle for converting dry herb quantities to their fresh equivalents: multiply the dry quantity 3 or 4 times. The only exception is chopped basil; the more you use the nicer it is, so use as much as you like to taste.

Remember when using fresh herbs to add the soft-leaf herbs – parsley (the best is the flat-leafed variety), basil, coriander, mint, chives and spring onion – towards the end of the cooking time.

Use different coloured sweet peppers in place of green peppers; use a real vanilla pod in place of the essence; use wonderful Italian tinned whole, chopped and crushed tomatoes in place of whole tomatoes or tomato puree. Ingredients have become so exciting!

What's good and what's not when it comes to fats? The fact that we need to use as little fat in our cooking as possible has not changed. But when I want the flavour and luxury, I still prefer butter and extra virgin olive oil in all my cooking and baking. The vegetable oils of choice are now extra virgin olive oil and canola. Whenever I used sunflower seed oil previously, I now use olive or canola oil.

Vinegars and juices. There are such interesting vinegars available. Balsamic vinegar can be used for dressings, seasoning and cooking. Try white balsamic vinegar, rice vinegar, sherry vinegar, or one of the flavoured vinegars – and my all-time favourite, fresh lemon or lime juice.

Sausages and cured meats. There is a large choice of smoked and cured meats and sausages (some with lower fat content) to choose from. You can now use authentic chorizo sausage in all the Cajun and Creole recipes.

Thickening sauces. The addition of wheat flour, corn flour, potato flour, emulsified butter, egg yolk and simple reduction are the methods used. If you watch the cooking channel on television, you will soon realise the fashionable methods are either emulsified butter (I don't like to add all that extra fat) or reduction. Reduction is the best method, but often the sauce becomes too concentrated and you end up with too little. Usually I thicken with a little starch – either flour or corn flour. Flour is the easiest to use as it is added at the beginning of the cooking process – simply sprinkled onto the sautéed vegetables or into the remaining fat. Flour also adds colour and flavour when browned (see the introduction to the meat section). Corn flour and especially potato flour mixed with a little cold water and then added to food, gives you a more shiny sauce, using half the quantity of flour, but it must be added at the end of the cooking process, brought to the boil and then served. On reheating, the sauce will thin down again.

Equipment

Ovens. The biggest change in equipment is the downsizing of most domestic ovens to fit into the European 60 cm module. This affects temperatures, especially for baking. All the recipes in this book were tested in a large South African oven, which has the same heating element as the smaller 60 cm oven. The result is that the smaller oven will reach the desired temperature more quickly and return to that temperature more quickly after the oven door is opened and closed. If you have a 60 cm oven, the general rule is to lower the temperature by 5–10 °C. The next problem is that *every* oven (and microwave oven), even the same make and size, has its own 'personality' – varying hot spots and slightly differing temperatures. The secret is to experiment with the recipes. If your dishes and baked goodies brown before they are cooked through, lower the temperature 5–10 °C. If they dry out before they have browned, increase the temperature by 5–10 °C. Once you have reached 'perfection', write the correct temperature for your oven in the book.

Bakeware. Your choice of baking tins will greatly affect the results. Good old-fashioned tin or aluminium baking tins are still the best. Shiny stainless steel, glass, non-stick and the new silicon forms will change the texture of the crust, and you may have to increase or decrease the temperature or cooking time. The only way to achieve perfect results is to experiment and then write on the recipe what you have changed.

I hope *My Way With Food*, with its emphasis on the practical, the why and the how, will give you the confidence to find your way with food.

Pamela Shippel
Cape Town
2005

MEASURING

Two very important requirements for successful
cooking are careful measuring and timing.

- All cooking recipes in this book may be adapted to your taste. Once you have it just right, jot down on the recipe exactly what changes you have made so you can repeat your creation.
- Baking recipes should be carefully and accurately measured. Variations can be made as long as the basic proportions are not altered.
- All the recipes in this book use standard metric measures. Check your measuring equipment and make sure it is South African Bureau of Standard metric. Imported glass measuring jugs often have 1 cup measures not equal to 250 ml (see chart below).
- An accurate scale makes your measuring very easy but they are expensive. The cheap kitchen scales are generally inaccurate when weighing off small quantities.
- Measuring spoons and cups are inexpensive. The best is to have 2 sets of cups and a set of spoons, which will then have every combination possible in millilitres, cups and spoons.

For example:
  Set of cup measures
  250 ml (1 cup), 125 ml ($^1/_2$ cup), 82 ml ($^1/_3$ cup), 62 ml ($^1/_4$ cup)
  Metric measuring set (4 cups)
  250 ml, 100 ml, 50 ml, 25 ml
  Set of spoons
  15 ml (1 Tbs), 5 ml (1 tsp), 2 ml ($^1/_2$ tsp), 1 ml ($^1/_4$ tsp)

- Use a measuring jug for liquids rather than measuring cups. The best is to use a South African or metric product, where the 250 ml measure is a cup. Be careful that you use the *ml* scale and not the *rice, flour, etc.* scale on the jug.

Volumes

Note: American and British cup, pint and quart measures are not the same. Check your measuring jug!

The standard metric measures are used throughout in this book.
Do not use household cutlery and crockery for measuring, especially in baking.

Comparative Measures	British Fl.oz	ml	American Metric Fl.oz	ml	ml
Teaspoon (tsp)	no standard			5	5
Tablespoon (Tbs)	$^1/_2$	14	$^1/_2$	15	15
Cup	10	284	8	236	250
Pint	20	568	16	473	
Quart	40	1136	32	946	

1 litre = 1000 ml = 3 $^1/_2$ British cups = 4 $^1/_4$ American cups = 4 metric cups

MY WAY WITH FOOD

Using standard cup measures

1 cup	=	250 ml
3/4 cup	=	185 ml
2/3 cup	=	165 ml
1/2 cup	=	125 ml
1/3 cup	=	80 ml
1/4 cup	=	60 ml
3 Tbs	=	45 ml
2 Tbs	=	30 ml
1 Tbs	=	15 ml
1 tsp	=	5 ml
1/2 tsp	=	2 or 3 ml
1/4 tsp	=	1 ml

(1 standard tea cup = 200 ml)

Using standard metric measures

250 ml	=	1 cup		
200 ml	=	1 teacup	=	3/4 cup + 1 Tbs
100 ml	=	7 Tbs	=	1/3 cup + 1 Tbs
75 ml	=	5 Tbs	=	1/4 cup + 1 Tbs
50 ml	=	3-3 1/2 Tbs		
25 ml	=	5 tsp		
15 ml	=	1 Tbs		
5 ml	=	1 tsp		
2-3 ml	=	1/2 tsp		

Weights

1 Kg	=	1000 g	=	2,2 lb = 2 lb 3 oz
100 g	=	3 1/4 oz		
1 lb	=	16 oz	=	450 g (454 g exactly)
8 oz	=	230 g (227,2 g exactly)		
1 oz	=	30 g (28,4 g exactly)		

To convert ozs to grammes: ozs x 28   =   grammes
To convert grammes to ozs: grammes ÷ 28   =   ozs
Note: American and British weight measures are identical.

To measure from 500g butter or margarine

500 g

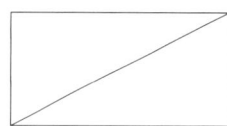
2x250 g

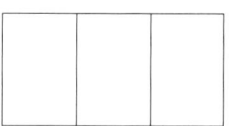
3x16 g

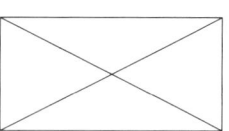
4x125 g

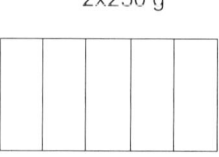
5x100 g

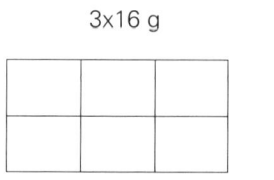
6x83 g

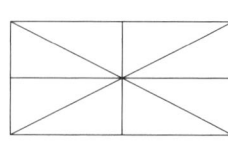
8x62 g

Length

305 mm	=	30,5 cm	=	1 foot
1 metre	=	100 cm	=	39 inches

Oven Temperatures

Deg C	Deg F	Gas	Deg C	Deg F	Gas
100	200		200	400	5
120	250	½	220	425	6
140	275	1	240	475	7-8
160	325	2	260	500	8
180	350	3			
190	375	4			

Approximate mass and volume equivalents

Note: All measurements are level and dry ingredients are measured before sifting.

	Volume in millilitres		
	5 ml (1 tsp)	15 ml (1 Tbs)	250 ml (1 cup)
Baking and desserts			
Baking Powder	4 g	12 g	
Bicarbonate of Soda	4 g	12 g	
Bran			50 g
Butter or Margarine	5 g	16 g	230 g
Cocoa	2 g	6 g	100 g
Coconut	1,5 g	5 g	80 g
Cornflour (Maizena)	3 g	9 g	150 g
Cream of Tartar	3 g	9 g	
Coffee	1,5 g	5 g	70 g
Custard Powder	3 g	9 g	150 g
Flour (all types)	3 g	9 g	150 g

(**Note:** The South African Bureau for Standards works on 120g flour = 250 ml. This is inaccurate. Accurate measure is 120g flour = 200ml

Gelatine	3 g	9 g	
Jam	6 g	18 g	330 g
Sugar: Brown, White, Yellow	4 g	12 g	200 g
Icing	3 g	10 g	160 g
Castor	4 g	12 g	210 g
Yeast (dried)	4 g	12 g	
Cheese			
Cheddar and Sweetmilk		6 g	100 g
Cottage and Cream		15 g	250 g
Gruyere and Roquefort		6 g	120 g
Parmesan	3 g	8 g	120 g

Approximate mass and volume equivalents

	Volume in millilitres		
	5 ml (1 tsp)	15 ml (1 Tbs)	250 ml (1 cup)
Crumbs			
Biscuits		6 g	100 g
Dry Bread		7 g	120 g
Fresh Bread		4 g	60 g
Dried Fruit			
Apple Rings (dried)			100 g
Apricots (dried)			100 g
Cherries (glacé)	3 g	9 g	150 g
Currants	3 g	9 g	150 g
Dates	3 g	9 g	150 g
Peaches (dried)	3 g	9 g	150 g
Peel		9 g	150 g
Prunes (dried, stoned)	3 g	9 g	150 g
Raisins		9 g	150 g
Sultanas		9 g	150 g
Farinaceous			
Maltabella			140 g
Milk Powder (blends)	3 g	9 g	100 g
Milk Powder (granules)		5 g	180 g
Mealie Meal	3 g	9 g	150 g
Oats	2 g	6 g	90 g
Pasta (all shapes)			110 g
Rice	4 g	12 g	200 g
Sago	4 g	12 g	180 g
Samp			200 g
Tapioca		10 g	170 g
Nuts			
Almonds (shelled)	3 g	9 g	150 g
Almonds (ground)	2 g	6 g	100 g
Peanuts (shelled)	3 g	9 g	150 g
Pecan (shelled)			100 g
Walnuts (shelled)			100 g
Spices			
Ground Spices and Curry Powder	2 g	6 g	
Pepper	1 g	3 g	
Salt	5 g	15 g	280 g

STARTERS & SALADS

There are many main course dishes that make delightful starters when served in small portions, and many starters that in larger portions make excellent light main courses. Look through the other sections, and use the index and your creative skills to put together the most suitable menu for the occasion.

I have put starters and salads together. Very often salads on individual plates make beautiful and fresh, light starters. Served as a separate course rather than left in a bowl in the middle of the table, the flavour of the raw and sometimes cooked vegetables can be fully appreciated.

A variety of salads with suggested salad dressings are given, as well as several recipes for low-fat salad dressings. Many of the dressings are interchangeable and by experimenting you can create different flavour combinations.

PÂTÉS

Piped or piled onto bread, biscuits, melba toast and vegetables or served in individual ramekins, pâtés are easy and versatile, and they can be prepared in advance.

AUBERGINE PÂTÉ

This is a chunky, crunchy pâté. Serve it with melba toast.

Serves 6 to 8

2	large aubergines
3	cloves garlic, peeled and sliced
10 ml (2 tsp)	soy sauce
45 ml (3 Tbs)	olive oil
1	medium tomato, peeled and chopped
1	stick celery, diced
10	black olives, stoned and chopped
	fresh lemon juice to taste
45 ml (3 Tbs)	sultanas
80 ml (1/3 cup)	slivered almonds or *pine kernels, roasted*
45 ml (3 Tbs)	chopped coriander

▶ Slice the aubergines in half lengthwise and place slices of garlic in slits in the flesh. Sprinkle lightly with salt.
▶ Bake for 1 hour at 180 °C. Leave to cool.
▶ Press the aubergines lightly on absorbent paper to remove the excess moisture.

- Remove the flesh from the skin and process or mash with the garlic until smooth.
- Remove from the processor and mix the remaining ingredients, *except the almonds*, in by hand and season to taste. Do not overmix. Mixture must be coarse and crunchy.
- Refrigerate overnight.
- Before serving, stir the pâté and fold in the almonds and chopped coriander.
- Serve with melba toast.

Melba toast

Melba toast is very easy to make and keeps for weeks in an air-tight container.

- Use at least day-old bread (older if possible) and chill for several hours or partially freeze. This makes it easier to cut into paper-thin slices.
- Using a serrated knife, slice the bread as thin as possible in a sawing action without putting any pressure on the knife. By letting the knife do the work, you will cut straight and in thin slices.
- Place the slices on a baking sheet and bake in an oven at 180 °C for 15 to 25 minutes, depending on the moisture content in the bread and the thickness of the slices. Keep an eye on them; they burn very quickly.
- Turn the slices to brown them on both sides.
- Cool and store in an air-tight container.

MUSHROOM PÂTÉ

The hint of blue cheese in this pâté makes a big difference to the taste. If you hate blue cheese, leave it out and use a little smooth cottage cheese instead. This pâté is perfect for stuffing baby tomatoes, chicory leaves, or as a topping for baby potatoes, if you are making elegant cocktail snacks. It has a perfect piping consistency. It is best chilled overnight before serving.

Serves 6 to 8

80 g	butter
1	medium onion, *chopped*
250 g	brown mushrooms, cut in large pieces
1	clove garlic, crushed
10 ml (2 tsp)	soy sauce
30 g (±3 Tbs, grated)	blue cheese
15 ml (1 Tbs)	fresh lemon juice
15 ml (1 Tbs)	sherry
180 ml ($^3/_4$ cup)	fresh white breadcrumbs
	salt and freshly milled black pepper

- Sauté the onion lightly in half the butter.
- Add the mushrooms and garlic and sauté until soft.
- Cook uncovered until all the water has evaporated.
- Place all the ingredients in a food processor for a rougher texture, or liquidiser for a smoother texture.
- Blend until smooth.
- Check seasoning and chill overnight before serving.

SNOEK PÂTÉ

This pâté can also be made with cooked kippers, smoked angelfish or smoked mackerel.

Serves 4 to 6

250 g	smoked snoek, boned and flaked
15 g	butter
1	large onion, *chopped*
125 g	smooth cottage cheese (approximately)
60 ml ($^1/_4$ cup)	cream
60 ml ($^1/_4$ cup)	mayonnaise
15 ml (1 Tbs)	sherry
2 ml ($^1/_2$ tsp)	freshly ground black pepper
15 ml (1 Tbs)	fresh lemon juice
45 ml (3 Tbs)	chopped parsley

- Sauté the onion in butter until glassy.
- Place all the ingredients in a food processor and blend until smooth.
- Adjust seasoning and chill for several hours.
- Serve on fresh wholewheat bread.

CHOPPED LIVER

Chopped liver is a coarser, less rich version of a chicken liver pâté. It is best made with a mincer or food mill rather than in a food processor.

Serves 8 to 10

500 g	chicken livers
2	onions, chopped
1	Telma chicken stock cube
or 1 tsp	chicken stock powder
80 ml (1/3 cup)	boiling water (approximately)
	olive oil or schmaltz for frying
3	hard boiled eggs
	salt and pepper to taste

- Fry the onions in schmaltz until soft and beginning to brown.
- Add liver and fry until cooked through but still a little pink inside.
- Dissolve the stock cube in the boiling water and add to the pan.
- Mince the liver, onions and 2 of the hard-boiled eggs.
- Season to taste.
- Spread the chopped liver in a shallow plate.
- Grate remaining hard-boiled egg over liver to decorate, and serve with fresh kitke (under *Yeast in baking*), or fresh white bread.

CHICKEN LIVER PÂTÉ

For a smooth texture, blend in a liquidiser rather than in a food processor. For a smooth texture, blend in a liquidiser rather than in a food processor.

Serves 8 to 10

60 g	butter
500 g	chicken livers
2	onions, sliced
1	clove garlic, chopped
1 tsp	chicken stock powder
or 1	chicken stock cube, crumbled and dissolved in
30 ml (2 Tbs)	boiling water
5 ml (1 tsp)	dried thyme
60 ml (1/4 cup)	cream
30 ml (2 Tbs)	sherry, or to taste
10 ml (2 tsp)	lemon juice
8 ml (1 1/2 tsp)	Worcestershire sauce
60 g	soft butter (not melted)
	salt and freshly milled black pepper

- Sauté the livers, onion and garlic in butter until just cooked. The liver must still be slightly pink inside.
- Place all the ingredients in a food processor and purée until smooth. The mixture will have a very soft texture when it is hot but will firm up as it cools.
- Pour a layer of melted butter on the surface to prevent the liver from discolouring.

MIDDLE EASTERN PÂTÉS, SALADS AND MEZZE

The 'mezze table' consists of a collection of salads, spreads, dips and pickles served with bread or pita. It is served as a starter before the main meal. This is a wonderful way to entertain informally.

HUMMUS

This traditional dish of chickpeas with tehina (sesame seed paste) is eaten as a spread with pita bread. To enjoy hummus at its best, make it the day before, but check the seasoning and lemon juice before serving. Tehina is available from many supermarkets and health shops.

Serves 6 to 8

125 g	chickpeas, soaked overnight
juice of 2	lemons, or to taste
3	cloves garlic
125 ml (1/2 cup)	tehina
	salt to taste
10 ml (2 tsp)	cumin (optional)

- Simmer chickpeas until very soft (3 to 4 hours).
- Drain and place in a food processor with the remaining ingredients.
- Blend very well, adding a little water if it is too thick.
- Before serving, check seasoning and lemon juice.
- Serve, liberally sprinkled with paprika, and drizzled with olive oil.

Hints
- The best hummus I have made was when I cooked the chickpeas all day; the longer you cook them, the creamier and more delicious they become.
- Chickpeas can be quick-soaked rather than overnight: Bring them to the boil and leave to stand for an hour. Bring them back to the boil, pour off the water, add clean water and cook for 3 to 4 hours.

SMOKED AUBERGINE PÂTÉ

Baba ganoush
Scorching the aubergines (brinjals, eggplant) imparts the characteristic smoked flavour that makes this a very unusual pâté.

Serves 8 to 10

3	medium sized aubergines
2	cloves of garlic
80 ml (1/3 cup)	tehina, or to taste
45 ml (3 Tbs)	lemon juice, or to taste
5 ml (1 tsp)	cumin
45 ml (3 Tbs)	chopped parsley
200 g	black olives, pitted

- Scorch the whole aubergines over an open flame or close to the grill element, or place them directly on a stove plate on high, or over the coals at a braai, until the skin is black and blistered and the flesh is soft.
- Rub off blackened skin under running water.
- Squeeze the flesh to remove as much moisture as possible.
- Place in a food processor with the remaining ingredients, except parsley and process till smooth. Add a little water to get a thick, creamy consistency.
- Season to taste and chill before serving
- Serve sprinkled with parsley and garnished with black olives.

Variation
Use thick yoghurt (p. 186) or mayonnaise instead of tehina.

TURKISH SALAD

Hot tomato relish
This adds a kick to boerewors rolls and to other braaied meat or fish.

Serves 6 to 8

500 g	very ripe tomatoes
or 2 x 410 g	tins tomatoes
125 ml (1/2 cup)	tomato purée
5 ml (1 tsp)	salt
4	cloves garlic
1-2	chillies, seeded (depending on taste)
15 ml (1 Tbs)	sugar
45 ml (3 Tbs)	olive oil
45 ml (3 Tbs)	chopped fresh coriander leaves
1/4	English cucumber, finely diced
1/2	small onion, finely chopped
1/2	green pepper, finely chopped

- Scald tomatoes in boiling water, skin and chop.
- Chop garlic and chillies.
- In a frying pan, cook the tomatoes, purée, garlic and chillies, with the sugar and salt, in the olive oil until the tomato is pulpy and most of the moisture has evaporated.
- Allow to cool.
- Stir in the finely chopped coriander leaves and chopped vegetables.
- Serve with pita bread and other mezze, or as a chilli relish, or as a salad with any food.

CAÇIK

Turkish tzatzikki
This is the Turkish version of the Greek tzatzikki. I use a mixture of cottage cheese and yoghurt, because our yoghurt is much thinner than Turkish yoghurt. If you make your own yoghurt (see under *This and That*), or if you can get thick Greek yoghurt, replace the cottage cheese with the same quantity of yoghurt.

Serves 8

375 g	Greek style yoghurt
or 250 g tub	smooth cottage cheese plus
125 ml (1/2 cup)	plain yoghurt
125 ml (1/2 cup)	English cucumber
3	cloves garlic, crushed
30 ml (2 Tbs)	chopped fresh mint
10 ml (2 tsp)	fresh dill,
or 2 ml (1/2 tsp)	dried dill
	fresh lemon juice to taste
	salt and freshly milled black pepper to taste

- Coarsely grate the cucumber.
- Combine all the ingredients and leave to stand for several hours before serving.
- Serve with pita bread as part of a mezze table.

Hint
For Greek tzatzikki, omit the mint and dill.

LABANEH

Yoghurt cheese

This Middle Eastern yoghurt cheese is a thick, rich, fermented cheese usually made from sheep's or goats' milk. I made it for a large party and although it has an unusual tart flavour, it was so popular that my guests were soon wiping the empty dish with their pita bread.

Makes about 750 g

2 litres	full-cream milk
175 ml ($^2/_3$ cup)	full-cream milk powder
5 ml (1 tsp)	salt
175 ml ($^2/_3$ cup)	natural yoghurt

- Pour the milk into a large pot and stir in the powdered milk and salt.
- Bring to the boil, stirring to prevent catching on the bottom.
- Remove from heat and leave to cool to just above body temperature (about 40 °C).
- Stir in the yoghurt, cover well and leave in a warm place for 24 to 36 hours. (I place mine in a bowl, in a cooler box and stuff newspaper around the bowl to keep the heat in.)
- Pour the yoghurt into a piece of clean muslin and hang it over a bowl for 24 to 36 hours, out of the fridge.
- Remove from muslin, place in a bowl and beat until smooth.
- Place in the fridge until required.
- Serve sprinkled with Za'atar (see below) and olive oil. Eat with pita bread.

ZA'ATAR

This is a blend of herbs, mostly hyssop and toasted sesame seeds, which is readily available in the Middle East. This recipe is not quite as good as the Middle Eastern original, but on the labaneh or on toasted pita bread, with olive oil, it is still delicious. Make sure that all your dry herbs are fresh and fragrant.

Makes 85 ml (1/3 cup)

30 ml (2 Tbs)	dried marjoram
10 ml (2 tsp)	dried origanum
5 ml (1 tsp)	dried mint
10 ml (2 tsp)	dried parsley
5 ml (1 tsp)	salt and vinegar spice
30 ml (2 Tbs)	toasted sesame seeds

- Mix all the ingredients and store in an air-tight container.

Hint

As a change from garlic bread, try pita breads, cut in half, sprinkled with olive oil, crushed garlic or garlic flakes, salt, pepper and plenty of Za'atar. Pop it under the grill for a minute to toast lightly, cut into wedges and pass them around.

TARAMASALATA

A creamy paste with tarama (smoked fish roe) as a base. That wonderfully smooth, lemony Greek flavour of taramasalata is very easy to achieve. Serve it garnished with olives on a bed of different salad greens and with pita or warm, crusty white bread. It makes an elegant starter to any meal, and a welcome addition to a mezze table.

Serves 4 to 6

65 g	fresh tarama
30 ml (2 Tbs)	chopped onion
125 ml ($^1/_2$ cup)	olive oil
250 ml (1 cup)	fresh, crustless white breadcrumbs
2	cloves garlic, crushed
125 ml ($^1/_2$ cup)	smooth cottage cheese (optional)
	juice of 1 lemon, or to taste
	a little milk or water, if needed
	black olives for garnish

- Lightly sauté the onion in a little of the olive oil.
- Place the tarama, breadcrumbs, garlic, cottage cheese and onion in a food processor and blend until smooth. Gradually add the rest of the olive oil and lemon juice to taste. Add a little milk or water if the flavour is right but the consistency is too thick.
- Leave it to stand for several hours and check seasoning and consistency before serving.
- Garnish with pitted olives and serve with pita bread, melba toast or crusty white bread.

Hints
- Often the bread for the crumbs is soaked in milk. I find it makes the tarama too runny.
- Cottage cheese is not traditional, but by using it you can cut down on the quantity of olive oil given.
- The real smoked tarama is available only in speciality food stores. If you can't find any, a tin of pressed

cod's roe can be used but use much less bread and the whole 200 g tin of roe. Add a drop of pink food colouring for the desired colour.
- For a very creamy consistency, blend the taramasalata in a liquidiser after you have made it in the food processor.

TUNA MOUSSE

Crunchy and light, this tuna mousse is an elegant and inexpensive starter or buffet dish. The taste of the evaporated milk disappears completely, but it adds lightness and creaminess to the texture.

Serves 6 to 8

2 x 185 g	tins tuna in oil, drained
45 ml (3 Tbs)	cold water
15 ml (1 Tbs)	gelatine
80 ml ($^1/_3$ cup)	mayonnaise
30 ml (2 Tbs)	tomato sauce
15 ml (1 Tbs)	lemon juice
	salt and pepper to taste
60 ml ($^1/_4$ cup)	finely chopped radishes
60 ml ($^1/_4$ cup)	finely chopped black olives
125 ml ($^1/_2$ cup)	finely diced celery
30 ml (2 Tbs)	chopped green pepper
1 x 175 g	tin evaporated milk, well chilled

- Soak the gelatine in cold water, then dissolve over boiling water.
- Place the tuna, mayonnaise, tomato sauce, lemon juice and seasoning to taste in a blender and blend until smooth.
- Add dissolved gelatine and blend.
- Remove from the blender and stir the chopped vegetables in by hand.
- Whip the evaporated milk and carefully fold into the fish mixture.
- Pour into one large or 6 to 8 small moulds and refrigerate until set.

Hint
For a more chunky texture, do not blend the tuna. Mix everything by hand.

FALAFEL

These delicious little 'vegetarian frikkadels' are the street food of the Middle East – their answer to our 'boerewors roll'. Falafel (also spelled *felafel*) make an interesting and tasty light meal, piled into a pita bread, with a salad and tehina (sesame seed dressing). Or serve as cocktail snacks, or add to the mezze table.

Makes about 48

250 g	chickpeas, soaked overnight
1	large onion, chopped
2	cloves garlic
180 ml ($^3/_4$ cup)	water (approximately)
250 ml (1 cup)	self-raising flour
20 ml (4 tsp)	ground cumin
15 ml (1 Tbs)	lemon juice
5 ml (1 tsp)	paprika
2 ml ($^1/_2$ tsp)	cayenne pepper
10 ml (2 tsp)	salt, or to taste
80 ml ($^1/_3$ cup)	chopped parsley

- Place chickpeas, onion and garlic in a food processor and process until fine. Remove from the food processor.
- Add water and mix until the mixture is like a thick, coarse batter.
- Add the remaining ingredients and mix well with a wooden spoon.
- Check seasoning.
- Form into small balls with 2 teaspoons and fry in fairly hot oil until well browned. They must not brown too quickly, as the inside is raw and needs time to cook.
- Drain on absorbent paper and serve with tehina, salad (see below) and pita bread.

MIXED SALAD

Make a salad with cabbage, tomato, cucumber, green pepper, celery, raw onion and plenty of fresh parsley.

- Chop or cut the vegetables into small cubes.
- Finish it with a simple dressing of lemon juice, olive oil and salt and pepper.

TEHINA SALAD DRESSING

250 ml (1 cup)	tehina paste
310 ml (1 1/4 cup)	water
80 ml (1/3 cup)	lemon juice
2	cloves garlic
	salt and pepper to taste

- Blend all ingredients to the consistency of cream.
- Check seasoning.

STUFFED MUSHROOMS AND HOLLANDAISE SAUCE

Elegant, full of flavour, and always a special treat.

Serves 4

250 g	large, brown mushrooms
50 g	chopped almonds or cashew nuts
80 g	butter
1	large onion, finely chopped
250 ml (1 cup)	fresh breadcrumbs
125 g	chopped ham, tuna or smoked snoek
30 ml (2 Tbs)	chopped parsley
5 ml (1 tsp)	dried origanum
	salt and pepper
	extra soft butter

- Remove the stalks from the mushrooms, but leave mushrooms whole and set aside. Chop and reserve stalks for the stuffing.
- Sauté the nuts in some of the butter, remove and set aside.
- Sauté the onion and chopped mushroom stalks in the remaining butter. Remove and leave to cool.
- Combine nuts, onion and the rest of stuffing ingredients, blending in a little extra soft butter to bind.
- Butter a flat casserole dish and place the mushrooms in it in a single layer.
- Pile the stuffing onto the mushrooms and cover the dish with a lid or aluminium foil.
- Bake at 180 °C for 30 minutes; mushrooms must be hot but still firm.
- Change oven setting to grill. Remove the lid and brown the mushrooms under the grill before serving with Hollandaise sauce (see under *Sauces*), or pour the Hollandaise sauce over the mushrooms and then brown under the grill.

Variation
Use shrimps, smoked mussels, smoked salmon or smoked chicken, turkey or salami in place of the ham.

AUBERGINE ROLLS WITH BASIL CHEESE

With a distinctive Italian flavour, these stuffed slices of aubergine make a tasty and elegant starter or light meal.

Serves 4 to 6

	olive oil
2	large aubergines
	salt
250 g	ricotta cheese
125 g	mozzarella cheese, coarsely grated
45 ml (3 Tbs)	grated Parmesan or *any strong cheese*
15 ml (1 Tbs)	chopped fresh basil
or 3 ml (1/2 tsp)	dry basil
15 ml (1 Tbs)	olive oil
	salt and pepper

- Leaving the skin on, slice each aubergine lengthwise into about 5 mm thick slices.
- Lightly salt and brush with olive oil.
- Grill, braai or fry the aubergines until soft and brown.
- Drain and cool.
- Mix cheeses with basil, oil, salt and pepper to taste.
- Place a spoonful of the cheese mixture on each aubergine slice and roll up.
- Arrange rolled up slices loosely in an ovenware dish.
- Bake, uncovered, at 180 °C for about 15 minutes or until the cheese has melted.
- Serve with a simple tomato sauce.

Hint
I never salt and leave aubergines to draw water. I find they lose flavour with the water.

Tomato sauce

1	large onion, finely chopped
30 ml (2 Tbs)	olive oil
2 x 410 g	tins tomatoes, drained and finely chopped
5 ml (1 tsp)	sugar
3	bay leaves
2	cloves garlic, crushed
	salt and pepper to taste

- Sauté the onion in oil until glassy.
- Add the tomatoes without the juice (the juice makes a great Bloody Mary!)
- Add remaining ingredients and simmer for 10 minutes or until fairly thick.
- Serve with the aubergine rolls.

Hint
If you can't get ricotta, use chunky cottage cheese. It becomes runny when baked, so only bake until the hard cheese has melted.

Variation
Vary this recipe by using large baby marrows, mushrooms or cooked large pasta shells instead of the aubergines.

CRUMBED VEGETABLES

For a light and simple starter, try crumbed mushrooms (either button or brown), cauliflower, baby marrow, broccoli or sliced aubergine with a piquant sauce.

- Be sure to use very fresh vegetables, as you will be heating them through and crisping the outside rather than cooking them completely.
- If you want to soften firm vegetables such as cauliflower and broccoli slightly, blanch them very quickly in boiling water before crumbing. They must be in the water only long enough to heat through, not to cook.
- Cut vegetables into large, bite sized pieces.
- In a plastic bag, place flour seasoned with salt, pepper and paprika.
- In another plastic bag, place dried crumbs of your choice. Grated Parmesan cheese added to the crumbs makes a delicious coating.
- In a deep bowl, beat an egg with 5 ml salt and 30 ml water. (Two eggs may be needed, depending on the quantity of vegetables.)
- Any left-over flour and crumbs may be kept in the deepfreeze.

To coat vegetables
- Wash and dry vegetable chunks.
- Toss them in the bag of flour.
- Remove from flour and shake off excess flour.
- Dip vegetables in the beaten egg, then toss in the bag of crumbs.
- Chill crumbed vegetables on a baking sheet in the fridge for several hours, or until needed.
- Just before eating, fry vegetables in hot deep oil until well browned. The inside of the vegetables should be hot but still crunchy.
- Drain on absorbent paper.

To serve
Crumbed vegetables can be served with a hot or cold sauce of your choice. Choose your favourite from Hollandaise sauce, mayonnaise, home made tomato sauce, mushroom sauce, curry sauce, sweet and sour sauce, or mustard sauce (see *Sauces in the index*)

CRÊPES

Crêpes can be served as starters or as light main courses as well as desserts, depending on the fillings and sauces used. These thin pancakes are versatile to make a whole range of elegant dishes using small quantities of filling. For dessert crêpe fillings, see *Desserts*.

Depending on the size of your pan and the thickness of the crêpes, this recipe makes 18 to 24 crêpes. Do not be concerned if you spoil the first crêpe; the first always goes to the cook, the dog or the bin!

BASIC CRÊPE BATTER

180 ml ($^3/_4$ cup)	flour
2 ml ($^1/_2$ tsp)	salt
2-3	eggs (see Hint below)
45 ml (3 Tbs)	oil
250 ml (1 cup)	milk

- Sift dry ingredients into a bowl. Add the eggs and oil and beat until smooth.
- Beat in the milk and leave to stand for 2 hours.
- Lightly grease a frying pan for the first crêpe only.
- Place the batter in a jug and pour some into the hot pan to cover the bottom evenly. Count to 5 and pour the excess back into the jug. This will give you a fairly thin crêpe. For a thicker crêpe, leave the mixture in the pan a little longer before pouring the excess back.

- Make all the crêpes, pile them one on top of the other, cover with clingfilm until they can be filled.

Hint
Using 3 eggs for the batter makes the crêpes paper thin and very delicate. If you prefer a more substantial crêpe, use only 2 eggs.

WHOLEWHEAT SESAME CRÊPES

165 ml (²/₃ cup)	wholewheat flour
2 ml (¹/₂ tsp)	salt
250 ml (1 cup)	milk (approximate)
3	eggs
45 ml (3 Tbs)	sesame seeds, toasted or raw
45 ml (3 Tbs)	oil

- Prepare batter, following the basic crêpe method above.

COURGETTE AND FETA FILLING

A tasty filling with a Greek flavour.

Serves 6

1 quantity of the crêpe batter of your choice.

Filling

45 g	butter
300 g	courgettes, coarsely grated
4	chopped spring onions
60 ml (¹/₄ cup)	crumbled feta cheese
125 g	chunky cottage cheese
	salt and freshly ground black pepper
30 ml (2 Tbs)	chopped fresh dill
or 5 ml (1 tsp)	dried dill

- Make the crêpes and then prepare the filling.
- Melt the butter and very quickly stir-fry courgette and spring onions. Leave to cool.
- Mix in the remaining filling ingredients.
- Place a spoonful of the filling on each crêpe, roll up and place crêpes in a greased ovenware dish or in individual dishes.
- Brush liberally with melted butter.
- Bake at 200 °C for about 20 minutes or until lightly browned and slightly crisp.
- Serve with lemon wedges.

SEAFOOD FILLING WITH HOLLANDAISE SAUCE

This filling requires a little more work than most others, but the reward is a very elegant beginning for your dinner party or a perfect light summer meal. The fish and seafood for the filling should total about 750 g use any combination you want to.

Serves 6 to 8 as starter

1 quantity of the crêpe batter of your choice

Filling

50 g	butter
2-3	leeks, thinly sliced
250 g	mushrooms, thinly sliced
1	clove garlic, crushed
200 g	calamari, cleaned and cut into rings
150 g	shrimps
150 g	frozen mussels
250 g	filleted fresh fish, cut into cubes
15 ml (1 Tbs)	tarragon vinegar or *lemon juice*
2 ml (¹/₂ tsp)	dried tarragon
45 ml (3 Tbs)	chopped parsley
	salt and black pepper

- Make the crêpes and then prepare the filling.
- Sauté the leeks, mushroom and garlic in the butter.
- Add all the fish/seafood and sauté very gently for 1 minute.
- Mix in the rest of the ingredients, seasoning to taste.
- Cover with lid and steam for about 3 minutes. *Do not overcook.*
- Place a heaped tablespoon of the filling in a crêpe, roll up and place 2 or 3 filled crêpes on each plate.
- Serve with Hollandaise sauce (see under *Sauces*), or pour Hollandaise sauce over filled crêpes and brown under oven grill.

PEPPERED MACKEREL FILLING

Something different and very tasty, served with Hollandaise or cheese sauce.

Serves 6

1 quantity of the crêpe batter of your choice.

Filling

50 g	butter
2	onions, chopped
1	clove garlic, crushed
250 g	mushrooms, chopped
15 ml (1 Tbs)	flour
125 g	peppered mackerel, flaked
3	bay leaves
2 ml ($\frac{1}{2}$ tsp)	dried mixed herbs
125 ml ($\frac{1}{2}$ cup)	sour cream or crème fraîche
	salt and pepper to taste

- Make the crêpes and then prepare the filling.
- Sauté the onion, garlic and mushrooms in the butter until glassy.
- Stir in the flour.
- Add the mackerel and the rest of the ingredients and simmer for 2 minutes.
- Discard the bay leaves.
- Place a spoonful of the filling in each crêpe, roll up and place 2 or 3 crêpes on each plate.
- Serve with Hollandaise or cheese sauce (see *Sauces*), or pour the sauce over the filled crêpes and brown under oven grill.

CHEESE BLINTZES

Make them savoury as starters, or sweet and served with warmed jam as a simple dessert (see *Desserts*).

Makes 12 to 18 crêpes

1 quantity basic crêpe batter

Filling

250 g	low fat cream cheese
250 g	ricotta cheese or more cream cheese
30 ml (2 Tbs)	boiling water (only if using ricotta cheese)
5 ml (1 tsp)	castor sugar
5 ml (1 tsp)	finely grated lemon rind and lemon juice to taste
2 ml ($\frac{1}{2}$ tsp)	ground cinnamon
2 ml ($\frac{1}{2}$ tsp)	salt
	pinch ground nutmeg
2	egg yolks
	melted butter for baking

- Make the crêpes and stack them, ready to be filled, then make the savoury filling.
- If using ricotta, beat the boiling water into the ricotta cheese and beat until smooth and creamy with an electric beater.
- Mix all the filling ingredients until smooth and chill until required.
- Place a spoonful of filling on each crêpe and fold up into a small parcel.
- Brush a square ovenware dish liberally with melted butter and arrange the filled blintzes in a single layer in the dish.
- Brush liberally with melted butter and bake, uncovered, in a preheated oven at 200 °C for 15 minutes, or until golden.
- Remove and leave to stand for 5 to 10 minutes to allow cheese to set.

Variation

Mix some flaked smoked snoek, peppered mackerel, lumpfish caviar or chopped smoked salmon into the basic cheese filling.

SOUFFLÉS

Relax if you can whip egg whites and make a cheese sauce, you can make a soufflé! There's no magic and certainly very little skill needed but don't tell your guests! Soufflés make light, delicious starters. In bigger portions they are filling but light meals. They're at their best straight from oven to table, but they can also be made in advance and reheated for a slightly different texture. Serves 6 to 8 as a starter, or 3 to 4 as a main meal (using 4 eggs).

BASIC CHEESE SOUFFLÉ

60 g	butter
60 ml (4 Tbs)	flour
250 ml (1 cup)	milk
250 ml (1 cup)	mature cheddar cheese, grated
5 ml (1 tsp)	mustard powder
4	eggs, separated

- In a small pot, melt the butter over medium heat.
- Stir in the flour.
- Add the milk, bring the sauce to the boil and boil for 1 minute, stirring constantly with a wire whisk (this will cook the flour).
- Remove from heat and stir in the cheese and mustard.
- Leave to cool for 5 minutes. Stir in the egg yolks.
- Whisk egg whites until they form soft peaks. Do not over-beat.
- Fold the cheese sauce into the egg whites and pour into a greased soufflé dish, or a deep ovenware dish.
- Bake in a preheated oven at 180 °C for about 40 minutes, or until soufflé is well risen and browned on top.
- Serve immediately.

Hint
Using a wooden spoon often results in a lumpy sauce. Use a wire (balloon) whisk – it is a cinch!

HADDOCK AND SPRING ONION SOUFFLÉ

Follow the basic cheese soufflé recipe and add …

1	bunch spring onions, sliced
150 g	haddock, cooked and flaked

- Sauté spring onion in the butter until soft.
- Add haddock and sauté for 1 minute more.
- Stir in the flour and continue as for basic cheese soufflé.

Variations
Instead of the spring onions and haddock, try adding any of the following to the basic cheese sauce: smoked snoek, peppered mackerel, fried mushrooms, creamed spinach, shredded lettuce, or left over roast chicken (diced). Be creative!

COURGETTE ROULADE WITH CREAM CHEESE AND SMOKED SALMON

A roulade is a soufflé which is baked in a Swiss roll tin and then rolled up like a Swiss roll. It can be eaten hot or cold as a starter or as a light meal. Served cold, sliced into attractive wheels, it makes a sophisticated starter. Use the variation ideas from the soufflé recipes and a filling of your choice to create different flavours.

Serves 6 to 8 as a starter

Roulade

60 g	butter
80 ml ($^1/_3$ cup)	flour
250 ml (1 cup)	milk
4	eggs, separated
3 ml ($^1/_2$ tsp)	dried marjoram
250 g	courgettes, grated

Filling

250 g	cream cheese
80 g	smoked salmon, chopped

- In a saucepan, melt the butter. Add flour and salt, and cook to form a roux.
- Add the milk and bring it to the boil, stirring constantly until sauce has thickened.
- Remove from the heat, cool slightly and add egg yolks, courgettes and marjoram.
- Season with salt and pepper.
- Beat egg whites until it forms soft peaks and fold into courgette mixture.
- Line a Swiss roll tin with baking paper and pour prepared mixture into tin.
- Bake at 180 °C for about 15 to 20 minutes, or until puffed and set.
- Remove from the oven and turn onto a cooling rack covered with a clean dishcloth.
- Leave for 10 minutes and then carefully remove paper and cool completely.
- Spread evenly with cream cheese. Sprinkle lightly with freshly ground black pepper.
- Spread salmon over cream cheese.
- Roll up like a Swiss roll.

Variation
Try using smoked snoek, peppered mackerel, or grilled, chopped bacon in place of the salmon.

FLOATING CHEESE ISLANDS

This is a 'twice-baked' soufflé made in advance and then puffed up again before it is served. It will never be as light as a soufflé eaten immediately, but it is still light and delicious.

Serves 6

250 ml (1 cup)	milk
½	onion, sliced
2	bay leaves
	pinch of ground nutmeg
45 g	butter
45 ml (3 Tbs)	flour
250 ml (1 cup)	mature cheddar cheese, grated
3	eggs, separated
	salt, pepper and a pinch of mustard powder
125 ml (½ cup)	cream
	or a mixture of cream and sour cream or crème fraiche

- To infuse the milk, place the onion, bay leaves and nutmeg in the milk and bring it to the boil. Remove from heat and leave to cool.
- Strain off the onion and bay leaf.
- In a pot, melt the butter and stir in flour.
- Add the milk and bring to the boil, stirring continually with a wire whisk.
- Remove from heat and stir in three-quarters of the cheese.
- Allow to cool, then stir in the egg yolks and seasoning.
- Beat egg whites until stiff and fold into the mixture.
- Grease 6 teacups or small glass ramekins and spoon in the mixture.
- Bake in a Bain Marie: Place the filled cups in a deep roasting pan and add warm water to the pan to reach halfway up the sides of the cups.
- Bake in preheated oven at 180 °C for about 20 minutes until risen and set.
- Allow to cool and sink.
- Butter an attractive, shallow ovenware dish or individual ovenware dishes.
- Loosen the soufflés and turn them out.
- Sprinkle with the remaining cheese.
- Season the cream with salt and pepper and pour over soufflés.
- Bake at 220 °C for about 10 minutes until risen.
- Serve immediately.

Variations
Try different cheeses such as blue cheese or camembert, or ring the changes with the variations given for the basic cheese soufflé.

SALADS TO MIX & MATCH

Hints for perfect salad making

- Salads are always at their best served at room temperature. Remove your salads from the fridge several hours before serving them.
- All salads improve if made in advance and allowed to stand. Dishes made with mayonnaise or lemon/vinegar and oil need time for the flavours to blend and mellow. Because of this, always recheck the seasoning and lemon/vinegar before serving. Where no quantities are given for salt and pepper, season to taste.

Please note, however, that any salad made with lettuce must be dressed and eaten immediately.

- To revitalise parsley, dip the bunch into cold water, shake off the excess moisture and place the stems in a jar of fresh cold water. Leave it uncovered in the fridge and within a few hours it will be fresh and perky. Fresh parsley will keep for up to 2 weeks in this way, if you change the water in the jar every couple of days.
- Soak raw onion in cold, lightly salted water for 30 minutes before using it in salads. This will give it a milder flavour and prevent it repeating and causing heartburn.
- I use a less acid mayonnaise in my recipes, such as Hellman's, Crosse & Blackwell Frenchstyle or Kraft, and then add the acid in the form best for that dish: lemon juice, wine vinegar, or other vinegars. Adjust the acid content to your taste.
- The oil used in salad dressings can be changed according to taste. Sunflower oil is light and has no flavour. The best grade of olive oil is called 'extra virgin' and is prized for its flavour. Nut and sesame seed oils can be used in small quantities for their distinctive flavours.
- All vinegars contain approximately the same percentage acid (5-6%). The differences are in the flavours. Fresh lemon juice, cider vinegar and wine vinegar are all interchangeable depending on the flavour you prefer. Spirit vinegar has no flavour. It is made from ascetic acid distilled from sugar cane, which is then diluted with water.
- Removing the skin of green, yellow and red peppers improves the flavour and prevents peppers from repeating and causing heartburn. This is really worth the trouble in any recipe using peppers. Char the skin of the peppers until it is black over an open flame or under the grill. (The best and quickest way is to use a gas blowtorch if the man in the house has one.) Place the scorched peppers in a plastic bag and leave them to sweat for 15 minutes. The skin will then rub off easily under cold running water.

- Don't let names confuse you. Aubergine, brinjal and eggplant are different names for the same vegetable. Courgette, zucchini and baby marrow are all the same vegetable.
- Sharp knives are essential for good salad making. Use a good serrated knife for soft vegetables and fruit such as tomatoes.
- Dressings should always taste too strong and overseasoned when tasted on their own. They have to flavour all the salad ingredients.
- When cutting up vegetables for salads:
  chopped   =   cut very finely
  diced   =   cut into small blocks
  cubed   =   cut into larger blocks

DRESSINGS

HONEY AND MUSTARD DRESSING

This quantity makes enough dressing for several salads and keeps well in the fridge. Shake it before using.

185 ml ($^3/_4$ cup)	freshly squeezed lemon juice (approximate)
330 ml (1 $^1/_3$ cups)	olive oil or sunflower oil, or a mixture of these
2	cloves garlic, crushed (optional)
30 ml (2 Tbs)	prepared mustard
30 ml (2 Tbs)	honey
10 ml (2 tsp)	dried origanum
	salt and freshly milled black pepper

- Place all the ingredients in a liquidiser and blend or mix all the ingredients well with a wire whisk.
- The dressing should taste overseasoned when tasted on its own.

Variation
In summer, when sweet basil is in season, add 12 leaves to the liquidiser instead of the origanum. Of all the herbs, basil is the best in a salad dressing but only when it is fresh.

PARSLEY DRESSING

45 ml (3 Tbs)	freshly squeezed lemon juice
45 ml (3 Tbs)	vinegar of your choice
165 ml ($^2/_3$ cup)	olive oil or sunflower oil
1	clove garlic
2 ml ($^1/_2$ tsp)	mustard powder
2 ml ($^1/_2$ tsp)	Maggi liquid seasoning (optional)
2 ml ($^1/_2$ tsp)	sugar
$^1/_3$	bunch parsley (approximate)
	salt and freshly milled black pepper

- Place all the ingredients in a liquidiser and liquidise until thick and green.
- Keep in the fridge and shake before using. It lasts for 7 to 10 days before losing its colour.

Variation
Use a mixture of fresh herbs with the fresh parsley.

BLUE CHEESE SALAD DRESSING

Try this flavoursome dressing over blanched broccoli and scatter toasted, flaked almonds over the salad.

170 g	blue cheese
250 ml (1 cup)	sour cream or crème fraiche
125 ml ($^1/_2$ cup)	mayonnaise
1-2	cloves garlic, crushed
45 ml (3 Tbs)	fresh lemon juice
45 ml (3 Tbs)	oil
	freshly milled black pepper to taste

- Cut the cheese into large pieces.
- Place all the ingredients in a food processor.
- Pulse until the cheese is crumbly.
- Leave to stand for several hours before using.
- Check seasoning and consistency, adding a little milk for a thinner dressing.

LOW-OIL SALAD DRESSINGS

The low-oil salad dressings are more acidic than the richer dressings, so use less to achieve the same flavour.

MUSTARD DRESSING

80 ml ($^1/_3$ cup)	fresh lemon juice
	or *good vinegar of your choice*
30 ml (2 Tbs)	water
45 ml (3 Tbs)	olive oil
15 ml (1 Tbs)	sugar
	or *equivalent to taste in sweetener*
2	cloves garlic, crushed
15 ml (1 Tbs)	good prepared mustard
2 ml ($^1/_2$ tsp)	paprika
10 ml (2 tsp)	origanum
	salt and freshly milled black pepper

▶ Place all ingredients in a liquidiser and blend, or mix with a whisk.

Hint
For a thicker green dressing, add several sprigs of fresh parsley when liquidising.

YOGHURT DRESSING

250 ml (1 cup)	drinking yoghurt
30 ml (2 Tbs)	olive oil
60 ml ($^1/_4$ cup)	lemon juice
2	cloves garlic, crushed
	fresh or dried herbs to taste
	(e.g. dill, tarragon, oreganum)
	salt and black pepper to taste

▶ Place all the ingredients in a liquidiser and blend, or mix with a wire whisk.

Hint
For a thicker dressing, use the thicker Bulgarian yoghurt or add some smooth cottage cheese when blending.

MAYONNAISE AND BUTTERMILK DRESSING

250 ml (1 cup)	buttermilk
80 ml ($^1/_3$ cup)	low fat mayonnaise
15 ml (1 Tbs)	good prepared mustard
30 ml (2 Tbs)	lemon juice
15 ml (1 Tbs)	tomato purée (optional)
	salt and black pepper to taste

▶ Place all the ingredients in a liquidiser and blend, or use a wire whisk.

CURRY DRESSING

1	medium onion, finely chopped
10 ml (2 tsp)	oil
30 ml (2 Tbs)	Cartwright's Traditional,
	or *any mild curry powder*
45 ml (3 Tbs)	tomato purée
60 ml ($^1/_4$ cup)	water
15 ml (1 Tbs)	smooth apricot jam
60 ml ($^1/_4$ cup)	any light mayonnaise
175 ml (1 carton)	plain yoghurt
15 ml (1 Tbs)	lemon juice
	salt to taste

▶ Sweat the onion in oil until glassy by cooking it with a lid on over a low heat.
▶ Add the curry powder, tomato purée, water and jam and simmer gently for 5 minutes.
▶ Remove from heat and leave to cool.
▶ Stir in the mayonnaise and yoghurt and season to taste.

SALADS

MIXED SALAD

Here is a suggested combination for a colourful salad. You can use any ingredients, provided they are fresh, and ring the changes with the dressing variations given.

Serves 6 to 8

1	*crisp lettuce, washed, dried and torn into pieces*
2	*spinach leaves, washed, dried and finely shredded*
2	*large tomatoes, cut into large pieces*
or 8	*cocktail tomatoes, horizontally halved*
5 cm	*English cucumber, sliced*
2	*sticks table celery, sliced*
2	*baby marrows, sliced or shredded*
1/2	*bell pepper, seeded and sliced vertically, not in rings*
1	*small onion, sliced in rings*
2	*small carrots, sliced or shredded*
12	*baby green beans*
	or *mange tout peas, blanched and chilled*
	assorted sprouts

▶ Arrange all the ingredients in an attractive bowl. Just before serving, pour the salad dressing over the salad and toss it.

CAESAR SALAD

This classic salad is the perfect way to start any meal. It is light, appetising, easy to prepare and complements any main course.

Serves 4 to 6

1	*lettuce of your choice*
	or *a variety of different greens*
4	*slices white* or *brown bread, crusts removed*
	oil for frying croutons
40 g	*grated parmesan cheese*

Dressing

2	*eggs*
50 g	*real anchovy fillets (with oil)*
16	*capers*
1	*clove garlic*
125 ml (1/2 cup)	*olive oil (plus oil from anchovies)*
45 ml (3 Tbs)	*red wine vinegar*
30 ml (2 Tbs)	*freshly squeezed lemon juice*
2 ml (1/2 tsp)	*mustard powder*
5 ml (1 tsp)	*sugar*
	freshly milled black pepper

▶ *Make the dressing first* Boil the eggs for 3 minutes. Immediately shell and scoop into a liquidiser or processor bowl. Hold the hot eggs with a dishcloth.
▶ Add anchovies, capers and garlic; blend well with eggs.
▶ Add a little of the measured oil and blend.
▶ Gradually add all the oil, vinegar and lemon juice, blending till dressing is thick and pale.
▶ Add mustard, sugar and pepper to taste.
▶ Chill before serving. It thickens on cooling; to thin, add a little oil or water.
▶ *Continue with the main salad* Wash and dry the lettuce and arrange in individual bowls.
▶ Cut bread into small cubes for croutons. Fry in hot oil until crisp, then drain well on absorbent paper.
▶ Scatter croutons and grated Parmesan over lettuce.
▶ Just before serving, pour on dressing liberally.

Hint

Instead of frying the croutons, you can dry-bake them on a baking tray at 180 °C until brown. The time it takes will depend on the freshness of the bread.

This egg based salad dressing is delicious as a sauce for grilled or roast fish (see *Fish*).

TOSSED SALAD

Use the salad ingredients of your choice, such as different varieties of lettuce, watercress, cucumber, celery, bell pepper and tomato. Arrange it in an attractive shallow bowl and immediately before serving pour on the dressing.

Serves 6 to 8

Marinated vegetable dressing

	carrots in julienne strips
3	brown mushrooms, thickly sliced
2	turnips, cut in julienne strips
1	onion, sliced into rings
125 ml ($^1/_2$ cup)	olive oil
125 ml ($^1/_2$ cup)	vinegar of your choice
15 ml (1 Tbs)	sugar
2 ml ($^1/_2$ tsp)	mustard powder
2 ml ($^1/_2$ tsp)	paprika
5 ml (1 tsp)	salt
2 ml ($^1/_2$ tsp)	freshly milled black pepper
2	cloves garlic, crushed
5 ml (1 tsp)	dried origanum

- Place the *dressing vegetables* in a small bowl and pour on the olive oil.
- Place remaining dressing ingredients in a pot and bring to the boil.
- Pour the hot mixture over the vegetables and carefully stir through to coat.
- Chill for 2 hours.
- Pour the marinated vegetables onto the main salad just before serving it.
- Don't make the dressing too long in advance, as the vegetables could become very acidic.

Hint

This can be done with any oil-and-vinegar style salad dressing recipe.

DAFNA'S HOT JUMPED MUSHROOM SALAD

I tasted this salad in Israel at a little sidewalk café. The name of the salad was translated for me from Hebrew as 'jumped mushroom salad'. (The French word 'sauté', which we would have used, literally means 'jumped'.)

Ideally, this salad is made with different types of mushrooms such as oyster, straw, button, brown and, best of all, wild mushrooms such as pine rings and seps. Served with fresh bread, it is offered as a light meal.

Serves 4 as a light meal; 8 as a starter

80 ml ($^1/_3$ cup)	olive oil
250 g	large brown mushrooms
250 g	small button mushrooms
2-3	red peppers
2-3	young leeks
$^1/_2$	bunch spinach

Dressing

45 ml (3 Tbs)	*balsamic* or *wine vinegar*
2	cloves garlic, crushed
2 ml ($^1/_2$ tsp)	freshly ground black pepper
5 ml (1 tsp)	salt
2 ml ($^1/_2$ tsp)	sugar
2 ml ($^1/_2$ tsp)	dried dill
or 7 ml (1 $^1/_2$ tsp)	fresh chopped dill

- Choose the smallest button mushrooms but the biggest brown mushrooms.
- Leave the button mushrooms whole and thickly slice the brown mushrooms. Set aside.
- Cut the red peppers into strips.
- Slice the leeks into very thin rings.
- Shred the spinach very finely. Place in an attractive shallow bowl, or on fish plates if serving as a starter.
- In a large frying pan, heat the olive oil until very hot and add all the mushrooms. Cook over high heat, stirring constantly until the mushrooms are heated through but still raw.
- Remove from heat, combine dressing ingredients and add to the hot pan. Stir until the sugar has dissolved.
- Mix in the reserved red pepper and leek and pour the hot mixture onto the shredded spinach.
- Serve immediately.

WALDORF SALAD

A popular salad made with celery, walnuts and apple. By adding a tin of flaked tuna, smoked chicken or sliced cold chicken breast, you have a crunchy, light starter.

Serves 4 to 6 as a starter

1	lettuce for presentation (optional)
4-6	celery stalks with leaves, sliced
100 g	walnuts or pecan nuts, broken into quarters
2-3	green apples, cubed
1	large bunch black grapes, halved and pitted
or 75 ml	raisins soaked in warm water for 30 minutes and drained
185 ml ($^3/_4$ cup)	mayonnaise
60 ml ($^1/_4$ cup)	orange juice
2 ml ($^1/_2$ tsp)	dried thyme
or 10 ml (2 tsp)	fresh thyme
	salt and pepper to taste

- In a bowl combine celery, nuts, apple and grapes.
- Mix mayonnaise, orange juice, thyme and seasoning. Pour onto salad and toss. Leave to stand for 1 to 2 hours before serving.
- Serve on a bed of lettuce leaves.

SAUSAGE AND CHEESE SALAD

A great summer alternative to winter's sausages, mash and sauerkraut.

Serves 6

200 g	shell noodles, cooked and drained
350 g	Russian or any other spicy sausage
1	onion, diced
45 ml (3 Tbs)	oil
150 g	mild cheddar cheese, cubed
2	apples, peeled and cubed
3	sticks celery, with leaves, diced
185 ml ($^3/_4$ cup)	tinned sauerkraut

Dressing

125 ml ($^1/_2$ cup)	mayonnaise
175 ml	carton plain, thick yoghurt
15 ml (1 Tbs)	vinegar
60 ml ($^1/_4$ cup)	chopped parsley
1	clove garlic, crushed
5 ml (1 tsp)	dried dill
5 ml (1 tsp)	caraway seeds
	salt and pepper

- Cut the sausages into cubes.
- Stir-fry the onion and sausage in the oil over high heat.
- Place all the salad ingredients in a bowl, mix the dressing ingredients and mix into the salad.
- Leave to stand for a few hours before serving and serve at room temperature.

CURRIED CHICKEN SALAD

Also known as 'Coronation chicken'. This is an ideal recipe for using up left-over chicken or roast turkey.

Serves 6

1	chicken, cooked and diced
4	sticks of celery with leaves, diced
1	green pepper, diced
	or $^1/_2$ green and $^1/_2$ red pepper
1	large onion, diced
2	green apples, diced
125 ml ($^1/_2$ cup)	raisins
125 ml ($^1/_2$ cup)	chopped parsley
45 ml (3 Tbs)	chopped fresh coriander leaves
$^1/_3$	lettuce, shredded

Dressing

15 ml (1 Tbs)	oil
1	medium onion, chopped
20 ml (4 tsp)	curry powder
10 ml (2 tsp)	tomato paste
30 ml (2 Tbs)	lemon juice
10 ml (2 tsp)	apricot jam
60 ml ($^1/_4$ cup)	dry white wine
80 ml ($^1/_3$ cup)	chicken stock
45 ml (3 Tbs)	chutney
375 ml (1 $^1/_2$ cup)	mayonnaise
	salt and pepper to taste

- To make the dressing, sauté onion in oil until glassy.
- Add curry powder, tomato paste, lemon juice and jam and cook until the jam has melted. The grainy texture and raw taste of the spices is removed by cooking.
- Add the wine and stock and simmer for a few minutes.
- Stir in the chutney and set aside to cool.
- Stir in the mayonnaise and season to taste.
- Combine all the salad ingredients and fold in the dressing.

Variation
For a more substantial salad, add 150 g cooked noodles of your choice instead of the shredded lettuce.

PEPPER MACKEREL SALAD

Any smoked fish or meat can be used instead of the mackerel. Try snoek, sausages or smoked chicken. The *stampkoring* (pearl wheat, or wheat rice) gives the salad a nutty texture.

Serves 4

1 x 200 g	packet pepper mackerel fillets
1	avocado, cubed
2	celery sticks, diced
1	green pepper, diced
1	onion, diced
$1/4$	English cucumber, diced
200 g	black olives, drained and stoned
150 g	pasta shells or stampkoring, *cooked*
250 ml (1 cup)	frozen corn, blanched

Dressing

250 ml (1 cup)	mayonnaise
125 ml ($1/2$ cup)	sour cream or yoghurt
60 ml ($1/4$ cup)	parsley
1	clove garlic
2	spring onions or chives
60 ml ($1/4$ cup)	wine vinegar or tarragon vinegar
5 ml (1 tsp)	Worcestershire sauce
2 ml ($1/2$ tsp)	mustard powder
	salt and pepper

- Cut the fish into small pieces and place in an attractive bowl with the vegetables.
- Liquidise all the dressing ingredients and add to the salad.
- Leave to stand for a couple of hours before serving.

PEPSI'S POTATO SALAD

Made with baby potatoes in their skins, this is one of the tastiest potato salads I know. If you don't want to use commercial dressings, make your own oil and vinegar dressing.

Serves 6 to 8

1 $1/2$ kg	baby potatoes
2	bunches spring onions, sliced
250 ml (1 cup)	bottled Italian dressing or *any preferred bottled dressing*
250 ml (1 cup)	mayonnaise
175 ml	carton plain yoghurt
1	punnet sprouts, any kind, for garnish

- Boil the potatoes in their jackets.
- Cut the potatoes in half, mix in the spring onion and pour bottled dressing over while the potatoes are hot.
- Leave to cool, allowing dressing to be absorbed.
- Mix the mayonnaise and yoghurt and pour over the marinated potatoes. Mix through very carefully, using your fingers or a metal spoon.
- Garnish with sprouts.

Variation
For curried potato salad, use the dressing for Curried rice salad.

CURRIED RICE SALAD

The curry dressing in this salad is delicious when poured over sliced bananas. This makes a wonderful accompaniment to braaied boerewors.

Serves 8

375 ml (1 $1/2$ cups)	rice, cooked with
2 ml ($1/2$ tsp)	turmeric *for colour*
1	large onion, diced
2	green peppers, diced
500 ml (2 cups)	frozen mixed vegetables, blanched and cooled
180 ml ($3/4$ cup)	seedless raisins
1 x 410 g	tin peaches or apricots, cubed
60 ml ($1/4$ cup)	chopped parsley to garnish

Dressing

1	medium onion, chopped
45 ml (3 Tbs)	oil
45 ml (3 Tbs)	mild curry powder
7 ml (1 1/2 tsp)	paprika
45 ml (3 Tbs)	tomato purée
185 ml (3/4 cup)	water
15 ml (1 Tbs)	apricot jam
250 ml (1 cup)	mayonnaise

- *Make the dressing first* Sauté onion in oil until soft.
- Add the curry powder, paprika, tomato purée, water and jam and simmer gently for 7 to 10 minutes.
- Strain and cool.
- Add curry mixture to the mayonnaise.
- Combine all the salad ingredients and add curry dressing.
- Leave to stand for several hours before serving, garnished with parsley.

CAPREZZA-HERB MARINATED MOZZARELLA AND TOMATO

This classic Italian salad must be made with fresh basil, so it is really a summer salad. The secret is to use firm, ripe tomatoes and freshly picked herbs.

Serves 6 to 8

2-3	firm, ripe tomatoes, sliced
500 g	mozzarella, well chilled and thinly sliced with a serrated knife

Marinade

80 ml (1/3 cup)	olive oil
30 ml (2 Tbs)	balsamic or wine vinegar
45 ml (3 Tbs)	chopped parsley
30 ml (2 Tbs)	chopped sweet basil
30 ml (2 Tbs)	chopped chives
1	clove garlic, crushed
2 ml (1/2 tsp)	paprika
	salt and freshly ground black pepper
	basil leaves for garnish

- Layer the tomato and mozzarella slices in a flat serving dish.
- Combine all the marinade ingredients and pour over the cheese and tomato.
- Cover with clingwrap and chill for at least 4 hours.
- Garnish with basil leaves.

COUSCOUS SALAD

Best made the day before, this is a very unusual salad, with the flavour of roasted almonds, coriander leaves, honey and mustard. Couscous, a type of fine semolina made from wheat grain, is precooked and needs only soaking. Cooked white rice can be used instead of couscous.

Serves 6 to 8

250 ml (1 cup)	couscous
80 ml (1/3 cup)	dried chickpeas, soaked overnight or drained tinned chickpeas
60 ml (1/4 cup)	currants
100 g	slivered almonds
1	green pepper, chopped or 1/2 green and 1/2 red pepper
	bunch of spring onions, sliced
3	sticks celery, with the leaves, chopped
45 ml (3 Tbs)	chopped parsley
45 ml (3 Tbs)	chopped coriander leaves

Dressing

165 ml (2/3 cup)	freshly squeezed lemon juice
165 ml (2/3 cup)	olive oil
15 ml (1 Tbs)	whole mustard seeds
15 ml (1 Tbs)	honey
1	clove garlic, crushed
	salt and black pepper

- Boil soaked chickpeas for several hours until soft, or drain tinned chickpeas.
- Soak the couscous in 1 litre of cold water for one hour.
- Soak currants in a cup of boiling water for 1 hour.
- Place nuts on a baking tray and roast in the oven at 180 °C until lightly browned.
- Drain the couscous very well through a strainer, shaking out all the excess water. Couscous must be dry and fluffy.
- Drain the currants well and add to the couscous with the remaining ingredients.
- Mix all the dressing ingredients.
- Pour on the dressing and leave to stand for several hours before serving. This salad is best made the day before.

Hint

I always soak and cook at least 250 g chickpeas at a time. They freeze perfectly and are much nicer than the tinned kind.

BROWN RICE AND LENTIL SALAD

This nutty, fruity salad is full of fibre and flavour!

Serves 8

310 ml (1 1/4 cups)	brown rice
250 ml (1 cup)	brown lentils
125 ml (1/2 cup)	seedless raisins
125 ml (1/2 cup)	sunflower seeds
180 ml (3/4 cup)	chopped dried apricots (optional)
250 ml (1 cup)	coarsely grated carrot
250 ml (1 cup)	chopped celery
125 ml (1/2 cup)	chopped green or red pepper
125 ml (1/2 cup)	chopped onion
125 ml (1/2 cup)	chopped parsley

Dressing

185 ml (3/4 cup)	sunflower or olive oil
15 ml (1 Tbs)	curry powder
3 ml (1/2 tsp)	cumin
5 ml (1 tsp)	soy sauce
20 ml (4 tsp)	honey
125 ml (1/2 cup)	lemon juice, or cider vinegar
	salt and pepper

- Cook the rice and lentils in separate pots.
- Mix the hot rice and lentils with the raisins, sunflower seeds and apricot.
- Combine all the dressing ingredients and add to the warm rice mixture. Leave to cool.
- Add remaining salad ingredients and leave to stand for several hours before serving.

RUSSIAN POTATO SALAD

The mixed vegetables and the flavour of horseradish make this a potato salad with a difference.

Serves 6 to 8

6	large potatoes
1 x 410 g	tin mixed vegetables, drained, but juice reserved
4	hard-boiled eggs, diced
1	bunch spring onions, thinly sliced
250 ml (1 cup)	mayonnaise
20 ml (4 tsp)	bottled white horseradish (approximate)
	juice of 1/2 lemon
5 ml (1 tsp)	good prepared mustard
125 ml (1/2 cup)	chopped parsley
	salt and pepper

- Boil the potatoes in their jackets.
- When cool enough, peel and cut into cubes.
- Combine the potatoes, mixed vegetables, egg and spring onion in a salad bowl.
- Mix the mayonnaise, horseradish, lemon juice, mustard and parsley.
- Add salt and pepper to taste and thin down with a little reserved vegetable juice as needed.
- Pour this over the warm potato mixture and toss gently but well.
- Leave to stand for several hours before serving.

Hints

- Always pour the mayonnaise onto the potatoes while they are warm. They absorb more flavour and the final salad will have a much smoother taste.
- Certain types of horseradish are milder than others, so taste before adding this ingredient.

TABBOULEH

Cracked wheat salad

This traditional salad is served in every restaurant in the Middle East. It should be made from bulgar or cracked wheat, but if it is not available, use wheat rice (*stampkoring*) or brown rice. Bulgar wheat is precooked and only needs soaking. If you use *stampkoring* or rice, be sure to cook both thoroughly.

Serves 8

250 g	bulgar wheat or stampkoring
2	bunches spring onions, chopped
2	cloves garlic, crushed
3	sticks celery, with leaves, chopped
½	bunch parsley, chopped
45 ml (3 Tbs)	chopped fresh mint
5 ml (1 tsp)	dried dill
or 15 ml (1 Tbs)	chopped fresh dill
2	firm tomatoes, pipped and diced
⅓	English cucumber, diced
80 ml (⅓ cup)	fresh lemon juice
125 ml (½ cup)	olive oil
	salt and black pepper
2	tomatoes, sliced, for garnish

▸ Soak the bulgar wheat in lots of cold water for 3 to 4 hours. Rinse and drain well.
▸ If you are using *stampkoring*, first soak it in boiling water for 2 hours. Boil for about 7 minutes or until chewy but do not boil it until completely soft. Drain well and chill. If you are using brown rice, cook it until almost soft but still chewy.
▸ Add all remaining ingredients and chill for several hours before serving.
▸ Garnish with slices of tomato.

Hints

This salad is at its best served 8 hours after making it. Check seasoning before serving as the lemon and salt is absorbed.

CABBAGE SALAD WITH CARAWAY AND BACON

The hot salad dressing wilts the cabbage but keeps it crunchy. Served with sausages and mashed potato, this salad is nicer than sauerkraut.

Serves 6 to 8

80 ml (⅓ cup)	oil (approximate)
1	large onion, diced
125 g	rindless streaky bacon, diced (optional)
60 ml (¼ cup)	vinegar (approximate)
	salt and pepper
½	small cabbage, shredded
15 ml (1 Tbs)	caraway seeds, or more to taste

▸ In half the oil, sauté onion and bacon until the onion is glassy and bacon cooked.
▸ Add the remaining oil, vinegar and season to taste.
▸ Place the cabbage and caraway seeds in a dish and pour on the still warm onion mixture. Toss well and leave to cool.
▸ Make the salad hours in advance and serve at room temperature.
▸ Check seasoning before serving. More vinegar and oil may be needed, depending on the size of the cabbage.

BEETROOT SALAD

The secret of this raw beetroot salad is to use young, small beetroots that are not woody.

Serves 8 and more

4	raw beetroots, finely grated
4	stalks celery, finely sliced
¼	cabbage, finely shredded
60 ml (¼ cup)	chopped parsley
2	carrots, finely grated
2	cloves of garlic, crushed
30 ml (2 Tbs)	chopped walnuts or pecan nuts

Dressing

165 ml (²/₃ cup)	apple cider vinegar
15 ml (1 Tbs)	wholegrain prepared mustard
15 ml (1 Tbs)	sugar
185 ml (³/₄ cup)	oil
	salt and pepper

▸ Mix the dressing ingredients.
▸ Combine all the salad ingredients and mix in the dressing.
▸ This salad is best when made the day before. Check the seasoning before serving.

CAULIFLOWER AND WALNUT SALAD

This salad was our staple lunch at Leith's Cookery School in London. We ate it piled into hot baked potatoes or on its own with fresh bread. Make sure the nuts are fresh. Stale walnuts will ruin the salad!

Serves 6 to 8

½	cauliflower, cut into tiny florets
500 ml (2 cups)	grated cheddar cheese
100 g	walnuts, roughly chopped
1	bunch spring onions, thinly sliced

Dressing

80 ml (¹/₃ cup)	apple cider vinegar
10 ml (2 tsp)	whole-seed mustard
	or any good prepared mustard
15 ml (1 Tbs)	sugar
160 ml (²/₃ cup)	oil
	salt and pepper

▸ First combine the dressing ingredients.
▸ Mix all the salad ingredients, then mix in the dressing.
▸ This salad improves with standing and should be made in advance. It will keep for several days.

BEER COLESLAW

The slight bitterness of the beer gives this coleslaw an unusual flavour.

Serves 6 to 8

½	white cabbage, shredded
3	carrots, grated
1	medium onion, very finely sliced
1	green pepper, finely sliced

Dressing

250 ml (1 cup)	mayonnaise
80 ml (¹/₃ cup)	beer
5 ml (1 tsp)	molasses, warmed
	salt and pepper

▸ Mix the dressing ingredients.
▸ Place the salad vegetables in a bowl and mix in the dressing.
▸ Leave to stand for several hours.

PAWPAW AND AVOCADO SALAD

Barbara Newman introduced me to this salad, and it's one of my favourites. Add thinly sliced poached chicken breasts and it becomes a delightful light starter or light meal.

Serves 6 to 8

1	papino or ½ pawpaw, peeled, pipped and sliced
2-3	avocados, peeled and sliced
1	medium onion, thinly sliced
3	sticks table celery, thinly sliced

Dressing

15 ml (1 Tbs)	honey, warmed
80 ml (¹/₄ cup)	cider vinegar
125 ml (½ cup)	oil
1	clove garlic, crushed
5 ml (1 tsp)	dried thyme
	salt and black pepper
30 ml (2 Tbs)	chopped parsley

▸ First combine all the dressing ingredients.
▸ Layer all the salad ingredients in a large shallow bowl.
▸ Dribble the dressing evenly over the salad and leave to stand for 2 to 3 hours before serving.

APPLE AND AVOCADO SALAD

This recipe follows the same idea used in the Pawpaw and avocado salad, of combining avocados with fruit. The apples and nuts give it a very crispy and crunchy texture.

Serves 6 to 8

4	Granny Smith apples
2-3	ripe, firm avocados
3	sticks celery with the leaves
100 g	salted cashew nuts

Dressing

- 60 ml (¼ cup) cider vinegar
- 15 ml (1 Tbs) good, strong prepared mustard
- 30 ml (2 Tbs) castor sugar
- 160 ml (⅔ cup) oil
- salt and pepper

▶ First mix all the dressing ingredients and check seasoning.
▶ Peel and core apples.
▶ Cut the apples and avocados into cubes.
▶ Thinly slice the celery and chop the leaves.
▶ Layer the salad ingredients in a shallow salad bowl.
▶ Scatter the nuts over, and pour on the dressing.
▶ Leave to stand for a couple of hours before serving.

COLD RATATOUILLE SALAD

By roasting the vegetables in the oven, you get a browned, slightly smoky taste that makes this salad very different.

Serves 6 to 8

- 3 aubergines, skin on, cut into large cubes
- 80 ml (⅓ cup) olive oil
- 8 courgettes (baby marrows), thickly sliced
- 250 g small button mushrooms, left whole
- 1 large onion, cut into thin rings
- 1 green pepper, cut into thin rings or ½ red and ½ green pepper

Dressing

- 80 ml (⅓ cup) freshly squeezed lemon juice
- 2 cloves garlic, crushed
- 5 ml (1 tsp) origanum
- salt and black pepper

▶ Toss the aubergine cubes in half the oil and roast on a baking sheet in a very hot oven at 220 °C until cooked and brown.
▶ Repeat this process with the courgette slices and mushrooms, using the remaining oil.
▶ Carefully toss the hot vegetables with the raw onion and pepper.
▶ Combine dressing ingredients, seasoning to taste.
▶ Pour dressing over vegetables and chill for several hours.
▶ Check seasoning before serving.

LENTIL AND SPINACH SALAD

I discovered this salad in Marmaris, a small seaside town in Turkey. It has an unusual combination of textures and the spicy flavour of cumin.

Serves 6 to 8

- 250 ml (1 cup) green or brown lentils
- 7 ml (1 ½ tsp) cumin
- 2 ml (½) salt
- 1 bunch spring onions, thinly sliced
- 2-3 large firm tomatoes or 15 cherry tomatoes, halved
- 8-12 fresh spinach leaves, shredded
- 150 g feta cheese, crumbled

Dressing

- 2 cloves garlic, crushed
- 7 ml (1 ½ tsp) origanum
- 5 ml (1 tsp) cumin
- 80 ml (⅓ cup) lemon juice
- 125 ml (½ cup) oil
- salt and pepper

▶ Cook the lentils in salted water with 7 ml cumin until soft.
▶ Drain and chill.
▶ Remove the seeds from the tomatoes and dice the flesh.
▶ Combine all the dressing ingredients, seasoning to taste.
▶ Layer the salad ingredients on a shallow platter and pour on the dressing.

REAL QUICKIES

BAKED BEAN SALAD

Very quick and simple. This salad with a slight hint of chilli is delicious with a braai.

Serves 4

1 x 410 g	tin baked beans in tomato sauce
1	onion, finely chopped
45-60 ml (3-4 Tbs)	mango atjar, finely chopped
45 ml (3 Tbs)	mayonnaise

▸ Combine all the ingredients.

THREE BEAN SALAD

Of all the many three bean salads I have tasted, Rhona's is my favourite. The salad dressing almost marinates the beans, so serve it with a slotted spoon to leave the liquid behind.

Serves 8 to 12

1 x 410 g	tin cut green beans, drained
1 x 410 g	tin butter beans, drained
1 x 410 g	tin baked beans
1	red pepper, seeded and chopped
1	green pepper, seeded and chopped
1	onion, finely chopped

Dressing

250 ml (1 cup)	vinegar
125 ml (½ cup)	oil
125 ml (½ cup)	brown sugar
125 ml (½ cup)	sultanas

▸ Mix all the salad ingredients in a bowl.
▸ Bring the dressing ingredients to the boil and simmer for 5 minutes, stirring until the sugar has dissolved.
▸ Pour the hot dressing over the salad and cool completely before serving.

BUTTERNUT SALAD

If you like mangoes, you'll love this salad. Lesley Hamlyn's simple recipe combines flavours that result in a mango taste.

Serves 6

1	medium butternut
1	medium pineapple
250 ml (1 cup)	fresh orange juice
	salt
1	sliced orange and 2 sprigs of mint for garnish

▸ Grate the raw butternut and the pineapple.
▸ Mix in the orange juice and salt to taste.
▸ Chill for several hours before serving, garnished with slice of oranges and mint.

QUICK MIDDLE EASTERN SALADS

Add these salads to your mezze table or just serve on their own.

BUTTER BEAN SALAD

This salad may be eaten hot or cold.

Serves 6 to 8

1 x 410 g	tin whole tomatoes, drained
1	large onion, sliced
60 ml (¼ cup)	olive oil
2 x 410 g	tins butter beans
15 ml (1 Tbs)	fresh lemon juice
2	cloves garlic, crushed
	salt and pepper
	chopped parsley for garnish

▸ Cut the tomatoes into thick slices.
▸ Sauté onion lightly in the olive oil.
▸ Add the rest of the ingredients and mix with the hot oil.
▸ Cool before serving, garnished with parsley.

STARTERS & SALADS

AUBERGINE IN YOGHURT

This recipe is especially for aubergine lovers. It can be served hot or cold.

Serves 6 to 8

4	aubergines, skin on, cut in large pieces
60 ml (¼ cup)	olive oil
250 ml (1 cup)	drinking yoghurt
2	cloves garlic, crushed
5 ml (1 tsp)	dried origanum
	salt and pepper

- Toss the aubergine in the olive oil
- Roast on a baking sheet at 220 °C until soft and browned.
- Combine the yoghurt, garlic, origanum, salt and pepper to taste and pour over the warm aubergine.

LEEKS IN TOMATO

This salad can be eaten hot or cold. The leeks are stewed rather than fried in the olive oil. Try this recipe using baby pickling onions instead of leeks.

Serves 6 to 8

2	bunches leeks
60 ml (¼ cup)	olive oil
1 x 410 g	tin whole tomatoes, drained
15 ml (1 Tbs)	fresh lemon juice
2	cloves garlic, crushed
	salt and black pepper
	chopped parsley for garnish

- Cut the leeks into 5 cm lengths and wash well.
- Cover and stew the leeks slowly in oil until soft.
- Increase the temperature and cook uncovered until they start to brown.
- Cut the tomatoes in thick slices.
- Carefully toss all the ingredients together in the hot oil.
- Cool before serving.
- Garnish with chopped parsley.

SOUPS

Soup is the most versatile course in the meal. It can be made smooth or chunky, thin or thick, and served hot or cold as a starter, or as a main course. In China, Russia and Switzerland it is often served after the main course, and in China a sweet soup is served for dessert!

Use up left-over vegetables that are just not fresh enough to be eaten raw.

Most soups freeze very well and are lifesavers when unexpected guests arrive, or as a last-minute meal. *However, do not freeze soups that contain pieces of potato.*

If you are going to store your soups, stews or casseroles, *chill them as quickly as possible* to prevent souring and bacterial contamination. The golden rules are:

- Place the pot of hot food in a sink of cold water.
- Remove the lid so that the heat can escape.
- Leave to cool, changing the water as it warms.
- Place the food, luke-warm and without the lid, in the fridge. (Placing warm food in the fridge is not bad for the food, it simply makes the fridge work harder to lower the temperature.)
- The chilled food can then be frozen in sealed containers.

Stock cubes

Try the different types of stock cubes on the market and find the flavour you like best. They vary in their content of salt, flavour and MSG (monosodium glutamate), a flavour enhancer.

I like to use the Israeli *Telma* cubes and Ina Paarman's MSG-free stock, because they have an excellent flavour and are not too salty. Telma cubes come in a variety of flavours: chicken, beef, chicken-flavoured vegetable, vegetable clear and with 'bits', and onion and mushroom. Being imported, they are sometimes not easy to find but when I do, I stock up.

Ina Paarman's stock powders are excellent and contain no MSG. They, however, contain no meat extract and the vegetable stock tastes very much like dehydrated vegetables.

Local brands of stock cubes tend to be a little saltier than Telma, and it is often wise to use less of the local product, and to bear this extra saltiness in mind when seasoning with additional salt, or when the recipe contains an ingredient which is naturally salty.

The Swiss stock Plantaforce is available from most health shops. This vegetable yeast extract contains no MSG. It also comes in a sodium-free, blander, version.

Cream of vegetable soup with variations

Cream of vegetable soups are the most versatile and useful soups to use as starters, or as light meals served with fresh bread and cheese.

Because these soups are thickened with potato and the vegetables themselves rather than with flour in the old fashioned way, they can be served hot or cold.

This is a basic recipe that can be adjusted to suit your taste and according to the ingredients you have available. With a little imagination you can make up your own variations and combinations. Try using beetroot, sorrel, carrot and parsnip together, or spinach, brinjals and sweet potato.

All soups are better the day after making. They freeze well as long as there are no pieces of potato in them, though grated or pureed potato in soups is fine for freezing.

If you intend freezing soup, it is best not to add the cream before freezing. But if you already have, it's not serious the soup may lose its velvety texture, but that's about all.

Quantities

The quantities given for vegetables, potato and stock are approximate. The water content, bulk and strength of flavour vary with the kind and age of the vegetables. Baby marrows are more watery than carrots. Celery has a very strong flavour but not so much bulk. Pumpkin and butternut vary in flavour and sweetness, depending on the season.

If the soup is a little watery, simply boil away the excess water. Check seasoning. The only way to get a really delicious soup is to taste it just before serving and season it then. Soup to be served cold will need more seasoning and more liquid in the preparation stock, milk or cream.

BASIC CREAM OF VEGETABLE SOUP

This vegetable soup freezes well, especially if frozen before adding the milk or cream.

Serves 6 to 8

2	large onions
or 1	bunch leeks
50 g	butter
750 g	vegetables of your choice (broccoli, cauliflower, pumpkin, etc.)
1-2	potatoes
750 ml – 1 litre (3-4 cups)	chicken or *vegetable stock squeeze of fresh lemon juice or other desired flavouring such as ground nutmeg, cinnamon or cumin to taste*
125 ml ($^1/_2$ cup)	cream or milk

- Sauté sliced onion or leeks in butter.
- Add vegetables, potatoes and stock and simmer until vegetables are soft.
- Purée the mixture in a liquidiser or food processor, or press through a sieve.
- Add the cream or milk, heat through, check seasoning and serve.

Hint
I always add a little fresh lemon juice to my soups. It brings out the flavours and you need less salt.

This basic cream of vegetable soup is used as the base for these variations:

Curried cream of broccoli or peas
- Use the basic recipe for cream of vegetable soup, but use broccoli or frozen peas and add 15 ml (1 Tbs) mild curry powder to simmering vegetables. After liquidising, season to taste.

Vichyssoise
- This soup is traditionally served cold, but is also delicious hot.
- Use the basic recipe for cream of vegetable soup, but use 3 bunches of leeks and 2 to 4 potatoes in the 750 g desired vegetables.
- Season with 2 to 5 ml ($^1/_2$ to 1 tsp) ground nutmeg to taste.

Courgette and brie soup
- Use the basic recipe for cream of vegetable soup, but use 750 g courgettes (baby marrows) and add 80 g ripe brie or camembert cheese to the soup while liquidising it.

Butternut or pumpkin soup
- Use the basic recipe for cream of vegetable soup, but use 750 g ripe butternut or pumpkin cut into large blocks.
- Season with a little ground cinnamon or nutmeg For something different, add 1 peeled apple, cut into cubes, and 5 ml (1 tsp) cumin to the vegetables while cooking.

Pea soup with apple and cumin
- Vary the basic cream of vegetable soup by using frozen peas, a peeled Granny Smith apple and 5 ml (1 tsp) cumin.
- This is a fairly sweet soup; season it with plenty of fresh lemon juice.

Celery soup

- Follow the basic recipe for cream of vegetable soup, but use a bunch of soup celery or the thicker but milder table celery, leaves and all. This is enough celery, even though it is not 750 g.
- Use large potatoes.
- For lovers of blue cheese, add 80 g blue cheese when liquidising the vegetables.

Waterblommetjie soup

- Follow the recipe for basic cream of vegetable soup, using 750 g fresh, well washed waterblommetjies and season with extra lemon juice and nutmeg.

Carrot and orange soup

- Use carrots in the basic cream of vegetable soup. For this variation, make the stock with the juice of 2 oranges topped up with chicken stock to make up the required 750 ml (3 cups) liquid.
- Add 5 ml (1 tsp) orange rind and a little sugar to simmering vegetables. The quantity of sugar depends on the acidity of the orange.
- A stick of cinnamon can be added to the simmering pot, if desired, and then be removed before liquidising.

Potage bonne femme

- Follow the recipe for basic cream of vegetable soup, using a variety of vegetables of your choice, such as celery, carrots, parsley, tomato, leeks, mushrooms, broccoli, turnips, cauliflower – whatever is handy.
- Cook the vegetables with 3 bay leaves, but discard the bay leaves before liquidising.

Lettuce soup

- Use the basic recipe for cream of vegetable soup, but use 1 to 2 lettuces, especially the green outer leaves, as part of your vegetables. The more outer green leaves you use, the tastier and greener your soup will be. The best lettuce to use, if you can get it, is Cos.
- Season with a little ground nutmeg.

Cauliflower and mushroom soup

- Use the recipe for basic cream of vegetable soup, but make up the 750 g vegetables with half a small cauliflower and 250 g brown mushrooms.
- Simmer with 2 bay leaves and discard these before liquidising.
- Season with 20 ml sherry and fresh lemon juice.

CREAM OF TOMATO SOUP

The method for this soup is exactly the same as that of the basic cream of vegetable soup, but the quantities are slightly different because of the high water content and higher acid content of tomatoes.

Serves 6 to 8

50 g	butter
2	onions, sliced
2	sticks celery, sliced
2 x 410 g	tins tomatoes
20 ml (4 tsp)	tomato paste
1-2	potatoes, peeled and cubed
250 ml (1 cup)	strong chicken stock
30 ml (2 Tbs)	sugar
2 ml ($^1/_2$ tsp)	black pepper
2 ml ($^1/_2$ tsp)	ground nutmeg
6	bay leaves
250 ml (1 cup)	cream or milk

- Sauté the onion and celery in the butter until glassy.
- Add all the remaining ingredients *except cream*, and simmer until potatoes are completely soft. This takes longer than normal, because the acid in the tomatoes slows down the softening process. Cook for 30 to 45 minutes.
- Remove bay leaves and purée the mixture in a liquidiser or food processor, or press through a sieve. For a very smooth texture, pass it through a sieve after liquidising.
- Add cream or milk, heat through, check seasoning and serve with croutons.

SPECIAL CREAM OF MUSHROOM SOUP

A fragrant, thick soup with a touch of luxury.

Serves 6

500 g	brown mushrooms, thickly sliced
1	large onion, thinly sliced
50 g	butter
80 ml ($^1/_3$ cup)	cake flour
1 litre (4 cups)	water
2	Telma mushroom stock cubes
15 ml (1 Tbs)	sherry
	fresh lemon juice to taste
	salt and black pepper to taste
125 ml ($^1/_2$ cup)	cream
	or *sour cream*

- Sauté the onion in the butter until glassy.
- Add half the mushrooms and sauté for 1 minute.
- Stir in flour to coat the vegetables.
- Add rest of the ingredients *except cream and remaining mushroom slices*.
- Simmer until mushroom slices are soft and soup is thick.
- Just before serving, add cream and remaining mushroom slices and simmer until mushrooms are almost tender.
- Do not overcook the mushrooms at this stage.
- Check seasoning.

MINESTRONE

More Italian you cannot get! To make a pure vegetarian soup called *minestra*, omit the bacon and use vegetable stock instead of the chicken stock.

Serves 8

45 ml (3 Tbs)	olive oil
4	rashers bacon, chopped
1	large onion, chopped
2	cloves garlic, chopped
1	leek, chopped
3	carrots, chopped
1	turnip, chopped
1	small piece cabbage, shredded
¼	cauliflower, cut up
2	sticks celery with leaves, chopped
125 ml (½ cup)	chopped parsley
1	large potato, chopped
2 litres (8 cups)	chicken stock
250 ml (1 cup)	frozen peas
250 ml (1 cup)	fresh or *frozen* sliced beans
410 g	tinned butterbeans
15 ml (1 Tbs)	tomato paste
125 ml (½ cup)	noodles, uncooked
	salt and pepper to taste

- Heat the olive oil and sauté onion, garlic and bacon.
- Add all the remaining fresh vegetables, stock and tomato paste.
- Simmer for 45 minutes.
- Add the frozen vegetables, butterbeans and noodles.
- Simmer for further 15 minutes.
- Check seasoning.
- Serve with plenty of grated Parmesan cheese.

CHICKEN SOUP

Here's Mama's penicillin chicken soup with all the trimmings. Prepare the soup the day before. Serve clear as it is, or use it as a base for other soups such as sweetcorn soup, or add plenty of sliced mushrooms to make chicken mushroom soup.

It can also be accompanied by *kneidlach* (Jewish matzo meal dumplings), *kreplach* (Eastern European ravioli) (see recipes). Or serve it with *perogen*, which are small meat pies (see *Pastry* under *Baking*).

Although the list of ingredients seems long, this is actually the simplest soup to make. The piece of shin adds flavour and depth to the soup without overwhelming the chicken taste.

Serves 6 to 8

1	chicken, cut into portions
250 g	chicken giblets
250 g	chicken necks
1	large piece of shin, cut into pieces
2-3	Telma chicken cubes, crumbled
	or *stock powder of your choice*
2 litres (8 cups)	water
45 ml (3 Tbs)	oil
	or *schmaltz (mock chicken fat; see Odds and ends)*
4-5	carrots, chopped
1	bunch leeks, chopped
1	turnip, chopped
2	large onions, chopped
½	bunch soup celery, with leaves, chopped
½	bunch parsley, with stalks, chopped
3 ml (½ tsp)	coarse black pepper
5 ml (1 tsp)	salt
4	extra carrots for serving, thinly sliced
50 g	vermicelli (optional)

- In a large pot sauté onions and leeks in oil or schmaltz. Add remaining vegetables and sauté until glassy.
- Remove from the heat. Place remaining ingredients in the pot and allow to soak for a few hours before cooking.
- Bring to the boil and simmer for 2 hours.
- Remove chicken pieces from soup, take all the meat off the bones, break up the bones and return them to the soup. (Reserve the cooked meat to use in a chicken salad, pie or sauces.)
- Continue simmering the soup, covered, for further 2 to 3 hours.

- Place pot (with lid off) in cold water until cool. When cool enough, place in the fridge overnight.
- Remove from fridge and remove all the fat from the top of the soup.
- Warm the soup and strain through a colander or strainer to remove all the solids. Discard solids.
- Return the soup to the pot and add the sliced carrot. Bring to the boil and break in vermicelli if you want chicken noodle soup.
- Check seasoning and simmer until carrots and noodles are soft.

FOOLPROOF KNEIDLACH

These traditional Jewish dumplings are made of matzo meal, and may be plain, or stuffed. Schmaltz, or mock chicken fat, is available at all kosher deli counters in supermarkets or make your own (see *Odds and ends*).

Makes about 15

- 250 ml (1 cup) water or *chicken soup*
- 80 ml ($^1/_3$ cup) *schmaltz* or *oil*
- 5 ml (1 tsp) salt
- 250 ml (1 cup) matzo meal
- 2 ml ($^1/_2$ tsp) ground cinnamon
- 5 ml (1 tsp) sugar
- 2 jumbo eggs

- Place the water, schmaltz and salt in a pot. Bring to the boil.
- Remove from the heat and immediately add matzo meal mixed with cinnamon and sugar.
- Stir well and leave to cool for 5 minutes.
- Beat eggs and add to the matzo meal, beating in very well.
- In the meantime, bring a pot of lightly salted water to the boil.
- Divide the mixture into 30 ml (2 Tbs) measures and lightly roll into balls.
- Drop them into the boiling water.
- Turn the heat down so that water is just boiling.
- Boil with the lid on for 30 to 40 minutes.

Stuffing (optional)

- 1 medium onion, finely *chopped*
- 2 carrots, finely *chopped*
- 45 ml (3 Tbs) *schmaltz*
- salt and white pepper

- In a frying pan, fry onion and carrot over medium heat for a long time until vegetables brown and caramelise (be careful not to burn them).
- Season with plenty salt and white pepper and leave to cool.
- When shaping kneidlach, place half a teaspoonful of the stuffing in the centre before forming into a ball.

LOKSHEN, FARFEL AND KREPLACH

These are made with a basic pasta and used in chicken soup.

Basic pasta

- 750 ml (3 cups) flour
- 15 ml (1 Tbs) oil or *melted schmaltz*
- 5 ml (1 tsp) salt
- 2-3 eggs, depending on size

- Place all the ingredients in a food processor and form into wet crumbs.
- Turn out and form into a dough.

Lokshen

- Make the basic pasta and roll out the dough, using a pasta machine. Or roll it out very thin with a rolling pin.
- Dredge well with flour and roll sheets up like Swiss rolls.
- Using a sharp knife, thinly slice the roll into ribbons.
- Boil in soup just before serving.
- The lokshen cooks very quickly. All you have to do is bring the soup back to the boil once you have added the lokshen and they will be cooked.

Farfel

- Make the basic pasta dough and roll into thin sausages like thick spaghetti.
- With a pair of scissors, snip the sausages into tiny pieces and place them on a well-floured surface.
- Drop the farfel into the boiling soup just before serving. They cook in less than 1 minute. If you overcook them, they will become mushy.

Kreplach

- Make 1 quantity of the basic pasta dough.
- *Make the filling by* straining or scooping out with a slotted spoon all the vegetables and some of the chicken meat from the chicken soup.
- Place in a food processor or mince it.
- Season very well with plenty salt, pepper and a little extra schmaltz. An extra onion chopped and fried in schmaltz added to the food processor adds a lot of flavour.
- Roll out the basic pasta dough very thin and cut into squares.
- Place a little of the filling on each pasta square, cover with another and seal edges well. (They may be frozen at this stage.)
- Boil for 1 to 2 minutes in salted water if fresh and a little longer if frozen. Do not overcook.
- *To freeze*, place well-floured kreplach on a tray and freeze. Once they are frozen individually, they can be packed into a container and kept in the freezer.

BORSCHT

Sweet and sour beetroot soup

There are as many different kinds of borscht as there are Russians. Every *babushka* has her own recipe!

This soup is served ice-cold, with a dollop of sour cream and a hot boiled potato. To serve it at a dinner party, I boil baby potatoes and place 2 or 3 in the cold soup with the sour cream on top. Will your guests be surprised by the different temperatures!

The colour of this soup varies, depending on the season. Sometimes the beetroots are very red and sometimes not. The soup tastes just as delicious, no matter what the colour is.

Borscht can also be served as a drink. Strain off the solids and serve ice-cold in a glass with sour cream or serve it hot as a cream of beetroot soup.

Serves 6 to 8

60 g	butter
1	onion
1	carrot
1	stick celery, with leaves
2	potatoes
2	ripe tomatoes
1	bunch beetroot
2	cloves garlic
15 ml (1 Tbs)	vinegar or *lemon juice (approximate)*
15 ml (1 Tbs)	sugar (approximate)
	4 bay leaves
3 ml (½ tsp)	dried thyme
750 ml (3 cups)	beef or *vegetable stock*
	salt and pepper to taste
250 ml (1 cup)	sour cream
	or *thick yoghurt*

- Chop or grate all the vegetables.
- Fry the onion in butter until soft.
- Add all remaining ingredients and simmer for about 1 ½ hours until all the vegetables are soft.
- If the soup is too thick, thin it down with extra stock.
- Serve as is, or liquidise for a smoother texture.
- Serve hot or chilled, garnished with sour cream or yoghurt.

Hint

If the soup is being served chunky, shred a large piece of cabbage and add it to the vegetables.

FRENCH ONION SOUP

Traditionally, slices of bread are placed in a heat-resistant bowl, the soup poured over and grated cheese sprinkled on top. The bowl is then placed under the grill to melt the cheese. The bread becomes very mushy this way. I prefer the texture of the cheesy toasted slices of bread served to accompany this hearty soup.

Serves 6 to 8

80 g	butter
4	onions, thinly sliced
30 ml (2 Tbs)	flour
1,5 litre (6 cups)	boiling beef stock
4	bay leaves
	black pepper

To serve

3	rolls or French loaf
	cut in 3 cm slices
	olive oil
	grated cheddar or *parmesan cheese*
	chopped parsley for garnish

- Heat the butter and sauté the onion until glassy. Increase the temperature and allow the onion to start browning. This caramelises the sugar in the onions.
- Sprinkle flour over onions.
- Add crumbled cubes and boiling water.
- Add bay leaves and black pepper to taste.
- Simmer with lid on for 30 minutes.

- Lightly brush the slices of bread with olive oil and toast lightly on both sides under the grill.
- Top with grated cheese and replace under oven grill.
- Sprinkle slices with parsley and float the toast on top of the onion soup.

GOULASH SOUP

A hearty Hungarian soup with the distinctive flavour of sweet paprika. Goulash soup is an inexpensive main course soup for the cold winter months. *Remember, your paprika must be fresh and red!*

Serves 4

5 ml (1 tsp)	salt
5 ml (1 tsp)	black pepper
30 ml (2 Tbs)	paprika
500 g	lean stewing steak or *chuck, cut into small cubes*
75 g	butter
2	large onions, thinly sliced
2 ml (½ tsp)	ground cumin
2	cloves garlic, crushed
45 ml (3 Tbs)	flour
1,5 litres (6 cups)	beef stock
2	large potatoes, cubed
410 g	tinned tomatoes, chopped
	sour cream for garnish

- Combine salt, pepper and paprika.
- Roll the meat in the spices, then brown in butter.
- Add onion and fry with the meat over medium heat until onions are glassy.
- Add cumin, garlic and flour and cook for 2 minutes.
- Add the beef stock, bring to the boil, and simmer for 2 to 3 hours.
- Add potatoes and tomato and simmer for another hour.
- Serve garnished with sour cream.

BEAN SOUP AUGIER

This soup has a distinctly Middle-Eastern flavour and is most reminiscent of the traditional bean dish called *Ful Medames*. I first tasted this soup made with little black beans, which were delicious. I have found these black beans occasionally, but generally I make the soup with speckled sugar beans. Served as a main meal with hot, crusty white bread, followed by a salad and cheese board, there is nothing to beat it on a cold winter's evening. I have divided this recipe into three stages which are very easy to follow.

Serves 6 to 8

First stage

250 g	black beans or *any dark beans*
1	large potato, peeled and cubed
5 ml (1 tsp)	dried thyme
1,5 litres (6 cups)	strong beef or vegetable stock

- *Quick-soak the beans:* Pour 2 litres water over the beans and bring to the boil. Leave to stand for 1 hour. Bring back to the boil and pour off the water. (Pouring off the water helps to prevent flatulence!)
- *Or soak beans overnight*, but again pour away this water.
- Place beans, potato and thyme in the stock in a pot and simmer for about 1 hour or until beans are soft.

Second stage

2	onions, chopped
410 g	tinned tomatoes (with juice), chopped

- Add the onion and tomato (with the juice) to the beans and simmer for another hour.
- With a potato masher, mash some of the beans in the soup to make it thicker. Alternatively, place 2 cups of the soup in a food processor and process until smooth, then return to the rest of the soup. This thickens the soup slightly and makes it creamy.

Third stage

  30 ml (2 Tbs) olive oil
  15-30 ml (1-2 Tbs) wine vinegar
    or *lemon juice*
  2 cloves garlic, chopped
    dash of Tabasco sauce

Note: The soup should have just enough vinegar to give a slightly acid flavour, and just enough Tabasco to give it a kick.

▶ Add the oil, vinegar, garlic and Tabasco to the soup.
▶ Simmer for 1 minute.
▶ Check seasoning and serve with plenty of garnish

Garnish

  2 hard boiled eggs, finely chopped
  1 large onion, finely chopped
    finely chopped parsley

▶ Place garnishes in 3 separate bowls and let people help themselves.

RUSSIAN CABBAGE SOUP

This classic Russian soup derives its flavour from the sauerkraut and dill, and the garnish of sour cream. Served with fresh rye or wholewheat bread, it makes a tasty, unusual winter's meal-in-one.

Serves 6 to 8

Stock

  500 g lean boneless brisket, cubed
  6 marrow bones
  1 large onion, quartered
  2 carrots, in large pieces
  2 sticks and leaves celery, in large pieces
  3 sprigs parsley
  1 parsnip, in large pieces
  5 bay leaves
  2 litres (8 cups) weak beef stock
    black pepper

▶ Place all ingredients in a pot and simmer for 3 hours.
▶ Strain off solids, keeping the meat and marrow bones and discarding the vegetables.
▶ Skim off and discard the fat.

Soup

  80 g butter
  1 litre (4 cups) finely shredded cabbage
  250 ml (1 cup) sauerkraut, rinsed under cold water
  1 carrot, in julienne strips
  1 large onion, chopped
  1 turnip, chopped
  2 sticks celery, chopped
  150 g brown mushrooms, sliced
  410 g tinned tomatoes (with juice), chopped
  2 cloves garlic, crushed
  10 ml (2 tsp) chopped fresh dill
  or 3 ml (½ tsp) dried dill
    salt and pepper to taste
    sour cream or *yoghurt* to garnish

▶ In a large pot sauté cabbage and sauerkraut in half the butter over a high heat until just beginning to brown.
▶ Remove from pot.
▶ Add remaining butter and sauté remaining vegetables *except tomato*, until glassy.
▶ Replace cabbage mixture and add strained stock, meat and bones, tomato and seasoning.
▶ Simmer for 20 minutes. For best results, leave in fridge for 24 to 48 hours before using.
▶ Serve garnished with sour cream or yoghurt.

BOUILLABAISSE

This superb, rich fish soup is of French Provençale origin, made by the fishermen with their unsold fish. It is served as the main dish with the rouille sauce and warm crusty bread.

It is often difficult to get enough bones and heads. Whenever you buy fish for grilling or frying, ask for the heads and bones and freeze them. When you have enough in the freezer, all you need is the fish served in the stock, which is much easier to come by.

It takes time, patience and effort to make bouillabaisse, so make enough for at least 8 people. You could make the large quantity of stock and freeze what you don't need, adding just enough fish for the number of people you are feeding when you want it. The stock is also wonderful to use for poaching fish in, or as the base of a sauce for grilled, poached or baked fish. The addition of the spice saffron is traditional and imparts a delicious flavour.

Although the court bouillon (fish stock) is better made a day in advance, once the fish has been added, the soup should be eaten immediately. The rouille sauce served with the soup adds life, texture and a slight kick to the already tantalising flavour.

Avoid game or oily fish such as yellowtail or tunny, as these can make the soup bitter. If you want to, add a lobster body (with shell), if available.

Four kilograms of a variety of whole line fish will give you about 2,5 kg bones and heads, and about 1,5 kg filleted fish.

Serves 8 to 10

Court bouillon (stock)

125 ml ($\frac{1}{2}$ cup)	olive oil
2	large onions
1	bunch leeks
3	cloves garlic
$\frac{1}{2}$	bunch parsley
4	sticks celery, with leaves
2 litres (8 cups)	water
500 ml (2 cups)	off-dry white wine
410 g	tinned tomatoes
30 ml (2 Tbs)	tomato paste
1	large pinch saffron
	juice of 1 lemon
2	strips lemon peel
2	Telma onion stock cubes, crumbled (optional)
5 ml (1 tsp)	dried thyme
5 ml (1 tsp)	dried tarragon
3	bay leaves
	salt and black pepper
2-2,5 kg	fish heads and bones of assorted line fish

▸ Wash and very roughly cut up all the vegetables, leaving the onion skins and garlic skins on and the stalks on the parsley (that's where most of the flavour is!)
▸ In a very large pot, sauté all the vegetables in the olive oil until the celery and onions are glassy.
▸ Add all the remaining ingredients, using only enough water to cover the heads and bones.
▸ Bring to the boil, lower the heat and simmer very gently for 2 hours. Do not boil.
▸ Strain off all solids and return stock to the pot.
▸ Season to taste.
▸ For the best flavour, cool and chill for 24 hours before straining.

To complete
Make rouille sauce (recipe follows), then continue with the soup as follows:

250 g	pasta shells
2 kg	fresh line fish of your choice, filleted and skinned (e.g. kabeljou, Cape salmon, hottentot, silver fish, steenbras, stumpnose, lobster tails, shrimps, mussels in or out of their shells, calamari)
125 ml ($\frac{1}{2}$ cup)	chopped parsley

▸ Cut the fish into large cubes.
▸ Bring the chilled stock to the boil and add pasta. Cook until the pasta is just cooked.
▸ Check seasoning.
▸ When you are ready to eat, add the fish to the boiling soup and bring back to the boil. The moment it comes back to the boil the fish is cooked do not overcook it.
▸ Serve sprinkled with plenty of parsley.
▸ Eat it with a good spoonful of rouille sauce on top of the soup, and plenty hot crusty white bread.

Rouille sauce

1 large	red pepper
1 large	green pepper
1 large	potato
5 ml (1 tsp)	dried basil
or 15 ml (1 Tbs)	fresh, chopped basil
2	cloves garlic, crushed
1	chilli, finely chopped
or 15 ml (1 Tbs)	chilli sauce
15 ml (1 Tbs)	olive oil
	a little fish stock

- Remove the seeds from the peppers and peel the potato.
- Cut vegetables into large pieces and boil in a little water until soft.
- Place the vegetables in a food processor with basil, garlic, chilli and olive oil and process.
- If sauce is too thick, add a little fish stock to make it the consistency of cream cheese.
- Season to taste and serve a liberal dollop on the soup.

CHICKEN AND SMOKED SAUSAGE GUMBO

A traditional Cajun or Creole soup from New Orleans. Cajun foods contain all the peppers, sweet and hot, making it very spicy. The combination of onions, celery, sweet peppers and tomato appear in many of the dishes. I have toned the cayenne pepper down a little. If you want it hotter, increase the quantity of cayenne to taste.

This soup is usually made without the rice and then served as a meal on cooked rice. I like to cook a little rice in the soup for more flavour and to serve the soup with crusty bread.

The soup is at its best if the stock and roux are made the day before and left in the fridge. Pour the excess oil off the roux. Remove the bones from the stock. Complete the soup the next day.

A quicker version is to use only commercial stock instead of making your own stock with the bones.

Serves 8

8	medium chicken portions of your choice
10 ml (2 tsp)	garlic salt
2 ml ($^1/_2$ tsp)	cayenne pepper
10 ml (2 tsp)	paprika
2 ml ($^1/_2$ tsp)	black pepper

- Remove the skin from the chicken, cut all the meat off the bones and cut into cubes. Reserve skin and bones.
- Mix salt, cayenne pepper, paprika and black pepper and coat chicken pieces with this mixture. Set aside.

Stock

2,5 litres (10 cups)	weak chicken stock
	all chicken bones and skin from portions
2	sticks celery, with leaves
2	bay leaves
1	onion
	peppercorns

- Place all the ingredients in a pot and simmer for 1 $^1/_2$ to 2 hours.
- Reduce to about 2 litres by boiling rapidly.
- Meanwhile make black roux.

Black roux

80 ml ($^1/_3$ cup)	flour
80 ml ($^1/_3$ cup)	oil

- Mix the flour and oil in a pot and cook gently, stirring continually until roux is almost black. Be careful not to scorch it. (It will smell slightly burnt.)
- This can be made very easily in a microwave oven starting on high for about 5 minutes and switching to medium. Stir very often until the flour is very dark.
- Before using the roux, refrigerate it for several hours and pour off all the excess oil that rises to the surface.

To complete gumbo

	reserved chicken pieces, coated with seasoning
45 ml (3 Tbs)	oil
250 ml (1 cup)	chopped onion
250 ml (1 cup)	chopped celery, with leaves
250 ml (1 cup)	chopped green pepper
2	cloves garlic, crushed
410 g	tinned tomatoes with juice, chopped
250 g	fresh okra (lady's fingers)
or 410 g	tinned okra with juice, sliced (optional)
2 litres (8 cups)	strained stock
125 ml ($^1/_2$ cup)	rice
300 g	coarse-grained smoked sausage (e.g. chorizo sausages), thickly sliced
	enough black roux to thicken
	salt, pepper and cayenne pepper to taste

- Brown chicken in oil.
- Add onions, celery and green pepper and sauté till glassy.
- Add garlic, tomato, okra, stock and rice and simmer until rice is cooked.
- Add sausage.
- Stir in the roux to form thick soup consistency.
- Check seasoning and serve.

HOT AND SOUR SOUP

A South African version of a peppery, slightly tart Chinese soup. For vegetarians, simply omit the chicken and shrimps and use vegetable stock. Wood ears, also called cloud ears, are an edible fungus that grows on trees. Tofu are soy bean cakes, and both are available from Chinese restaurants and speciality shops and very often from health shops.

Serves 4 to 6

1,2 litres (5 cups)	strong chicken stock
2	chicken breasts
or 150 g	lean pork
125 g (½ punnet)	brown mushrooms
30 ml (2 Tbs)	dried wood ears (optional)
150 g	frozen shrimps
2	tofu cakes
1	bunch spring onions
30 ml (2 Tbs)	frozen peas
1	egg
15 ml (1 Tbs)	sesame seed oil (optional)
	chopped coriander leaves to garnish

Hot and sour mixture

30 ml (2 Tbs)	soy sauce
45 ml (3 Tbs)	vinegar
5 ml (1 tsp)	sugar
15 ml (1 Tbs)	medium dry sherry
5 ml (1 tsp)	black pepper
30 ml (2 Tbs)	cornflour
45 ml (3 Tbs)	water
	salt to taste

- Soak dried wood ears in boiling water for 30 minutes.
- Pour stock into a large pot.
- Add soaking water to stock.
- Cut chicken and mushrooms into fine julienne strips.
- Cut tofu into small blocks. Coarsely chop spring onions.
- Tear up wood ears and coriander leaves.
- Add mushroom, chicken, wood ears, shrimps, tofu, spring onion and peas and bring to the boil.
- Mix ingredients of hot and sour mixture and pour into soup.
- Stir until thickened, being careful not to break up the tofu.
- Beat egg with a little salt and gradually pour into boiling soup.
- Add sesame seed oil
- Garnish with chopped coriander leaves and serve immediately.

 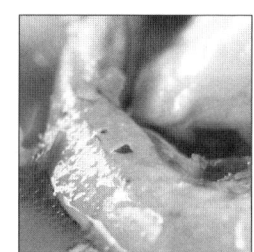 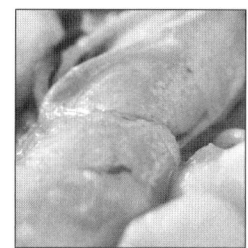

FISH FROM SOUTH AFRICAN WATERS

When buying fish make sure that it is fresh:
- The fish should not smell 'fishy', but rather like the sea.
- The eyes must be clear, wet and protrude from the head a little.
- The fish should look wet and shiny, with all the scales still in place.
- Fish should feel firm and springy to the touch.

Have the fish gutted and scaled and, if you prefer, the skin removed. Have it filleted or butterflied, but remember, there will always be a few bones remaining for you to remove before cooking. Whenever possible, I leave the skin on, especially on hake. It holds the fish together and, when fried, becomes crisp and delicious.

Before cooking fish, rinse it under cold water to remove any loose scales. Pat it dry with roller towel and keep it on a plate in the fridge, covered with clingfilm.

Most fish recipes can be used for any kind of fish.

Traditionally, the types of fish are divided into two groups *oily fish* and *white fish*. The trickiest types to cook are a few of the very soft, white fish, and those that toughen easily. I have listed those separately.

Oily fish
All game fish belong in this group. Besides being more oily, they are also much firmer than most of the white fish (with the exception of elf). Examples include snoek, galjoen, mackerel, elf (shad), bonito, swordfish, tunny, yellowtail, barracuda.

White fish
Hake, kingklip, kabeljou (cob), Cape salmon (geelbek), red roman, stumpnose (red and white), steenbras (red and white), silverfish, hottentot, John Dory, blue fish, gurnard, musselcracker, sole, monkfish, angelfish (a white fish, although it contains a layer of oil just under the skin).

Tricky fish
- Kingklip and monkfish become very tough if overcooked.
- Tunny is very dry and needs moisture while cooking, or, best of all, cook medium-rare.
- Hake is very soft.
- Snoek can be limp or 'wormy'. If it is not firm-fleshed, don't buy it.
- The small types of fish tend to be soft and can be overcooked easily and fall to pieces.

If the recipe calls for white fish (which is softer than the oily types) and you have only oily fish available, there is no problem. Simply use the oily fish exactly the same way.

If, however, the recipe calls for a fish that is firm or from the oily fish group, and you want to use a softer white fish, first coat it with flour and seal it in a hot pan in a little butter and oil. Then continue with the recipe.

THE BASICS OF COOKING FISH

There are certain herbs and spices that go particularly well with fish. If in doubt, use a combination of the following and you will always be sure of success:

Musts: Salt, freshly ground black pepper, fresh lemon juice, parsley and fresh paprika (it must have a bright red colour and a fresh, sweet aroma if not, throw it out!)

Also good: Garlic, dill, basil, tarragon, fennel, bay leaves. Thyme, marjoram and origanum are also suitable.

Filleting fish

Many people miss out on the pleasure of eating fish because of the bones. Even after filleting, fish will always have a few bones. Run your finger down the centre of each fillet and you will feel any remaining bones. It is very easy to remove those few bones before you cook the fish. I keep a small pair of jewellery pliers especially for this job. (A strong pair of eyebrow tweezers will also do.) I learnt this trick in London while working at Leith's Catering Company, where I once had to fillet 150 salmon! I smelled of fish for days, but my hands were baby soft from the salmon oil.

When is fish done?

Test for doneness by parting the flesh: as soon as it is opaque right through, the fish is nicely done.

Fish cooks very quickly and must never be overcooked!

Grilling fish

- Preheat the oven to 250 °C very hot! If you don't preheat the oven, the fish will end up drying out before it is browned and cooked.
- Change oven setting to grill and wait for grill to get red hot.
- Place fish in an ovenware dish, not on a rack, and brush with lemon juice, butter and seasoning to taste.
- Place fish very close to grill and close the oven door to keep the heat in.
- Grill for only a few minutes until fish is brown (3 to 5 minutes).
- Turn the fish carefully, repeat the seasoning on the other side, and grill for a further 3 minutes.

Frying fish

- Fish is generally coated with seasoned flour or batter before it is fried.
- The sequence for coating and frying always remains the same: *wet* food – *dry* flour – *wet* egg – *dry* flour or crumbs. You can stop this sequence at any point depending on how you want the food coated.

SEASONED FLOUR FOR FRIED FISH

Mix the following:

   250 ml (1 cup)   cake flour
   7 ml (1 ½ tsp)   paprika
   10 ml (2 tsp)   salt
                    pinch of pepper

- Lightly coat fish with seasoned flour.
- Using half butter and half oil, fry fish in a little fat in a hot pan to seal it on both sides.
- Reduce heat and cook slowly until cooked through.

THIN BATTER COATING FOR FRIED FISH

- Coat fish on all sides with seasoned flour. Shake off excess.
- Beat an egg with a little water and a pinch of salt.
- Dip floured fish in egg mixture. Let excess egg drip off.
- Shallow fry (oil depth half-way up the side of the fish) in hot oil.
- Turn fish, then reduce heat and cook on medium until done.
- Drain on absorbent paper.

SOFT BATTER FOR FRIED FISH

   250 ml (1 cup)   cake flour
                1   egg, beaten
   160 ml (⅔ cup)   water
                     salt, pepper and paprika to taste

- Mix all the ingredients and leave to stand for 30 minutes.
- Dip *dry* fish in batter, allow excess to run off and fry in deep oil until golden.

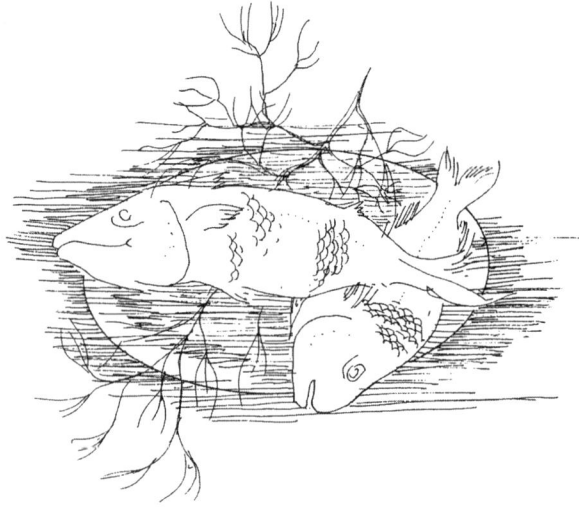

CRISP BATTER FOR FRIED FISH

180 ml (³/₄ cup) self-raising flour
60 ml (¹/₄ cup) cornflour
185 ml (³/₄ cup) water or beer (approximate)
plenty of salt, pepper and paprika to taste

- Mix all ingredients and leave to stand for 30 minutes before using.
- Dip *dry* fish into seasoned flour and then into batter, and let excess run off.
- Fry in deep oil until done and golden.

Hint
For a more 'glassy' crisp batter, increase the amount of cornflour; use half cornflour and half self-raising flour in the mix of 250 ml (I cup).

CRUMB COATING FOR FRIED FISH

- Lightly coat fish in seasoned flour.
- Dip fish into mixture of beaten egg and water.
- Coat well in dry crumbs of your choice.
- Refrigerate for at least 2 hours or place in the deep freeze for 15 minutes before frying in deep or shallow oil.

POACHING FISH

- Make a well flavoured stock using water or vegetable stock, a little wine or lemon juice, slices of onion, bay leaves, freshly milled black pepper, herbs of your choice (preferably fresh), or a good fish stock (see *recipe*).
- Bring stock to the boil.
- Place the fish in a frying pan or roasting pan and pour on just enough boiling stock to cover the fish.
- Brush greaseproof paper or aluminium foil (not waxed paper) with butter and place on top of the fish.
- Place in a very hot oven (220 °C) for 10 minutes or until the fish is just cooked. Cooking time depends on the thickness of the fish. Alternatively, simmer gently on top of the stove for 7 to 10 minutes, but be careful not to overcook it.
- The stock may then be strained and used to make a sauce for the fish.

FISH STOCK

Using fish stock (instead of milk, water, vegetable stock or wine) for cooking fish and for all your fish sauces transforms an ordinary dish into a gourmet dish. And it is so easy to make!

Makes about 750 ml

1 kg assorted fish bones and heads (not oily game fish)
750 ml (3 cups) cold water
250 ml (1 cup) dry white wine
2 sticks celery with leaves
3 sprigs parsley
1 onion, sliced
1 carrot, sliced
juice and skin of ¹/₂ lemon, cut into 4 pieces
4 bay leaves
1 Telma onion stock cube (optional)
3 ml (¹/₂ tsp) black pepper
5 ml (1 tsp) salt

- Simmer all ingredients very gently for 1 hour.
- Leave to cool, preferably overnight in the fridge. Then strain and discard the solids.
- This stock can be made in advance and frozen in small quantities until required.

BRAAIED FISH

Use plenty of coals, but allow them to burn down until they are grey. Oil the grid lightly.

In restaurants, chefs first dip fish into flour to prevent it sticking to the grill. I decided to try this for braaied fish, because the skin, which is the nicest part when it is crispy, usually sticks to the grid. It works perfectly for whole fish or for fillets; the only exception I found was hake, which is just too soft. Use seasoned flour, as described at the beginning of this chapter.

1 large fresh line fish, filleted but preferably not skinned
250 ml (1 cup) seasoned flour, with herbs of your choice added

- If desired, the fish can be marinated in lemon juice for 30 minutes before cooking.
- Coat both sides of the *dry* fish with seasoned flour and shake of excess.

- Dip the flour-coated fish into a basting mixture of your choice. Let the excess run off.
- Place, skin side down, on the grid and braai for about 15 minutes (for large fillets).
- Turn and braai the other side for about 5 minutes.
- In a Weber or other kettle braai, the fish will cook faster than on open coals; braai the first side for 7 to 10 minutes and the other side for a further 7 minutes.
- Serve with a sauce made from the remaining basting mixture, diluted with vegetable stock and slightly thickened with cornflour.

BASIC BASTING FOR FISH

125 g	melted butter
125 ml ($^1/_2$ cup)	sunflower or olive oil
	juice of 1 lemon

- Mix and dip the flour-coated fish in the basting before placing it on the grid. Baste while braaiing.

SWEET AND SOUR BASTE

The apricot jam and lemon juice in this basting sauce gives the fish a sweet and sour taste that is especially delicious with yellowtail.

125 g	butter
60 ml (4 Tbs)	oil
45 ml (3 Tbs)	smooth apricot jam
45 ml (3 Tbs)	lemon juice
30 ml (2 Tbs)	soy sauce
10 ml (2 tsp)	crushed, dried tarragon

Sauce

125 ml ($^1/_2$ cup)	vegetable or fish stock
5 ml (1 tsp)	cornflour
	remaining basting mixture

- Combine the first six ingredients in a saucepan and cook over low heat, stirring constantly, until the jam has melted.
- Combine the sauce ingredients, *except the remaining basting mixture*, and bring to the boil.
- Stir in the remaining basting mixture and check seasoning.

BASIC FISH CAKES

Although fish cakes can be made with raw minced fish, I find that they are juicier and tastier when made with cooked fish. My favourite mix is half haddock and half hake.

Makes 8 to 12 cakes

500 g	raw fish of your choice
1	large potato, peeled and quartered
1	onion, sliced
1	stick celery, with leaves, chopped
2	sprigs parsley, with stalks
4	bay leaves
	water or vegetable stock
1	large onion, finely chopped
	butter
80 ml ($^1/_3$ cup)	chopped parsley
1	egg, beaten
	salt and black pepper to taste

- Place the fish and potato in a pot with sliced onion, celery, parsley, bay leaves, salt and black pepper.
- Cover with water or stock and simmer until fish is cooked.
- Remove the fish and continue cooking until the potatoes are soft. Remove potatoes and discard the rest.
- Flake the fish, removing all the bones.
- Mash the cooked potato *without* milk or butter. Add to fish.
- Sauté the chopped onion well in butter and add, with chopped parsley, beaten egg and plenty of seasoning to fish and mashed potato. Mix well.
- Shape into fish cakes and continue following all the steps for crumbing (see method at the beginning of this chapter).
- Serve fish cakes with a variety of sauces (See under *Sauces* for those suitable for fish).

Hint

Cook the potatoes in large pieces and only until soft enough to mash, otherwise the mixture may become mushy. If the mixture is a little too wet, omit the egg and add enough instant mashed potato (Smash) or matzo meal to make it firm enough to shape.

THE BASICS OF SEAFOOD

Calamari
- Clean the calamari well by removing the inside body and the piece of plastic material.
- Slice the tube into thick rings and cut off the legs. Discard the rest.
- Dry on absorbent paper.

Fried calamari
- Place the rings of calamari in fresh lemon juice for 30 minutes.
- Drain well.
- Dip into well-seasoned flour (see under *Basics of cooking fish*).
- Shake in a sieve to remove the excess.
- Fry *very quickly* in *very hot oil* in small batches.
- Drain on absorbent paper and serve immediately with lemon juice, sauce tartar, or lemon garlic butter (see *Sauces*).

Prawns
- Thaw the prawns in cold water.
- With a sharp knife, slit down the back of each prawn.
- Remove black 'vein' and remove dark matter from head.
- Dry very well.
- Deep-fry in oil for 1 minute.
- *Do not overcook.*
- Serve with lemon garlic butter or peri peri sauce (see *Sauces*)

Crayfish (South African rocklobster)

Grilled
- Drop fresh crayfish, preferably alive, into a small quantity of vigorously boiling water for 5 minutes (frozen crayfish boils for an extra 2 minutes). The crayfish will be parcooked.
- Remove from water and, with a pair of scissors, cut down the back and head.
- Remove dark 'vein' and remove green matter from head.
- Place on baking sheet and thickly spread on garlic butter (see *Sauces*). Place under grill for 5 minutes.
- *Do not overcook.*

Boiled crayfish
- For fresh crayfish, boil for 8 minutes.
- For frozen crayfish, boil for 10 minutes.
- *Do not overcook.*

Perlemoen (Abalone)
- Slice the well-cleaned perlemoen into paper thin slices using a very sharp knife. If the slices are not very thin, place them between two sheets of clingfilm and flatten them with a meat mallet or a rolling pin.
- Dip the slices in well-seasoned flour and flash fry in butter. Fry over a high heat until it is brown on both sides. Ten seconds should be long enough!
- Drain and serve with fresh lemon or lemon garlic butter.

Mussels

Frozen
- Remove the mussels from the packet and place on an ovenware dish.
- Pour the hot sauce over the frozen mussels.
- Heat through in the oven at 180 °C for 15 to 20 minutes.

Off the rocks
- Scrub the fresh mussels and remove the beard and any seaweed.
- Cook only the mussels that are closed. Discard the rest.
- Steam the mussels in a closed pot. No extra liquid is needed as there is enough liquid in the mussels that will drain as they open; or add a little wine for the flavour. Do not overcook them.
- Once you have steamed and de-bearded them, rinse under running water to remove any remaining sand.

Cultivated mussels
- Many fresh cultivated mussels will have opened before you cook them. This does not mean they are off. Tap them with a knife and most of them will slowly close. You will quickly smell if they are not fresh!
- Steam the mussels in a little salted water or wine, only until the shells open. *Do not overcook them.*
- Remove the beards and discard any mussels that have not opened.
- Serve with garlic butter, lemon garlic sauce, the tomato sauce from the calamari in tomato sauce, cream and white wine sauce, or any sauce of your choice (see *Sauces*).

PAN-FRIED LINE FISH WITH JULIENNE VEGETABLES

The secret of this recipe lies in the freshness of the fish. It must be cooked at the last minute and eaten immediately. Served on a bed of fresh stir-fried vegetables with simple lemon butter, this plain pan-fried fish becomes a very special dish.

Serves 4

800 g	fillets of firm, fresh fish
80 g	butter
	seasoned flour
50 g	butter
2	carrots
2	sticks of celery
2	leeks
5 cm	cucumber
2	sticks fennel *when available*
2	turnips
	salt and pepper
	fresh lemon juice

- Cut the fish into 4 to 6 even-sized pieces.
- Cut all the vegetables into julienne strips (thin matchsticks).
- Dry fish and dip into seasoned flour.
- Fry in butter until cooked through and lightly browned.
- In a separate pan, sauté the vegetables in butter until almost soft.
- Season with salt, pepper and lemon juice.
- Place a bed of vegetables on each plate and the fish on top, or arrange ingredients the other way around.
- Pour on lemon garlic butter. (See under *Basics of cooking fish*)

SPICY RED FISH

The famous Cajun 'blackened red fish' is unusual and delicious, but very tricky to make at home, because an extremely high heat is needed. In fact, I know someone who uses a blowtorch! It can only be done outside; I use high-pressure gas on full blast and a cast-iron pan. The secret is to coat the fish with spices and then burn them onto the fish. Once the spices are burnt black, the bite of the chillies is lessened.

Traditionally, this dish is served with melted butter and lemon juice. I have taken the conventional combination of spices and added them to seasoned flour. Pan-fried and served with lemon juice, fish done in this way has the same flavour profile as the real thing and you won't need to call in the fire department!

Serves 4

4	fillets firm line fish, skin left on (e.g. red roman, red stumpnose)

Coating mixture

15 ml (1 Tbs)	paprika
5 ml (1 tsp)	onion salt
5 ml (1 tsp)	garlic salt
1 ml (pinch)	cayenne pepper
5 ml (1 tsp)	black pepper
7 ml (1 ½ tsp)	dried thyme
7 ml (1 ½ tsp)	dried origanum
80 ml (⅓ cup)	flour
	butter and oil for frying

- Combine all the ingredients.
- Coat the fish in the spicy flour mixture.
- Fry in a mixture of butter and oil until cooked through.
- Serve with lemon butter sauce (see *Basics of cooking fish*) or lemon wedges for squeezing.

FISH MILANESE

The fresh soft breadcrumbs give the marinated fish a light, crisp, buttery coating. Served with a browned butter sauce, this is something really special.

Serves 4

750 g	fish fillets

Marinade

1	onion, chopped
1	clove garlic, crushed
45 ml (3 Tbs)	lemon juice
30 ml (2 Tbs)	oil
	salt and pepper
	seasoned flour (see *The Basics of cooking fish*)
1	egg, beaten with a little milk or water
250 ml (1 cup)	fresh white breadcrumbs
30 ml (2 Tbs)	grated parmesan cheese
100 g	butter (approximate)
45 ml (3 Tbs)	oil

- Mix the marinade ingredients and marinate fish for 2 hours.
- Mix breadcrumbs and parmesan cheese.
- Dry the fish and dip it in the flour, then the egg and then coat with crumbs.
- Place in the freezer for 15 minutes.
- Fry in a mixture of butter and oil and drain on absorbent paper.
- Serve with brown butter sauce.

Brown butter sauce

60 g	butter
1-2	cloves garlic, crushed
30 ml (2 Tbs)	fresh lemon juice
30 ml (2 Tbs)	finely chopped parsley
	salt and pepper to taste

- Just before serving, melt the butter with the garlic.
- Heat until butter turns brown.
- Add lemon juice and parsley and pour over the fish.

KINGKLIP SESAME GUJONS

Gujons are small, fat fingers of fish perfect to serve hot or cold as a starter, a snack or at a cocktail party. Piled up on a plate with a good sauce, they are delicious as a main course.

Serves 4

750 g	kingklip or other line fish, cut into gujons about 6 cm long and 3 cm thick

Batter

250 ml (1 cup)	self-raising flour
125 ml ($^1/_2$ cup)	sesame seeds
3 ml ($^1/_2$)	tsp salt
5 ml (1 tsp)	paprika
250 ml (1 cup)	water (approximate)

- Mix the batter ingredients and leave to stand for 1 hour.
- Dip the gujons into the batter and fry in deep oil until golden brown.
- Drain on absorbent paper and serve with the sauce of your choice my favourite is avocado sauce (see under *Sauces*).

Hint

If you are going to serve the fish cold, fry the gujons twice, and they will remain crisp even when cold. First fry them until they are just starting to brown. Remove and drain on absorbent paper. Then fry again in very hot oil, a few pieces at a time, very quickly, until they turn golden brown. Drain again on absorbent paper.

SESAME FRIED PRAWNS

This recipe is equally successful using any fresh fish cut into gujons small, thick fingers of fish. Serve the prawns with fried rice.

Serves 4 as a main course, 8 as a starter

20-24	king prawns

Marinade

30 ml (2 Tbs)	lemon juice
5 ml (1 tsp)	soy sauce
30 ml (2 Tbs)	medium cream sherry
5 ml (1 tsp)	grated fresh ginger
5 ml (1 tsp)	castor sugar
1	clove garlic, crushed

Batter

1 x batter	from Kingklip sesame gujons recipe

- Remove the heads and shell prawns, leaving the tail attached.
- Slit the prawn along back and almost, but not quite, through.
- Remove vein and open prawn out like a butterfly.
- Combine the marinade ingredients and pour over prawns.
- Leave to marinate for 1 to 2 hours.
- Make the batter with flour, seeds, salt and water. Leave to stand for 1 hour.
- Dip the prawns into the batter and fry in hot deep oil until golden.
- Serve with sauce tartar (see under *Sauces*) or green mayonnaise (see recipe).

Green mayonnaise

1-2	*spinach leaves*
80 ml (about $^1/_3$ cup)	*mayonnaise*
1	*clove garlic, crushed*
15 ml (1 Tbs)	*lemon juice*
	salt and black pepper
5 ml (1 tsp)	*soy sauce*
3 ml ($^1/_2$ tsp)	*grated fresh root ginger*

▸ Place all the ingredients in a liquidiser and blend well.

ROAST LINE FISH

Roasted open in a very hot oven, the fish becomes crisp on the outside while remaining juicy inside. Or stuff the fish with the mixture given, tie up and braai whole over the coals. Work on *300 g raw fish per person* (including the bones and head).

1-1,5 kg	*line fish, filleted* or *butterflied, but not skinned*
1	*large onion*
2	*carrots*
2	*celery sticks*
1	*large* or *2 small turnips*
125 g	*mushrooms*
125 g	*butter*
2	*sprigs fennel (optional)*
5 ml (1 tsp)	*dried dill, if not using fennel*
	salt and pepper
	juice of 1 lemon
	lemon wedges for serving

▸ Preheat the oven to 220 °C.
▸ Slice the onion, and cut other vegetables into julienne strips.
▸ Fry the vegetables in the butter until just changing colour.
▸ Add dill, salt and pepper to taste.
▸ Place one fillet, skin side down, in a buttered baking dish.
▸ Season with salt, paprika and some lemon juice.
▸ Spread vegetables on top of the fish.
▸ Place the remaining fillet on top, skin side up.
▸ Place toothpicks through the two fillets, joining them together loosely, with the filling inside.
▸ Pour more lemon juice over the fish and check seasoning.
▸ Dot with extra butter.
▸ Bake, uncovered, for 20 to 30 minutes at 220 °C.
▸ Serve with extra fresh lemon or lemon butter sauce.

Braaiing
▸ Butterfly the whole fish, slitting open on the belly side but keeping hinged at the backbone.
▸ Prepare and cook the vegetables as for oven roasting.
▸ Place on one half of the butterflied fish, fold over and tie together with string.
▸ Diagonally slash the skin on both sides to allow the flavour of the basting sauce to penetrate.
▸ Coat the fish with seasoned flour.
▸ Dip into, or paint with a mixture of melted butter and oil.
▸ Braai in a Weber or similar braai oven for about 20 minutes, depending on the size and thickness of the fish, turning and basting once.
▸ Or braai for 30 to 40 minutes or until done (depending on the size and thickness) over open coals, basting as needed with butter and oil mixture.

ISRAELI CRISPY FRIED FISH

On a visit to Israel, we ate St Peter's fish from the Sea of Galilee. We tasted it cooked in different ways, but it was at its best when cooked in the following simple way. I have been cooking the small South African fish the same way and the taste of this usually unexciting fish is extraordinary.

Because the oil is so hot, the fish, after draining, is dry and non-oily, even though fried in deep oil, while the outside remains beautifully crisp.

Even people who hate the bones will be able to handle the fish, because the flesh falls off the bones and the fins just pull out. The skin is also crisp and delicious.

	small pan-sized fish of your choice, scaled but not skinned
1 x 750 ml	*bottle sunflower oil*
	lemons

▸ Preheat the oven to 160 °C to keep the fish hot for a few minutes.
▸ Make 3 deep diagonal slashes on each side, from the top to the bottom of the fish.
▸ Use a wok or a large, deep frying pan.
▸ Set the plate at its highest, or preferably use a gas ring.
▸ Heat all the oil until it begins to smoke.
▸ Fry the fish one or two at a time, depending on the size of the fish and pan and heat.
▸ Place the fish in the oil, being careful to stand clear – it spatters dangerously.
▸ Turn the fish after about 2 minutes, depending on the size, and cook 1 to 2 minutes longer.
▸ Remove and drain on paper
▸ Place in the oven to keep warm (but not for too long!) while frying the rest.

- Make sure the oil is again just beginning to smoke before frying the next fish.
- All you need to serve with the fish are wedges of fresh lemon.

Hints
- Although a lot of oil is needed, it can be reused. Keep oil in the fridge with a couple of cloves of garlic and a chilli in it. It will keep for several months like this and can be used over and over again, as very little is absorbed by the fish.
- Cooking fish outside on a gas burner prevents fishy odours pervading the house.

BAKED LINE FISH EN PAPILOTTE

En papilotte means 'cooked in paper'. Cooking suitable food in greaseproof paper is one of the most efficient ways of keeping it juicy. It is better than aluminium foil, because it keeps the juices in while allowing some of the steam to escape. Use a large sheet of greaseproof paper. Be sure that it is greaseproof paper and not waxed paper.

Serves 4 to 6

250 g	melted butter
	or *a mixture of butter and oil*
	(approximate)
1	line fish of your choice (about 1,5 kg)
1	large onion, sliced
4	brown mushrooms, sliced
4	bay leaves
1	ripe tomato, sliced
5 ml (1 tsp)	dried dill, tarragon, fennel, or marjoram
or 15 ml (1 Tbs)	of the fresh herb
	juice of 1 lemon
4	sprigs parsley
	salt and black pepper

- Leave the fish whole and make 2 large slashes: from stomach cavity, along the bones, towards the tail, and on the top of the fish, from the tail to the head along the fin.
- Stuff these slashes with the remaining ingredients, except the butter.
- Dip a sheet of greaseproof paper in the melted butter and loosely wrap the fish in it.
- Bake on a baking sheet at 200 °C for 40 minutes.
- Serve with herb mayonnaise, sauce tartar, Hollandaise sauce, or other preferred sauce (see under *Sauces* in index).

Hints
- To make it really tasty, fry the onion and mushrooms in a little butter before stuffing the fish.
- If you want to use less butter, crumple up the paper and wet it under the tap, as if it were a piece of cloth. Shake off the excess water and then brush the paper with butter where it will come into contact with the fish.

BAKED FISH AU GRATIN

Baked on a bed of vegetables and topped with a tasty cheese sauce, this is a favourite variation of the basic fish bake.

2	large onions, sliced
2	green or red peppers, sliced
250 g	mushroom (button or brown), thickly sliced
	salt and pepper
15 ml (1 Tbs)	flour
2-3	large, ripe tomatoes, skinned and thickly sliced
3	bay leaves

Cheese sauce

45 g	butter
45 ml (3 Tbs)	flour
375 ml (1 1/2 cups)	milk
125 ml (1/2 cup)	grated cheddar cheese
	extra grated cheddar cheese for topping

- Brown fish as described for *Basic fish bake*.
- In the butter remaining from browning the fish, sauté onion, mushroom and pepper.
- Season to taste.
- Sprinkle on 15 ml flour.
- Add tomatoes be careful not to overmix, to prevent mushiness.
- Add bay leaves.
- Place the fish on top of vegetables in an ovenware dish.
- Melt the butter for the cheese sauce and stir in the flour.
- Add the milk and bring to the boil, whisking continually.
- Remove from heat and stir in cheese.
- Pour the cheese sauce over the fish and top with scattering of extra grated cheese.
- Bake, uncovered, for 30 to 40 minutes in oven preheated to 200 °C.

BASIC FISH BAKE

A wonderful variety of quick fish bakes or casseroles can be made using the same simple method, but substituting one of many different sauces. Very often chicken sauce recipes are also delicious with fish. Simply use fish or vegetable stock instead of chicken stock.

Serves 4 to 6

750 g	fish of your choice, *fresh* or *frozen*
185 ml ($^3/_4$ cup)	flour seasoned with salt, pepper and plenty of paprika
60 ml (4 Tbs)	oil, olive oil, butter *or* a mixture

- Leave the fish in large fillets, or cut into portions if preferred.
- Coat fish in some of the seasoned flour and brown over medium heat in oil, butter or a mixture of these. The fish will be brown, but still raw inside.
- Place fish in an ovenware dish and set it aside while preparing a sauce of your choice.
- Pour the sauce over the fish.
- Bake, uncovered, for 30 to 40 minutes in oven preheated to 200 °C.

Italian sauce

2	medium onions, diced
125 g	rindless streaky bacon, diced
1	green pepper, diced
1	red pepper, diced
15 ml (1 Tbs)	flour remaining from the seasoned flour mixed for the fish
250 ml (1 cup)	white wine or *fish stock* or *vegetable stock*
15 ml (1 Tbs)	tomato paste
2	cloves garlic, crushed
30 ml (2 Tbs)	fresh sweet basil
or 5 ml (1 tsp)	dried origanum
5 ml (1 tsp)	sugar
	salt and pepper
2	ripe tomatoes, skinned and cubed
8-10	baby potatoes, boiled and halved
30 ml (2 Tbs)	grated parmesan cheese

- In the oil remaining from browning the fish, sauté onion, bacon and green and red peppers until bacon is cooked.
- Stir 15 ml flour into the onion mixture.
- Stir in wine or stock, tomato paste, garlic, herbs and seasoning to taste.
- Bring to the boil, stirring constantly.
- Remove from the heat and carefully fold in the tomatoes. Do not overmix, or the tomatoes will become mushy. Add extra liquid if required.
- Arrange the potatoes around the fish in the ovenware dish.
- Pour the sauce over the fish, sprinkle with the parmesan cheese and place in the oven.
- Bake, uncovered, for 30 to 40 minutes in oven preheated to 200 °C.

Greek flavour fish bake

- Brown the fish as described for *Basic fish bake*.
- Follow the recipe for Italian sauce, with these variations:
- Leave out the bacon and parmesan cheese.
- Stir 12 pitted and halved black olives in with the tomatoes.
- Crumble 250 g feta cheese over the fish before pouring the sauce over fish.
- Bake, uncovered, for 30 to 40 minutes in oven preheated to 200 °C.

Spicy yoghurt sauce

This sauce is delicious on braaied fish.

15 ml (1 Tbs)	finely grated fresh ginger
3	cloves garlic
30 ml (2 Tbs)	chopped coriander leaves
2	red *or* green chillies
1	small onion, cut in pieces
10 ml (2 tsp)	ground cumin
30 ml (2 Tbs)	chutney
15 ml (1 Tbs)	tomato paste
45 g	butter, melted
30 ml (2 Tbs)	oil
45 ml (3 Tbs)	lemon juice
175 ml	carton Bulgarian yoghurt
10 ml (2 tsp)	flour

- Prepare the fish as described for *Basic fish bake*.
- Place all the sauce ingredients in a liquidiser and blend until smooth.
- Pour the sauce over fish.
- Bake uncovered for 30 to 40 minutes in oven preheated to 200 °C.

HERBED FISH FILLETS

    60 g butter
    1 clove garlic, crushed
    1 large onion, finely chopped
    30 ml (2 Tbs) lemon juice
    60 ml (1/4 cup) chopped parsley
    3 ml (1/2 tsp) dried tarragon or dill
    3 ml (1/2 tsp) dried thyme
    80 ml (1/3 cup) dry bread crumbs

- Brown the fish as for *Basic fish bake*.
- Sauté the onion and garlic in the remaining butter until glassy.
- Add remaining ingredients and mix well.
- Spread the mixture over fish.
- Bake, uncovered, for only 15 to 20 minutes in oven preheated to 200 °C, because this is a topping rather than a sauce.

JEANS FISH BAKE

    500 g fresh or frozen stir-fry vegetables of your choice (e.g. carrots, onions, mushrooms, baby marrows, celery), all cut into matchsticks or thinly sliced
    250 ml (1 cup) grated cheddar cheese
    250 ml (1 cup) sour cream or pouring cream
    60 ml (1/4 cup) finely chopped parsley
    125 ml (1/2 cup) grated cheddar cheese (extra)
    125 ml (1/2 cup) fresh breadcrumbs
    30 g butter

- Brown the fish as for *Basic fish bake*.
- Stir-fry the vegetables in the remaining butter.
- Place the fish on top of stir-fry. Sprinkle the 250 ml (1 cup) grated cheddar cheese over fish.
- Mix the sour cream and chopped parsley and pour over the cheese on the fish.
- Mix extra cheese and breadcrumbs and sprinkle on top of sour cream.
- Dot with butter.
- Bake, uncovered, for 30 to 40 minutes in oven preheated to 200 °C.

FISH BAKE WITH SOUR CREAM OR YOGHURT

For this delicious fish bake you need sour cream or, as an alternative, one quantity of cooked yoghurt sauce (see *Sauces*).

Sauce
    250 ml (1 cup) sour cream or cooked yoghurt
    80 ml (1/3 cup) mayonnaise
    60 ml (1/4 cup) freshly chopped parsley
    80 ml (1/3 cup) milk
    salt and pepper

Topping
    125 ml (1/2 cup) fresh wholewheat bread crumbs
    125 ml (1/2 cup) grated cheddar cheese

- Brown the fish as for *Basic fish bake*.
- Mix all the sauce ingredients in a liquidiser, or with a spoon.
- Pour over the fish.
- Mix the topping ingredients and scatter over fish and sauce.
- Bake, uncovered, for 30 to 40 minutes in oven preheated to 200 °C.

Further variations
- To ring the changes, use any creamy salad dressing in place of the mayonnaise. Try adding diced apple or grapes, drained asparagus or fried mushrooms to the fish before you pour on the sauce.
- Some of the sauces used for chicken dishes are ideal for fish bakes, but in this case use a vegetable stock for the fish sauce instead of chicken stock. Try the sauces given for the following chicken dishes (see *Poultry*): Polynesian chicken, Paprika chicken, Chicken marengo, Chicken bonne femme, or Chicken a la king.

CALAMARI IN TOMATO SAUCE

Served hot or cold, the subtle flavour of bay leaves enhances the natural taste of calamari. For a change, use mussels instead of calamari for an equally delicious dish.

Serves 4

Sauce

50 g	butter
1	large onion, chopped
6	button mushrooms, chopped
1	stick celery, chopped
2	cloves garlic, crushed
410 g	tinned tomatoes
30 ml (2 Tbs)	tomato paste
125 ml ($^1/_2$ cup)	white wine
15 ml (1 Tbs)	sugar
125 ml ($^1/_2$ cup)	cream
6-8	bay leaves
	salt and pepper to taste
	chopped parsley for garnishing

- Gently sauté the onion, garlic, mushrooms and celery in butter.
- Add tomatoes, tomato paste, wine, bay leaves and seasoning – simmer gently for 10 minutes.
- Remove bay leaves (do not discard) and liquidise sauce if a smooth sauce is desired.
- Add cream and check seasoning.
- Replace bay leaves and reduce to desired thickness.
- Add calamari and either serve immediately or chill well before serving.

For chilled calamari

500 g	cleaned calamari
375 ml (1 $^1/_2$ cups)	vegetable or fish stock
125 ml ($^1/_2$ cup)	white wine

- Combine stock and wine in a pot.
- Cut calamari into rings.
- Bring stock to the boil and drop calamari into pot.
- Cook for about 30 seconds or until calamari is opaque.
- Drain and place in sauce.

For hot calamari

500 g	calamari
100 g	butter

- Heat butter and fry gently until calamari is just opaque.
- Add to hot sauce and serve immediately.

For mussels

- Place frozen mussels in their shells or half shells in the boiling sauce and return to the boil. *Do not overcook.*
- Serve immediately.

POACHED LINE FISH WITH LEMON SAUCE

Serves 4

1,5 kg	line fish (fillets or whole fish)
1	quantity fish stock
	(see Basics of cooking fish)

Lemon sauce

250 ml (1 cup)	fish stock
60 g	butter
30 ml (2 Tbs)	flour
2	eggs, separated
30 ml (2 Tbs)	fresh lemon juice
	pinch of cayenne pepper
125 ml ($^1/_2$ cup)	cream
60 ml ($^1/_4$ cup)	chopped parsley

- Pour stock into a deep roasting pan.
- Add the fish and cover with buttered paper.
- If using fillets, place in an oven preheated to 220 °C for 10 to 15 minutes, or on top of the stove for 7 to 10 minutes. If using whole fish, place in the oven at 180 °C for about 30 minutes, or on top of the stove for about 20 minutes. Cooking time depends on the size and thick-ness of the fish and on degree of heat; test for doneness.
- Place the fish on a serving dish and make the sauce.
- Boil the stock to reduce still further. It must be very rich when you taste it.
- In a small pot, melt the butter and stir in flour.
- Add the stock, lemon juice and cayenne pepper and bring to the boil.
- Remove from heat and combine it with egg yolks and cream.
- Check seasoning.
- Pour over the fish, garnish with chopped parsley and serve with lemon wedges.

Variations

Poached fish can also be served with many other sauces (see *Sauces*). Also try sauce tartar, lemon butter sauce, tarragon cream sauce, mustard mayonnaise (see *Herring* recipes).

GINGER PINEAPPLE YELLOWTAIL

This is a Chinese recipe with a difference. The fish is quickly fried, the vegetables are stir-fried and then everything is quickly cooked in a delicious sweet and sour sauce. Serve on steamed rice.

This recipe works best with a firm game fish.

Serves 4

750 g	filleted yellowtail, or *any firm fish*, cut into thick strips
60 ml (¼ cup)	lemon juice
60 ml (¼ cup)	soy sauce
45 ml (3 Tbs)	cornflour
	oil
150 g	small button mushrooms, left whole
1	onion, sliced in julienne strips
2	bamboo shoots, sliced
6	baby marrows, thickly sliced
or 250 g (1 cup)	broccoli florets
2	pieces glacé ginger, sliced
240 g	tinned pineapple pieces
45 ml (3 Tbs)	sliced water chestnuts
1	bunch spring onions, finely chopped
15 ml (1 Tbs)	sesame seed oil (optional)

Sauce

30 ml (2 Tbs)	syrup
30 ml (2 Tbs)	tinned pineapple juice
30 ml (2 Tbs)	lemon juice
15 ml (1 Tbs)	soy sauce
5 ml (1 tsp)	cornflour
45 ml (3 Tbs)	water
	salt to taste

▸ Mix the lemon juice and soy sauce and marinate fish in this mixture for 15 minutes.
▸ Reserving the remaining marinade, drain the fish well and lightly coat with cornflour.
▸ Fry the fish quickly in shallow oil and remove. Pour off excess oil.
▸ Stir-fry the mushrooms, baby marrows and onion in a little of the remaining oil.
▸ Add the bamboo shoots, ginger, pineapple and water chestnuts.
▸ Lightly toss in the fish, but be careful not to break it up.
▸ Combine all the sauce ingredients, add remaining marinade and pour over fish and vegetables.
▸ Cook the sauce through.
▸ Remove from heat and sprinkle with sesame oil and spring onion.

YELLOWTAIL OR KABELJOU BIRYANI

This recipe was given to me by Amina Petersen who trained all the Pick 'n Pay fish shop staff in Cape Town. Her knowledge of Cape fish is amazing and it was a treat to watch her work with the fish. Cook the rice and lentils in advance.

Serves 6

750 g	yellowtail, Cape Salmon, or kabeljou, cut into pieces
15 ml (1 Tbs)	fish masala
15 ml (1 Tbs)	biryani masala
15 ml (1 Tbs)	turmeric
15 ml (1 Tbs)	ginger and garlic paste
3	cloves garlic, crushed
10 ml (2 tsp)	grated ginger
	oil
2	onions, chopped
2-3	ripe tomatoes, chopped
30 ml (2 Tbs)	chutney
	lemon juice and salt to taste
250 g	rice, cooked with
2 ml (½ tsp)	turmeric
250 g	lentils, cooked
	butter

▸ Mix all the spices with 3 Tbs oil and coat the fish. Leave to stand for 1 hour.
▸ Seal the fish in hot oil and remove from heat.
▸ Fry the onion until glassy.
▸ Add the chopped tomato, chutney, lemon juice and salt to taste and simmer for 2 minutes.
▸ Return the fish to the pan.
▸ Check seasoning.
▸ Layer half the rice, half lentils, all the fish mixture, remaining lentils, and top with remaining rice.
▸ Dot with butter and steam on low heat for 1 hour or in oven preheated to 140 °C for 1 hour.

GEFILTE FISH

Gefilte fish probably originated in Eastern Europe as a poor man's dish. It was a way of using all the bits and pieces of the fish and to prevent waste – perhaps their equivalent of fish biryani or bouillabaisse?

Makes about 16

Stock for gefilte fish

1,5-2 kg	fish bones and heads (no oily or game fish!)
10 ml (2 tsp)	salt
1	onion
2	carrots
	celery
	parsley
2 litres	water
2	vegetable or onion stock cubes (optional)

Fish

2	carrots, chopped
1	large onion, chopped
30 ml (2 Tbs)	oil
1 kg	minced fish (any kind, but preferably a mixture of hake and 2 kinds of line fish)
5 ml (1 tsp)	dried dill or tarragon
80 ml (1/3 cup)	freshly chopped parsley
15 ml (1 Tbs)	matzo meal
or 1 slice	of bread
1/2	vegetable or onion stock cube, dissolved in
125 ml	boiling water
or 125 ml	fish stock
1	egg
	salt and pepper
2-3	extra carrots, left whole

- *To make the stock,* cover the fish and vegetables with water. Add salt to taste and simmer for 1 1/2 hours. Strain off stock.
- *For the fish,* sauté carrot and onion in oil then mince or chop very fine.
- Combine all the ingredients, except the 2 extra carrots.
- With wet hands shape into balls the size of a golf ball or flattened ovals.
- In a large pot bring strained stock to the boil.
- Carefully drop in the fish balls.
- Add the whole carrots.
- Simmer for 45 minutes.
- Remove the fish balls and place in a deep, attractive serving bowl.
- Slice the whole cooked carrots and decorate each fish ball with a carrot ring.
- Carefully strain the cooking liquid over fish balls to cover completely.
- Cool, then refrigerate.

Hint

If the stock does not gel, pour all the stock from the fish into another bowl. Mix 10 ml (2 tsp) of gelatine in a little cold stock. Heat in a pot until gelatine has dissolved and add 1-2 cups of the cold stock to the hot dissolved gelatine. Then add this to the remaining cold stock. Return to the fish balls and chill.

PICKLED FISH

Firm-fleshed fish is generally used for pickled fish, but you can use hake in this recipe.

Serves 4 to 6

750 g	hake
2	eggs, beaten with
45 ml (3 Tbs)	water
	seasoned flour (see Basics of cooking fish)
	oil for frying
3	onions, sliced

Pickle

250 ml (1 cup)	vinegar
325 ml (1 1/3 cup)	water
6	bay leaves
6	white peppercorns
5 ml (1 tsp)	salt
20 ml (4 tsp)	flour
20 ml (4 tsp)	mild curry powder
60 ml (1/4 cup)	smooth apricot jam
30 ml (2 Tbs)	sugar

- Bring the vinegar, water, bay leaves and peppercorns to the boil.
- Mix salt, flour and curry powder with a little cold water and add to the boiling vinegar with the jam and sugar.
- Add onions and boil for 30 seconds; onion must still be crisp.
- Cut the hake into serving portions dip into flour and egg and fry until golden.

- Remove from the oil and simmer in the pickle for 1 minute.
- Remove the fish from the pickle and place in a shallow glass dish.
- Pour over remaining pickle and chill for 24 hours before using.

PICKLED CALAMARI

This delicious pickle can be used with any mixture of fish and seafood.

Serves 6 to 8

800 g	frozen calamari rings, thawed
4	carrots
1	head fennel with leaves
or 4	sticks of celery

Pickle

375 ml (1 $\frac{1}{2}$ cups)	water
375 ml (1 $\frac{1}{2}$ cups)	white wine vinegar
15 ml (1 Tbs)	pickling spice
6	bay leaves
30 ml (2 Tbs)	sugar
10 ml (2 tsp)	salt
4	cloves garlic
125 ml ($\frac{1}{2}$ cup)	olive oil
3	stalks of the fennel leaves
or 10 ml (2 tsp)	dried dill, if using celery

- Thaw the calamari.
- Cut the carrots into julienne strips.
- Slice fennel or celery in thickish slices and retain leaves for pickle.
- *To make the pickle*, place vinegar, water, pickling spice, bay leaves, sugar and salt in a large pot.
- Bring to the boil and then leave to stand for 1 hour to infuse flavours.
- Strain and return liquid and bay leaves to the pot. Discard pickling spices.
- Add garlic, olive oil and fennel leaves and bring to the boil.
- Add the thawed calamari, sliced carrot and fennel. *Remove from the stove immediately.*
- Pour into a dish, stand to cool, cover and chill overnight in the fridge.

'SMOKED' FISH SHANGHAI

The combination of sweet and sour and Oriental spices makes this a pickled fish with a difference.

Serves 6

1 kg	line fish steaks or fillets, cut into 3 cm thick slices
	oil for frying

Marinade

1	small piece root ginger
45 ml (3 Tbs)	soy sauce
30 ml (2 Tbs)	medium dry sherry

Sauce

500 ml (2 cups)	water
1	star anise
1	stick cinnamon
2	pieces naartjie or orange peel
3	spring onions
5 ml (1 tsp)	grated ginger
6	peppercorns
30 ml (2 Tbs)	wine vinegar
80 ml ($\frac{1}{3}$ cup)	apricot jam

- *For the marinade*, roughly chop the ginger and mix soy sauce and sherry.
- Marinate the fish in this for 2 hours.
- Meanwhile, make the sauce. Place all ingredients, *except* vinegar and jam, in a pot.
- Boil to reduce to about 375 ml (1 $\frac{1}{2}$ cups).
- Strain off the solids.
- Return to the pot, adding vinegar and jam.
- Bring to the boil.
- Drain the fish and fry in oil until brown. (If you are using a soft fish such as hake, coat it in flour before you fry it.)
- Strain the remaining marinade into the pot and keep sauce simmering.
- Simmer fried fish in the sauce for 1 to 2 minutes.
- Lift out the fish and place in a large shallow dish.
- After cooking all the fish, reduce the sauce to a syrupy consistency and pour over the fish. Chill and serve.

HERRINGS

Herring is very popular in Holland and the Scandinavian and Baltic countries. It is a fish rich in Omega 3 oils.

Herrings are stored in salt and must always be soaked before being prepared whole herrings for 12 to 18 hours and fillets for 6 to 8 hours.

Herring makes a most impressive starter, but remember to make the dishes days in advance.

They go well with vodka!

CHOPPED HERRING

Chopped herring is an acquired taste. You either love or hate the sweet and sour flavour of this salty fish. Serves 8

600 g (about 4)	salted herring
1	medium onion, chopped
500 g (about 3)	apples
4	hard-boiled eggs
24	Marie biscuits or *matzo* or *kichel*
30 ml (2 Tbs)	castor sugar
3 ml ($^1/_2$ tsp)	acetic acid or vinegar, to taste extra hard-boiled eggs for garnish

- Fillet, skin and then soak the herrings for 6 hours. If you soak fillets for longer, you'll lose all the flavour.
- Mince all the ingredients *except* the extra eggs for garnish.
- Season to taste.
- Leave in the fridge for several hours for the flavours to develop.
- Decorate with extra hard boiled egg, grated.
- Serve on kichel (a thin sweet biscuit), melba toast, or cream crackers.

Hints

- The number of Marie biscuits in the list of ingredients depends on the size and saltiness of the herrings.
- I use acetic acid, available from any pharmacy, rather than vinegar because it is the vinegar acid without the water. The chopped herring then does not become watery. *Be very careful not to get acetic acid on your skin it's pure acid!* Wash off any splashes immediately under plenty of cold running water.

PICKLED HERRING

This is a beloved traditional delicacy.

8	salt herrings, soaked for 12 to 18 hours
or 16	fillets soaked for 6 hours
3-4	onions, sliced
750 ml (1 bottle)	white or natural vinegar
330 ml (1 $^1/_3$ cup)	water
15 ml (1 Tbs)	pickling spice
15 ml (1 Tbs)	sugar
3 ml ($^1/_2$ tsp)	mustard powder
4	bay leaves

- Layer the herring and onion in a glass container.
- Place the vinegar and water in a pot with pickling spice, sugar, mustard and bay leaves.
- Bring to the boil and boil for 30 seconds, then switch off the stove and leave to cool.
- Remove bay leaves and place in the container with the herrings.
- Strain the vinegar over herrings through muslin or a fine sieve.
- Allow to stand in the fridge for 2 to 3 days before using.

Cream sauce for pickled herring

2	eggs
80 ml ($^1/_3$ cup)	vinegar from pickle mixture
30 ml (2 Tbs)	lemon juice
15 ml (1 Tbs)	sugar
125 ml ($^1/_2$ cup)	cream

- In a double boiler heat the eggs, vinegar, lemon juice and sugar, whisking until it is thick and pale. Cool.
- Whip the cream and fold in.
- Serve on pickled herring.

Tarragon cream

2	eggs
45 ml (3 Tbs)	sugar
80 ml ($^1/_3$ cup)	tarragon vinegar
125 ml ($^1/_2$ cup)	cream

- Follow the method for the cream sauce.

Mustard sauce

    250 ml (1 cup)   mayonnaise
    125 ml ($1/2$ cup)   sour cream
    45-60 ml (3-4 Tbs)   good prepared dijon mustard, or *mixture of mustards*
    3 ml ($1/2$ tsp)   dried dill
    black pepper

- Blend the sauce ingredients.
- Leave to stand for several hours before using.
- Serve on pickled herring.

DANISH HERRING

Try this variation of the traditional Danish way with salt herrings.

    1 kg   salt herrings
    125 ml ($1/2$ cup)   Old Brown sherry or *any fortified sweet wine*
    250 ml (1 cup)   white or *brown* vinegar
    185 ml ($3/4$ cup)   sugar
    125 ml ($1/2$ cup)   oil
    410 g   tinned tomato purée
    65 g   tinned tomato paste
    500 g   apples, cubed
    500 ml (2 cups)   diced onion
    10 ml (2 tsp)   prepared mustard
    12   black peppercorns

- Clean and soak the herrings for 12 hours.
- Drain, fillet and cut the herrings into small, bite-sized pieces.
- Combine the vinegar, wine and sugar and heat to dissolve the sugar. Cool.
- Mix all the ingredients into the vinegar and pour over the herring.
- Refrigerate for at least 36 hours before using.

PINEAPPLE HERRING

Herrings with an intriguing difference.

    600 g (about 4)   salt herrings
    1   onion, sliced
    440 g   tinned pineapple chunks
    15 ml (1 Tbs)   mustard powder
    250 ml (1 cup)   mayonnaise
    250 ml (1 cup)   pineapple juice (*don't use juice from pineapples*)

- Clean and soak the herrings for about 16 hours.
- Cut into fillets and cut each fillet in 3.
- In a glass jar or a bowl, layer the herring with onion and pineapple pieces.
- Mix remaining ingredients and pour over herrings.
- Place in fridge for a few days before using.

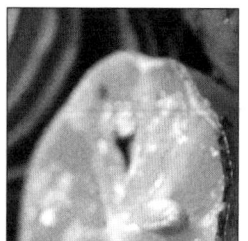 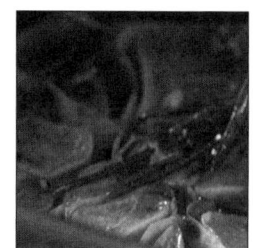 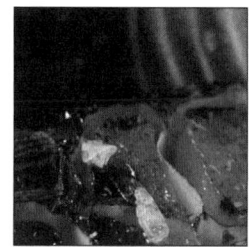

MEAT

Cooking meat is very easy once you are familiar with the different cuts and the best cooking methods for each cut.

Meat can be divided into two broad groups of *tough* and *tender*. Lamb, mutton and pork offer tender meat, but with beef most cuts are tough. It is important to know which are the best cuts for a particular dish. Until you know all the cuts available, talk to the butcher, tell him what you want to make and let him suggest what is best. Don't stick to the same cuts – experiment with different cuts of various kinds of meat, and you'll soon widen your cooking range and find your favourites.

Tender and tough cuts of meat

- All meat can be cooked soft by long, slow, moist cooking. The tougher the meat, the longer it will take to cook it soft, but it will never be tender and have the texture of steak!
- *Pork* All pork cuts are tender. Certain cuts have more fat than others.
- *Lamb* All lamb cuts are tender. Certain cuts contain more fat and more connective tissue and are therefore better for stewing than for other methods of cooking.
- *Mutton* is the flesh of bigger and older sheep, and is much fattier and tastier than lamb, but only the ribs, loin and chump are really tender enough for dry-heat cooking. The tender cuts of mutton correspond to those similarly named in beef.
- *Beef* is the most difficult to understand because there are so many different cuts and only a few are tender.

Tender beef cuts

Hind-quarter Sirloin, rump, wing rib and fillet, and all the cuts made up of these muscles are tender.

- Entrecôte, T-bone, porterhouse steak all come off the sirloin.
- Rump can be cut into steaks or roasted whole.
- Wing rib can be cut into club steaks or rib-eye steaks, or roasted whole.
- Fillet can be cut into thick steaks or roasted whole.

Fore-quarter Prime rib and the cuts made up from this are the only tender cuts on the fore-quarter. These include rib-eye steak, club steak and scotch fillet.

Tougher beef cuts

The tough cuts of beef hind-quarter are denser and have a close, dry texture. These are best cooked slowly by moist cooking.

- Tough cuts include silverside, topside and thick flank.
- Aitchbone is less dense and more juicy but still tough.
- Some people dry-roast a large piece of topside, but I find it very dry and tough unless it is well hung and thinly sliced.
- The tastiest beef cuts are all from the fore-quarter. For all stews, casseroles and potroasts I use fore-quarter

cuts – the flavour is completely different from hind-quarter cuts.
- My first choice is always chuck. The flavour and texture of chuck is the best for moist-heat cooking methods, and can be used on the bone or off the bone. It generally is the same price as stewing beef (on the bone). If you ask for stewing beef or stewing steak, you will usually end up with hind-quarter; if you want chuck or brisket, which is my second choice for moist-heat cooking, be sure to specify this.
- Other tasty cuts are flat rib and neck. The best is to experiment and see which cuts you like best.

Ripening meat is also called ageing or maturing. Ripening breaks down the fibres of the meat by the action of enzymes, making it more tender and improving the flavour. Ripening is achieved by hanging large cuts or sides of the carcass in a coolroom, or vacuum-packing them for at least 14 days.

Lamb and mutton may be ripened for a few days, but generally it is beef, which is tougher, that is aged.

Ripening thin cuts of meat such as steak or chops at home can be done only if the meat is vacuum packed. It can then be kept for a couple of weeks in the fridge, rather than in the freezer.

When you are buying beef, ask your butcher if he has hung the meat (most butchers do, but there are some who do not).

COOKING METHODS

The most important step when cooking meat is the browning, which is needed to develop the flavour.

The two basic methods of cooking meat are by *dry heat*, and by *moist heat*.

Dry-heat methods are those in which no water is used. These include dry- or open-roasting or rotisserie roasting, (not in a double roaster, foil or cooking bag), grilling, braaiing, frying (oil gets much hotter than water, so frying is classed as dry, not moist-heat cooking).

Dry-heat cooking is suitable only for tender cuts that do not need slow, moist cooking to soften them.

Moist-heat cooking occurs when water or steam is present during the cooking process. The three main moist-heat methods for meat are pot-roasting in a pot on top of the stove or in the oven (using foil, double roasters or cooking bags all result in a potroast because the meat cooks in the steam), casseroling and stewing.

All three methods can be done on top of the stove or in the oven. The main difference between these three methods is the size of the pieces of meat used.

Basic method for dry-roasting
- Season meat with black pepper and herbs of your choice. (See *recipes* in this chapter for ideas.)
- *Do not salt the meat until it is browned.* This precaution prevents the salt from drawing out the juices.
- Brown the meat well in a pan on top of the stove in a little oil or a mixture of oil and butter.
- Place the browned meat in a roasting pan, preferably on a roasting rack in the pan, and pour 250 to 500 ml (1 to 2 cups) stock into the pan under the rack to catch the dripping juices. This will be used to make the gravy once the meat is cooked. If you are roasting without a roasting rack, *do not* add the stock. The meat must not come into contact with the liquid.
- Preheat the oven and cook at 170 °C to 180 °C.
- For all large cuts of meat except whole beef fillet and entrecôte (sirloin off the bone) and a butterflied leg of lamb, work out the cooking time according to the following timetable.

Dry-roasting time table

Meat weight	Rare	Medium	Well-done
	x 40 min/kg + 30	50 min/kg + 30	60-70 min/kg + 30
1 kg	1 hr 10 min	1 hr 20 min	1 hr 40 min
1,5 kg	1 hr 30 min	1 hr 45 min	2 hr 15 min
2 kg	1 hr 50 min	2 hr 20 min	2 hr 50 min
2,5 kg	2 hr 10 min	2 hr 40 min	3 hr 25 min
3 kg	2 hr 30 min	3 hr	4 hr

Meat thermometer settings
60 °C – 65 °C   65 °C – 70 °C   70 °C – 75 °C

- Beef can be roasted rare, medium or well-done.
- Pork, lamb and mutton are usually roasted to medium or well-done.

Important Because of the even thickness of a whole (unsliced) cut of beef entrecôte, fillet or butterflied leg of lamb, do not use this chart. Cook as follows, no matter what the weight is:

- *Fillet* Well-browned in a very hot pan, then 20 to 30 minutes in the oven at 200 °C.
- *Entrecôte or boned leg of lamb* Well-browned in a very hot pan, then 45 to 55 minutes at 180 °C.

The shorter period in these times will give you rare to medium-rare meat.

Always remember to leave meat to stand for 10 minutes out of the oven to rest before serving. The meat will be more tender and the juices will not run out as you cut it.

Basic method for grilling
I find that grilling meat in a domestic stove is not very successful. The elements are just not hot enough to seal and brown the meat before it is overcooked. For best results

- Preheat your oven as hot as you can (about 240 °C), and then change the setting to grill.
- When the element is red, place your meat very close to the element and grill on both sides.
- The total cooking time should be no more than 5 to 7 minutes.

I find that pan-frying, or at least browning the meat in a pan before grilling it, produces much tastier, juicier steaks. This is also best when using a small TV grill.

Basic method for pan-fried meat
For me this is the best way of cooking steak and chops. For pan-frying meat, you need a good heavy-based pan, because the pan must be able to get very hot and retain its heat.

- Seal the meat in the same way as for grilling and roasting – in a very hot pan in a little oil or oil and butter. (You can brush the oil or butter on the meat itself if you want to use less fat.)
- For fat-free cooking, use a cast-iron griddle pan with ridges. Seal the meat on both sides. As soon as the meat is well browned, reduce the heat to low and cook the meat more slowly.
- A steak of 4 to 5 cm thick will take about 7 minutes to cook to medium. When pink juices start to ooze out of the meat, it is medium.
- Leave it to stand for a few minutes before serving. The meat will be more tender and it will lose less of the juices.

Remember, if you keep the steaks warm for any length of time, they will dry out and toughen. If you are going to cook a large number of steaks or chops that won't fit in your frying pan at the same time, the best way of cooking them is to brown them first quickly on both sides, a few at a time, in a very hot pan on top of the stove. Then place them, well browned but still raw, on a grilling rack and follow the grilling instructions.

Basic method for braaiing meat
For braaiing over the coals, use the same method as for frying.

- Seal the meat on both sides by placing it close to the hot coals.
- Then raise the grid a little farther from the heat and cook more slowly. This should take about 7 minutes altogether.
- When the meat is almost cooked, dip it into the basting mixture and return to the hot fire for 1 to 2 minutes, or brush on the basting mixture.

Basting mixtures usually contain sugar and therefore burn quickly. If you cook the meat from the raw stage with the basting mixture, you end up with a layer of burned sauce on the meat.

Basic method for potroast/casserole/stew
Any potroast, casserole or stew recipe can be made following these easy steps.

- Cut vegetables according to the size of the meat. For a potroast using a large piece of meat, the onions and vegetables should be whole or cut in big chunks. For a casserole the vegetables should be smaller, while for a stew the pieces should be even smaller, keeping pace with the size of the pieces of meat. The vegetables should be very small when cooking mince.
- Heat a heavy-based pan over a high heat until it is very hot. Pour just enough oil in the pan to coat the bottom. If desired, a little butter can be added.
- Sear and brown the meat on all sides as quickly as possible. This will seal it and prevent the juices from seeping out and it will give the meat extra flavour and colour (see *Hint*).
- If you are using smaller pieces of meat, brown them a few pieces at a time. Repeat till all the pieces are sealed and browned. If needed, add a little extra oil and butter and heat it thoroughly before adding the next batch of meat.
- Remove the meat and lower the heat. In the remaining oil, sauté your onions until they just start to brown.
- If you are going to thicken the dish with flour, add the flour to the onions and cook until the flour is brown. This gives the dish a good colour and a rich nutty flavour. If you have a basic brown roux in your fridge, skip this step and add the roux to the sauce before replacing the meat.
- Add the remaining ingredients the recipe calls for to make a good sauce.
- Return the meat to the pan and sauce and cover.

Simmer slowly till the meat is soft. If it is necessary to add liquid during cooking, add boiling water or stock, a little at a time. Adding cold liquid would drop the temperature in the pan. Check the seasoning before serving. The cooking can be done on top of the stove or in the oven at 160 °C.

Hint
Don't toss your meat in flour before you brown it. The flour burns on the bottom of the pot. Brown the meat on its own and add the flour to the oil afterwards, then cook till the flour is brown.

SIMPLE GRAVIES WITH YOUR MEAT

This is where you use your creative skills …

Basic roux
Cook equal quantities of flour and oil over medium heat, or in the microwave, until dark brown. This toasts the flour and gives your gravies flavour and colour, while at the same time thickening them. Cool and leave in the fridge overnight. By the next day the oil will have risen to the top and can be poured off. The roux keeps indefinitely in the fridge and can be used to thicken any gravy, sauce or stew.

Pan gravy
Once you have cooked the meat, remove it and pour all the pan juices into a glass jug. Leave it to stand till the fat comes to the top. Skim off the fat and return the fat to the pan with about 20 ml (4 tsp) flour per 250 ml (1 cup) liquid, and stir well. (You will need more flour than normal, because browning the flour removes some of its thickening properties.) Cook over medium heat until the flour is brown and toasted. Add the pan juices in the jug to the roux in the pan and bring to the boil, stirring constantly with a whisk rather than a wooden spoon.

Flavour the gravy with any of the following: red or white wine (simmer the sauce for several minutes to 'mellow' the wine), sherry, a little of any of the bottled sauces, prepared mustard, horseradish, and/or herbs of your choice. The most important item is a little freshly squeezed lemon juice – it's a natural flavour enhancer.

Another way of thickening gravies and sauces is to mix cornflour with cold water to form a smooth paste – 20 ml (4 tsp) per 500 ml (2 cups) stock – instead of the browned flour, but you will not get the same flavour, and on reheating gravy thickened with cornflour, it will thin down again.

ROASTS, GRILLS AND FRIES

Basic marinade
Marinades and basting mixtures are generally used on meat when roasting, braaiing or grilling.

125 ml ($\frac{1}{2}$ cup) oil
375 ml (1 1/2 cups) red or white wine
    or orange juice
juice of $\frac{1}{2}$ lemon
1 clove garlic, crushed
1 onion, sliced
3 bay leaves
freshly ground black pepper

Any combination of the following may be added to taste:

herbs
mustard
soy sauce
Worcestershire sauce
Maggi liquid seasoning
curry powder
tomato purée
sweet wine or sherry
mayonnaise

The following 4 ingredients contain sugar, which may result in easy burning, so use sparingly

tomato sauce
chutney
honey
apricot jam

▶ Mix the ingredients. Pour into a dish, or a large, strong plastic bag and marinate the meat in it for several hours before cooking.

Basting
▶ Basting is done during the cooking process – the meat does not lie in the mixture before it is cooked.
▶ A basting mixture that contains sugar in any form should be brushed on towards the end of the cooking time to avoid burning.
▶ A basic basting mixture uses the same ingredients as the basic marinade mixture, but with much less wine or liquid. It should be thicker and have a stronger flavour than a marinade.

ROSEMARY ROAST BEEF

A succulent roast, with rosemary adding a subtle sweetness. Use a whole cut of entrecôte, rump, fillet, prime rib roast or rolled beef roast of your desired weight.

Allow 170 g of raw meat (without bone) per person

	beef of any of suggested cuts
	coarsely ground black pepper
	dried rosemary
	oil and/or butter for roasting
500 ml (2 cups)	beef stock

▶ Preheat oven to 180 °C.
▶ Coat meat well in black pepper and rosemary.
▶ In a heavy-based pan on top of the stove, brown the meat very well in oil or a mixture of butter and oil.
▶ Place the meat, fatty side up, on a grid in a roasting pan and pour the stock into the bottom of the pan to catch the meat juices. (This will become the gravy.)
▶ Roast according to the cut and mass of the meat (see roasting chart at the beginning of this chapter).
▶ While roasting, ensure that the liquid in the pan does not dry up. Top up with a little water if necessary.
▶ Once the meat is cooked, remove from the pan and leave to rest while you make the gravy.
▶ Serve with a basic simple gravy made with the pan juices (see *Gravies*) or any of the following sauces (see *Sauces*): béarnaise, horseradish, mushroom or monkey gland sauce, or use the pepper sauce from the pepper steak recipe.

RARE ROAST FILLET

Roasted to perfection, a whole fillet is an impressive main course. While it is expensive, it's all meat and beautifully tender. The weight of the fillet does not affect the roasting time.

Allow 170 g per serving

1	whole fillet
60 g	butter or oil, or a mixture
	freshly ground black pepper
	dried rosemary
30 ml (2 Tbs)	soy sauce

▶ Preheat oven to 180 °C.
▶ Melt the butter in a roasting pan.
▶ Coat fillet with black pepper and rosemary.
▶ Place roasting pan on a very hot plate on top of stove and brown fillet well on all sides.
▶ Add soy sauce and coat meat well.
▶ Roast fillet in the same pan in the oven for 20 to 30 minutes.
▶ Remove fillet and leave to rest for 10 minutes before serving.
▶ Serve with béarnaise, horseradish or mushroom sauce (see *Sauces*).

ROAST LAMB WITH ROSEMARY

Leave lamb whole or ask the butcher to bone and butterfly it for you. Use the bones for the gravy. A gravy for lamb made with bones rather than beef or chicken stock cubes is very easy to make and much tastier, but you must have the stock made, preferably the day before you start roasting the meat.

Allow 170 g per serving, or 250 g before being boned.

1	leg or rack of lamb
1	large sprig rosemary
or 5 ml (1 tsp)	dried rosemary
2	cloves garlic
	black pepper
	butter or olive oil, or a mixture
500 ml (2 cups)	water

Gravy

	lamb bones from boning the leg
or 200 g	stewing lamb with plenty bone
1	large sprig fresh rosemary
or 7 ml (1 1/2 tsp)	dried rosemary
2	cloves garlic
125 ml (1/2 cup)	red wine
500 ml (2 cups)	water
	salt and pepper
	squeeze of lemon juice
45 ml (3 Tbs)	sherry
45 ml (3 Tbs)	cream
	or sour cream (optional)

- Preheat oven to 180 °C.
- Stuff the meat with garlic by making small incisions in it with a sharp-pointed knife and pushing slivers of garlic into the incisions. Season liberally with rosemary and black pepper.
- In a very hot roasting pan on top of the stove, brown meat in a little oil, or in oil and butter mixed.
- Place lamb, fatty side up, on a grid in a roasting pan.
- Pour 500 ml (2 cups) water into the bottom of the pan to catch the meat juices.
- Roast according to the roasting chart in this chapter. (If the leg has been deboned and butterflied, work on the roasting time for entrecôte.) Baste occasionally.
- *Gravy* Place bones, rosemary, whole garlic, wine, water, salt and pepper in a pot and simmer for 1 hour (preferably the day before). Have this ready before roasting the lamb.
- Once the meat is cooked, remove it from the pan and set aside to rest.
- Add the pan juices to the pot of gravy stock.
- Skim off the fat from the gravy and return 30 ml (2 Tbs) of the fat to the roasting pan.
- Add 45 ml (3 Tbs) flour to the 30 ml fat and cook in the roasting pan on top of the stove until the flour is brown in colour. (This step can be left out if you have basic roux in your fridge.)
- Strain the gravy liquid onto the roux and boil to reduce it until flavour and consistency are correct.
- Stir in lemon, sherry and cream. Serve the gravy with the meat.

LEMON-HONEY ROASTED OR BRAAIED LAMB

Lamb roasted or braaied with this marinade/basting sauce is unforgettable. Make the marinade first; the meat has to lie in it for 24 hours before roasting.

Allow 170 g per serving, or 250 g with bone

1	boned leg of lamb

Marinade

45 ml (3 Tbs)	honey
45 ml (3 Tbs)	lemon juice
30 ml (2 Tbs)	good prepared mustard
10 ml (2 tsp)	dried rosemary
5 ml (1 tsp)	chicken stock powder
3 ml (1/2 tsp)	black pepper
15 ml (1 Tbs)	oil

- Combine marinade ingredients in a small pot and heat until honey has melted. Stir well.
- Cool and pour into a strong plastic bag.
- Score the fatty side of the meat and marinate lamb for 24 hours in the plastic bag.
- Wipe off all the marinade before browning.
- *Oven-roasting* Preheat oven to 180 °C.
- In a little oil or butter, brown the meat in a very hot pan on top of the stove.
- Place the meat, fatty side up, in a roasting pan and pour on any remaining marinade.
- Roast, uncovered, in the roasting pan with no grid inside (meat must lie in marinade) for 40 to 50 minutes. Baste periodically.
- *Braaiing* Braai over low coals, basting often with the marinade, for about 50 minutes, or on a Weber or other hooded braai for 40 minutes.

EASTER LAMB ANDROS

This traditional Greek dish, which is usually cooked on an open fire, is a superb dinner party dish. It can be cooked in the oven, on a rotisserie or on a Weber. The lamb, stuffed with spinach and feta cheese, is prepared in advance and needs very little last-minute attention. Serve it with a ratatouille or with Jams Californian vegetables (see *Vegetable side dishes*) and extra rice or crusty white bread.

Allow 170 g of meat per serving, or 250 g with bone

1	boned shoulder or *leg of lamb*
	juice of 1 lemon
45 ml (3 Tbs)	melted butter
45 ml (3 Tbs)	olive oil
	salt and black pepper

Stuffing

1	bunch spring onions, chopped
45 ml (3 Tbs)	olive oil
1	bunch fresh spinach, chopped
250 ml (1 cup)	cooked rice
125 g	feta cheese, crumbled
100 g	pine nuts toasted in olive oil (optional)
5 ml (1 tsp)	dried dill
2 ml ($^1/_2$ tsp)	dried mint
or 5 ml (1 tsp)	fresh chopped mint
	salt and black pepper

- Preheat oven to 180 °C.
- *Stuffing* Sauté spring onions in olive oil until glassy.
- Add spinach and cook until wilted.
- Add cooked rice, crumbled cheese, nuts, herbs and season to taste.
- Stuff lamb and tie with string.
- *Meat* Mix lemon juice, butter, oil, salt and black pepper.
- In a little oil or butter, or a mixture of the two, brown the meat well in a very hot pan on top of the stove and then roast, uncovered, basting well with the lemon-butter mixture. Check the roasting chart for roasting times.

RAAN ROASTED LAMB

This lamb, with its spicy Eastern flavour, is delicious roasted in the oven or cooked over the coals in a Weber. Begin with making the marinade in which to soak the meat for 24 hours.

Allow 170 g per serving, or 250 g with bone

1	leg of lamb, boned and butterflied

Marinade

15 ml (1 Tbs)	finely grated fresh ginger
30 ml (2 Tbs)	chopped fresh coriander (dhania) leaves
15 ml (1 Tbs)	curry powder
10 ml (2 tsp)	cumin
30 ml (2 Tbs)	chutney
4	cloves garlic, crushed
15 ml (1 Tbs)	tomato paste
45 ml (3 Tbs)	melted butter
350 ml	Bulgarian yoghurt
	pinch of cayenne pepper
	salt and black pepper

- Place all marinade ingredients in a liquidiser and blend till smooth.
- Completely coat lamb with mixture and marinate in a thick plastic bag for 24 hours.
- *Oven-roasting* Preheat oven to 180 °C.
- Place the marinated lamb in a roasting pan and roast for 50 minutes to 1 hour, depending on how well-done you like the lamb.
- Do not turn the meat, but baste periodically; the marinade will form a crust on top of the meat.
- *Braaiing* To cook the lamb over the coals in a Weber, cook by indirect method for 50 minutes to 1 hour, basting periodically. The marinade must be on top – do not turn the meat.

SCHWARMA

Döner kebab
To make a real Schwarma you need a vertical rotisserie. You also need to prepare your meat by slicing it thinly, marinating it for 12 hours, and then placing it in layers on the rotisserie skewer. The meat is cooked by a gas or electric element running vertically next to the rotisserie.

In Turkey, the best Döner kebab I tasted was surrounded by a caged, vertical wood fire. As the outside edges of the meat were cooked by the fire, they were thinly sliced off and piled on Turkish pita bread. Browned butter was then dribbled over it. By using the same marinade on a boned shoulder or leg of lamb, braaiing or roasting it and serving it with or without the browned butter (omit the butter if you want a less rich dish), you'll come very close to the original. *Allow 250 g of meat per serving before boning*

1	boned shoulder *or* leg of lamb
125 g	butter for browning (optional)

Marinade

80 ml ($^1/_3$ cup)	olive oil
30 ml (2 Tbs)	dried origanum
1	onion, grated
4	cloves garlic, crushed
20 ml (4 tsp)	cumin
2 ml ($^1/_2$ tsp)	black pepper
	juice of 1 lemon

- Mix all the marinade ingredients and marinate for 12 hours in a thick plastic bag.
- Braai or roast the meat, uncovered, in oven preheated to 180 °C for 50 minutes to 1 hour.
- Heat butter until it turns brown, taking extreme care not to burn it.
- Slice lamb and season with browned butter. Serve with pita bread.

CHINESE BARBECUED SPARE RIBS

These ribs are really gooey and rich, and irresistible straight from the oven or coals.

Serves 4

1 kg	pork spare ribs, sliced

Basting sauce

45 ml (3 Tbs)	sugar
125 ml ($^1/_2$ cup)	vinegar
45 ml (3 Tbs)	smooth apricot jam
45 ml (3 Tbs)	tomato purée
30 ml (2 Tbs)	HP sauce
30 ml (2 Tbs)	soy sauce
45 ml (3 Tbs)	sherry
3 ml ($^1/_2$ tsp)	grated green ginger
1-2	cloves garlic, crushed
	good pinch cayenne pepper
3 ml ($^1/_2$ tsp)	barbecue spice
80 ml ($^1/_3$ cup)	water

- Caramelise the sugar in the vinegar by boiling rapidly till sugar takes on light caramel colour, and immediately add all remaining basting ingredients.
- Bring back to the boil and stir until sugar has dissolved.
- *To oven-roast the ribs,* place them in an open roasting pan and pour over basting mixture.
- Roast, uncovered, in oven preheated to 180 °C for 30 minutes, turning ribs periodically.
- Remove ribs from the pan and place on a grilling rack.
- Grill on all sides until brown and sticky.
- *To braai the ribs,* first cook in the oven as above, but instead of placing ribs under the oven grill, braai over the coals. (If you braai them over the coals from the raw stage, they will burn black because of the fat and the sugar.)

QUICK COOKS

The next few recipes are neither dry-heat or slow-cooked moist-heat dishes. They use tender cuts that are cooked very quickly in a sauce or fried in oil.

STEAK WITH PEPPER SAUCE

In this recipe the steaks are flamed with brandy, which doesn't really affect the flavour of the meat and sauce very much, but impresses the guests no end. If you don't want to use cream in the sauce, use sour cream, which has half the fat content of cream.

Serves 4

	4 steaks of your choice, 2-3 cm thick
	freshly ground black pepper
15 ml (1 Tbs)	oil
15 ml (1 Tbs)	butter or extra oil
	brandy for flaming

Pepper sauce

30 ml (2 Tbs)	brandy
30 ml (2 Tbs)	sherry
45 ml (3 Tbs)	tinned green peppercorns
250 ml (1 cup)	cream or sour cream
10 ml (2 tsp)	good prepared mustard
5 ml (1 tsp)	powdered beef stock
or $^1/_3$	stock cube
	squeeze of lemon juice (if using fresh cream)
	salt

- Sprinkle steaks liberally with pepper.
- Over a high heat, heat a heavy-based pan until very hot. Add the oil and when oil is hot, add the butter.
- As the butter starts to change colour, add the steaks. (Add them two at a time if you think your pan won't remain hot enough to seal the steaks quickly. This depends on the size and quality of the pan.)
- Once the steaks are browned on both sides, reduce the heat to low and cook slowly so that the total cooking time will be about 7 minutes – this will give you a medium steak.
- Pour the brandy onto the steaks and light quickly with a match. Shake the pan and the flames will spread over the steaks. The brandy can be poured straight into the pan with the remaining ingredients for the sauce, if you do not want to flame them.
- Remove the steaks from the pan and keep on a heated plate.
- With a fork, crush half the green peppercorns and leave the remainder whole.
- Add all the remaining sauce ingredients to the pan and simmer for a few minutes until the sauce has thickened slightly.
- Add lemon juice and season with salt.

Hint

For a slightly thicker, less rich sauce, proceed as follows:
- Once you have removed the steaks, use a wire whisk to stir 7 ml (1 $^1/_2$ tsp) flour into the remaining pan juices.
- Add all the remaining ingredients for the sauce, but use half cream and half water in place of 250 ml cream. Use a little more stock powder to taste.

VEAL MARSALA

Simple to prepare in just a few minutes, this tasty veal makes an impressive dinner party dish. Try this recipe also with chicken breasts or pork fillets.

Serves 4

8	veal schnitzels
125 ml ($^1/_2$ cup)	seasoned flour
45 ml (3 Tbs)	olive oil
1	medium onion, halved vertically and sliced
375 g	button mushrooms, sliced
125 ml ($^1/_2$ cup)	marsala
3	cloves garlic, chopped
5 ml (1 tsp)	dried tarragon
250 ml (1 cup)	sour cream
	salt and pepper

- Lightly toss the schnitzels in seasoned flour.
- Heat oil in a pan and brown meat on both sides over very high heat. Remove the meat from the pan and set aside.
- Add onion and mushrooms to the pan and sauté until the onion is soft and the liquid from the mushrooms has evaporated.
- Add the marsala, garlic and tarragon.
- Add sour cream and salt and pepper to taste and bring to the boil.
- Return veal to the pan and simmer for about 5 minutes.
- Serve with ribbon noodles and vegetables of your choice.

Hint

If you do not have marsala, use sherry or port. It is almost as good.

BEEF STROGANOFF

This traditional Russian dish is very quick and easy to make. The compliments will fly and no one will know how little effort it took!

Very tender meat is a must for a stroganoff. The meat is very quickly browned, a few strips at a time. Once the sour cream and mushroom sauce is made, the steak is merely heated through and served. The browning of the meat and the sauce can be done in advance, but once the meat goes into the sauce it must be eaten immediately or else the meat overcooks.

Serves 4

750 g	fillet or *well-hung rump,* cut into strips
75 g	butter
2	large onions, thinly sliced
500 g	button mushrooms, halved
15 ml (1 Tbs)	flour
5 ml (1 tsp)	powdered beef stock
250 ml (1 cup)	sour cream or *cream soured with lemon juice*
15 ml (1 Tbs)	dijon or *any good prepared mustard*
10 ml (2 tsp)	fresh dill
or 3 ml (½ tsp)	dried dill
	salt and pepper
	chopped parsley for garnishing

- In a very hot pan brown the meat in butter, a few strips at a time, and set aside.
- Sauté onion and mushrooms in remaining butter until glassy.
- Sprinkle on flour and add remaining ingredients.
- Return meat to the pan and heat through to just on boiling point, but do not overcook.
- Serve on buttered pasta or rice, garnished with chopped parsley.

SIZZLING STEAK

The meat used in this 'Chinese' flavoured steak is topside. Generally topside is not at all as nice as a steak, but because the meat is sliced very thinly and beaten like a schnitzel, it becomes tender enough for a quick-cooking recipe.

This recipe is especially for those who love the flavour of steakhouse barbecue sauces.

Serves 4

750 g	topside, sliced into very thin schnitzels
	oil
4	onions, peeled, cut into 6 wedges, leaves separated

Sauce

45 ml (3 Tbs)	HP sauce
80 ml (⅓ cup)	tomato sauce
45 ml (3 Tbs)	brown sugar
30 ml (2 Tbs)	soy sauce
80 ml (⅓ cup)	dry white wine
45 ml (3 Tbs)	water

- Mix all the sauce ingredients and reserve.
- With a mallet or rolling pin, beat the meat until very thin. Cut into pieces about 5 cm square.
- In a little oil in a very hot frying pan or wok, quickly brown the meat, a few slices at a time.
- Remove and set aside.
- Quickly stir-fry the onion pieces; they must still be crisp and just starting to brown around the edges.
- Remove the onions from the pan.
- Return meat to the pan and pour on the sauce mixture.
- Simmer with the lid off until almost all the liquid has evaporated.
- Toss in the onions and heat through. The onions must still be crisp.
- Serve with noodles or rice.

SWEET AND SOUR PORK

I have tried many different recipes for sweet and sour pork. The lightness of the batter, the leanness of the meat and the richness of the sauce puts this recipe at the top of my Chinese hit parade. Instead of the pork, cubed rump steak, chicken breasts or any firm fish can be used.

Serves 4

750 g	pork goulash
30 ml (2 Tbs)	soy sauce
	salt

Batter

125 ml (1/2 cup)	cornflour
125 ml (1/2 cup)	self-raising flour
1	egg
125 ml (1/2 cup)	water

Sauce

1	onion, cut into julienne strips
5 cm	cucumber, cut into julienne strips
1	green pepper, seeded, trimmed, in julienne strips
60 ml (1/4 cup)	sugar
45 ml (3 Tbs)	vinegar, or *more*, to taste
30 ml (2 Tbs)	soy sauce
30 ml (2 Tbs)	dry sherry
125 ml (1/2 cup)	orange juice
125 ml (1/2 cup)	water
30 ml (2 Tbs)	cornflour
2	slices pineapple, cubed (optional)

- Marinate the pork in salt and soy sauce for 1 hour, then drain and pat dry.
- Mix the self-raising flour, cornflour, egg and water to form a batter. Leave to stand for 1 hour.
- In the meantime, make the sauce by stir-frying the onion, green pepper and cucumber.
- Combine all the remaining sauce ingredients, except pineapple, and pour over the vegetables.
- Bring the mixture to the boil and allow to thicken. Don't overcook the sauce. Add pineapple.
- Dip the pork into the batter and fry in deep oil over medium heat until golden. Drain well.
- Pour the sauce over the pork and serve.

WIENER SCHNITZEL

Tender and tasty marinated veal in a crumb coating. The schnitzels have to be marinated for 1 to 2 hours, and then chilled for 2 to 3 hours, before frying.

Serves 4

4-5	thin veal escalopes

Marinade

45 ml (3 Tbs)	lemon juice
60 ml (1/4 cup)	olive oil
30 ml (2 Tbs)	chopped parsley
5 ml (1 tsp)	mixed dried herbs
	black pepper

Coating

125 ml (1/2 cup)	flour, seasoned with plenty of salt, pepper and paprika
30 ml (2 Tbs)	grated parmesan cheese (optional)
1	egg, beaten with
30 ml (2 Tbs)	water
	dry breadcrumbs
	oil for frying

- Trim the veal schnitzels and beat to flatten.
- Mix marinade ingredients and place the veal in the marinade for 1 to 2 hours.
- Pat dry and coat with seasoned flour mixed with Parmesan cheese (if you are using this).
- Dip floured schnitzels into egg beaten in water, then coat with crumbs.
- Chill for 2 to 3 hours before frying to prevent the crumbs from coming off in the oil.
- Fry in shallow oil until golden. Oil must be halfway up the schnitzel so that when you turn it, the other half is in the oil. The oil must be fairly hot but not so hot that the crumbs brown immediately. It should take 3 to 5 minutes on each side to cook through and brown.
- Drain on absorbent paper and serve with a little lemon butter or sauce tartare (see *Sauces*).

HAMBURGERS

Home-made hamburgers or meat balls are very often dry and leathery. The secret of moist, juicy hamburgers is to add a little bread to separate the mince crumbs, and plenty of liquid in the mixture to keep it juicy. Serve on hamburger rolls or on fluffy mashed potatoes with onions fried in the remaining oil.

Serves 3 to 4

500 g	lean mince
1	onion, finely chopped
	butter or oil for frying
1	slice white bread, crusts removed
125 ml (½ cup)	beef stock
30 ml (2 Tbs)	tomato sauce
15 ml (1 Tbs)	Worcestershire sauce
30 ml (2 Tbs)	freshly chopped parsley
1	egg
	salt and pepper

- Sauté the onion in a little butter or oil and leave to cool.
- Soak the bread in the stock.
- Combine the rest of the ingredients. Mix very well, preferably with your hand. The mixture must be very wet, otherwise the hamburgers become dry. Season well with salt and pepper.
- Form into patties and fry in a frying pan in a little oil over medium heat. (If the heat is too high they will burn because of the sugar in the tomato sauce.) To prevent the burger breaking, don't turn it until you can see it is cooked halfway up, then carefully turn it, using a lifter and a fork.

Hint
This recipe makes the most delicious braaied burgers. To braai over coals, leave the egg out of the mixture. Brush the hamburgers with oil and once they are on the braai grid, do not turn them until they are cooked almost right through. If you turn them too soon they will break.

Variation
Serve these burgers with a spicy cheese sauce (see *Sauces*).

LIVER AND ONIONS IN ORANGE

The flavour of the onion and orange juice balance perfectly with the slightly 'irony' taste of the liver. Even if you are not fond of liver, try this recipe.

Serves 4

600 g	lamb or calf liver, trimmed, skin removed, sliced into thin schnitzels
	seasoned flour
50 g	butter
45 ml (3 Tbs)	oil
2	onions, sliced
1	clove garlic, chopped
125 ml (½ cup)	beef stock
250 ml (1 cup)	fresh orange juice
15 ml (1 Tbs)	brown sugar
10 ml (2 tsp)	Worcestershire sauce
1	orange, peeled and thickly sliced
	salt and pepper
45 ml (3 Tbs)	freshly chopped parsley for garnish

- Coat the liver with seasoned flour and fry quickly in mixture of butter and oil for 1 to 2 minutes. Remove from pan and place in a warmed dish.
- Fry the onions until just beginning to brown. Add garlic.
- Sprinkle on 30 ml (2 Tbs) of the seasoned flour.
- Add stock, orange juice, sugar and Worcestershire sauce. Bring to the boil and taste for seasoning.
- Replace the liver and heat through.
- Add sliced orange and heat through.
- Garnish with scattering of chopped parsley and serve on fluffy mashed potatoes.

POTROASTS, STEWS AND CASSEROLES

> Please read the *basics of potroasts and stews* in the introduction to this chapter. It will make all these recipes child's play.
> Veal and pork may be used instead of chicken in all the chicken recipes in this book.

BASIC POT-ROASTED BEEF

The technique of this basic potroast can be applied to most potroasts.

Serves 8

1,5 kg	*topside, aitchbone* or *whole chuck*
15 ml (1 Tbs)	oil
30 g	butter (optional)
2	large carrots, sliced
2	large onions, sliced
30 ml (2 Tbs)	flour

Sauce mixture

250 ml (1 cup)	beef stock
125 ml (½ cup)	red wine
15 ml (1 Tbs)	Worcestershire sauce
10 ml (2 tsp)	tomato paste
5 ml (1 tsp)	sugar
4	bay leaves
	salt and pepper

- Preheat oven to 160 °C.
- In a very hot pan, brown the meat well in oil or butter and oil mixed. Remove the meat from the pan.
- Lower the heat and sauté carrot and onion until the onion is translucent.
- Sprinkle the flour on the onion mixture and cook over medium heat until flour is dark brown. (Leave out this step if you have a basic brown roux to hand – see introduction to this chapter.)
- Mix the sauce ingredients, add to the pan and bring to the boil.
- Place the meat and sauce in a heavy-based saucepan and cook with the lid on for about 3 hours on top of the stove on low, or covered in an ovenproof dish.
- Check the liquid content while the meat is cooking and add a little boiling water if the sauce is evaporating.
- Once the meat is soft, remove it from the pot and leave to rest on a warmed plate.
- In the meantime, complete the gravy.
- The onion and carrot in the pan juices can be strained out for a smooth gravy, or liquidised for a thicker consistency, or left as they are for a chunky sauce.
- Check the flavour and seasoning, adding a little extra water or seasoning if needed.
- Slice the meat and serve it with the gravy, and with rice, roast potatoes and vegetables.

Variations

- Add any of the following to the potroast with the onions and carrots: cubed sweet potato, swedes, green or red peppers, celery, button or brown mushrooms.
- Instead of roasting your potatoes, place halved potatoes in the saucepan/casserole with the meat halfway through the cooking time.

STUFFED SMOTHERED BEEF

Cajun spicy potroast

For those who like it hot and spicy, this is the tastiest potroast yet! Choose any meat suitable for pot-roasting. I like chuck off the bone best, and pot-roast it in the oven. Once stuffed, the beef should ideally stand for 8 hours for the flavour to develop.

Serves 6 to 8

1,5 kg	beef
45 ml (3 Tbs)	oil
45 g	butter (optional)
1	large onion, cut in 8 pieces
½	large red pepper, cut in large pieces
½	large green pepper, cut in large pieces
250 ml (1 cup)	beef stock
15 ml (1 Tbs)	flour to thicken gravy

Stuffing

1	large onion, finely chopped
½	large red pepper, finely chopped
½	large green pepper, finely chopped
3	cloves garlic, crushed
15 ml (1 Tbs)	sugar
5 ml (1 tsp)	salt
15 ml (1 Tbs)	good prepared mustard

2 ml (¹/₂ tsp) *cayenne pepper*
2 ml (¹/₂ tsp) *black pepper*
10 ml (2 tsp) *vinegar*
15 ml (1 Tbs) *flour*

Seasoned mustard

30 ml (2 Tbs) *prepared mustard*
15 ml (1 Tbs) *sugar*
5 ml (1 tsp) *salt*
1 ml (pinch) *black pepper*

▸ In a heavy-bottomed pan (preferably one that has a lid and that can go in the oven), heat the oil. Add the butter if you are using it.
▸ Over a high heat, brown the meat very well, then remove it from the pan and reserve.
▸ *To make the stuffing*, sauté chopped onion and red and green pepper until soft.
▸ Add remaining stuffing ingredients and mix well.
▸ Cut the meat in thick slices but do not cut all the way through. Place stuffing in the cuts between the slices.
▸ Mix the ingredients for the seasoned mustard and spread it over the browned meat.
▸ Add a little more oil (and butter) to the pan and sauté large pieces of onion and pepper (from the main list) until glassy.
▸ Place the stuffed meat on top of these vegetables. For the best flavour, cool and leave it to stand in the fridge for about 8 hours before cooking.
▸ Pour the beef stock (main list) over the vegetables in the bottom of the saucepan/ovenware dish and pot-roast, covered, for 2 ¹/₂ to 3 hours at 160 °C in the oven, or on low on top of stove.
▸ Remove the meat and leave it to stand for 10 minutes.
▸ For gravy, skim off the fat and mix 15 ml (1 Tbs) of it with 15 ml (1 Tbs) flour. Add the flour mixture to the pan juices and simmer for 3 minutes on top of the stove, stirring constantly.
▸ Check seasoning and serve the sauce with the meat, with Brabant potatoes, and/or rice, and Jams Californian vegetables (see *Vegetables*).

GIOUVETSI

Greek pot-roasted lamb with orzo

The flavour of lamb is very strong in this Greek recipe. The orzo (rice-shaped noodles) are cooked in the meat juices, resulting in a rich, delicious combination.

Serves 8

1 *leg of lamb, about 2,5 kg*
2 *cloves garlic, slivered*
45 ml (3 Tbs) *olive oil*
500 g *orzo*
Parmesan cheese, grated

Roasting mixture

250 ml (1 cup) *chicken stock*
60 ml (¹/₄ cup) *lemon juice*
10 ml (2 tsp) *dried origanum*
salt and pepper

Gravy/sauce

2 *medium onions, diced*
80 ml (¹/₃ cup) *tomato purée*
salt and pepper

▸ Preheat oven to 160 °C.
▸ With a sharp knife, make slits in the meat and stuff the leg with slivers of garlic.
▸ In a roasting pan, brown the lamb well in hot olive oil.
▸ Mix the stock, lemon juice, origanum and pepper and season to taste with salt and pepper. Pour this roasting mixture over the lamb.
▸ Cover roaster with lid or very loosely with aluminium foil and pot-roast in the oven for 3 to 3 ¹/₂ hours until the lamb is soft. Baste and turn lamb periodically.
▸ Tip orzo into boiling salted water and cook until it is 'al dente'.
▸ When lamb is ready, remove from the pan and leave to rest for 15 minutes before serving.
▸ Pour off the pan juices, leaving only enough fat to sauté the onion in. Sauté until they are glassy.
▸ Add orzo and sauté for 1 minute.
▸ Return some of the pan juices and the tomato purée to form a wet stew and bring it to the boil.
▸ Simmer to reduce the liquid, but do not let it boil away.
▸ Check seasoning.
▸ Thicken remaining pan juices with cornflour or flour and serve with the meat.
▸ To serve, heap the orzo around the leg of lamb and offer the grated Parmesan cheese separately to scatter on the pasta.

KASSLER BIGARADE

Kassler are cured, smoked pork chops with the rich, sweet flavour of smoked meats. The bigarade sauce, made with 'burned' sugar and orange juice, is usually served with duck or poultry. I find it complements the kassler beautifully.

Serves 4 to 6

6	*kassler chops* or *gammon steaks*
30 ml (2 Tbs)	*oil, butter,* or *a mixture*
1	*small onion, sliced*
1	*carrot, sliced*
1	*stick celery, with leaves, chopped*
	large sprig parsley
6	*peppercorns*
4	*bay leaves*
500 ml (2 cups)	*water*

Bigarade sauce

1	*large onion sliced*
30 ml (2 Tbs)	*fat from pan juices*
80 ml ($^1/_3$ cup)	*sugar*
80 ml ($^1/_3$ cup)	*white vinegar*
250 ml (1 cup)	*cooking liquid*
250 ml (1 cup)	*fresh orange juice*
10 ml (2 tsp)	*cornflour*
30 ml (2 Tbs)	*cold water*
1	*orange, unpeeled, sliced in 6*

▶ Brown the chops in butter and oil. Remove chops from pan.
▶ Sauté onion, celery and carrot in remaining fat in pan.
▶ Add parsley, peppercorns, bay leaves and water and bring to the boil.
▶ Return chops to the pan and simmer, covered, for about 20 minutes.
▶ Remove the chops and strain the cooking liquid, discarding the vegetables but keeping the stock for the sauce.
▶ Skim off all the fat and keep just enough for the sauce.
▶ *Bigarade sauce* Sauté onion in the fat.
▶ Add sugar and vinegar and boil until all the liquid has evaporated and the sugar caramelises to dark brown. Be careful not to burn it.
▶ As soon as the colour is right, pour in the stock and orange juice and bring back to the boil.
▶ Stir in the cornflour mixed with the water, and add orange slices.
▶ Return chops to sauce and heat through.
▶ Serve with roast baby potatoes or buttered noodles.

BRISKET FLAUMEN TZIMMES

Winter would not be the same for me without a slightly sweet, rich carrot and prune tzimmes. It is the easiest pot-roast to make, because after the meat has been browned, the vegetables are added as they are without sautéing.

Serves 8 to 10

1,5 kg	*brisket off the bone*
30 ml (2 Tbs)	*oil*
2	*bunches carrots*
2	*large onions*
2	*swedes* or *turnips*
4	*large potatoes*
2	*sweet potatoes*
250 g	*pitted prunes*
1,5 litres (6 cups)	*beef stock*
	salt and freshly ground black pepper
30 ml (2 Tbs)	*flour* or *cake meal*
30 ml (2 Tbs)	*syrup*

▶ Preheat oven to 160 °C.
▶ Clean all the vegetables and cut into very large chunks.
▶ Use a heavy-based saucepan that can go into the oven, or a roaster or casserole which has a well-fitting lid.
▶ Seal the brisket, uncovered, on top of the stove in the very hot oil.
▶ Remove the meat, place all the vegetables in the pan, then place the meat on top of the vegetables, fatty side up.
▶ Add enough stock to cover the vegetables.
▶ Season with salt and black pepper.
▶ Make sure the lid seals well.
▶ Pot-roast, covered, in the oven for 3 to 4 hours.
▶ Check periodically that the liquid level has not dropped and top up with a little boiling water if necessary.
▶ When the meat is very soft, remove it from the pot.
▶ Place the pot on top of the stove, sprinkle the flour onto vegetables and add syrup to taste.
▶ Bring to the boil and stir carefully until the vegetables thicken.
▶ Serve the vegetables with slices of brisket and kitke or crusty white bread.

GLAZED GAMMON

With the bone, allow 250 g per serving

5-6 kg	gammon
1 litre	ginger beer
	cold water
12	black peppercorns
1	large onion, peeled, studded with 6 cloves
4	bay leaves

Glaze

250 ml (1 cup)	soft brown sugar
250 ml (1 cup)	smooth apricot jam
15 ml (1 Tbs)	dijon or any good prepared mustard
30 ml (2 Tbs)	sherry
5 ml (1 tsp)	soy sauce

To serve

sliced fresh pineapple or fresh yellow cling peaches

- Place the gammon in a large saucepan, pour on the ginger beer and add enough water to cover the gammon.
- Add the remaining ingredients.
- Bring to the boil, cover with the lid and reduce the heat.
- Simmer, allowing 30 minutes per 500 g.
- Remove the gammon from the cooking liquid, leave to cool for a few minutes and then peel off the outer skin.
- Return gammon to saucepan and leave to cool in the liquid before glazing (this will ensure a more succulent gammon).
- Score the fat in a diamond pattern and push several cloves into the fat.
- Place gammon on a roasting pan just large enough to hold the meat. This will prevent the glaze from burning onto the pan.
- Preheat oven to 180 °C.
- Melt the glaze ingredients in a saucepan on top of the stove.
- Pour the sauce over the scored surface of the cooked gammon.
- Place gammon in the oven for 30 minutes. Baste regularly.
- Remove the gammon from the pan.
- Slice the fruit and add to the remaining glaze in the pan.
- Simmer on top of the stove for a few minutes until the fruit is hot through and sticky on the outside.
- Serve hot or cold with the gammon.

STEWS

The same basic method is used in all these recipes. Please read the introduction to this chapter. Once you have made one delicious stew, others can be made in the same way.

RICH BROWN STEW

This is a basic stew. Use it with whatever suitable ingredients you have in the fridge plus a little imagination and it will be deliciously different every time.

Serves 6

750 g	stewing beef, cubed
45 ml (3 Tbs)	oil, butter, or a mixture
2	onions, diced
30 ml (2 Tbs)	flour
2	carrots, sliced
2	ripe tomatoes, skinned and chopped
2	large potatoes, cubed
500 ml (2 cups)	beef stock
15 ml (1 Tbs)	Worcestershire sauce
5 ml (1 tsp)	mixed herbs for beef
410 g	tinned sliced green beans
or 250 g	fresh or frozen green beans (either optional)
or 410 g	tinned butterbeans

- In a *very* hot saucepan, brown the meat well, a little at a time, in oil or butter and oil mixed. Remove meat and reserve.
- Lower the heat and sauté the onions until glassy.
- Sprinkle on the flour and cook over medium heat until flour is dark brown.
- Add all the remaining ingredients except the beans and bring to the boil.
- Return the meat to the saucepan and simmer for 1 ½ to 2 hours or until the meat is almost soft enough.
- Check seasoning and add potatoes; cook for further 20 minutes or until potatoes are almost soft.
- Add beans and cook for 10 minutes more until beans are soft.
- Serve with rice and a green as well as a yellow vegetable.

CARBONADE OF BEEF

The flavour of the beef is enhanced by the beer, mustard and nutmeg in this hearty stew.

Serves 4

750 g	chuck or *any stewing beef, cubed*
45 ml (3 Tbs)	oil, butter, or *a mixture*
2	onions, diced
1	clove garlic, crushed
45 ml (3 Tbs)	flour
250 ml (1 cup)	beef stock
250 ml (1 cup)	beer
1	bouquet garni
or 5 ml (1 tsp)	mixed dried herbs for beef
15 ml (1 Tbs)	prepared mustard
5 ml (1 tsp)	lemon juice
5 ml (1 tsp)	sugar
2 ml (½ tsp)	grated nutmeg

- In a *very* hot, heavy-based saucepan, brown the meat well, a little at a time, in oil or butter and oil mixed. Remove the meat from the saucepan and reserve.
- Lower the heat and sauté the onion and garlic until onion is glassy.
- Sprinkle on the flour and cook over medium heat until flour is dark brown.
- Add all the remaining ingredients and bring to the boil.
- Return meat to saucepan and simmer for about 2 ½ hours or until meat is soft.
- Season to taste.
- Serve with rice and vegetables.

HUNGARIAN GOULASH

This traditional stew has the distinctive flavour of paprika and a hint of cumin. Paprika is made of roasted sweet red (bell) peppers, and is sweeter and milder than cayenne or chilli pepper. The Hungarians maintain that paprika is the secret of their genius!

Serves 4

750 g	beef cubes (goulash)
45 ml (3 Tbs)	oil, butter, or *a mixture*
2	onions, chopped
1	clove garlic, crushed
15 ml (1 Tbs)	flour
15 ml (1 Tbs)	very red and fresh paprika
3 ml (½ tsp)	cumin
15 ml (1 Tbs)	tomato paste
410 g	tinned tomatoes, with the juice, thickly sliced
500 ml (2 cups)	beef stock
3	potatoes, cut into chunks
2	red peppers, sliced
125 ml (½ cup)	sour cream
	salt and black pepper

- In a very hot saucepan brown the meat well, a little at a time, in oil or butter and oil mixed. Remove meat from pan and reserve.
- Lower the heat and sauté the onion and garlic until onion is glassy.
- Stir in the flour, paprika and cumin.
- Return the meat to the saucepan and add tomato paste, reserved liquid from tomatoes and the stock.
- Simmer until the meat is almost soft (about 2 hours).
- Add the potato chunks, red pepper and tinned tomato.
- Simmer until potatoes are soft.
- Serve with a good dollop of sour cream.

RENDANG

Mild and spicy Indonesian curried beef

It looks like a long list of ingredients, but once you have put them together, this rewarding curry is quick to make.

Masala is a mixture of ground spices used when making curry. Curry powder is a commercially prepared masala. Dhania or dhunia leaves are coriander leaves, also known as Chinese parsley and calintro. Dhania and the other spices are usually available at supermarkets, or at Indian speciality shops. This is a fairly mild curry. If you want the curry stronger, simply add more meat masala or curry powder.

Serves 6 to 8

1,5 kg	chuck on the bone, cubed
45 ml (3 Tbs)	oil
2	large onions, chopped
2	cloves garlic, crushed
10 ml (2 tsp)	grated fresh ginger
15 ml (1 Tbs)	flour
15 ml (1 Tbs)	meat masala, or *curry powder of your choice*
10 ml (2 tsp)	ground cumin
6	curry leaves
15 ml (1 Tbs)	sugar
30 ml (2 Tbs)	chutney
2	sticks cinnamon
5 ml (1 tsp)	turmeric
2	large, ripe tomatoes, skinned and chopped,

or ½ 410 g	tin tomatoes
4	potatoes, quartered
2	medium aubergines, diced
500 ml (2 cups)	water
175 ml (carton)	yoghurt
or 250 ml (1 cup)	sour cream
15 ml (1 Tbs)	lemon juice
30 ml (2 Tbs)	garam masala
60 ml (4 Tbs)	chopped dhania (coriander) leaves
	salt

- Brown the meat in oil in a very hot saucepan, a few pieces at a time.
- Remove the meat from the saucepan and set aside.
- Sauté the onion over a medium heat in the same pan until beginning to brown.
- Add garlic, ginger and stir in the flour and all the spices.
- Add all the remaining ingredients, except garam masala and dhania leaves.
- Return the meat to the saucepan and simmer, covered, for 2 to 3 hours or until the meat is soft.
- Stir in the garam masala and dhania leaves, and serve.

Variations
Chicken, or neck, shoulder or leg of lamb may be used in place of beef.

NAVARIN OF LAMB

This rich lamb stew has a hint of a bacon flavour.

Serves 4

750 g	boned shoulder of lamb, cubed
45 ml (3 Tbs)	oil, butter, or a mixture
20 ml (4 tsp)	flour
375 ml (1 1/2 cup)	chicken or lamb stock
1	clove of garlic, crushed
80 ml (⅓ cup)	tomato purée
8	small pickling onions
75 g	rindless bacon, chopped
15 ml (1 Tbs)	oil or butter
2	small turnips, diced
8	baby potatoes, peeled
75 g (⅓ cup)	mixed frozen peas and carrots
15 ml (1 Tbs)	chopped parsley

- In a *very* hot saucepan, brown the meat well, a little at a time, in oil or in butter and oil mixed. Remove the meat and reserve.
- Sprinkle the flour into the pot and cook over medium heat until flour is dark brown.
- Add the stock, garlic and tomato purée, stir until the sauce boils, reduce heat and return the meat to the pot.
- Simmer, covered, for 30 minutes. Check the liquid and add extra boiling water if the stew is becoming dry.
- In a separate pan, sauté onions and bacon in a little oil or melted butter.
- Add the onions, bacon, turnips and potatoes to the pot with the meat and simmer, covered, for about 30 minutes longer, or until the meat and vegetables are soft.
- Add the frozen peas and carrots and simmer for further 5 to 10 minutes.
- Add chopped parsley and serve.

TOMATO BREDIE

The Malay exiles and slaves brought their traditional dishes with them to the Cape. These have become a cornerstone of South African cuisine. This tomato bredie is rich and spicy and one of my favourites. Instead of the lamb, use stewing beef or chuck if you prefer beef.

Serves 6 to 8

1,2-1,5 kg	lamb neck or knuckles
60 ml (4 Tbs)	oil, butter, or a mixture
30 ml (2 Tbs)	flour
3	large onions, chopped
410 g	tinned tomatoes, chopped (with juice)
250 ml (1 cup)	tomato purée
3	cloves garlic, crushed
6	cardamom pods
or 3 ml (½ tsp)	ground cardamom
10 ml (2 tsp)	grated fresh ginger
1 ml (pinch)	cayenne pepper
4	bay leaves
4	sticks cinnamon
625 ml (2 1/2 cups)	chicken or lamb stock
15 ml (1 Tbs)	sugar
4	medium potatoes, each cut in 6 pieces
	salt

- Split the cardamom seeds by gently hitting them with a rolling pin or meat mallet.
- In a *very* hot pot, brown the meat well, a little at a time, in oil or in butter and oil mixed. Remove the meat and reserve.

- Lower the heat and sauté the onions until glassy.
- Sprinkle the flour into the pan and cook over medium heat until flour is dark brown.
- Add all the remaining ingredients except the potatoes, and bring to the boil.
- Return the meat to the pot and simmer for about 2 hours (3 hours for beef) until the meat is soft.
- Add the potatoes and season to taste.
- Simmer for another 30 minutes or until potatoes are soft.

Variation

Half a shredded cabbage may be added when adding the potatoes.

OSSO BUCCO

Traditionally made with veal shin, this Italian stew can be made with any stewing meat for an equally delicious meal.

Serves 8

1,5-2 kg	meaty veal shin, cut in 2 cm slices
45 ml (3 Tbs)	olive oil
2	onions, diced
2	large carrots, diced
3	sticks celery, diced
45 ml (3 Tbs)	flour
410 g	tinned tomatoes, chopped
80 ml ($1/3$ cup)	tomato purée
3	cloves garlic, chopped
125 ml ($1/2$ cup)	dry white wine
750 ml (3 cups)	chicken stock
5 ml (1 tsp)	dried basil
5 ml (1 tsp)	dried thyme
3	bay leaves
10 ml (2 tsp)	sugar
10 ml (2 tsp)	finely grated lemon rind
	salt and pepper
60 ml ($1/4$ cup)	freshly chopped parsley

- Preheat the oven to 160 °C.
- In a *very* hot saucepan brown the meat well, a little at a time, in olive oil. Remove the meat from the pan and place in a casserole.
- Lower the heat and sauté the onion, carrot and celery until onion is glassy.
- Sprinkle on the flour and cook over medium heat until flour is dark brown.
- Add all the remaining ingredients, except the parsley and lemon rind, and bring to the boil.
- Pour the sauce over the meat and casserole, covered, in the oven for about 1 $1/2$ hours until the meat is soft.
- Toss in plenty of chopped parsley and serve on rice, garnished with grated lemon rind.

STEAK IN RED WINE

This stew requires a little more effort than the others, but the puréed vegetables give the sauce a rich flavour with a thick, non-starchy texture. It's easier to cook in the oven, because the thick sauce can easily burn on the bottom if you don't watch it carefully on top of the stove.

Serves 6 to 8

1,5 kg	boned chuck, cubed
60 ml (4 Tbs)	oil, butter, or a mixture

Sauce

30 ml (2 Tbs)	oil or butter
45 ml (3 Tbs)	flour
1	onion, finely chopped
1	clove garlic
410 g	tinned tomatoes, chopped
2	carrots, sliced
250 ml (1 cup)	red wine
375 ml (1 $1/2$ cup)	beef stock
4	bay leaves
5 ml (1 tsp)	sugar
5 ml (1 tsp)	dried thyme
	salt and black pepper
45 ml (3 Tbs)	cream (optional)

- Preheat oven to 160 °C.
- In a *very* hot frying pan, brown the meat well, a little at a time, in oil or butter and oil mixed. Remove the meat from the pan and place in a casserole dish.
- Add the extra butter or oil to the pan and sauté the chopped onion till glassy.
- Stir in the flour and cook over medium heat until flour is well browned.
- Add remaining ingredients, except cream, and simmer until the vegetables are very soft (about 15 minutes).
- Remove the bay leaves and place them with the meat.
- Liquidise the sauce and pour over the meat and bay leaves.
- Casserole, covered, for 2 to 3 hours or until meat is soft.
- Just before serving, stir in the cream.
- Serve with rice and vegetables.

STEAK AND KIDNEY WITH VEGETABLES AND HERB DUMPLINGS

This recipe really stretches the meat. Because of the strong flavour of the kidneys and well-browned meat, everyone gets enough meat and vegetables even though you are using only 1 kg of meat

Putting the herb dumplings on top of the meat is lighter, less fatty than a pastry and much tastier. The dumplings soak up the gravy, so no rice is needed. This is definitely a one-pot meal. The recipe for the dumplings follows, but you must have the mixture ready to drop spoonfuls on the stew 30 minutes before serving.

If you prefer, make a pie, using either rough puff pastry or hot-water pastry (see *Pastry*, where oven temperatures for pastry are also indicated). If using pastry, cut back on the stock by 250 ml (1 cup).

Serves 6

750 kg	chuck on the bone or *any stewing meat*
3	sheep's kidneys
or 250 g	ox kidney
3	large onions, chopped in fairly large pieces
60 ml (4 Tbs)	oil, butter, *or a mixture*
30 ml (2 Tbs)	flour
625 ml (2 $^1/_2$ cups)	beef stock
3 ml ($^1/_2$ tsp)	ground allspice
4	bay leaves
30 ml (2 Tbs)	Worcestershire sauce
	salt and black pepper
1	large potato, unpeeled, cut in 8 pieces
1	large sweet potato, peeled and cut in 8
1	small butternut, unpeeled, pips removed, cut into chunks
1-2	aubergines, unpeeled, cut in large pieces

Herb dumplings

375 ml (1 $^1/_2$ cups)	cake flour
125 ml ($^1/_2$ cup)	wholewheat flour
5 ml (1 tsp)	salt
15 ml (1 Tbs)	baking powder
80 g	butter
10 ml (2 tsp)	mixed herbs
125 ml ($^1/_2$ cup)	grated mature cheddar cheese
3 ml ($^1/_2$ tsp)	dry mustard
1	egg
185 ml ($^3/_4$ cup)	water

▶ Cut meat into large cubes and the kidneys into small cubes.
▶ In a *very* hot saucepan, brown the meat well, a little at a time, in oil or in butter and oil mixed. Remove the meat and set aside.
▶ Lower the heat and sauté the onions until glassy.
▶ Sprinkle the flour into the saucepan and cook over medium heat until flour is dark brown.
▶ Return the beef and kidney cubes to the pot, with 1 $^1/_2$ cups of the stock and all the seasoning.
▶ Simmer until meat is soft, checking the liquid content and adding stock as needed. Season to taste with salt and pepper.
▶ For the last hour, add all the vegetables and simmer until they are soft.
▶ Meanwhile, make the dumplings by mixing the cake and wholewheat flour, salt and baking powder together and rubbing the butter into the mixture.
▶ Add remaining dry ingredients for dumplings.
▶ Beat egg in the water and mix the liquid into the dry mixture, using a knife and a cutting rather than a stirring action.
▶ Drop spoonfuls of the dumpling mixture on top of the stew 30 minutes before you are ready to serve.
▶ Cover saucepan and steam till dumplings are cooked through (about 30 minutes).
▶ Serve immediately.

Hint
If left to stand, the dumplings absorb the liquid and the stew will become dry. If you have any stew left over, remove the dumplings and store the stew and the dumplings separately.

TWO-DAY OXTAIL STEW

This is well worth the time and effort! By cooking this oxtail stew over two days, you can remove all the fat and develop the maximum flavour.

Serves 6 to 8

Day 1

2	oxtails, cut into pieces
60 ml (4 Tbs)	olive oil, butter, or a mixture
2	large onions, quartered
45 ml (3 Tbs)	flour
2	large carrots, cut into chunks
1	swede or turnip cut into chunks
3	sticks celery, with leaves, chopped
4-6	rashers of bacon, chopped (optional)
6	bay leaves
10 ml (2 tsp)	dried thyme
	or large sprig fresh thyme
3	cloves garlic, crushed
3 ml (½ tsp)	black pepper
10 ml (2 tsp)	sugar
750 ml (3 cups)	beef stock
500 ml (2 cups)	red wine (reserve rest of bottle)
80 ml (⅓ cup)	tomato purée
	large sprig parsley, with stalks

▸ Preheat oven to 130 °C to 140 °C.
▸ In a *very* hot saucepan brown the meat well, a few pieces at a time, in oil or butter and oil mixed. Remove the meat from the pan.
▸ Lower the heat and sauté the onion until just beginning to brown.
▸ Sprinkle on the flour and cook over medium heat until flour is dark brown.
▸ Add all the remaining ingredients and bring to the boil.
▸ Return meat to the sauce and cook (using an ovenproof casserole) in a slow oven for 3 to 4 hours.
▸ Cool, uncovered, in a sink of cold water and leave in saucepan/casserole in the fridge overnight.

Day 2

16	small pickling onions
16	baby carrots
4	sticks celery, cut into chunks
16	baby potatoes, peeled
2 x 410 g	tins butter beans
or 250 g	dry beans of your choice, cooked
250 ml (1 cup)	red wine
	salt and pepper

▸ Remove all the fat from the top of the chilled oxtail, but retain enough to sauté the vegetables and discard rest.
▸ Heat the stew through. Strain off all the vegetables (and bacon) and discard. The vegetables can be puréed, strained and returned to the sauce for a thicker consistency.
▸ In a separate pan, sauté the small onions, carrots, celery and baby potatoes in a little of the fat.
▸ Add these vegetables, with the beans and wine, to the meat in the pot and simmer for about 1 ½ hours, or until the vegetables are cooked.
▸ Check seasoning and serve with rice or samp.
▸ If using tinned beans, add 10 minutes before serving.

SPICED LAMB WITH SPINACH AND YOGHURT

This rich Turkish dish, flavoured with cumin and yoghurt, is perfect for an adventurous dinner party (see *Vegetables* for a vegetarian version of this recipe)

Serves 8

1,5 kg	leg or shoulder of lamb
1 large onion,	diced
60 ml (4 Tbs)	olive oil, butter, or a mixture
30 ml (2 Tbs)	flour
30 ml (2 Tbs)	tomato paste
10 ml (2 tsp)	sugar
8 ml (1 ½ tsp)	dried dill
2 ml (½ tsp)	ground cinnamon
8 ml (1 ½ tsp)	cumin
325 ml (1 ½ cups)	chicken stock
2-3	packets fresh spinach
3	cloves garlic, crushed
	salt and pepper
	cooked yoghurt

Cooked yoghurt

350 ml	plain yoghurt (not drinking)
1	egg white
5 ml (1 tsp)	salt
15 ml (1 Tbs)	cornflour

▸ Cut the lamb into large cubes.
▸ In a *very* hot saucepan, brown the meat well, a little at a time, in oil or butter and oil mixed. Remove the meat and reserve.
▸ Lower the heat and sauté the onions in the same saucepan until glassy.
▸ Stir in the flour.

- Return meat to the pot and add tomato paste, sugar, dill, cinnamon and stock.
- Simmer, covered, for 1 1/2 to 2 hours until the meat is tender.
- Wash and roughly chop the spinach and add, with garlic, to the stew.
- Simmer until the spinach is wilted.
- Meanwhile, pour yoghurt into a small saucepan.
- Lightly whisk egg white and add to yoghurt with salt and cornflour.
- Stirring constantly, heat until mixture begins to boil.
- Reduce heat and leave to simmer for 2 minutes until thick.
- Just before serving, stir the cooked yoghurt into the stew. Heat through and check seasoning.
- Serve with basmati or plain rice.

BASIC MINCE SAUCE

(ragu or bolognaise)

This is a good basic mince sauce that can be used plain on pasta, or as a filling base for lasagne or moussaka.

Serves 4 to 6

600 g	minced lamb or beef, or a mixture of the two
45 ml (3 Tbs)	oil
2	onions, finely chopped
2	sticks celery, with leaves, finely chopped
2	carrots, finely grated
410 g	tinned tomato purée
125 ml (1/2 cup)	white wine
125 ml (1/2 cup)	strong beef stock
15 ml (1 Tbs)	sugar
5 ml (1 tsp)	dried origanum
5 ml (1 tsp)	dried thyme
5 ml (1 tsp)	dried basil
or 45 ml (3 Tbs)	fresh basil
125 ml (1/2 cup)	freshly chopped parsley
3	cloves garlic, crushed
	salt and black pepper

- Brown the mince well in a little oil, breaking it up with the back of a fork or slotted spoon as it is browning. Remove it from the pan and set aside.
- In remaining oil, sauté the onion and celery until onion is glassy.
- Add all the remaining ingredients, seasoning to taste with salt and pepper.
- Cover and simmer for 45 minutes. Check and adjust seasoning.

Hint

Ask the butcher to mince the meat 3 times instead of twice.

SIMPLE MOUSSAKA

Layered mince with aubergines has the authentic taste of Greece.

Serves 4 to 6

1	quantity basic mince sauce
1	quantity béchamel sauce (see Lasagne)
3-4	potatoes, unpeeled
3-4	aubergines, unpeeled
	extra grated cheese for topping

- Prepare mince sauce and béchamel sauce.
- Preheat oven to 160 °C.
- Boil potatoes in their jackets. Cool, peel and slice.
- Slice brinjals, brush each side lightly with oil and brown quickly in a hot dry pan or under the grill. (If you fry them in oil, they become very oily.)
- Layer half the mince sauce, potato and aubergine slices and béchamel sauce in sequence. Repeat, ending with béchamel.
- Top with a sprinkling of grated cheese.
- Bake for 45 to 60 minutes.

Hint

If you want to cut back on the oil, boil the brinjals in their skins until they are soft. Leave to cool and then slice. I never salt and sweat aubergines. By drawing out the water, you also draw out the flavour!

LASAGNE

This is my quick variation on the Italian theme. Made in small individual ovenware dishes, the lasagne looks more attractive and is easier to serve.

Serves 4 to 6

1	quantity basic mince sauce
200-300 g (about $^1/_3$ packet)	precooked lasagne sheets or *flat ribbon noodles*
1	quantity béchamel sauce

Béchamel sauce

500 ml (2 cups)	milk, infused with 1 onion, 4 bay leaves and 12 peppercorns
45 ml (3 Tbs)	flour
50 g	butter
125 ml ($^1/_2$ cup)	grated cheddar cheese
	salt and white pepper
2	egg yolks
25 ml	grated parmesan cheese

- Preheat oven to 180 °C.
- Prepare the basic mince sauce.
- *For the béchamel sauce, melt the butter and, off the heat, stir in the flour.*
- Strain the infused milk (see *Hint*) into butter and flour and bring it to the boil, stirring constantly with a wire whisk. Remove from the heat.
- Stir in the cheddar cheese and season with salt and pepper.
- Add the sauce to the egg yolks and beat well. *Do not return to stove.*
- Layer half the mince sauce, lasagne sheets or cooked noodles and béchamel in a large ovenproof dish. Repeat the sequence, ending with béchamel sauce.
- Sprinkle with grated parmesan cheese and bake for 40 minutes.

Hint

To infuse the milk, place the milk, chopped onion, bay leaves and peppercorns in a pot. Bring to just under boiling point and leave to stand for 15 minutes to absorb the flavour.

Variation

For a simpler version, use 300 g of any pasta of your choice. Place the cooked pasta at the bottom of a large ovenproof dish. Pour on all the meat sauce, then all the béchamel sauce. Sprinkle with cheese and bake at 180 °C for 30 minutes.

BOBOTIE

South Africa's favourite, this recipe is fruity and spicy.

Serves 4

500 g	mince (beef, lamb or *mixture*)
2	onions, chopped
60 ml (4 Tbs)	oil, butter, or *a mixture*
1	slice bread
125 ml ($^1/_2$ cup)	beef stock
15 ml (1 Tbs)	garlic and ginger paste
or 15 ml (1 Tbs)	grated fresh ginger, mixed with 2 crushed cloves garlic
10-15 ml (2-3 tsp)	apricot jam or *chutney*
1	small apple, grated
15 ml (1 Tbs)	curry powder
5 ml (1 tsp)	mixed herbs
5 ml (1 tsp)	turmeric
15 ml (1 Tbs)	lemon juice
125 ml ($^1/_2$ cup)	chopped dried apricots and raisins
	salt and pepper

Topping

250 ml (1 cup)	sour cream
	salt and pepper
2	eggs
6	bay or *lemon* leaves

- Preheat oven to 180 °C.
- In a frying pan on top of the stove, brown the mince well in a little oil, breaking it up with the back of a fork or slotted spoon as it is browning. Remove and set aside.
- Sauté the onion in butter and oil until glassy. Remove the pan from the stove and then return the meat.
- Remove the crusts from the bread and soak in the stock. Work bread into mince mixture, ensuring that there are no lumps of bread.
- Add the rest of the ingredients in main list and mix well. Season to taste.
- Transfer to a casserole.
- Mix all topping ingredients, except bay or lemon leaves, and pour over meat.
- Push bay or lemon leaves into mixture.
- Bake, uncovered, for 30 to 40 minutes until custard is set.

BITKIS

Meat patties in tomato sauce
This Russian dish of meat balls in a tomato and sour cream sauce makes a delicious family meal or an inexpensive dish for guests.

Serves 4 to 6

Sauce

30 g	butter
45 ml (3 Tbs)	flour
410 g	tinned tomatoes, chopped
375 ml (1 1/2 cups)	beef stock
5 ml (1 tsp)	dried thyme
2	bay leaves
5 ml (1 tsp)	sugar
	salt and pepper
250 ml (1 cup)	sour cream

Beef patties

750 g	lean mince
1	large onion, finely chopped
	oil for frying
30 ml (2 Tbs)	freshly chopped parsley
1	slice white bread
80 ml (1/3 cup)	beef stock
1	egg yolk
	salt and pepper

- Melt the butter for the sauce and stir in the flour.
- Cook over medium heat until the flour is well browned.
- Add the remaining ingredients, except the cream, season to taste, and simmer for 15 minutes.
- Remove the bay leaves and liquidise the sauce with the sour cream
- Return bay leaves to the sauce and set aside while making the patties.
- Preheat oven to 160 °C.
- Finely chop the onions and sauté in a little oil until glassy.
- Remove the crusts from the bread and soak bread in beef stock.
- Mix all the ingredients, making sure there are no lumps of bread, and season to taste with salt and pepper.
- Form mixture into smallish meat balls and brown well in a little oil.
- Place the browned patties in a casserole and pour on the tomato sauce and bay leaves.
- Casserole, covered, for 45 minutes.
- Serve with buttered noodles.

SPICY CHILLI MINCE

Mexican tacos filled with chilli mince topped with guacamole, shredded lettuce, salsa, sour cream and grated cheese. This tasty, easy and economic dish is fun to prepare for informal entertaining. If you can't find ready-made tacos or tortillas in the shops, serve the mince in a bowl, offering various toppings and lots of crusty white bread.

Serves 8

16-20	taco shells
1 kg	lean beef mince
60 ml (1/4 cup)	oil
2	onions, chopped
3	cloves garlic, crushed
2	fresh hot green chillies, seeded and chopped
1	large red pepper, seeded and chopped
1	large green pepper, seeded and chopped
15 ml (1 Tbs)	ground coriander
15 ml (1 Tbs)	ground cumin
5 ml (1 tsp)	ground cinnamon
3 ml (1/2 tsp)	ground allspice
10-15 ml (2-3 tsp)	chilli powder
5 ml (1 tsp)	dried origanum
60 ml (1/4 cup)	finely chopped parsley
2 x 410 g	tins tomatoes
65 g	tinned tomato paste
	salt and milled black pepper

- In a heavy frying pan, brown the mince well in a little hot oil, breaking it up with the back of a fork or slotted spoon as it is browning. Remove from the pan and set aside.
- Sauté the onion in the remaining oil till glassy.
- Add the remaining ingredients and return the mince to the pan.
- Bring to the boil.
- Cover, reduce the heat and cook very gently, stirring now and again, for 1 to 1 1/2 hours or until very soft and saucy. Check seasoning.
- As a topping, use guacamole, salsa cruda (see *Sauces*), thick sour cream, grated mild cheddar cheese, fresh coriander leaves and shredded lettuce.

STUFFED CABBAGE LEAVES

This dish is spicy rather than herby and can be made plain or sweet and sour. For a variation, use the vegetarian stuffed cabbage recipe (see *Vegetables*) and add 500 g of browned mince to the filling.

Serves 4

1 cabbage

Filling

500 g	lean mince
1	large onion, finely chopped
	oil for frying
1	slice white bread
180 ml ($^3/_4$ cup)	beef stock
1	ripe tomato, skinned and chopped
60 ml ($^1/_4$ cup)	uncooked rice
7 ml (1 $^1/_2$ tsp)	ground cinnamon
5 ml (1 tsp)	allspice
5 ml (1 tsp)	mixed herbs
	salt and pepper

Sauce

1	large onion, sliced
45 ml (3 Tbs)	oil
2 x 410 g	tins tomatoes, with juice, sliced
180 ml ($^3/_4$ cup)	beef stock
15 ml (1 Tbs)	sugar
	salt and pepper

- Preheat oven to 160 °C.
- Chop the onions finely and fry well in oil.
- Remove from the stove and add the remaining ingredients, with the sautéed onion, soaked bread and rice, mixing well and ensuring that there are no lumps of bread. Check seasoning.
- Place the whole cabbage in a large pot of boiling water.
- Remove leaves, one at a time, and plunge each leaf into cold water.
- Cut out the bottom of the very thick white vein of the leaf.
- Spoon some of the filling onto each leaf and wrap it around the filling. Repeat the process, using up the filling mixture.
- Pack stuffed cabbage leaves in a casserole, close together, so that the leaves won't unroll.
- Sauté the onion for the sauce in heated oil.
- Add remaining sauce ingredients and bring to the boil.
- Season to taste with salt and pepper
- Pour sauce over stuffed cabbage leaves and casserole, covered, for 1 hour.

Variation

For sweet and sour stuffed cabbage leaves, add about 100 ml (7 Tbs) brown sugar and 30 ml (2 Tbs) vinegar to the sauce.

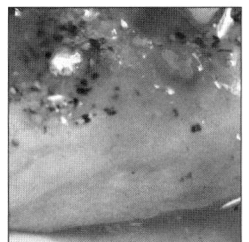  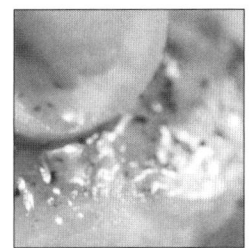

POULTRY

This chapter deals in turn with whole birds (chicken, turkey and duck), chicken portions, and filleted chicken breasts.

Most of the chickens we buy are more or less the same age and size. This makes cooking chicken very simple. The occasional 'pot bird' must be treated like any tough cut of meat, which means long, slow cooking. For a Cornish hen or large, tough bird, use any of the pot-roasted chicken recipes, but cook it for double the time, or until it is soft.

Turkey is the most underrated poultry in South Africa. We tend to eat it only on special occasions. In fact, it is a very inexpensive, flavoursome protein that should be used throughout the year. The turkeys we get now are smaller and juicier than in the past. In this chapter there are a few recipes for whole turkey, but the chicken casserole recipes are delicious when made with turkey in place of chicken. Simply double the cooking time.

Many people are somewhat afraid of cooking duck because of the extremely high fat content. As you will see in the recipe in this chapter, this problem is easily solved and you will be able to achieve the unique flavour of crisp duck that the Chinese are famous for.

WHOLE BIRDS

Wash the body cavity of the bird under running water, making sure that you remove any pieces of internal organs that remain. The lung often remains in the rib cage and if left imparts a slight taste of offal to the breast meat. Remove it with your fingers.

Remember to remove the preening gland on the 'pope's nose' ('parson's nose') on the tail. This oil gland is used by the bird to keep the feathers waterproof, and has a bitter taste. If it is not removed, it will affect the taste of the pope's nose, which many people regard as a choice bit.

There are often little feathers left unplucked. I remove them with a small pair of tweezers I keep in the kitchen for this purpose.

There is always an extra flap of skin on the neck. Don't cut it off before it is cooked. The remaining skin will shrink as the chicken cooks and if you cut off this flap, the shrinking skin will leave the breast exposed.

Trussing
Trussing is tying the wings and drumsticks against the body of the bird to form one solid mass of meat that will cook more evenly, preventing the drumsticks and wings from drying out, and preserving a neat shape. If the chicken is trussed, the skin between the body and the wing and drumstick is not exposed to the dry heat and remains pale and soft. With the juicy, tender and quick-cooking chickens available today, drying out is no longer a problem. I have stopped trussing chickens and ducks, although I will truss a turkey.

Butterflying
Unless the bird is to be stuffed, I prefer to 'butterfly' the chicken or turkey before roasting it. Using a large, heavy, sharp knife, or a strong pair of kitchen scissors, cut down the backbone. Cut through the point of the wishbone. *Do not* cut down the breastbone, or the breast meat will dry out more quickly. Open the bird out with the skin facing up and press down hard on the breastbone to flatten it out. To butterfly a turkey, follow the same procedure as for chicken; you need strong hands, and this is definitely a job for the man of the house.

Butterflied chicken cooks much more quickly, browns and becomes crisp more evenly and is easier to baste and season. The roasting time for a chicken is 45 to 55 minutes. Cooking time for a butterflied turkey is about 2 hours, depending on how much stuffing there is!

Cooking time
The oven roasting time for an average chicken of 1,5 to 2 kg is about 1 to 1 1/2 hours depending on how dry and how crisp you want it on the outside. For roasting times of turkey or duck, follow the recipe instructions in this chapter.

To test if a whole bird is cooked, stick a thin knife into the thigh joint, which always takes the longest to be done. The juices should run out clear; if they are pink, the bird is still underdone.

Overcooked poultry becomes dry and stringy, especially the breast. For a crisper skin, increase the temperature rather than the cooking time and liberally salt the skin for the last 30 minutes of the cooking time.

Flavouring
With roasting, very little flavour from the seasoning will penetrate the skin into the meat. Many people do not eat the skin because of its high fat content. Once the skin has been removed, there is very little flavour left unless you have seasoned the meat. Loosen the skin of the breast and thigh by putting your hand in between the layers. You can then pour some of the basting mixture and seasoning directly onto the meat.

Gravy
To make a gravy, the general procedure is to skim off the fat from the basting sauce/roasting liquid. In some cases the remaining strained liquid can be used as a gravy or sauce on its own, or you can thicken it to the consistency you need for your gravy as follows:

Into a little of the fat, mix 30 ml (2 Tbs) flour for every 500 ml (2 cups) of the sauce/roasting liquid remaining as pan juices. Use less flour for a thinner gravy.

Or mix 5 to 10 ml (2 tsp) cornflour with a little cold water, stir it into the pan juices and bring it to the boil.

STUFFINGS

Use any of the turkey or chicken stuffing recipes in this chapter and add your personal touch.

In place of the usual sausage meat or minced veal, add 1 or 2 filleted chicken breasts or thighs that have been finely chopped. It adds subtle flavour, texture and quality to an otherwise starchy, fatty stuffing.

For a change use your favourite stuffing recipe and place the stuffing between the skin and meat instead of in the cavity. The flavour penetrates the meat more easily.

SALAMI STUFFING

500 g	pork sausage meat
125 ml (1/2 cup)	fresh breadcrumbs
30 ml (2 Tbs)	chopped parsley
100 g	salami, chopped
	salt and pepper to taste

▶ Combine ingredients and stuff poultry.

MUSHROOM OYSTER STUFFING

1	stick celery, chopped
4-6	rashers bacon, chopped
100 g	tinned oysters, chopped
250 g	mushrooms, chopped
50 g	butter, melted
375 ml (1 1/2 cups)	fresh breadcrumbs
	salt and pepper to taste

▶ Mix ingredients and stuff poultry.

PRUNE AND SWEET POTATO STUFFING

The sweet potato gives this stuffing the texture and flavour of chestnuts.

150 g	prunes, chopped
250 g	sweet potatoes
2	apples, finely chopped
500 g	pork sausage meat
	or *chopped chicken breasts*
1	turkey liver
or 3	chicken livers, chopped
1	egg
60 ml (1/4 cup)	chopped parsley
10 ml (2 tsp)	grated orange rind

```
           2  onions, chopped
           2  sticks celery with leaves, chopped
60 ml (¼ cup)  brandy
   5 ml (1 tsp)  instant chicken stock powder
          or 1  cube
750 ml (3 cups)  breadcrumbs
  10 ml (2 tsp)  mixed dried herbs
         250 g  cream cheese
    juice of 1  orange
```

- Sauté the onions and celery and leave to cool.
- Add all the remaining ingredients and use as stuffing for turkey, or make half the quantity for a chicken.

ROASTING POULTRY

Roasting, pot-roasting, butterflying, braaiing – it's all in the sauce or basting mixture! Without a recipe, using whatever comes to hand, your recipe could be the nicest you have ever tasted. But what a pity if the next time you don't remember what you put into it! Here are a few ideas for basting your simple, open-roast chicken.

Be careful with any basting mixture containing tomato paste or sugar. It makes the chicken go black before it is cooked, and should therefore be used only towards the end of the cooking time.

Whenever possible, coat chicken in basting mixture hours before cooking it. This will allow the chicken to marinate and absorb the flavour.

All the following recipes for roast chicken are also perfect for the Weber or kettle braai. Cook by indirect method for 60 minutes.

BASTING SAUCES

SPICY SOY SAUCE

```
125 ml (½ cup)  oil
 15 ml (1 Tbs)  soy sauce
 15 ml (1 Tbs)  herb blend for chicken
 10 ml (2 tsp)  chicken seasoning
  5 ml (1 tsp)  barbecue spice
```

- Mix all the ingredients.

Variation
10 ml (2 tsp) of curry powder instead of the chicken and barbeque seasoning is delicious.

SIMPLE LEMON AND ROSEMARY BASTING SAUCE

```
80 ml (⅓ cup)  oil
     juice of  2 lemons
10 ml (2 tsp)  dried rosemary
               plenty salt and black pepper
```

- Mix ingredients.

LEMON, HONEY AND MUSTARD BASTING SAUCE

```
30 ml (2 Tbs)  oil
30 ml (2 Tbs)  sweet white wine
15 ml (1 Tbs)  honey, warmed
30 ml (2 Tbs)  lemon juice
10 ml (2 tsp)  mustard
10 ml (2 tsp)  dried rosemary
 5 ml (1 tsp)  salt
 5 ml (1 tsp)  pepper
```

- Warm all the ingredients and stir to dissolve the honey.

PERI PERI SAUCE

```
    45 ml (3 Tbs)  oil or melted butter
    10 ml (2 tsp)  powdered chicken stock
             or 1  cube, crumbled and dissolved
                   in a little hot water
 or 5 ml (1 tsp)   salt
                3  cloves garlic, crushed
2-5 ml (½-1 tsp)  peri peri powder, or to taste
     5 ml (1 tsp)  paprika
    10 ml (2 tsp)  thyme
    30 ml (2 Tbs)  lemon juice
    10 ml (2 tsp)  honey or castor sugar
```

- Heat all the ingredients and stir to dissolve honey or sugar. Leave to stand for a couple of hours before using.

BASIC DRY-ROASTED CHICKEN

    1 *chicken, washed and dried*
       prepared basting mixture

- Butterfly chicken if desired.
- Brush the basting mixture on the chicken and in between the skin and meat.
- Place chicken on a rack in a roasting pan to catch the juices and roast in a preheated oven at 180 °C to 200 °C for 1 1/4 to 1 1/2 hours (if butterflied, for 45 to 55 minutes). Baste periodically.
- If you want to make a gravy to go with the chicken, pour 500 ml of water into the roasting pan under the rack. Make sure that during the roasting, it does not all evaporate, topping up if necessary. Use this as a base for the gravy as described in this chapter.

TURKISH STUFFED CHICKEN

I love Middle-Eastern flavours. They are warm, spicy and rich. The base for this stuffing is couscous, which is a staple food in many Mediterranean countries. It is made from semolina and is precooked, making it very quick and easy to use. If you prefer, use rice, preferably basmati or any short-grain rice that will become sticky when cooked. This recipe is delicious when cooked on the Weber. Cook by indirect method for 45 to 50 minutes.

Serves 4 to 6 (8 if chicken is deboned)

    1 *fresh chicken, whole* or *deboned*
    2 *filleted chicken breasts (4 if you are using a deboned chicken)*

Stuffing
125 ml (1/2 cup) couscous
1 small onion, finely chopped
1/2 green pepper, finely chopped
45 ml (3 Tbs) olive oil
50 g pinenuts
   or *almonds, roasted*
   or *pistachio nuts*
30 ml (2 Tbs) currants, soaked in boiling water
3 ml (1/2 tsp) allspice
1 ml (1/4 tsp) ground cinnamon
7 ml (1 1/2 tsp) tomato paste
80 ml (1/3 cup) freshly chopped parsley
2 cloves garlic, crushed
15 ml (1 Tbs) lemon juice
5 ml chicken stock powder
   or *salt to taste*
3 ml (1/2 tsp) coarse black pepper
2 filleted chicken breasts
60 ml (1/4 cup) water

Basting mixture
45 ml (3 Tbs) olive oil
45 ml (3 Tbs) lemon juice
3 ml (1/2 tsp) allspice
5 ml (1 tsp) salt
3 ml (1/2 tsp) black pepper

- Beforehand, soak couscous in 500 ml cold water for at least 2 hours. If using rice, soak in boiling water for half an hour.
- Sauté the onion and green pepper in olive oil and leave to cool.
- Chop the chicken breasts very finely in a food processor.
- Drain the couscous very well in a strainer.
- Mix all the stuffing ingredients with a spoon, but preferably with your hands.
- Stuff the chicken in the cavity or between the skin and flesh. (Or spread a layer on a deboned chicken, placing the 2 extra breasts in the middle. Roll into a large sausage. Tie with string and place in a roasting pan.)
- Combine the basting ingredients and pour over the bird in the roasting pan.
- Roast, uncovered, at 180 °C for about 1 1/2 to 2 hours, basting several times. Use the pan juices to make a gravy.

STARTERS AND SALAD: Hummus and Turkish salad pages 9 and 10, Lavash page 242.

MY WAY WITH FOOD

STARTERS AND SALAD: Lentil and spinach salad page 29.

SOUPS: Chicken and smoked sausage gumbo page 41.

MY WAY WITH FOOD

Aubergine Rolls step 1.

Aubergine Rolls step 2.

STARTERS AND SALAD: Aubergine rolls with basil cheese page 13.

STARTERS AND SALAD: Falafel being formed into balls page 12.

POULTRY: Chicken Breast with Bigarade sauce page 112.

MY WAY WITH FOOD

SOUPS: Bouillabaisse page 40.

SOUPS: Steps for Bouillabaisse page 40.

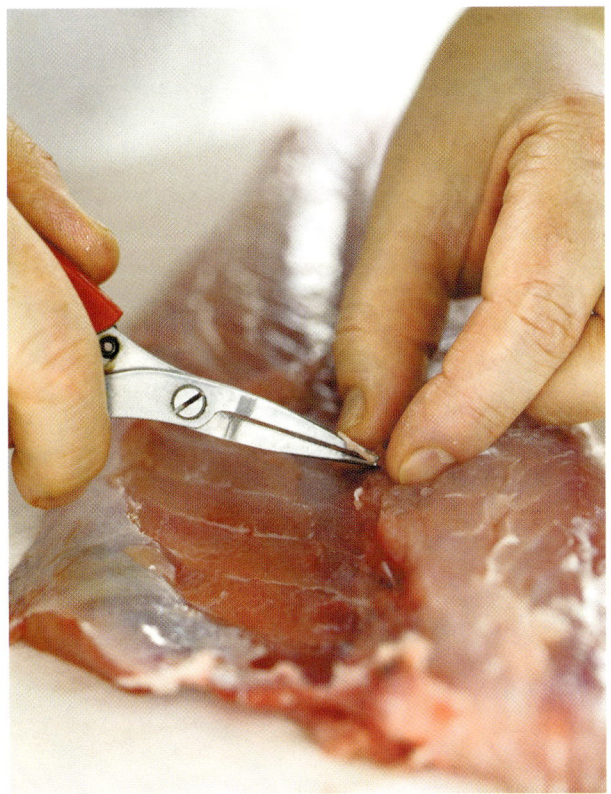

Step1: remove pin bones from fish.

Step 2: Chop ingredients for Bouillabaisse.

Step 3: Fish and vegetable in stock pot.

Step 4: Blending ingredients for rouille sauce.

MEAT: Roast lamb with rosemary page 64.

POT-ROASTED CHICKEN

It is all in the sauce! Pot-roasted chicken is very soft, full of flavour from the sauce it is cooked in, but it is never as crisp as a dry-roasted chicken.

A whole chicken is very difficult to brown all over before it is cooked. After it is pot-roasted, it is usually open-roasted at a high temperature to brown it. The sauce can then be completed while the chicken is browning.

STUFFED CHICKEN IN ORANGE CARAMEL SAUCE

This caramelised sugar and orange sauce is used in different ways in many of the recipes in this book. It has become one of my firm favourites. Using 2 baby chickens in this recipe is even tastier.

Serves 4 to 6

  1 chicken or 2 petit poussin

Stuffing

- 1 small onion, chopped
- 1 stick celery, chopped with leaves
- 2 brown mushrooms, chopped
- 30 ml (2 Tbs) butter or oil
- 250-375 ml (1-1 $\frac{1}{2}$ cups) fresh breadcrumbs
- 45 ml (3 Tbs) freshly chopped parsley
- 5 ml (1 tsp) finely grated orange rind
- 5 ml (1 tsp) dried rosemary
- 5 ml (1 tsp) chicken stock powder
- 45 ml (3 Tbs) orange juice
- 1 egg
- 2 chicken breasts, chopped in food processor

Orange sauce

- 45 ml (3 Tbs) butter, oil or *schmaltz*, or a combination
- 1 onion, chopped
- 80 ml ($\frac{1}{3}$ cup) sugar
- 80 ml ($\frac{1}{3}$ cup) vinegar
- 185 ml ($\frac{3}{4}$ cup) chicken stock
- 250 ml (1 cup) orange juice
- 5 ml (1 tsp) rosemary
- salt and pepper
- 10 ml (2 tsp) flour for thickening, if desired

▸ *For the stuffing*, sauté onion, celery and mushrooms in butter.
▸ Remove pan from the heat and leave to cool.
▸ Add remaining ingredients and check seasoning.
▸ Stuff the chicken.
▸ *For the sauce*, heat oil or butter in flameproof casserole.
▸ Sauté onion until glassy.
▸ Add sugar and vinegar and boil to reduce until sugar caramelises and turns a dark golden colour. *Be careful not to burn it.*
▸ Add stock, orange juice and rosemary and stir until caramel has dissolved.
▸ Place the chicken in the orange sauce. Cover with lid and pot-roast in the oven for 1 $\frac{1}{4}$ hours at 180 °C, basting periodically.
▸ Remove chicken from the sauce and change oven setting 200 °C.
▸ Return to oven and roast, uncovered, to crisp skin.
▸ On top of the stove, reduce sauce until flavour is right.
▸ Strain and skim off as much fat as possible.
▸ Garnish chicken with orange segments and serve with the reduced orange sauce as gravy.
▸ Use the gravy as is or, if slightly thicker gravy is preferred, stir flour into a little of the fat. Add this to pan and boil for 1 minute.

POT-ROAST CHICKEN IN GINGER ALE

This recipe has no added fats. It is tasty with a slight sweet-sour taste and is extremely simple to make.

Serves 4 to 6

- 1 cleaned chicken
- 185 ml ($\frac{3}{4}$ cup) ginger ale
- 125 ml ($\frac{1}{2}$ cup) water
- 10 ml (2 tsp) chicken stock powder
- 15 ml (1 Tbs) chicken spice
- 10 ml (2 tsp) dried rosemary

To complete

- 10 ml (2 tsp) cornflour, mixed with a little cold water
- 30 ml (2 Tbs) lemon juice
- 15 ml (1 Tbs) dry or medium sherry
- 30 ml (2 Tbs) cream (optional)

- Place chicken in a roasting pan that has a lid.
- Mix the first 5 ingredients together and pour over the chicken.
- Cover the pan and pot-roast in the oven at 160 °C for about 1 1/2 hours, basting every 15 minutes.
- Place the chicken in the lid of the roaster, salt the skin lightly and return it to the oven. Brown, uncovered, at 220 °C for 15 minutes.
- Make a gravy from the liquid.
- Remove as much fat from the liquid as possible.
- Thicken with a little cornflour mixed with cold water.
- Season with lemon juice and sherry.
- Cream may be added just before serving, if desired.

ROAST TURKEY

This is a classic recipe for a wonderful Christmas turkey. Instead of the sausage meat and veal mince, you can use minced chicken thigh and breast.

3 to 4 kg serves 8 to 10

1	turkey
750 g	chipolata sausages
	melted butter
500 ml (2 cups)	stock from the giblets
	or *made with a chicken stock cube*
	greaseproof paper (not wax wrap)
	string
	canned cranberry sauce or *jelly (to serve)*

Crop stuffing

250 ml (1 cup)	cooked rice
2	hard-boiled eggs, chopped
100 g	olives, chopped
50 g	almonds, toasted and chopped
100 g	ham, chopped
	soft butter to bind
	salt and black pepper

Body cavity stuffing

100 g	butter
2	onions, chopped
2	sticks celery, chopped
250 g (1 cup)	minced veal
250 g (1 cup)	pork sausage meat
1	clove garlic
750 ml (3 cups)	fresh breadcrumbs
60 ml (1/4 cup)	chopped parsley
5 ml (1 tsp)	dried sage
5 ml (1 tsp)	dried rosemary
5 ml (1 tsp)	dried thyme
5 ml (1 tsp)	grated lemon rind
1	egg
125 ml (1/2 cup)	apricot fruit juice
1	chicken stock cube, crumbled
or 1 tsp	chicken stock powder
	salt and pepper

- Combine stuffing ingredients for the crop and stuff this cavity.
- For body cavity stuffing, first sauté the onions and celery and leave to cool.
- Add the rest of the ingredients for body cavity stuffing and mix well. Check seasoning and stuff into the body cavity.
- Truss turkey securely and season with salt and pepper.
- Dip sheets of greaseproof paper into melted butter and completely cover the turkey.
- Place it in a large, deep roasting pan.
- Roast at 170 °C, allowing 40 minutes per kilogram, plus an extra 20 minutes.
- One hour before the turkey is cooked, lift the greaseproof paper and drape the chipolata sausages over the turkey. Replace the paper and roast for the last hour.
- Remove turkey from oven and place it on a serving dish to rest for 15 minutes.
- Skim the fat off the pan juices and mix a little fat with enough flour to thicken (see *Gravy*).
- Stir this into the pan juices and bring to the boil. (The pan juices are very rich and you may have to add extra water or chicken stock, but taste it first.)
- Season to taste and strain into a gravy boat.
- Serve with the sausages and cranberry sauce or jelly.

POT-ROAST TURKEY IN ORANGE

This is my favourite roast turkey recipe. The flavour of horseradish and orange suit the strong turkey flavour very well.

3 to 4 kg serves 8 to 10

1	turkey

Stuffing

60 ml (1/4 cup)	butter, oil or *schmaltz*
2	onions, chopped
2	sticks celery with leaves, chopped
4-6	chicken thighs, depending on the size of the turkey
2	cloves garlic
1	orange, peeled
125 ml (1/2 cup)	chopped parsley
10 ml (2 tsp)	dried marjoram
30 ml (2 Tbs)	bottled horseradish
60 ml (1/4 cup)	red wine
30 ml (2 Tbs)	orange juice
5 ml (1 tsp)	chicken stock powder
1	egg
3-4 cups	fresh breadcrumbs

Orange basting sauce

185 ml (3/4 cup)	orange juice
185 ml (3/4 cup)	Fanta Orange
45 ml (3 Tbs)	lemon juice
80 ml (1/3 cup)	dry red wine
45 ml (3 Tbs)	horseradish
80 g	butter

- *For the stuffing,* Remove the chicken thigh meat from the bones and mince or chop in food processor.
- Sauté onion and celery in butter until soft and leave to cool.
- Mix all the remaining ingredients and season to taste.
- Stuff both the crop and large cavity with this mixture and truss turkey securely.
- *For the sauce,* combine ingredients and boil for 5 minutes.
- Place stuffed turkey in double roaster and pour over orange basting sauce.
- Pot-roast in oven at 160 °C for about 3 hours (40 minutes per 1 kg once stuffed plus an extra 20 minutes).
- Remove the lid for the last 30 minutes.
- Turn the oven to 200 °C to brown the turkey.
- Remove from roasting pan and leave to rest for 15 minutes – it will not get cold in this time.
- Strain all the pan juices into a measuring jug and see how much you have.
- Skim off as much fat as possible from roasting pan.
- Pour a little fat back in the roasting pan. Place pan on plate on top of stove and add flour to the fat (see *Gravy*).
- Mix flour into the fat and then add the balance of the pan juices.
- Bring the gravy to the boil and simmer until the desired flavour and consistency is reached.

ROAST DUCK

Duck has little meat but what there is of it is delicious. It also has lots of fat. The problem is to render down all the fat and then crisp the skin. The secret is to cook the duck in liquid first and then to dry-roast it to brown and crisp the skin.

Serve the duck with any of the chicken sauces using the skimmed, reduced roasting liquid as the stock.

Serves 2 to 3

1	large duck
3 ml (1/2 tsp)	black pepper
5 ml (1 tsp)	paprika
3 ml (1/2 tsp)	grated nutmeg
2	cloves crushed garlic
2	large sprigs parsley
1	onion, sliced
2	sticks celery, chopped with leaves

Roasting liquid

500 ml (2 cups)	water
1	chicken stock cube
	duck giblets (not the liver)
45 ml (3 Tbs)	red wine (optional)
or 30 ml (2 Tbs)	soy sauce

Quick orange sauce

	reduced liquid from roasting pan
50 g	butter
45 ml (3 Tbs)	flour
250 ml (1 cup)	fresh orange juice
250 ml (1 cup)	reserved cooking liquid from roasting pan
30 ml (2 Tbs)	brown sugar to taste
15 ml (1 Tbs)	vinegar
15 ml (1 Tbs)	brandy
15 ml (1 Tbs)	sherry
1	orange, thickly sliced, with the peel

Garnish

100 g	almond flakes, toasted (optional)

- Season the duck to taste.
- Combine ingredients for roasting liquid.
- Place the duck, breast down, in roasting pan in the roasting liquid and completely cover with foil.
- Cover and cook at 180 °C for 2 hours, turning the duck after 1 $\frac{1}{2}$ hours. (This is actually boiling the duck to remove all the fat.)
- Remove the duck from the liquid and place it breast side up on a rack.
- Pour off all the cooking liquid and leave it to stand to allow the fat to rise.
- Brush the duck with a little of the fat and salt lightly.
- Roast, uncovered, at 200 °C until skin is well browned and crisp, turning a few times to ensure that the duck is evenly browned all round. (See hint)
- Skim off as much fat as possible from the cooking liquid and boil remaining liquid vigorously to reduce it to little more than 250 ml (1 cup). Reserve reduced liquid as a base for the sauce.
- Melt the butter (or use duck fat) and stir in the flour.
- Add orange juice, cooking liquid, sugar and vinegar. Bring to the boil, stirring constantly.
- Stir in the brandy and sherry and add sliced oranges.
- Simmer for 1 minute.
- Serve, with the duck, garnished with toasted almond flakes.

Hint
I find it easier to cut the duck in half, lengthwise, before cooking it. The halves are placed, skin down, in the liquid, so you need not turn it during cooking. It also makes for even browning and crisping of the duck.

Variation
Instead of *Quick orange sauce*, try *Bigarade sauce* (see *Jiffy chicken casseroles*) or *Sour cherry sauce*.

POULTRY PORTIONS

The joy of cooking portions is that in a family of drumstick eaters you don't have to draw straws for the 2 drumsticks per chicken. Buy your portions according to you personal preference and the best cut for the dish. Filleted chicken breasts should be handled differently to other portions and I have dealt with them separately in this chapter.

Veal or pork can be substituted for chicken in all the recipes in this chapter.

DRY HEAT COOKING

For more information on the cooking methods, refer to the introduction to *Meat*.

Grilling
Grilling chicken portions, with the skin on, is not completely successful unless you are prepared to watch it all the time to stop it from burning. You must keep the chicken far from the element, but by the time the chicken is crisp, it is also dried out. I find by placing the portions on a grilling rack and roasting them at 200 °C, basting with any of the basting mixtures (see *Whole birds*) the result is as good as grilling but without the hassle.

Frying
Crumbed or Southern fried chicken is delicious.

For crumbing:
- Lightly coat the chicken in seasoned flour.
- Dip into beaten egg and water mixture.
- Coat well in dry crumbs of your choice.
- Refrigerate for at least 2 hours or place in the deep freeze for 15 minutes before frying in deep or shallow oil for 25 to 30 minutes.
- Drain on absorbent paper before serving.

To oven-fry the chicken
- Brush the well-chilled crumbed portions with oil.
- Place on a baking sheet and roast, uncovered, at 200 °C for 20 to 25 minutes turning once. Drain on absorbent paper before serving.

Note Chicken portions on the bone take about 25 to 30 minutes, while filleted chicken breasts take 15 to 20 minutes to cook through once they are coated in crumbs or flour. Always cook over a medium to low heat so the crust does not brown before the chicken is cooked through.

SPICY SOUTHERN FRIED CHICKEN

Succulent chicken in a crisp coat, with a kick of spices. The herb and sesame seed coating (recipe follows) is a milder, but equally delicious variation.

Serves 6 to 8

8	chicken portions of your choice, with or *without the skin and bones*
375 ml (1 1/2 cups)	flour
30 ml (2 Tbs)	paprika
10 ml (2 tsp)	cayenne pepper
20 ml (1 1/2 Tbs)	salt
10 ml (2 tsp)	dried thyme
160 ml (2/3 cup)	milk or *water*
2	eggs

- Wash and dry the chicken portions.
- Beat the egg and milk together in a bowl.
- Mix flour and seasoning and place in a plastic bag.
- Put the chicken portions in the bag and shake until they are completely coated.
- Shake off excess flour and dip the chicken in the egg mixture, allowing the excess to run off.
- Coat again with flour, making sure the chicken is well coated.
- Chill chicken for 30 minutes in the deepfreeze.
- Heat sufficient oil to reach halfway up the chicken portions (average depth 5 cm) in a deep pan and fry over medium heat for 25 minutes until crisp, golden brown and cooked through. If you are using filleted chicken breasts, cook for 15 minutes only.
- Drain on absorbent paper and serve with a squeeze of fresh lemon.

Variation
For a change, follow the Southern Fried Chicken recipe using the following coating mixture.

Herb and sesame seed coating

310 ml (1 1/4 cups)	flour
30 ml (2 Tbs)	Robertson's chicken spice
125 ml (1/2 cup)	sesame seeds
15 ml (1 Tbs)	salt
15 ml (1 Tbs)	dried thyme
15 ml (1 Tbs)	dried tarragon
15 ml (1 Tbs)	dried marjoram

HONG KONG CHICKEN WINGS

The sticky, sweet barbecue sauce will have you licking your fingers! It is a delicious recipe to use as a starter or as a snack and can be eaten hot or cold. For an authentic Chinese flavour, use the Hoi Sin sauce and 5 Spice powder for the sauce.

18	chicken wings
	oil for frying

Sauce

125 ml (1/2 cup)	sugar
80 ml (1/3 cup)	vinegar
125 ml (1/2 cup)	smooth apricot jam
50 ml (3 1/2 Tbs)	HP sauce or *Hoi Sin sauce*
30 ml (2 Tbs)	soy sauce
80 ml (1/3 cup)	water
3 ml (1/2 tsp)	barbeque spice or *5 spice powder*

- Cut the wings into 36 wing 'drumsticks', or just joint the wings, discard the tips, leaving 2 pieces per wing (see *Hint*).
- In a saucepan, dissolve the sugar in the vinegar and boil rapidly until sugar turns a dark golden colour. (Be careful not to breathe in the vinegar fumes.)
- Combine all the remaining sauce ingredients and have the mixture ready to add to the sugar mixture as soon as the sugar is a dark golden colour.
- Immediately add remaining sauce ingredients and, stirring constantly, bring back to the boil.
- In a frying pan, quickly fry chicken wings in hot oil, then simmer them in the sauce for 2 minutes.
- Once all the chicken wings are cooked, transfer to a serving dish.
- Boil the sauce, uncovered, to reduce until it is thick and sticky. Pour the sauce over the chicken wings.
- Serve on a bed of shredded Chinese cabbage.

Hints
- To make chicken wing 'drumsticks', cut each wing into 3 joints, discarding the tip. Using a sharp knife, cut the flesh away from one end of the bone and pull the meat back to form a small ball of meat at the end of the bone.
- When pulling back the meat on the segment with 2 bones, pull the small bone out and discard before pulling the meat back to form a drumstick.

STEWS AND CASSEROLES

There are several basic casseroles in this chapter, as well as a few with a difference.

Basic method for casseroles
- Cut the vegetables into fairly large pieces, according to the size of the chicken pieces.
- Wash and dry the chicken pieces very well to prevent oil splattering when you brown it. If preferred, the skin may be removed and discarded before the chicken is browned.
- In a heavy-based pan, preferably one that can go into the oven, heat a little oil, schmaltz, butter, or a mixture of oil and butter. Brown the chicken over a medium heat, making sure it does not burn.
- Remove the chicken from the pan, pour off most of the fat and lower the heat.
- In the remaining oil, sauté the onions until glassy and just starting to brown.
- If you are going to thicken the dish with flour, add it to the onions, stir until flour is coated with the fat and add the liquid in the recipe. Because this is not a traditional brown sauce, the flour does not have to be browned, unless that is the flavour you prefer. (See introduction to Meat.)
- If you thicken the dish with cornflour instead of flour, it must be mixed with a little cold water and then added to the dish, stirred through and brought to the boil just before serving. Cornflour added at the beginning of the cooking time will thin down again before the food is cooked. *Use half the quantity stated for flour.*
- Add the remaining ingredients (vegetables, liquid and seasoning and whatever you need for your special variation to make a good sauce).
- Return the reserved chicken to the sauce and simmer slowly, covered, on top of the stove, or in the oven at 160 °C for 45 minutes to 1 hour. Check seasoning before serving.

Any casserole or stew recipe can be made following these easy steps.

Hints
- Don't toss your chicken in flour before you brown it. The flour burns on the bottom of the pot. Brown the chicken on its own and add the flour to the oil afterwards.
- The skin can be removed and the browning left out to lower the fat content of the dish. It does not impair the flavour as much as with red meat.

POLYNESIAN CHICKEN

Sweet and sour, with plenty of pineapple, children love this dish.

Serves 4 to 6

8	chicken portions of your choice
45 ml (3 Tbs)	oil, butter, or a combination of the two
1	large onion, cubed
1	large green pepper, cubed
3	stalks celery, thickly sliced
45 ml (3 Tbs)	flour
375 ml (1 1/2 cups)	chicken stock
440 g	tinned pineapple chunks
125 ml (1/2 cup)	pineapple juice from the tin
30 ml (2 Tbs)	soy sauce
2	skinned tomatoes, quartered

- Brown the chicken well in oil, or a mixture of oil and butter.
- Remove chicken from the pan and pour off excess oil.
- In the remaining oil, sauté the onion, green pepper and celery.
- Stir in the flour.
- Add chicken stock, pineapple juice and chunks and soy sauce.
- Bring to the boil and check seasoning.
- Return the chicken pieces to the sauce and add tomato quarters.
- Simmer, covered, over a low heat for 45 minutes, or casserole in the oven at 160 °C for about 1 hour. Check seasoning again.

COQ AU VIN

This is a rich casserole with red wine and bacon. It is a good winter dish.

Serves 4 to 6

8	chicken portions of your choice
45 ml (3 Tbs)	oil, butter or a combination of the two
16	pickling onions, peeled and left whole
125 g	rindless streaky bacon, cut into large pieces
45 ml (3 Tbs)	flour

250-300 ml
(1-1 1/4 cups) red wine
375 ml (1 1/2 cups) chicken stock
30 ml (2 Tbs) sherry
2 cloves garlic, crushed
15 ml (1 Tbs) tomato paste
5 ml (1 tsp) dried thyme
5 ml (1 tsp) mixed dried herbs
3 bay leaves
black pepper to taste
250 g brown mushrooms cut in thick slices, or left whole if small enough
50 g butter
45 ml (3 Tbs) parsley, chopped

- Pour boiling water over the bacon to remove excess salt.
- Brown chicken well in oil, or a mixture of oil and butter.
- Remove chicken from the pan and pour off excess oil.
- In a little remaining oil, sauté onions and bacon until the onions begin to brown.
- Stir in the flour and cook until flour turns a nut brown colour.
- Add the wine, chicken stock, sherry, garlic, tomato paste and stir through. Add all the seasoning, except the chopped parsley.
- Bring to the boil and check seasoning.
- Return reserved chicken pieces to the sauce.
- Simmer, covered, over a low heat for 45 minutes, or casserole in the oven at 160 °C for about 1 hour.
- Meanwhile, quickly sauté the mushrooms in butter and set aside. Mushrooms must still be firm.
- Before serving, add sautéd mushrooms and parsley to casserole and check seasoning.
- Serve with rice.

CHICKEN BONNE FEMME

This is a classic French recipe, which is also delicious made with pork or veal.

Serves 4

8 chicken portions of your choice
45 ml (3 Tbs) oil or butter, or a combination of the two
4 rashers rindless bacon, diced
16 pickling onions
or 3 large onions, cut in quarters
250 g button mushrooms, left whole
30 ml (2 Tbs) flour
375 ml (1 1/2 cups) chicken stock
125 ml (1/2 cup) white wine
5 ml (1 tsp) dried rosemary
black pepper to taste
8 baby potatoes
or 2 large potatoes, quartered
125 ml (1/2 cup) cream
chopped parsley for garnish

- Brown chicken well in oil or a mixture of oil and butter.
- Remove from the pan and pour off excess oil.
- In a little remaining oil, sauté onions, bacon and mushrooms.
- Stir in flour.
- Add chicken stock, wine, rosemary, garlic and season to taste with salt and pepper.
- Bring to the boil and check seasoning.
- Return chicken pieces to the sauce and add potatoes.
- Simmer, covered, over a low heat for 45 minutes, or casserole in the oven at 160 °C for about 1 hour.
- Just before serving, check seasoning, stir in cream and sprinkle with chopped parsley.

CHICKEN CASSEROLE WITH HERBS

This is a very simple dish. The combination of different herbs makes it tasty and aromatic.

Serves 4 to 6

8 chicken portions of your choice
45 ml (3 Tbs) oil or butter, or a combination of the two
30 ml (2 Tbs) flour
16 pickling onions
250 g small button mushrooms
3 sticks celery, thickly sliced
375 ml (1 1/2 cups) chicken stock
125 ml (1/2 cup) white wine
2 cloves garlic, crushed
5 ml (1 tsp) dried tarragon
5 ml (1 tsp) dried marjoram
5 ml (1 tsp) dried thyme
125 ml (1/2 cup) freshly chopped parsley
salt and black pepper

- Brown chicken well in oil or a mixture of oil and butter.
- Remove chicken from the pan and pour off excess oil.
- In a little remaining oil, sauté onions, mushrooms and celery.
- Stir in flour.

- Add chicken stock, wine and herbs, including the parsley.
- Bring to the boil and check seasoning.
- Return chicken pieces to the sauce.
- Simmer, covered, over a low heat for 45 minutes, or casserole in the oven at 160 °C for about 1 hour.

Hint

Use fresh herbs wherever possible. Multiply dry quantities by 3.

PAPRIKA CHICKEN

The flavour of paprika and sour cream is reminiscent of Hungarian goulash.

Serves 4 to 6

8	chicken portions of your choice
45 ml (3 Tbs)	oil or butter, or a combination of the two
1	large onion, cubed
1	green pepper, cubed
1	red pepper, cubed,
30 ml (2 Tbs)	flour
15 ml (1 Tbs)	paprika
250 ml (1 cup)	chicken stock
250 ml (1 cup)	sour cream
or 175 ml	plain yoghurt
	salt and pepper

- Brown chicken well in oil or a mixture of oil and butter.
- Remove chicken from the pan and pour off excess oil.
- In a little remaining oil, sauté onions, green pepper and red pepper.
- Stir in flour and paprika.
- Add chicken stock and sour cream or yoghurt. The yoghurt will curdle, but the flavour is delicious.
- Bring to the boil and check seasoning.
- Return chicken pieces to the sauce.
- Simmer, covered, over a low heat for 45 minutes, or casserole in the oven at 160 °C for about 1 hour.

Hint

If you do not want the yoghurt to curdle, casserole the chicken without the yoghurt, but make half a quantity of cooked yoghurt (see under *Sauces*) and stir into the casserole once the chicken is cooked.

LEMON AND GARLIC CHICKEN

The lemony Greek flavour in this casserole is very special. The extra time it takes will be worth it when you receive all the compliments from your family and friends.

This recipe makes a wonderful chicken pot roast. Use a whole chicken and brown it, uncovered, in the oven while you are making the sauce (see *Whole birds*).

Serves 4 to 6

8	chicken portions of your choice
45 ml (3 Tbs)	oil or butter, or a combination of the two
1	large onion, chopped
2	carrots, chopped
2	celery stalks, with leaves, chopped
3-4	sprigs parsley
500 ml (2 cups)	strong chicken stock
5 ml (1 tsp)	dried rosemary
3	bay leaves
2	cloves garlic, chopped
	salt and pepper

To complete the sauce

45 ml (3 Tbs)	flour
125 ml ($^1/_2$ cup)	cream
30 ml (2 Tbs)	lemon juice
1 ml ($^1/_4$ tsp)	cayenne pepper
2	cloves garlic, crushed

- Brown the chicken well in oil or a mixture of oil and butter.
- Remove from pan and pour off excess oil. Keep the remainder for use when making the sauce.
- In a little remaining oil, sauté onions, carrots, celery and parsley, until the onion is glassy and soft.
- Add the stock, rosemary, bay leaves and garlic.
- Bring to the boil and check seasoning.
- Return the chicken pieces to the sauce.
- Simmer, covered, over a low heat for 45 minutes, or casserole in the oven at 160 °C for about 1 hour.
- *To complete the sauce,* remove the chicken pieces from the casserole and place on a serving dish in a warm oven.
- Strain the cooking liquid and reserve. Discard all the vegetables.
- Place the remaining fat (from browning the chicken) in a pot and stir in the flour. Add a little extra butter if the remaining fat is not enough to coat the flour.
- Pour on the strained stock and bring it to the boil, whisking until it is thick.

- Stir in the cream, lemon juice, cayenne pepper and garlic, and bring to the boil.
- Taste for seasoning and add more lemon juice or cayenne pepper to taste, if desired.
- Pour the sauce over the chicken and serve with parsley rice.

CHICKEN MARENGO

This is a variation of the classic French marengo and has an intriguing contrast of sweetness (from the large proportion of onions and sweet wine), balanced by a slight tartness from the white wine and tomatoes. Mushrooms round off the flavour.

Serves 4 to 6

8	chicken portions of your choice
45 ml (3 Tbs)	oil or butter, or a combination of the two
12	pickling onions
or 3	onions, diced
250 g	button mushrooms, left whole
2	cloves garlic, chopped
30 ml (2 Tbs)	flour
125 ml (1/2 cup)	dry white wine
125 ml (1/2 cup)	sherry
125 ml (1/2 cup)	chicken stock
15 ml (1 Tbs)	brandy
30 ml (2 Tbs)	tomato paste
4	bay leaves
	black pepper to taste

- Brown chicken well in oil or a mixture of oil and butter.
- Remove chicken from the pan and pour off excess oil.
- In a little remaining oil, sauté onions, mushrooms and garlic until the onions begin to brown.
- Stir in the flour and cook until flour turns a nut brown colour.
- Add wine, sherry, chicken stock, brandy, tomato paste, bay leaves and black pepper.
- Bring to the boil and check seasoning.
- Return the chicken pieces to the sauce.
- Simmer, covered, over a low heat for 45 minutes, or casserole in the oven at 160 °C for about 1 hour.

Variation

For something special, add 100 g pitted black olives to the casserole and heat through before serving.

RABIE'S CHICKEN CURRY

Rabie Abrahms worked as an assistant in the kitchen of the Pick 'n Pay School of Cooking for 10 years. Her chicken curry was in a class of its own.

If you can't find them at your local supermarket, the spices and dhania leaves are available at all Indian spice shops.

Serves 4 to 6

8	chicken portions of your choice
45 ml (3 Tbs)	oil or butter, or a combination of the two
2	large onions, diced
2	large tomatoes, grated
4	potatoes, quartered
15 ml (1 Tbs)	lemon juice
15 ml (1 Tbs)	sugar
	salt to taste

Spices

30 ml (2 Tbs)	Bombay special curry masala
15 ml (1 Tbs)	ground coriander
15 ml (1 Tbs)	ground fennel
15 ml (1 Tbs)	turmeric
6	cinnamon sticks
6	cardomom seeds
6	curry leaves
5 ml (1 tsp)	crushed garlic
5 ml (1 tsp)	grated ginger
15 ml (1 Tbs)	garam masala
45 ml (3 Tbs)	chopped coriander leaves

- Brown chicken well in oil, or a mixture of oil and butter, and remove it from the pan. (Rabie did not brown the chicken first, but I prefer the flavour.)
- In the remaining oil, sauté the onions until they begin to brown.
- Add tomatoes.
- Stir in all the spices, except the garam masala and coriander, but including the garlic and ginger.
- Add 500 ml (2 cups) boiling water, bring to the boil and add the chicken and potatoes.
- Add the lemon juice, sugar and salt to taste.
- Simmer until chicken is tender, adding extra water when needed.
- Before serving, add garam masala and coriander leaves. Bring back to the boil and serve. The garam masala spices and thickens the curry.

SPRING CHICKEN CASSEROLE WITH PARSLEY DUMPLINGS

A fragrant casserole topped with cheesy parsley dumplings.

Serves 4 to 6

8	chicken portions of your choice
50 g	butter
15 ml (1 Tbs)	oil
16	pickling onions, peeled
2	cloves garlic, crushed
45 ml (3 Tbs)	flour
410 g	tinned whole peeled tomatoes, roughly chopped (reserve juice)
500 ml (2 cups)	chicken stock
10 ml (2 tsp)	mixed, dried herbs
	salt and black pepper
4	medium carrots, cut in chunks

Parsley dumplings

500 ml (2 cups)	flour
5 ml (1 tsp)	salt
15 ml (1 Tbs)	baking powder
1	large egg and water, together equalling 160ml ($^2/_3$ cup)
60 g	butter
30 ml (2 Tbs)	freshly chopped parsley
160 ml ($^2/_3$ cup)	cheddar cheese, grated
7 ml (1 $^1/_2$ tsp)	lemon rind, finely grated

▶ Brown the chicken in the butter and oil. Remove chicken from the pan. Pour off excess fat, leaving a little in the pan.
▶ Add sliced onion and garlic to the pan and sauté until glassy.
▶ Stir in the flour.
▶ Drain the tomatoes. Add the liquid to the pan with stock and cook until the sauce has slightly thickened.
▶ Add the mixed herbs and season to taste.
▶ Place the chicken pieces in a casserole dish. Add tomatoes and carrots between the chicken pieces and pour on the sauce.
▶ Cover and cook in oven preheated to 160 °C for 1 hour.

▶ For the dumplings, rub the butter into the flour, salt and baking powder.
▶ Add the remaining ingredients, except for the egg and water.
▶ While the stew is cooking, break the egg into a measuring jug and add water until egg and water measure 160 ml. Beat the egg in the water.
▶ With a blunt knife, mix the liquid into the dry mixture using a cutting motion. Do not overmix.
▶ About 20 minutes before the end of the casserole cooking time, drop spoonfuls onto the stew. Return the pot to the oven and cook until dumplings are cooked through (about 30 minutes).

DHANSAK-CHICKEN WITH VEGETABLES AND LENTILS

This is a mild, Indian chicken curry with lentils and lots of vegetables.

Serves 6 to 8

8	chicken portions of your choice
425 g	tinned chickpeas
or 250 ml (1 cup)	cooked chickpeas
150 g	black lentils, soaked in boiling water for 1 hour
45 ml (3 Tbs)	butter or oil
15 ml (1 Tbs)	grated ginger
2	cloves garlic, crushed
1	large onion, chopped
2	medium aubergines, cut in cubes, skin on
1	butternut, pipped but skin on, cubed
1	large bunch spinach, roughly cut
410 g	tinned tomatoes
15 ml (1 Tbs)	chicken masala
5 ml (1 tsp)	tumeric
15 ml (1 Tbs)	chopped, fresh mint
125 ml ($^1/_2$ cup)	chicken stock

▶ Cut the chicken portions in half to get 16 small portions.
▶ Melt butter and add garlic and ginger.
▶ Sauté chicken in garlic and ginger until the chicken is beginning to brown. Remove chicken from the pan.
▶ In the remaining butter, sauté the onion until glassy, then add aubergines, butternut, spinach, tomatoes and spices.
▶ Return chicken to the sauce and add lentils and chickpeas, together with the stock.
▶ Casserole at 160 °C for 45 minutes to 1 hour.
▶ Serve with rice.

MEXICAN CHICKEN WITH FRUIT

This is an adaptation of the traditional Mexican recipe, *Chicken manchamanteles* (meaning *tablecloth stainer*), which was introduced to me by Phillipa Cheifitz. It is spicy, fruity and very unusual. Don't be put off by the long list of ingredients; it is worth the little bit of extra work.

Serves 4 to 6

8	chicken portions of your choice
45 ml (3 Tbs)	oil
3 ml (1/2 tsp)	crushed red chilli, or to taste
5 ml (1 tsp)	ground cinnamon
3 ml (1/2 tsp)	ground cloves
1	large onion, very finely chopped
3	cloves garlic, crushed
410 g	tinned tomatoes, chopped
3 ml (1/2 tsp)	black pepper
3 ml (1/2 tsp)	origanum
3 ml (1/2 tsp)	thyme
45 ml (3 Tbs)	fresh parsley, chopped
250 ml (1 cup)	chicken stock
500 g	sweet potatoes, peeled and cut into blocks
	butter or oil for browning the fruit
1	small pineapple, cut into blocks
2-3	bananas, sliced
60 ml (4 Tbs)	chopped fresh coriander leaves (dhania)

- In a large, paella-type pan, scorch the chillies, cinnamon and cloves. You will smell the aroma as they roast. Remove from pan.
- With or without the skin, brown the chicken in a little oil in the same pan.
- Remove the chicken and fry onions in remaining oil until they begin to brown.
- Add scorched spices, tomatoes (with the juice), remaining herbs, chicken stock, parsley and seasoning to taste (not coriander leaves).
- Bring to the boil and add browned chicken and sweet potato.
- Casserole at 160 °C for 1 hour, or until the sweet potatoes and chicken are soft.
- Just before serving, quickly fry the pineapple and banana in a little oil or butter, over a high heat in a separate pan.
- Add fruit and chopped coriander to casserole and heat through.
- Serve with rice.

CHICKEN A LA KING

No chapter on chicken would be complete without a good Chicken a la King recipe.

Serves 6 to 8

1	chicken
10 ml (2 tsp)	rosemary
5 ml (1 tsp)	thyme
4	bay leaves
500 ml (2 cups)	chicken stock
50 g	butter
1	green pepper, chopped
1	red pepper, chopped
1	onion, chopped
2	sticks celery with leaves, chopped
250 g	button mushrooms, thickly sliced
30 ml (2 Tbs)	flour
125 ml (1/2 cup)	white wine
125 ml (1/2 cup)	cream, sour cream, or cooked yoghurt (see Sauces)
250 ml (1 cup)	chicken stock from cooked chicken
	salt and black pepper to taste
250 ml (1 cup)	frozen peas
125 ml (1/2 cup)	fresh parsley, chopped

- In a large pot, place chicken, thyme, rosemary, bay leaves and stock. Simmer, covered, for about 45 minutes or until the chicken is soft.
- Remove the chicken from the pot and retain the stock for the sauce.
- Remove all the meat from the bones and cut into small pieces.
- In a pot, sauté onions, celery and peppers in the butter.
- Add mushrooms and cook for 3 minutes. Mushrooms must still be firm.
- Stir in the flour.
- Add wine, cream and chicken stock. Bring to the boil and allow it to thicken.
- Stir in the chicken, frozen peas and check seasoning. Stir in parsley.
- Serve with rice.

CHICKEN BREASTS

> I have separated the recipes for filleted chicken breasts from the rest of the chicken recipes, because they need special handling. Chicken breasts offer endless possibilities and are suitable for grilling, braaiing and casseroles. They absorb marinades beautifully, there is no skin to burn and they cook very quickly.
>
> Good news for kilojoule watchers is that chicken breasts contain very little fat. However, because of this, they can become stringy and dry very quickly if overcooked. Chicken breasts that are not in a coating such as crumbs, cook in 6 to 8 minutes. *Don't cook them for longer.*

To ensure that the breasts are soft and juicy:
- Always slash them diagonally on the fat side of the fillet, cutting across the grain of the meat and cutting 5 mm into the flesh. When the muscle contracts as it cooks it will not toughen.
- To see if they are cooked through, lift the tenderloin (the small separate piece of the fillet), and look at the colour in the middle. The breast is cooked to perfection when this colour is pinky white. It is overcooked if it is completely white.

Grilling and braaiing
Chicken breasts are the best part of the chicken to braai or grill with a marinade of your choice.

The best way to grill is to preheat the oven to 240 °C to 260 °C and then change the setting to grill. Once the element is red, grill the chicken on the second rack from the top. The chicken will then cook very quickly in the hot oven without drying out.

If you are braaiing the marinated chicken breasts, do so over very hot coals for no longer than 7 minutes. You could use chicken thighs with any of the marinades in this chapter, in which case they should be braaied a little further away from hot coals, or over cooler coals, for 25 to 30 minutes.

MARINADES

> Choose from one of the following marinades for grilling or braaiing, or use one of the basting sauces from the whole bird section. Marinated chicken breasts are delicious hot or cold.

Basic method
The quantities given here make enough marinade for 8 to 12 filleted chicken breasts, which should serve 6 to 8 people.

8-12 filleted chicken breasts
marinade of your choice

- Slash the chicken breasts (see introduction to this section).
- Place the chicken breasts in a plastic bag with the prepared marinade and leave the bag in the fridge for 5 to 6 hours, or overnight.
- Thickly coat the chicken with the marinade and then place on a grid for braaiing, or on a baking sheet for grilling.
- Braai over hot coals, or grill in a very hot oven for 7 minutes, turning once.
- *Be careful not to overcook them.*

Note The marinade will form a coating on the chicken as it cooks. The chicken itself will not brown.

PEPSI'S TOMATO MARINADE

This is a very simple but delicious marinade for chicken. For a low calorie marinade, leave out the oil.

410 g	tinned tomato purée
45 ml (3 Tbs)	white wine
45 ml (3 Tbs)	oil or *melted butter*
30 ml (2 Tbs)	soy sauce
30 ml (2 Tbs)	tomato sauce
45 ml (3 Tbs)	HP sauce
10 ml (2 tsp)	dried marjoram
or 30 ml (2 Tbs)	*fresh sweet basil, chopped*
3 ml (1/2 tsp)	salt
3 ml (1/2 tsp)	black pepper

- Mix all marinade ingredients together.

DEVILLED CHICKEN MARINADE

This list of ingredients may seem long, but you will have most of these ingredients in your cupboard.

60 ml (¼ cup)	tomato purée
30 ml (2 Tbs)	tomato sauce
10 ml (2 tsp)	Worcester sauce
10 ml (2 tsp)	soy sauce
15 ml (1 Tbs)	apricot jam
10 ml (2 tsp)	sugar
3 ml (½ tsp)	ground ginger
3 ml (½ tsp)	black pepper
5 ml (1 tsp)	chicken spice mix of your choice
3 ml (½ tsp)	mild curry
3 ml (½ tsp)	dried mustard
30 ml (2 Tbs)	oil

▶ Mix all marinade ingredients together.

SPICY YOGHURT MARINADE

15 ml (1 Tbs)	fresh ginger finely grated
3	cloves garlic
30 ml (2 Tbs)	chopped fresh coriander leaves
2	red or green chillies
1	small onion, chopped
10 ml (2 tsp)	ground cumin
30 ml (2 Tbs)	chutney
15 ml (1 Tbs)	tomato paste
50 g	butter, melted
175 ml	Bulgarian yoghurt
5 ml (1 tsp)	cornflour

▶ Place all the ingredients in a liquidiser or processor and blend until smooth.

CHICKEN BREASTS STUFFED UNDER THE SKIN

This makes a wonderful dinner party dish. Use the stuffing given here, or any of those given for whole birds.

Serves 6 to 8

8	chicken breasts with skin and bone

Spinach and feta cheese stuffing

60 g	butter
250 g	brown mushrooms, sliced
2	bunches spinach, cored, washed and shredded
15 ml (1 Tbs)	flour
250 g	crumbled feta cheese
5 ml (1 tsp)	dill
	salt and pepper to taste
	lemon juice to taste

Basting mixture

60 g	butter
15 ml (1 Tbs)	lemon juice
5 ml (1 tsp)	dill
5 ml (1 tsp)	salt
3 ml (½ tsp)	black pepper

▶ Fillet the chicken breasts, but leave the skin on (see *Hint*).
▶ Quickly brown the mushrooms in the butter. They must still be firm.
▶ Add the spinach and cook over low heat until the spinach has wilted.
▶ Stir in the flour.
▶ Remove from heat and leave to cool.
▶ Add the crumbled feta cheese, dill, salt, pepper and lemon juice to taste.
▶ Stuff the chicken breasts by placing the stuffing under the skin and tucking the short ends of the skin under the meat of the breast to form a rounded shape.
▶ Pack stuffed breasts tightly into a buttered ovenware dish.
▶ Prepare basting mixture by melting the butter and mixing in remaining basting ingredients.
▶ Roast, uncovered, for 20 to 25 minutes at 200 °C, basting often.

Hint
Buy chicken breasts with the bone and, using a small, sharp knife, run the blade between the bone and the meat to remove the bone. You will end up with a filleted chicken breast with the skin. If you keep the knife pressed up against the bone, the meat will come off quite easily.

BABY MARROW AND RICOTTA STUFFING

Follow the recipe for chicken breasts stuffed under the skin, but use this stuffing as an alternative. In the basting mixture, substitute marjoram for the dill.

500 g	courgettes
1	onion, finely chopped
50 g	butter
1	clove garlic, crushed
250 g	ricotta
	or *smooth cottage cheese*
45 ml (3 Tbs)	grated parmesan cheese
5 ml (1 tsp)	marjoram
2	egg yolks
250 ml (1 cup)	fresh breadcrumbs
	salt and pepper to taste

- Coarsely grate the courgettes and salt lightly. Leave to stand in a strainer for an hour to drain. Rinse and pat dry.
- Sauté the onion in the butter until glassy.
- Turn up the heat and add courgettes. Fry quickly over a high heat.
- Set aside and leave to cool.
- Add remaining ingredients.
- Continue as in the recipe for spinach and feta cheese stuffing, using marjoram instead of dill.

CHICKEN CHOW MEIN AND CHOP SUEY

Chicken breasts are perfect for stir-frying. Be careful not to overcook them. For this dish, Chinese noodles are the best. If they are available, boil them in chicken stock, drain well and coat in a little oil. For *Chop suey*, leave out the noodles and serve with rice.

There are two methods for stir-frying. I have used the simplest in this recipe. For the more traditional method, see the stir-fried vegetable recipe under *Vegetables*. A Chinese wok, with its rounded bottom, is ideal for stir-frying; it allows the juices to run down, so that the vegetables remain crisp. A heavy-based frying pan may also be used.

Serves 4 to 6

300 g	narrow ribbon egg noodles
4	filleted chicken breasts, cut into thin strips
750 g	vegetables of your choice, (e.g. cabbage, onions, carrots, broccoli, cucumber, celery, bean sprouts, bamboo shoots, water chestnuts, beans)
	oil for stir-frying

Marinade for chicken

5 ml (1 tsp)	sugar
5 ml (1 tsp)	salt
15 ml (1 Tbs)	sherry
15 ml (1 Tbs)	soy sauce
7 ml (1 1/2 tsp)	cornflour

Sauce

5 ml (1 tsp)	cornflour
125 ml (1/2 cup)	water
15 ml (1 Tbs)	soy sauce
15 ml (1 Tbs)	sherry
3 ml (1/2 tsp)	chicken stock powder
	or 1/2 cube, crumbled

- Mix the chicken with the marinade ingredients and leave to stand for 30 minutes.
- Mix all the sauce ingredients and set aside.
- Cut the vegetables into julienne strips, keeping them separately in piles on a tray.
- Stir-fry the vegetables in batches according to their toughness, starting with carrots, celery and onions together, then adding the broccoli, cabbage and beans before the first batch is cooked. Cucumber and bean sprouts, which need very little cooking, are added last and, almost immediately thereafter, the bamboo shoots and water chestnuts, which are already cooked. All the vegetables should have reached the same crispy texture at this point.
- Add salt to taste and remove from the wok or pan.
- Add a little more oil and quickly stir-fry the chicken, taking care not to overcook it.
- Replace vegetables and pour on the sauce. Simmer for 1 minute and remove from the wok or pan.
- Heat a little oil and quickly fry cooked mein (noodles).
- Toss in the chicken and vegetables.
- Serve chicken chow mein garnished with toasted sesame seeds.

STIR-FRIED CHICKEN WITH ALMONDS

Serves 4 to 6

4	filleted chicken breasts, cut into cubes
10 ml (2 tsp)	sugar
5 ml (1 tsp)	salt
15 ml (1 Tbs)	dry sherry
10 ml (2 tsp)	soy sauce
5 ml (1 tsp)	cornflour
5 ml (1 tsp)	green ginger, grated
	oil for frying
100 g	almonds, blanched or slivered
1	large onion, diced
1	stick celery, diced
5 cm	English cucumber, diced
500 g	frozen mixed vegetables, rinsed under cold water and well drained

Sauce

5 ml (1 tsp)	cornflour
125 ml (1/2 cup)	water
15 ml (1 Tbs)	soy sauce
15 ml (1 Tbs)	dry sherry
3 ml (1/2 tsp)	chicken stock powder

- Mix all the sauce ingredients and set aside.
- Coat chicken with a mixture of sugar, salt, sherry, soy sauce, cornflour and ginger and set aside.
- In a little oil, stir-fry almonds until golden and set aside.
- Stir-fry chicken until just cooked and set aside.
- Stir-fry onions and celery for 1 minute.
- Add cucumber and frozen vegetables and stir-fry until hot through.
- Add chicken and sauce mixture and heat through.
- Add almonds and serve immediately on rice.

JIFFY CHICKEN CASSEROLES

By using chicken breasts, you can make a delicious casserole in 30 minutes. All the chicken casserole recipes in this chapter can be made using chicken breasts, but once you have returned the browned chicken to the sauce, simmer it on the stove for no longer than 7 minutes before serving.

BASIC CHICKEN BREAST CASSEROLE

Vary this basic casserole with any of the simple sauces given in this chapter.

Serves 4

6-8	filleted chicken breasts
	casserole sauce of your choice

- Slash the chicken breasts as described in the introduction to this chapter.
- Brown chicken breasts quickly in a hot pan in a little oil or butter. Remove from pan.
- Make the sauce in the pan in the remaining fat.
- Place browned chicken in the sauce of your choice.
- Cover and simmer for 7 to 10 minutes.
- Serve with rice, pasta or baby potatoes.

JIFFY CASSEROLE SAUCES

Bacon and mushroom sauce

6	rashers rindless bacon, chopped
1	medium onion, chopped
250 g	brown mushrooms, thickly sliced
	oil for frying
1	tin chicken or mushroom soup
125 ml (1/2 cup)	dry white wine
	salt and pepper

- Sauté bacon, onion and mushrooms in a little oil.
- Add soup and wine and bring to the boil.
- Season to taste, return chicken to sauce, cover and simmer for 7 to 10 minutes.

Orange, ginger and honey sauce

10 ml (2 tsp)	grated ginger
2	cloves garlic, crushed
25 ml (1 1/2 Tbs)	flour
15 ml (1 Tbs)	honey
375 ml (1 1/2 cups)	fresh orange juice
2 ml (1/2 tsp)	dried thyme
1	orange, sliced
	salt and pepper
	sugar
100 g	slivered almonds, roasted

- After browning the chicken, stir garlic and ginger into remaining oil.
- Stir in flour and add orange juice, honey and thyme (depending how sweet the oranges are, more or less honey may be needed).
- Add salt, pepper and sugar to taste.
- Return chicken to the sauce and add sliced oranges.
- Simmer, covered, for 7 minutes.
- Sprinkle with almonds just before serving.

Lemon and honey sauce

30 g	butter
15 ml (1 Tbs)	flour
180 ml (¾ cup)	chicken stock
45 ml (3 Tbs)	honey
45 ml (3 Tbs)	lemon juice
45 ml (3 Tbs)	white wine
15 ml (1 Tbs)	prepared mustard
5 ml (1 tsp)	thyme

- Melt butter and stir in flour.
- Add remaining ingredients and bring to the boil, stirring as it thickens.
- Add chicken to sauce, check seasoning and simmer, covered, for 7 minutes.

Bigarade sauce

This versatile, piquant sauce of orange and caramelised sugar takes slightly longer, but it is well worth the extra time!

1	large onion, sliced
30 ml (2 Tbs)	oil
45 ml (3 Tbs)	sugar
45 ml (3 Tbs)	vinegar
250 ml (1 cup)	chicken stock
250 ml (1 cup)	fresh orange juice
25 ml (1 ½ Tbs)	flour, mixed with a little oil to form a paste

- Sauté onion in oil until glassy.
- Add sugar and vinegar and boil until vinegar has evaporated and sugar has caramelised. Take care not to burn it, but sugar should be brown and like toffee.
- Immediately add the stock and stir to dissolve the sugar.
- Add the remaining ingredients and bring to the boil.
- Return the browned chicken to the sauce and simmer, covered, for about 7 minutes.

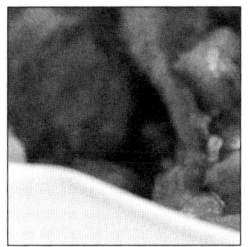  

VERSATILE MAIN COURSES

This chapter contains recipes for substantial meals, in which the main ingredient is of vegetable origin. In some cases this is combined with meat, while others are designed for vegetarians.

BOSTON BAKED BEANS

Dried pulses are full of protein and fibre. In this American recipe, beans are used for a warming and very economical meal. Serve with crusty white bread and a mixed salad.

Serves 6 to 8

500 g	haricot beans
200 g	gammon, or any smoked pork product (e.g. sausages)
2	onions
5 ml (1 tsp)	salt
30 ml (2 Tbs)	brown sugar
45 ml (3 Tbs)	molasses
10 ml (2 tsp)	dry mustard
10 ml (2 tsp)	vinegar
3 ml ($^1/_2$ tsp)	black pepper
500 ml (2 cups)	cold water

- Soak the beans overnight in plenty of cold water.
- Pour off the water, add fresh cold water to cover the beans and bring to the boil.
- Preheat oven to about 130 °C.
- Again pour off the water. (This reduces the substances in beans that cause flatulence.)
- Cut the onions into quarters, the meat into large cubes and place them in a casserole with the beans.
- Mix the remaining ingredients with the 500 ml cold water.
- Pour on the remaining ingredients. Beans should just be covered; add a little more water if necessary.
- Cover casserole and bake in a slow oven for 4 to 5 hours, or until the beans are soft.

Hint

If the casserole lid fits very well, you may find that you have to remove the lid for the last 30 minutes of the baking time in order to reduce the liquid. If the lid does not fit very well, check periodically to ensure that the beans do not dry out. The beans should be moist but not watery.

VEGETARIAN MAIN COURSES

INDIAN VEGETABLE CURRY

Leave the skin on the butternut, potatoes and aubergines. It gives the dish flavour and texture and prevents the vegetables from falling apart as they cook.

Serves 4 to 6

45 ml (3 Tbs)	oil or butter
1	large onion
3	cloves garlic
10 ml (2 tsp)	grated fresh ginger
2	medium aubergines
1	small butternut
3	medium potatoes
410 g	tinned tomatoes (with juice), sliced
15 ml (1 Tbs)	masala or curry powder
3 ml ($^1/_2$ tsp)	turmeric
125 ml ($^1/_2$ cup)	chicken or vegetable stock
375 ml (1 $^1/_2$ cups)	frozen peas
60 ml ($^1/_4$ cup)	chopped dhania (coriander) leaves
15 ml (1 Tbs)	garam masala

▶ Cut all the vegetables into large chunks, leaving the skin on the butternut, aubergines and potatoes.
▶ Fry the onions in the oil until they just begin to colour.
▶ Add the remaining ingredients except the peas, dhania leaves and garam masala.
▶ Simmer, covered, until the vegetables are soft.
▶ Check seasoning, adding salt to taste.
▶ Add the peas, dhania leaves and garam masala and mix carefully into the curry.
▶ Serve on a bed of rice.

VEGETARIAN CASSEROLE

This old favourite is a mixture of vegetables in season, served on a bed of *stampkoring* (wheat rice, pearled wheat), barley or brown rice. The chunky white cheese sauce and savoury crumble topping make this a tasty, wholesome meal in one pot.

Serves 4 to 6

250 ml (1 cup)	stampkoring or brown rice
30 g	butter
1	onion, chopped
1	vegetable stock cube
or 1 tsp	vegetable stock powder
100 g	grated cheddar cheese
500 g	diced vegetables of your choice (e.g. mushrooms, butternut, baby marrows, potatoes, cauliflower, broccoli cuts, diced carrots, peas, sweetcorn)
7 ml (1 $^1/_2$ tsp)	mixed dried herbs
	salt and black pepper

Cheese sauce

375 ml (1 $^1/_2$ cups)	milk
50 g	butter
45 ml (3 Tbs)	flour
125 ml ($^1/_2$ cup)	grated cheddar cheese
250 g	chunky cottage cheese
5 ml (1 tsp)	mustard
2 ml ($^1/_2$ tsp)	ground nutmeg
30 ml (2 Tbs)	freshly chopped parsley

Topping

Make the breadcrumbs in a food processor, liquidiser or grate slices of bread on a coarse grater.

125 ml ($^1/_2$ cup)	fresh breadcrumbs, white or wholewheat
125 ml ($^1/_2$ cup)	grated cheddar cheese
30 ml (2 Tbs)	grated parmesan cheese

▶ Preheat oven to 180 °C.
▶ Boil the wheat rice or brown rice in vegetable stock.
▶ Stir-fry the onion in a little butter.
▶ Mix the onion and cheese into the wheat rice.
▶ Spread this mixture in a casserole dish.

- Boil all the vegetables for 5 minutes, drain and season well.
- Place vegetables on top of the wheat rice.
- *For the cheese sauce, melt the butter in a small pot and stir in the flour.*
- Add the milk and bring it to the boil, stirring continually until mixture thickens.
- Remove the pot from the heat.
- Add the grated cheese and seasoning and mix in the cottage cheese.
- Mix all the topping ingredients.
- Pour on the cheese sauce and sprinkle with the savoury crumble topping.
- Bake, uncovered, for 40 to 50 minutes, or until the crumble topping is well browned.

Hint
Mix a few roasted cashew nuts or sunflower seeds into the stampkoring layer for a special treat.

SAMP AND BEANS

Served as a main course with vegetable side dishes, this truly South African dish provides a substantial, balanced meal. Samp and beans are nutty, chewy, full of protein and complex carbohydrates and low in fats. As a side dish at a braai, it complements the fatty meat.

Serves 4 to 6

500 g	samp and beans, soaked in water overnight
3	litres vegetable, beef or chicken stock
15 ml (1 Tbs)	Worcestershire sauce
50 g	butter
	salt and pepper

- Place the samp and beans and stock in a medium-sized pot and simmer for about 3 hours or until soft.
- Add the butter, season to taste and serve.

Hint
Instead of soaking the samp and beans overnight, quick-soak them by bringing the water to the boil, leaving it to stand for an hour and then boiling until soft.

SPICED LENTILS WITH VEGETABLES AND YOGHURT

This cumin-flavoured vegetable casserole is thickened and enriched by the addition of cooked yoghurt.

Serves 6 to 8

300 g	*large green* or *black* lentils
500 ml (2 cups)	vegetable stock
1	large onion, diced
60 ml (4 Tbs)	*olive oil* or *butter*
2	packets spinach, washed and roughly chopped
1	small butternut, cubed but not peeled
250 g	whole button mushrooms
30 ml (2 Tbs)	tomato paste
10 ml (2 tsp)	sugar
7 ml (1 ½ tsp)	dried dill
2 ml (½ tsp)	ground cinnamon
7 ml (1 ½ tsp)	cumin
2 ml (½ tsp)	cayenne pepper
3	cloves garlic, crushed
	salt and pepper

Cooked yoghurt

350 ml	plain yoghurt, preferably full-cream
1	egg white
5 ml (1 tsp)	salt
15 ml (1 Tbs)	cornflour

- Boil the lentils in vegetable stock until almost soft.
- Sauté the onion well in the oil or butter.
- Add the spinach, butternut and mushrooms and a little water.
- Cook until the vegetables are soft and the spinach is wilted.
- Add the remaining ingredients and cooked lentils.
- Simmer for 10 minutes.
- *For the cooked yoghurt,* whisk the egg white, salt and cornflour lightly in a small pot. Whisk in the yoghurt.
- Stir constantly over medium heat until it begins to boil.
- Reduce the heat and leave to simmer for 2 to 3 minutes until thick.
- Stir yoghurt into lentil mixture and check the seasoning.
- Heat through.
- Serve with basmati rice.

VEGETARIAN STUFFED CABBAGE LEAVES

Stuffed cabbage leaves are always a little extra work but the end result is well worth it. Any cheese you prefer can be used in place of the Gruyere.

Serves 6 to 8

375 ml (1 1/2 cups)	brown rice
	or barley
	or stampkoring *(wheat rice)*
1	large onion, chopped
1	stick celery, chopped
1	green pepper, chopped
150 g	mushrooms, chopped
50 g	butter
100 g (1 cup)	grated Gruyere cheese
5 ml (1 tsp)	dried sweet basil
	salt and pepper
1	cabbage

Sauce

1	large onion, chopped
50 g	butter
45 ml (3 Tbs)	flour
375 ml (1 1/2 cup)	vegetable stock
410 g	tinned tomatoes
2	bouquets garni
or 3 ml (1/2 tsp)	thyme
2	bay leaves
	salt and pepper
125 ml (1/2 cup)	cream
	or sour cream

▸ Parboil the rice in vegetable stock or water. The rice should still be chewy.
▸ Sauté the onion, celery, green pepper and mushroom in butter and leave to cool.
▸ Mix in the cooked rice, cheese and season to taste.
▸ Preheat oven to 160 °C.
▸ Bring a large pot of water to the boil. Place the whole cabbage in the water and remove one leaf at a time. Dip it into cold water to cool it down.
▸ Remove the thick white stalk and place a large spoonful of the filling in the middle of the leaf.
▸ Fold over the edges and make into a parcel.
▸ Place the parcels in a casserole with the loose ends facing down.

▸ *Make the sauce* by melting the butter in a pot. Sauté the onion until glassy.
▸ Stir in the flour and cook over medium heat until the flour has turned nut-brown in colour (see introduction to *Meat*).
▸ Add the remaining ingredients, except the cream, and simmer for 5 minutes.
▸ Remove the bouquets garni and bay leaves.
▸ Add the cream and liquidise the sauce until smooth or leave it chunky if you wish.
▸ Return the bay leaves and bouquets garni.
▸ Pour the sauce over the stuffed cabbage leaves and casserole, covered, for 1 hour.

GREEN PEPPER DOLMA

Stuffed green peppers

Sweet and spicy, the unusual stuffing in this Turkish recipe can be used to stuff all kinds of vegetables. Hollow out the centre of large baby marrows, aubergines, onions, butternuts, and stuff with the filling, or wrap filling in cabbage or vine leaves. Use basmati or any short-grain white rice.

Serves 4 to 6

6-8	small sweet peppers
	(green, red or yellow)
165 ml (2/3 cup)	uncooked rice
60 ml (1/4 cup)	olive oil
1	large onion, chopped
50 g	pine nuts or slivered almonds
30 ml (2 Tbs)	currants, soaked in
125 ml (1/2 cup)	boiling water
7 ml (1 1/2 tsp)	tomato paste
5 ml (1 tsp)	allspice
3 ml (1/2 tsp)	ground cinnamon
125 ml (1/2 cup)	freshly chopped parsley
2	cloves garlic, crushed
15 ml (1 Tbs)	fresh lemon juice
5 ml (1 tsp)	sugar
	salt and pepper
2	tomatoes, sliced
5 ml (1 tsp)	tomato paste
125 ml (1/2 cup)	boiling water
15 ml (1 Tbs)	olive oil

VERSATILE MAIN COURSES

- Cut off the stalk end of the pepper to form a lid.
- Remove the pith and seeds from inside the peppers.
- Cook the rice until it is chewy.
- Preheat oven to 180 °C.
- Sauté the onion and nuts in oil.
- Add all the remaining ingredients.
- Check seasoning and add a little water if mixture is dry.
- Stuff the peppers and place the 'lids' on top.
- Line a casserole with sliced tomato.
- Arrange the stuffed peppers on top.
- Mix the 5 ml tomato paste with 125 ml boiling water and the 15 ml olive oil.
- Pour into the casserole and bake, covered, for 1 hour.
- Remove the lid and increase the oven temperature to 220 °C for 15 to 20 minutes until the peppers just begin to brown.
- Serve hot or cold as a main meal, or as part of the mezze table (see *Starters*).

EGG AND CHEESE DISHES

(For soufflés, see under *Starters*)
I receive many queries on how to fry eggs correctly and how to make a simple omelette. This is my advice:

FRIED EGGS

Frying eggs with the lid on removes the 'gooey' texture while still having a soft yolk. The top is slightly cooked by the steam trapped under the lid. It also avoids having to turn the egg. For a firmer yolk, cook it a little longer.

- Melt 15 ml (1 Tbs) of butter in a small pan over medium heat.
- Crack in the eggs and cook, covered, on medium to low for 3 to 4 minutes. (Any lid will do as long as it covers the eggs.)

With a little practice you will soon know exactly how long and at what temperature setting you need to fry your eggs. Make a note of what you did and, *Voila!* Perfect eggs every time!

OMELETTE

To make an omelette with 2 eggs, you need a frying pan 16 to 18 cm in diameter. The size of the pan is very important. Use 3 eggs if your pan is larger, otherwise your omelette will be too thin and more like a crêpe than an omelette. Filling suggestions follow.

Serves 1

> 2 eggs
> 25-30 ml (2 Tbs) water, not milk
> 15 ml (1 Tbs) butter
> salt and pepper
> desired filling

- Lightly beat the eggs with a fork. Beat in the water. The mixture must not be foamy.
- Do not add any salt at this stage. Salt breaks down the egg and the omelette will not fold easily. Add salt once the omelette is cooked, before adding the filling.
- Melt the butter in a 16 to 18 cm frying pan over a high heat until the butter is bubbling.
- Pour the beaten egg into the pan and immediately turn the plate down to medium-low (depending on your stove).
- Puncture the air bubbles as they form with the egg lifter.
- Carefully lift the cooked edges of the omelette with the egg lifter and tilt the pan to allow the raw egg to run onto the bottom of the pan.
- As soon as there is no more liquid egg, season with salt and pepper and place the filling on half of the omelette.
- Tilt the pan and, with the egg lifter held upside-down, carefully slide it under the omelette all the way to the centre of the pan. Tilt the pan and carefully roll the unfilled half of the omelette over the filled half.
- Switch off the plate, but leave the pan on the plate. Cover the omelette with a plate or lid to warm the filling slightly.
- Use the egg lifter to ensure that the omelette is not stuck to the pan. Place the serving plate over the pan and quickly invert the pan, dropping the omelette onto the plate.
- Serve immediately.

OMELETTE FILLINGS

These fillings are enough for 2 omelettes. Do not overfill the omelette, as it will break when you fold it.

Cheese, onion and tomato filling

　　　　　1 small onion, chopped
　　　　　1 small tomato, diced
　　　　　25 g butter
　　　　　　salt and pepper
125 ml ($^1/_2$ cup) finely cubed cheese of your choice

- Sauté onion in the butter until glassy.
- Add the tomato and heat through. Season to taste.
- Spread the onion and tomato over half of each omelette and top filling with cheese.

Apple and cheddar filling

　　　　　1 small Granny Smith apple, grated
125 ml ($^1/_2$ cup) finely cubed cheddar cheese

- Mix and use as filling.

Hint
For a slightly sweeter omelette, add 30 ml (2 Tbs) seedless raisins.

Avocado and bacon or salmon filling

　　　　　4 rashers rindless bacon, crisply grilled or fried and crumbled
　　　or 50 g smoked salmon
　　　　　1 small avocado, finely cubed

- Spread the avocado on half the omelette and sprinkle the bacon over the filling.

VEGETABLE FRITTATA

Almost like the filling of a quiche, but without the pastry and richness, a frittata makes a quick and tasty light meal.

Serves 4 as a main dish and 8 as a side dish

　　750 ml (3 cups) grated or chopped vegetables (e.g. baby marrows, mushrooms and spinach)
　　　　　1 onion, chopped
　　　　　50 g butter
　　45 ml (3 Tbs) flour
　　250 ml (1 cup) milk
　125 ml ($^1/_2$ cup) grated cheese
　　　　　4 eggs, well beaten
　　　　　　salt and pepper

- Preheat oven to 160 °C.
- Cook the vegetables in a little water until almost soft. Drain in a colander to remove any excess water.
- Sauté the onion in the butter.
- Stir in the flour.
- Add the milk and bring to the boil, stirring continually.
- Carefully fold in the vegetables, cheese and seasoning to taste.
- Add the beaten eggs.
- Pour into a greased shallow dish and bake for about 40 minutes, or until set.
- Cut into squares or wedges and serve with fresh bread.

FLAT COURGETTE OMELETTE

With a Middle-Eastern flavour, this is delicious served on its own or as a side dish.

Serves 4 as a main dish, or 8 as a side dish

　　750 ml (3 cups) grated courgette
　　50 ml (3 $^1/_2$ Tbs) chopped spring onion
　　　　　50 g butter
　　50 ml (3 $^1/_2$ Tbs) flour
　　250 ml (1 cup) sour cream
　125 ml ($^1/_2$ cup) crumbled feta cheese
　　　　　4 eggs, beaten
　　3 ml ($^1/_2$ tsp) dill
　　　　　　black pepper

- Preheat oven to 160 °C.
- Lightly salt the grated courgette and leave to drain in a colander for 30 minutes.
- Sauté onion and courgette in the butter.
- Stir in the flour. Add the sour cream and bring to the boil, stirring continually.
- Remove from the heat and stir in the feta cheese and beaten eggs.
- Pour into a large shallow greased dish and bake for about 40 minutes until firm enough to cut into wedges.

FONDUE A LA BEER

This cheese fondue has a completely different flavour to the traditional Swiss one. The slightly spicy and faintly bitter flavour is delicious with vegetables or crusty white bread. Serve as a light winter meal with mulled wine (see *This and that*).

Serves 4 to 6

75 g	butter
45 ml (3 Tbs)	flour
15 ml (1 Tbs)	prepared mustard
5 ml (1 tsp)	Worcestershire sauce
500 ml (2 cups)	beer
250 g (2 cups)	Emmenthal cheese, grated
250 g (2 1/2 cups)	cheddar cheese, grated

To serve

French loaf
assorted vegetables,
cut into thick strips

- Melt the butter and stir in the flour.
- Add the mustard and Worcestershire sauce, and stir in the beer.
- Bring to the boil and then switch the plate to its lowest setting.
- Add cheese slowly, stirring continually until melted. Do not let the mixture boil.
- Serve with French bread and vegetables.

RICE DISHES

Rice of various kinds makes an excellent basis for a tasty and economical main meal.

The best rice for making an Italian risotto is the round-grained rice called *arborio*. For biryani, use the aromatic Indian basmati rice, and for rice puddings use short-grained white rice. Try different types of rice, brown, white, wheat – even barley 'rice' – to make risottos, paellas and pilaffs a little different from the ordinary.

VEGETARIAN RICE MOULD

This dish can be made with any rice. For a nutty flavour, use brown rice.

Serves 4 to 6

310 ml (1 1/4 cup)	rice of your choice
50 g	butter
500 ml (2 cups)	vegetable or mushroom stock
185 ml (3/4 cup)	brown lentils, cooked
1	onion, chopped
125 g	brown mushrooms, sliced
1	aubergine, diced
2	baby marrows, sliced
1	green pepper, diced
1	red pepper, diced
250 ml (1 cup)	frozen peas
185 ml (3/4 cup)	grated sweetmilk cheese
5 ml (1 tsp)	dried origanum
	salt and pepper
	chopped parsley for garnish

- Sauté the rice in half the butter for 2 minutes.
- Add the stock.
- Cook the rice until it is dry.
- Sauté the onion and other vegetables in the remaining butter until almost soft.
- Stir in the rice, lentils, grated cheese and origanum, and season to taste with salt and pepper.
- Press mixture into a greased pudding bowl to mould it. Invert the bowl, turning out onto a serving plate.
- Garnish with chopped parsley and serve with a simple tomato sauce or, if you like it more spicy, with Cajun tomato sauce (see *Sauces*).

BASIC ITALIAN RISOTTO

Use this as a basic recipe and add different vegetables in season or herbs. In a risotto, the rice and other ingredients are always cooked together in an open pan and the rice is not steamed at all.

Any rice can be used instead of arborio and the risotto will still be tasty, although it will definitely not be the same. This recipe should not take longer than 20 to 25 minutes to make.

Serves 4

l litre (4 cups)	chicken stock
25 g	butter
45 ml (3 Tbs)	olive oil
1	large onion, chopped
500 ml (2 cups)	arborio rice
375 ml (1 1/2 cups)	dry white wine
20 ml (4 tsp)	freshly chopped sweet basil (not dried)
2	cloves garlic, crushed
45 ml (3 Tbs)	grated parmesan cheese
	salt and pepper

- Heat the stock in a saucepan; keep it hot but do not boil.
- Heat the butter and olive oil in a deep frying pan.
- Add the onion and sauté until soft.
- Add the rice to the onion and cook for 2 minutes.
- Add half the wine to the rice and bring to the boil, stirring constantly.
- Lower the heat slightly, but keep the rice simmering all the time.
- Add 125 ml (1/2 cup) of the stock and then the remaining wine.
- Add the remaining stock 125 ml (1/2 cup) at a time, stirring continually until all the stock has been absorbed.
- Add the crushed garlic and sweet basil.
- Season to taste with salt and pepper.
- Remove from the heat and stir in the cheese.
- Serve with extra grated parmesan cheese.

Variations
- Try adding any of the following: spinach, frozen peas, mushrooms, aubergines or a little chilli. Also delicious is salami, bacon or left-over chicken. Chopped tomato or a little tomato paste can be added with the stock for a tomato risotto. Instead of the fresh sweet basil use marjoram, sage or even a little rosemary (fresh or dried), to taste.
- To make it rich and creamy, add 125 ml (1/2 cup) cream to the risotto just before serving.

For these variations, follow the basic recipe:
- Sauté the onion until glassy.
- Add any other vegetables or meat of your choice and sauté for a further 5 minutes. Continue with the basic recipe.
- If using tomato, add it only towards the end of the cooking process.

CHICKEN LIVER PILAFF

In a pilaff the rice is very often cooked separately and then added to the other ingredients and steamed to blend the flavours.

Serves 4

500 ml (2 cups)	rice of your choice
1 litre (4 cups)	chicken stock
50 g	butter
4-6	rashers rindless bacon, diced
1	large onion, diced
250 g	mushrooms, diced
250 g	chicken livers, cut up
5 ml (1 tsp)	dried marjoram or origanum
30 ml (2 Tbs)	sherry
2	cloves garlic, crushed
185 ml (3/4 cup)	extra chicken stock
	salt and pepper
60 ml (1/4 cup)	freshly chopped parsley
	grated Parmesan cheese

- Cook the rice in chicken stock until almost soft. Do not overcook.
- In a large, deep frying pan, fry the bacon and onion in the butter until the onion begins to brown.
- Add the diced mushroom and fry quickly over high heat.
- Add the chicken liver and fry quickly. Do not overcook; they should still be pink inside.
- Add the rice, marjoram (or origanum), sherry, garlic and enough of the extra stock to keep the mixture moist.
- Check seasoning, cover with a lid and steam for 10 to 15 minutes over a low heat to blend the flavours.
- Stir in the parsley and serve with grated Parmesan cheese.

CHICKEN AND SEAFOOD JAMBALAYA

Jambalaya is a Cajun or Creole rice dish from Louisiana. The assortment of meat and fish and the distinctive use of all the peppers, both sweet and hot, make this a warming main course dish.

Serves 6 to 8

4	chicken thighs, filleted, skinned and cubed
200 g	smoked pork or *kassler ribs*, cubed
3	spicy smoked sausages (e.g. chorizo), cubed
200 g	frozen shelled shrimp
2 x 105 g	tins oysters (optional)
80 ml ($^1/_3$ cup)	oil or butter
375 ml (1 $^1/_2$ cups)	finely chopped onion
250 ml (1 cup)	finely chopped celery
250 ml (1 cup)	finely chopped peppers – green, red and yellow (if possible)
410 g	tinned tomatoes, chopped
60 ml ($^1/_4$ cup)	tomato purée
4	cloves garlic, crushed
1	bunch spring onions, chopped
500 ml (2 cups)	chicken stock
375 ml (1 $^1/_2$ cups)	uncooked rice

Seasoning mix

4	bay leaves
8 ml (1 $^1/_2$ tsp)	salt
5 ml (1 tsp)	cayenne pepper
3 ml ($^1/_2$ tsp)	white pepper
3 ml ($^1/_2$ tsp)	black pepper
8 ml (1 $^1/_2$ tsp)	dried origanum
5 ml (1 tsp)	dried thyme
5 ml (1 tsp)	paprika

- Fry the pork cubes in butter until well browned.
- Add the onion, celery and peppers and sauté for a couple of minutes – the onions must still be crisp.
- Add the chicken and sausage and cook on high for 1 minute.
- Reduce the heat and add seasoning mix and garlic and cook gently for 3 minutes.
- Add tomato and stock and bring to the boil.
- Add the rice and simmer, covered, on a low heat for about 15 minutes until rice is almost cooked.
- Add seafood with some of the liquid from the oysters, and add the spring onion and heat through.
- At this point be careful not to overcook; rice should still be firm in a jambalaya.
- Serve as it is, or with spicy Creole sauce if desired (see *Sauces*).

Hint
For presentation, fill a small bowl with the jambalaya, using the bowl as a mould and then invert it onto the plate. Top it with Creole sauce.

PASTA DISHES

Pasta has become one of the most popular dishes in the Western world. Besides the fact that it is healthy, its versatility and speed of preparation makes it a winner in our hasty lives.

Cooking pasta
Pasta is always cooked in the same way, no matter what the shape or flavour.

- Bring a large pot of very lightly salted water to the boil with the lid on.
- Add the pasta. Over a high heat (without lid) and stirring continually, bring the water back to a rolling boil.
- Stop stirring and boil without the lid until the pasta is tender but still slightly chewy (al dente). Different types of pasta require different cooking times – follow the time recommended on the packet.
- Drain in a colander or strainer and serve. Do not rinse the pasta. If you are not serving the pasta immediately, toss in 15 to 30 ml (1 to 2 Tbs) oil to prevent it from sticking.

Sauces
The variety of sauces and pasta shapes is endless, from the simplest, olive oil and garlic, to elaborate seafood sauces. Refer also to *Sauces*, *Meat* and *Fish* for sauces to use on pasta.

Try any of the following:
- *Bolognaise meat* sauce See *Meat* for the mince sauce used for lasagne.
- *Seafood sauce* See the *Calamari casserole sauce* under *Fish* and *Misto di mare* under *Pasta*.
- *Chicken a la King* This sauce (see *Poultry*) is perfect to serve on pasta.
- *Roast ratatouille* See under *Vegetable side dishes*.
- Look under *Sauces* for other sauce ideas.

HOME-MADE PASTA

Fresh home-made pasta is quite different from dried pasta. With a little practice you can make enough pasta for 4 in 30 minutes. A small pasta machine is a great help!

Serves 4

500 ml (2 cups)	flour
5 ml (1 tsp)	salt
2	jumbo eggs
15 ml (1 Tbs)	olive oil
30 ml (2 Tbs)	water

- Place flour, salt, eggs and oil in a food processor and form into crumbles.
- Add just enough of the water to form large wet crumbs. *Do not form into a dough.*
- Turn out onto a floured surface and lightly knead into a dry dough.
- Divide the pasta mixture into 8 pieces and roll out each portion into a very thin rectangle. Sprinkle liberally with flour and roll each rectangle up like a Swiss roll. Slice to form ribbon noodles to the thickness that you want (tagliatelle or tagliarini). Unroll each strip and leave on a tray well dusted with flour until you are ready to eat.
- To cook the pasta, place it in a pot of vigorously boiling water for about 1 minute.
- Drain and serve.

Variations
- For a more tender pasta, use 3 eggs and leave out the water.
- For green spinach pasta, add 50 g cooked, chopped spinach that has been well drained.
- For red pasta, add about 15 ml (1 Tbs) tomato paste; it will give the pasta a good flavour.

PASTA WITH AVOCADO AND GARLIC

This amazing combination of hot pasta with cold avocado, garlic and olive oil makes a memorable starter.

500 g	shell noodles, cooked and drained
3-4	ripe avocado pears, cubed
4	thick sticks celery, coarsely chopped
4-6	cloves garlic, crushed
185 ml (3/4 cup)	olive oil
	salt and pepper to taste
	freshly chopped parsley

- In a bowl, combine the avocado, celery, garlic, olive oil, salt and pepper.
- Toss into the warm, drained pasta.
- Serve in a large platter and sprinkle with freshly chopped parsley.
- Serve the pasta at room temperature.

Variation
For something different, use the avocado and apple salad dressing (see *Salads*) as a cold sauce with hot pasta.

MIKI'S SALMON SAUCE

The most delicious sauce I have ever tasted! It is also the easiest.

Serves 4

200 g	smoked salmon cut in strips
375 g	Mascarpone cheese
or 125 g	cream cheese and 250 ml cream
3-5 ml (1/2-1 tsp)	freshly ground black pepper
3 ml (1/2 tsp)	dried dill
or 15 ml (1 Tbs)	fresh dill (optional)
400 g	tagliatelle or pasta of your choice

- If using cream cheese, mix it with the cream.
- On a flat serving dish, arrange the strips of salmon and blobs of the mascarpone or cream cheese.
- Sprinkle on the black pepper.
- Just before eating, boil the pasta in salted water until just cooked.
- While the pasta is cooking, place the serving dish in a hot oven for a few minutes to warm the dish and its contents.
- Drain the pasta well and toss into the salmon and cheese.
- Serve immediately.

BASIC TOMATO SAUCE FOR PASTA

'Less is more' is a golden rule that definitely applies to this simple tomato sauce. The cooked tomatoes are flavoured with bay leaf, garlic, sweet basil and olive oil. The combination of flavours of the pasta, tomatoes and cheese makes this my favourite tomato sauce. Use it on plain or filled pasta such as ravioli.

Serves 6

425 g	tinned tomato purée
or 115 g	tin tomato paste
2 x 410 g	tins chopped tomatoes,
or 410 g	tinned tomatoes, with the juice, chopped
2	bay leaves
45 ml (3 Tbs)	olive oil
3	cloves garlic
	salt, pepper and sugar to taste
45 ml (3 Tbs)	chopped fresh sweet basil
or 10 ml	dried origanum

- Simmer the tomato purée or paste, chopped tomatoes and bay leaves for about 10 minutes until thick.
- Add the oil, garlic and seasoning.
- Heat through and serve.
- If you are using dried origanum, simmer it with the tomatoes.

Variations
- Fry chopped onion, celery and mushrooms in the olive oil and then simmer in the tomato sauce.
- For a *salami and chilli sauce*, fry 1 chopped onion, 1 fresh red chilli and about 15 slices of salami (cut into strips) in the olive oil and then simmer in the tomato sauce.

HAM AND MUSHROOM SAUCE

This is the pasta sauce recipe that I am most often asked for. It is rich and creamy. Add diced left-over roast chicken and turn it into a sauce for mashed or baked potato or rice.

Serves 4

45 g	butter
1	stick celery, chopped
1	onion, chopped
250 g	button mushrooms, halved
30 ml (2 Tbs)	flour
150 g	ham, cubed
15 ml (1 Tbs)	origanum
125 ml (½ cup)	chicken stock
125 ml (½ cup)	white wine
125 ml (½ cup)	cream
	seasoning to taste
45 ml (3 Tbs)	fresh parsley, chopped

- Sauté the onions and celery in the butter.
- Add the mushrooms and fry quickly.
- Stir in the flour.
- Add the ham, stock, wine, cream and seasoning.
- Simmer until thick.
- Stir in the parsley and serve on tagliatelle with parmesan cheese.

Variations
- Use smoked turkey instead of the ham.
- For a plain Alfredo sauce, make the sauce but leave out the vegetables and ham. This will give you a simple cream sauce.

SAUCE PUTTANESCA

Tomato, anchovy, olives and chilli makes this a warming sauce for pasta. Bake fillets of yellowtail or tuna in the sauce, or just serve it with grilled fish.

Serves 4

1	large onion, chopped
45 ml (3 Tbs)	olive oil
3	cloves garlic, crushed
4	large ripe tomatoes, skinned and chopped
or 2 x 410 g	tinned tomatoes, chopped
15 ml (1 Tbs)	tomato paste
50 g	anchovy fillets, chopped
200 g	pitted green olives, sliced
2	cloves garlic, crushed
15 ml (1 Tbs)	chilli sauce, or fresh chilli to taste
30 ml (2 Tbs)	fresh basil, chopped
or 5 ml (1 tsp)	dried basil
125 ml (½ cup)	parsley, chopped

- Sauté the onion in oil.
- Add all the remaining ingredients.
- Season to taste and simmer for 2 minutes.
- Serve on pasta with parmesan cheese.

For Variation *see next page.*

Variation

Mix the sauce with cooked pasta shells or penne and place in an ovenware dish. Add cubes of mozzarella and mix through evenly. Sprinkle with grated mozzarella. Bake until the cheese has melted. Serve with parmesan cheese.

CHICKEN LIVER AND BACON SAUCE

The eggs added at the end give this rich pasta sauce a very creamy texture. It is delicious on baked potato, rice or mealie pap.

Serves 4

500 g	chicken livers, roughly chopped
2	onions, chopped
4	rashers bacon, chopped
45 ml (3 Tbs)	oil
250 ml (1 cup)	cream
15 ml (1 Tbs)	cornflour
2	eggs, well beaten
	salt and pepper
5 ml (1 tsp)	origanum
400 g	cooked pasta of your choice

- Sauté onion and bacon.
- Add liver and cook until liver changes colour.
- Mix the cream with the cornflour.
- Stir in cream and origanum and cook for 2 minutes.
- Remove from the heat and stir in beaten eggs.
- Adjust seasoning and serve over pasta with Parmesan cheese.

AUBERGINE AND TOMATO SAUCE

This is the same as a ratatouille, but the vegetables are cut into very small pieces to form a pasta sauce. It makes an excellent topping for baked potatoes.

Serves 4

45 ml (3 Tbs)	olive oil
1	onion
1	aubergine
1	green pepper
	or ½ red and ½ green pepper
3	baby marrows
125 g	brown mushrooms
30 ml (2 Tbs)	tomato paste
410 g	tinned tomatoes, chopped
2	cloves garlic, crushed
5 ml (1 tsp)	origanum
or ¼ cup	chopped fresh basil
	salt and pepper to taste
45 ml (3 Tbs)	parsley, chopped

- Chop up all the vegetables into fairly small pieces.
- Sauté the onion in olive oil until glassy.
- Add the remaining ingredients and simmer until vegetables are soft and sauce has reduced (about 20 minutes).
- Serve on pasta with parmesan cheese.

Variation

Use short pasta such as shells or penne. Cut 150 g mozzarella into small cubes and mix them into the pasta with the sauce. Place the mixture in an ovenware dish and either pour on a 500 ml béchamel sauce and sprinkle on Parmesan cheese, or simply sprinkle the top with grated mozzarella. Bake, uncovered, at 160 °C until the cheese on the top has melted and browned. Serve with Parmesan cheese.

QUICK SPINACH AND TUNA PASTA SAUCE

Serve this on pasta or a baked potato for a tasty light meal.

Serves 4

1	large onion, chopped
45 ml (3 Tbs)	butter, oil, or a mixture
250 g	frozen creamed spinach
1	tin tuna, drained
410 g	tinned tomatoes, chopped
5 ml (1 tsp)	origanum
	salt and pepper to taste
	parmesan cheese

- Sauté the onion until glassy.
- Add the remaining ingredients and simmer for 10 minutes.
- Check seasoning and serve with pasta and parmesan cheese.

Hint
1 bunch of fresh spinach, washed, chopped and steamed, will replace the 250 g frozen spinach to make the sauce even more delicious.

MACARONI CHEESE

Rhona's recipe transforms macaroni cheese from the ordinary to the very special.

Serves 4

250 g	macaroni or *elbow macaroni,* cooked
1	onion, diced
150 g	button mushrooms, sliced
40 g	butter
45 ml (3 Tbs)	flour
500 ml (2 cups)	milk
80 ml (1/3 cup)	tomato purée
250 ml (1 cup)	cream, sour cream, or *extra milk*
3	eggs, beaten
	salt and pepper
7 ml (1 1/2 tsp)	dry mustard powder
500 ml (2 cups)	grated cheddar cheese, preferably mature
80 ml (1/3 cup)	chopped parsley
	extra chopped parsley for garnish

- Preheat the oven to 180 °C.
- Cook the macaroni in boiling water until just tender.
- Sauté the onion and mushroom in butter until soft.
- Stir in the flour and cook for 1 minute, then add the milk and stir until boiling.
- Remove from the heat and stir in the tomato purée and cream.
- Add 30 ml (2 Tbs) of the hot sauce to the beaten egg and mix.
- Mix the egg mixture into the sauce and add seasoning, mustard, and salt and pepper to taste.
- Carefully mix half the cheese and all the parsley into the cooked macaroni.
- Pour the sauce over the macaroni and gently mix through.
- Sprinkle with remaining cheese and extra parsley.
- Bake at 180 °C for 30 to 40 minutes.

QUICK TUNA NOODLE BAKE

This variation of macaroni cheese makes a perfect light meal or a starter that can be made in advance.

Serves 3 to 4 as a main course, 6 as a starter

200 g	pasta of your choice, cooked
1 x 185 g	tin tuna in oil
30 g	butter
2	sticks celery, with leaves, chopped
1	green pepper, chopped, or 1/2 green and 1/2 red pepper
2	large onions, peeled, halved and thinly sliced
1	tin mushroom or *asparagus* soup
250 ml (1 cup)	milk
250 ml (1 cup)	grated cheddar cheese
60 ml (1/4 cup)	freshly chopped parsley
	salt and pepper
	extra grated cheese for topping

- Preheat oven to 180 °C.
- Drain the oil from the tuna into a saucepan.
- Sauté the onion, celery and green pepper in the tuna oil and butter until soft and slightly golden.
- Add the tin of soup.
- Add the milk and over medium heat, stir until the mixture comes to the boil.
- Remove from the heat and add the flaked tuna, grated cheese, parsley and cooked pasta.
- Season to taste.
- Transfer to an ovenware dish.
- Top with extra grated cheese.
- Bake in preheated oven at 180 °C for 20 to 30 minutes.
- Place under the grill to brown the cheese.

Variation
To serve as a special starter, add 100 g cashew nuts and an extra tin of tuna to the mixture.

MISTO DI MARE WITH PASTA

Pasta with seafood sauce

This piquant seafood sauce is perfect on pasta and, for a change, you could serve it with white or brown rice or couscous. By using 1 kg fish of your choice, the seafood may be left out and a simple fish sauce can be made.

Serves 6 to 8

500 g	tagliatelle or pasta of your choice
	salted boiling water

Sauce

30 g	butter
30 ml (2 Tbs)	olive oil
1	bunch spring onions, sliced
2	cloves garlic, crushed
2	sticks celery, sliced
250 g	button mushrooms, sliced
45 ml (3 Tbs)	flour
2 x 410 g	tins tomatoes, with juice, chopped
5 ml (1 tsp)	dried origanum
	salt, pepper and sugar
250 ml (1 cup)	cream
125 ml (1/2 cup)	dry white wine
125 ml (1/2 cup)	freshly chopped parsley

Fish

	butter and olive oil for frying
250 g	calamari rings
250 g	kingklip, monkfish or crayfish
250 g	any other seafood (e.g. prawns, shrimps, scallops)
250 g	frozen mussels

- In a mixture of butter and oil, sauté the onion, garlic, celery and mushrooms until soft.
- Sprinkle on the flour.
- Add the chopped tomatoes with juice from the tin.
- Stir in the seasoning, cream and wine and simmer until thick, stirring continually to prevent it catching at the bottom.
- Check the seasoning and set aside.
- In a mixture of butter and oil, very gently sauté each type of fish individually and set aside. *Do not overcook.*
- Cook the pasta in plenty of salted water.
- Just before serving, bring the sauce just to simmering point and add all the fish.
- Heat through, but do not boil.
- Mix in the chopped parsley.
- Serve on the tagliatelle.

SPAGHETTI SICILIANA

This moulded pasta dish, covered with aubergine slices, looks very attractive on a serving dish.

Serves 4

3	large or 6 small aubergines
	oil for frying
250 ml (1 cup)	dry breadcrumbs
1	onion, chopped
2	cloves garlic, chopped
500 g	mince
30 g	butter
30 ml (2 Tbs)	olive oil
65 g	tinned tomato paste
125 ml (1/2 cup)	white wine
5 ml (1 tsp)	sugar
5 ml (1 tsp)	dried origanum
80 ml (1/3 cup)	freshly chopped parsley
	salt and pepper
250 ml (1 cup)	grated mozzarella or *Tussers* cheese
45 ml (3 Tbs)	grated parmesan cheese
250 g	frozen peas
250 g	spaghetti

- Preheat oven to 180 °C.
- Slice the aubergines into thin rings, dip them in flour and fry in shallow oil until well browned, or brush with oil and grill until soft and brown.
- Butter and crumb an ovenware dish or large pudding bowl.
- Line with the browned aubergine slices.
- Brown the mince well until crumbly, and then remove from pan.
- Sauté the onion and garlic in butter and oil.
- Add the mince, tomato paste, wine, sugar, origanum, parsley, peas and season to taste with salt and pepper. Cool slightly.
- Boil and drain the spaghetti.
- Stir the cheese into the mince and mix in the spaghetti.
- Spread the mixture into the bowl lined with aubergine slices.
- Press flat to make sure the bowl is completely filled.
- Bake, covered, at 180 °C for 45 minutes. Cool slightly.
- Turn out on a serving plate and slice as you would a cake.

HADDOCK AND SPINACH BAKE

A tasty, inexpensive one-pot meal.

Serves 4 to 6

250 g	elbow macaroni, cooked
375 ml (1 1/2 cups)	milk
500 g	frozen haddock
2-3	bunches fresh spinach, well washed, chopped and cooked in a little water
or 500 g	frozen spinach, thawed
50 g	butter
45 ml (3 Tbs)	flour
125 ml (1/2 cup)	grated mature cheddar cheese
	salt, pepper and nutmeg to taste

- Poach the haddock in the milk.
- Pour off the milk for use in the sauce.
- Flake haddock and carefully mix the fish and spinach into the cooked pasta.
- Make the cheese sauce by melting the butter and stirring in the flour.
- Add the milk and bring to the boil, stirring constantly.
- Remove the pot from the heat and stir in half the grated cheese.
- Pour the sauce over fish mixture, top with remaining cheese and bake at 180 °C for 30 to 45 minutes.

FISH LASAGNE

Serves 4 to 6

300 g	lasagne sheets (approximate)

Fish sauce

500 g	firm fish, poached and flaked
or 2 x 185 g	tins tuna
2	onions, chopped
2	cloves garlic, crushed
45 ml (3 Tbs)	olive oil
250 ml (1 cup)	tomato purée, or more depending on taste
80 ml (1/3 cup)	white wine
5 ml (1 tsp)	sugar
	salt and pepper
3 ml (1/2 tsp)	dried thyme
5 ml (1 tsp)	dried origanum
125 ml (1/2 cup)	freshly chopped parsley

Béchamel sauce

500 ml (2 cups)	milk, infused with
1	onion, sliced
4	bay leaves
12	peppercorns
50 g	butter
45 ml (3 Tbs)	flour
125 ml (1/2 cup)	grated cheddar cheese
2	eggs, separated
30 ml (2 Tbs)	grated parmesan cheese

- *To make the fish sauce,* sauté the onion in butter till glassy.
- Add the flaked fish and all the remaining ingredients.
- Simmer for about 5 minutes. Do not overcook.
- *For the béchamel sauce,* infuse by heating the milk in a pot with the onion, bay leaf and the peppercorns. Leave to cool.
- Melt the butter in a small pot and stir in the flour.
- Strain the milk into this pot and bring to the boil, stirring continually.
- Remove from the heat and stir in the cheddar cheese.
- Pour the sauce onto the egg yolks and mix well.
- *Very important:* Do not return it to the stove.
- If you are using uncooked lasagne, place 2 to 3 sheets at a time in a pot of salted boiling water. Once they are soft, remove them from the boiling water, dip them into cold water and then drain on a clean cloth.
- If you are using the precooked lasagne sheets, no further cooking is needed. Simply layer with the two sauces. The dry lasagne absorbs a lot of liquid, so make sure the fish sauce is very runny.
- To assemble the lasagne, layer the fish sauce, béchamel sauce and lasagne. Start with lasagne, then half the fish and half the béchamel. Repeat, ending with béchamel.
- Sprinkle on the parmesan cheese or extra cheddar, if you prefer.
- Bake for 40 minutes in oven preheated to 180 °C.

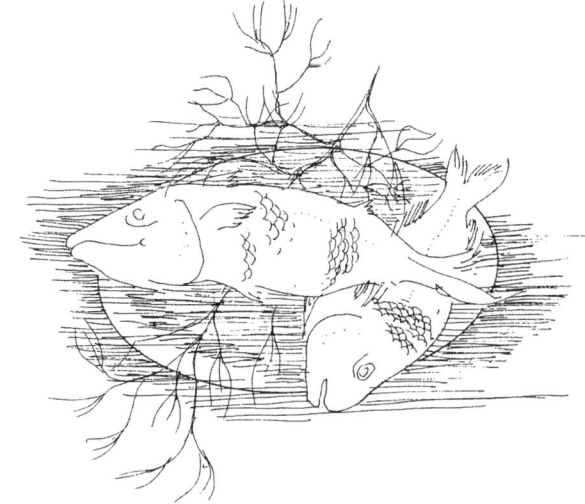

TUNA CANNELONI

If canneloni are not available, use lasagne sheets or even crêpes (see *Starters*). Serve as a main meal or as a starter.

Serves 4 to 6

1/2 x 500 g	box canneloni
	or *prepare 1 quantity basic crêpes*
250 ml (1 cup)	grated cheese (sweetmilk and cheddar mixed, or mozzarella)

Tuna filling

2 x 185 g	tins tuna, flaked
1	large onion, chopped
2	sticks celery with leaves, chopped
30 g	butter
250 g	frozen spinach
or 1-2 bunches	fresh spinach, blanched and chopped
250 g	mushrooms, chopped (brown or button)
125 ml (1/2 cup)	cream
5 ml (1 tsp)	dried origanum
80 ml (1/3 cup)	white wine
	salt and pepper

Tomato sauce

2	large onions, chopped
30 ml (2 Tbs)	olive oil
2 x 410 g	tins tomatoes, chopped
2	cloves garlic, chopped
	salt and pepper
5 ml (1 tsp)	dried origanum
5 ml	sugar (1 tsp)
30 ml (2 Tbs)	tomato paste
125 ml (1/2 cup)	cream
60 ml (1/4 cup)	chopped, fresh basil

Béchamel sauce
(See recipe for Fish lasagne)

- *For the tuna filling*, sauté the onion and celery in butter.
- Add the flaked tuna, spinach and mushrooms.
- Add all the remaining ingredients.
- Simmer for 15 minutes. Leave to cool.
- *For the tomato sauce*, sauté the onion in oil until glassy.
- Add chopped tomatoes, garlic and seasoning.
- Simmer for 15 minutes, stir in chopped basil, then leave to cool.
- *To make up*, place 3/4 of the tomato sauce in the bottom of a square ovenware dish.
- Fill each crêpe with tuna filling and roll up, or pipe into canneloni tubes.
- Place side by side on top of the tomato sauce and pour on remaining tomato sauce.
- Pour on the béchamel sauce and top with grated cheese.
- Bake in oven preheated to 180 °C for about 45 to 60 minutes.

Hint
Instead of the first 4 ingredients of the tomato sauce, use 2 x 410 g tins of tomato & onion mix, and add 5 ml origanum.

COLD PASTA SAUCES

ARRABIATA

Parsley, chilli and garlic sauce
This is the simplest sauce for pasta. It allows the full pasta flavour and texture to come through. Serve it as a starter before a braai or any meaty meal.

Serves 4 as a starter

250 g	spaghettini, fettuccini or *tagliarini* or *pasta of your choice*

Sauce

3	cloves garlic
1-2	chillies, chopped
45 ml (3 Tbs)	olive oil
80 ml (1/3 cup)	fresh parsley, finely chopped
	salt and pepper to taste
45 ml (3 Tbs)	parmesan cheese

- Sauté the garlic and chilli lightly in oil.
- Stir in the parsley, salt and pepper.
- Toss into cooked pasta with parmesan and serve immediately.

PESTO SAUCE

There is nothing like the flavour of fresh sweet basil and toasted pine kernels with garlic and olive oil!

Serves 4 as a starter

300 g	tagliarini, spaghettini or spaghelli or pasta of your choice

Sauce

3	large sprigs fresh basil
30 g	pinenuts
30 ml (2 Tbs)	olive oil
2	cloves garlic
60 ml (1/4 cup)	olive oil
45 ml (3 Tbs)	parmesan, pecorino or rigatello cheese

- Sauté pinenuts in a little olive oil until just golden.
- Place sweet basil, pinenuts and garlic in a food processor.
- Process, gradually adding remaining oil to form a mayonnaise type of consistency.
- Add salt and pepper and parmesan cheese.
- Cook pasta and serve with pesto sauce and extra cheese.

Variation
For something different and delicious, serve the sauce on grilled fish.

BASIC POTATO GNOCCHI

Gnocchi are not pasta, but rather little Italian potato dumplings that can be served with any of the pasta sauces. They make wonderful starter dishes or light main courses. Baking the potatoes means that very little flour is needed, resulting in light gnocchi with a strong potato flavour.

Serves 4 to 6

1 kg	potatoes (approximately 6 medium)
5 ml (1 tsp)	salt
2	egg yolks
1 ml (1/4 tsp)	dry mustard
1 ml (1/4 tsp)	grated nutmeg
185 ml (3/4 cup)	flour
5 ml (1 tsp)	baking powder
60 ml (1/4 cup)	cornflour

To serve
chopped sweet basil or crispy fried sage
grated parmesan cheese

- Prick the potatoes well with a fork and bake in their jackets at 180 °C for 1 1/2 to 2 hours or until very soft on the inside and dry on the outside.
- Peel and mash the potatoes while they are still hot then leave to cool for 10 minutes.
- Add the remaining ingredients, mix well and turn out onto a floured surface.
- Knead lightly until the mixture is soft but pliable. You may need extra flour if the potatoes are too wet.
- Roll the mixture into ropes as thick as the handle of a wooden spoon. Cut into 2 cm pieces, press with a fork to give a decorative pattern and lay out separately on a floured surface.
- Simmer the dumplings in a pot of lightly salted water only until they rise to the top (about 3 minutes).
- Serve with any sauce of your choice or simply with olive oil or melted butter.
- Sprinkle on sweet basil or crispy sage and plenty of Parmesan cheese.

Hint
For crispy sage, fry leaves in a little olive oil until crispy. Drain on absorbent paper.

SPINACH GNOCCHI

Follow the basic gnocchi recipe, but with these variations:

250 g	frozen spinach or 1 bunch of fresh spinach

- Thaw and drain frozen spinach very well, or steam and chop fresh spinach.
- Use only 1 egg yolk and add the spinach.
- Use extra flour and cornflour to absorb the moisture in the spinach.

VEGETABLE SIDE DISHES

When choosing vegetables for a meal make sure you have a variety of colour, texture and vegetable types – don't serve cabbage with Brussels sprouts or cauliflower, or butternut with gem squash and baby marrows. For the rest, I don't believe in rules that decide which vegetable should be served with what meat.

Secrets for serving vegetables
- Use fresh vegetables that are in season whenever possible. If you are going to use frozen vegetables, serve a fresh vegetable as well.
- Never overcook vegetables. They should be firm and tasty.
- Vary your cooking methods by baking, stir-frying, steaming or quick-boiling the vegetables.
- Use simple sauces to enhance the flavour of the vegetables.

The conservative method of quick-boiling is to cook the vegetables in a little vigorously boiling water in a covered pot, until the vegetables are cooked but still firm. This will retain most of the nutrients.

Other ways of moist-cooking are cooking in the microwave, using minimal amounts of water in 'waterless' pots, using a cooking bag, or steaming over boiling water.

Try the following vegetables with sauces (see under *Sauces*):
- carrots in orange sauce or a plain béchamel sauce with lots of chopped parsley
- green beans with a mushroom or lemon sauce
- beetroot with an orange or a béchamel sauce
- boiled baby onions or leeks in a light cheese sauce
- cauliflower and broccoli in a cheese sauce
- brussels sprouts with lemon sauce.

Stir-frying
There are different ways of stir-frying, depending on how much heat you have, what kind of pan you use and the type and size of the vegetables.

This is a basic stir-fry using a large variety of vegetables all cut into thin strips (julienne strips):

- Any combination of vegetables may be used (e.g. cabbage, broccoli, cauliflower, carrots, celery, cucumber, onion, bean sprouts, green beans, mushrooms, frozen peas, baby marrows (courgettes), tinned bamboo shoots, tinned water chestnuts).
- Use a wok or a large, shallow frying pan.
- Cut up the vegetables, keeping different types of vegetables separately. Keep them in piles according to their texture and how fast they will cook, because you have to begin with those that will take longest and end with those that cook very quickly.

Onion, carrot and celery can be stir-fried together.

Broccoli, cauliflower, green beans can be stir-fried together.

Shredded cabbage and spinach will cook very quickly. Mushrooms and baby marrows will also cook very quickly.

- Using very little oil in the wok or pan, heat it until it is smoking. Stir-fry vegetables in batches, frying the different types separately. Fry small quantities at a time to ensure the smallest possible drop in temperature. Working over a high heat and stirring constantly, cook the vegetables until they are just hot but still raw. Remove each batch from the pan before stir-frying the next. Season with salt and a sprinkling of sugar. (In Chinese cooking a little bit of sugar is always used to balance the salt. It gives the vegetables an authentic oriental flavour.)
- Once all the vegetables have been stir-fried, return them all to the wok or pan.
- Mix 15 to 30 ml (1 to 2 Tbs) soy sauce with 5 ml (1 tsp) cornflour and 45 ml (3 Tbs) water and stir this into the vegetables.
- Cook for 1 minute, stirring all the time, until the sauce has coated the vegetables and all the vegetables are hot but still raw and crunchy.
- Serve immediately.

Hint

If you are in a hurry and want a low-oil version, this method is almost as good. Mix all your vegetables together and pour a kettle of boiling water over them. Drain very well. Stir-fry the mixture in a little oil.

CHUNKY VEGETABLE STIR-FRY

If you are going to stir-fry large pieces of vegetables, always blanch them in boiling water before frying them. You then need much less oil and the stir-frying goes much quicker.

Serves 8

250 g	baby green beans
250 g	baby corn
300 g	broccoli
	oil for stir-frying
5 ml (1 tsp)	cornflour
30 ml (2 Tbs)	soy sauce
45 ml (3 Tbs)	water
3 ml ($^1/_2$ tsp)	salt
3 ml ($^1/_2$ tsp)	sugar

- Top and tail the beans.
- Cut the corn crosswise in half.
- Cut the broccoli into large florets.
- Blanch all the vegetables in batches in boiling water for 1 minute, then drain and cool.
- Mix cornflour, soy sauce and water.
- Heat a little oil in a wok or large frying pan until it smokes and stir-fry the vegetables quickly over high heat.
- Season with salt and sugar and pour on the cornflour mixture. Simmer for $^1/_2$ minute.
- Serve immediately.

JAMS CALIFORNIAN VEGETABLES

'Jams' is the name of the Californian restaurant where this recipe originated, but I was introduced to it at Leith's in London. Since then, it has become my favourite vegetable side dish.

Combining the Eastern method of stir-frying with the Western flavours of butter, black pepper and garlic, these vegetables are simply delicious. Use a mixture of vegetables, and this will be the only vegetable dish you need at a meal.

Combine any vegetables in season, such as:

small new potatoes
baby carrots or carrots, peeled and cut into diagonal chunks
red and yellow sweet peppers, cut into thick strips
baby corn on the cob
button turnips, or larger turnips, cut into thick strips
baby beans or mange tout, topped and tailed
cucumber, seeded and cut into strips
courgettes, cut into diagonal chunks
radishes
broccoli and cauliflower florets

> *butter, olive oil* or *oil*
> *salt and freshly ground black pepper*
> 1-2 *cloves garlic, crushed*

- Wash all the vegetables before cutting them.
- Boil the potatoes in water until they are soft, and the carrots until just tender. Drain.
- Blanch the rest of the vegetables, in batches, in boiling water for 1 minute. Drain. (This can be done well in advance.)
- Melt the butter in a large frying pan or wok.
- Heat the wok or pan on high until the butter just starts to bubble.

- Add the pepper and garlic and toss all the vegetables in the mixture until lightly glazed and hot through.
- Pile vegetables on a warmed serving dish and serve immediately. The vegetables will never be piping hot – to get them very hot, you must overcook them!

VEGETABLES WITH SAUCE AIOLI

I was introduced to this recipe by a friend many years ago. I don't remember what else we ate, but these vegetables have become a firm favourite. Try them at your next braai.

- Prepare and blanch an assortment of vegetables in the same way as for Jams Californian vegetables.
- Pile the blanched vegetables onto a plate. (If you use a microwave oven, make sure the plate will fit in.) Cover with clingwrap for the microwave, or with aluminium foil for the oven.
- Prepare a big bowl of the potato and garlic sauce aioli (see *Sauces*).
- About 15 or 20 minutes before serving, heat the vegetables in the oven preheated to 200 °C, or for 5 minutes in the microwave on high. The vegetables will be warm and crunchy.
- Place the platter of vegetables and the sauce on the table and let them help themselves. I promise there will be none left over!

HOT RAW BEETROOT

Stir-fried and seasoned with lemon juice and garlic, the beetroot is crisp, with a sweet and sour flavour. Use young beetroots and avoid the large woody ones.

Serves 4

1	bunch small beetroots
60 g	butter
2	cloves garlic, crushed
	fresh lemon juice to taste
	salt and fresh black pepper

- Peel and coarsely grate the beetroot.
- Melt the butter in a large frying pan.
- Over medium heat, toss the beetroot and garlic in the butter for about 2 minutes until hot but not cooked.
- Season with lemon juice, salt and pepper to taste.

Variation
Try this recipe with coarsely grated baby marrows instead of the beetroot, but cook for only 1 minute.

BABY BEANS WITH RED PEPPER

An interesting mix for a stir-fry.

Serves 6 to 8

500 g	baby green beans
1	onion
50 g	butter
2	red peppers
	salt and pepper

- Thinly slice the onion, working root to shoot. This will give you strips instead of rings.
- Slice the red peppers into strips.
- Fry onion and fresh red pepper strips in the butter until onion is glassy.
- Cook the beans until just tender and add to the onion and red pepper mix.
- Season to taste.

GREEN BEANS, CARROTS AND SALAMI

A colourful and tasty stir-fry.

Serves 6 to 8

300 g	baby green beans
6	carrots, sliced into julienne strips
125 g	salami, in 1 piece
2	cloves garlic, crushed
1	small onion
30 ml (2 Tbs)	olive oil

- Boil the beans and carrot strips, separately, in a little water until cooked but still firm. Drain.
- Slice the onion into strips from root to shoot.
- Cut the salami into thin julienne strips.
- Fry the onion and garlic in oil.
- Add the beans and carrot strips, together with the salami strips, and stir-fry until hot through.

EAST INDIAN PEAS AND RED CABBAGE

When served, the colours of this dish are as exciting as the unusual ginger and cumin flavour.

Serves 4

250 g	frozen peas
	small piece of fresh ginger, grated
2	cloves garlic, crushed
45 ml (3 Tbs)	oil
5 ml (1 tsp)	ground cumin
$1/2$	small red cabbage, shredded
	pinch of cayenne pepper
	salt and pepper to taste
45 ml (3 Tbs)	boiling water

- Place the peas in a strainer and rinse them under cold water to melt the ice.
- In a frying pan over a high heat, quickly fry the ginger and garlic.
- Add the cumin, cayenne pepper and seasoning to taste.
- Stir-fry the cabbage and peas.
- Add boiling water and boil for 3 minutes, uncovered, until the water has evaporated.
- Serve immediately.

JULIENNE CARROTS AND TURNIPS

Even those who do not like turnips love this recipe.

Serves 4

6	carrots
2-3	turnips
	juice of 1 orange
3 ml ($1/2$ tsp)	cornflour
15 ml (1 Tbs)	syrup
15 g	butter
	salt and pepper

- Cut the carrots and turnips in julienne strips.
- Simmer the carrots and turnips in a little water until almost tender. Remove the lid and boil off the water.
- Mix the orange juice with cornflour and add, with the syrup and butter, to the vegetables.
- Boil vigorously, uncovered, to evaporate most of the orange juice. The vegetables should be coated in the thick orange sauce.
- Season to taste with salt and pepper and make sure the vegetables are coated in the sauce.

CABBAGE AND TOMATO CASSEROLE

This vegetable dish (without the caraway) reminds me of my childhood in Johannesburg when I used to eat it with *stywe pap*. The cabbage also had a touch of chilli, which you can add if you like it hot!

Serves 4 to 6

2	ripe tomatoes, skinned and chopped
45 ml (3 Tbs)	oil
$1/4$-$1/2$	cabbage, thinly shredded
	salt and black pepper
5 ml (1 tsp)	caraway seeds (optional)
	chilli powder (optional)

- Sauté the tomato in oil until pulpy.
- Add the cabbage and season to taste. Add the caraway seeds.
- Cook, covered, over low heat until the cabbage is cooked.

BROCCOLI ROMAN STYLE

The red wine gives the broccoli an unusual flavour. The olive oil and garlic round it off beautifully.

Serves 4 to 6

500 g	broccoli
45 ml (3 Tbs)	olive oil
2	large cloves garlic, sliced
	salt and pepper
250 ml (1 cup)	dry red wine

- Trim the broccoli and cut into medium-sized florets. Wash well and drain.
- Heat the olive oil in a saucepan and lightly brown the garlic.
- Add the broccoli, salt and pepper to taste and cook for about 5 minutes.
- Add the red wine, cover and simmer over a low heat for about 12 to 15 minutes, or until broccoli is cooked but still firm. Stir the broccoli occasionally but be careful not to break the florets.

VEGETABLE POTJIE

A tasty mix, casseroled in the oven, or over the coals in a potjie. You can add any other vegetables of your choice. Add a few sausages or tinned butterbeans to make this a filling, nutritious main meal. Bear in mind that this dish is layered and that you have to add garlic and seasoning to each layer as you go.

Serves 6 to 8

3	soft gem squash, with skin, cut into quarters
12	baby potatoes, washed
1-2	sweet potatoes, peeled and cut into chunks
2	aubergines, cut in thick pieces
3	carrots, cut in large pieces
12	baby onions, peeled
1	butternut, with skin, cut into thick slices
6	brown mushrooms, halved
	any other vegetables of your choice
12	cloves garlic, unpeeled
	salt and pepper
30 g	melted butter
30 ml (2 Tbs)	olive oil

- Preheat oven to 160 °C.
- Layer the vegetables in a potjie or ovenware dish with the longest cooking vegetables on the bottom – first the gem squash, then the potatoes, sweet potatoes, carrots and butternut and ending with the mushrooms and aubergines.
- Add garlic and seasoning to taste to each layer.
- Mix the oil and butter and pour over the vegetables.
- Cook slowly for about 3 hours in the oven at 160 °C or for 2 hours in a potjie over the coals.

MEDITERRANEAN BRAAIED VEGETABLES

This recipe will change an ordinary braai into a gourmet feast. Cook the vegetables before the meat while the fire is still very hot. Make the marinade 6 hours before cooking to allow vegetables to lie in it.

Serves 4 to 6

1 kg	vegetables of your choice (e.g. mushrooms, onions, aubergines, coloured peppers, baby marrows, butternut, queen squash)

Marinade

125 ml ($^1/_2$ cup)	olive oil
45 ml (3 Tbs)	lemon juice
125 ml ($^1/_2$ cup)	semi-sweet white wine
3	cloves garlic, crushed
3 ml ($^1/_2$ tsp)	salt
5 ml (1 tsp)	black pepper
3 ml ($^1/_2$ tsp)	cumin

- Mix all the marinade ingredients and pour it into a plastic bag.
- Leave the mushrooms whole and peel the onions.
- Slice the remaining vegetables in thick slices, skin on.
- Marinate the vegetables for about 6 hours, but remove the mushrooms after 3 hours.
- Braai the vegetables over fairly hot coals for 10 to 15 minutes until brown and almost soft, but still fairly firm.
- Alternatively, preheat oven to 240 °C, then change the setting to grill. When the element is red-hot, place the vegetables on a baking tray one rack down from the top. Brown the vegetables on both sides.

Variation

Cut the vegetables into chunks and place on skewers to make vegetable kebabs.

BUTTERNUT IN SOUR CREAM

In all butternut recipes you can substitute pumpkin. Choose whichever is in season and the sweetest – the colour should be deep orange.

Serves 4 to 6

2	small butternuts, peeled and cubed
125 ml (½ cup)	flour
250 ml (1 cup)	sour cream
45 ml (3 Tbs)	olive oil
1	clove garlic, chopped
45 ml (3 Tbs)	freshly chopped parsley
	salt and pepper

- Preheat oven to 180 °C.
- Toss the butternut chunks in flour and place in an ovenware dish.
- Mix the sour cream, olive oil, garlic, parsley and seasoning to taste and pour over the butternut.
- Bake, covered, for 30 minutes.
- Remove lid and bake for another 30 minutes.

Variation
If you prefer, use butter instead of the olive oil and flavour the butternut to taste with cinnamon, nutmeg or a pinch of cumin.

LENTILS IN MILD CURRY SAUCE

Something different to serve at a braai, or with steak or a roast.

Serves 4

500 ml (2 cups)	cooked black lentils
2	onions, sliced
50 g	butter
5 ml (1 tsp)	cumin
5 ml (1 tsp)	curry powder
15 ml (1 Tbs)	lemon juice
15 ml (1 Tbs)	chutney
250 ml (½ cup)	our cream
	or *cooked yoghurt (see* Sauces*)*

- Sauté the onion in butter until glassy.
- Add sour cream or yoghurt, cumin, curry, lemon juice and chutney and bring to the boil.
- Add lentils and simmer for 5 minutes.

AUBERGINES IN TOMATO

Served hot or cold, aubergines cooked this way are equally delicious. Have the hot tomato sauce ready by the time the aubergine slices are cooked.

Serves 4 to 6

4	small or *2 large aubergines*
	seasoned flour
1-2	eggs, beaten
2 ml (½ tsp)	salt
	oil for frying

Tomato sauce

1	large onion, thinly sliced
45 ml (3 Tbs)	olive oil
2	ripe tomatoes, skinned and sliced
or ½ tin (205 g)	tomatoes
2	cloves garlic, crushed
	herbs of your choice (origanum, basil or *marjoram to taste*)
	salt and pepper
	pinch of sugar

- *For the tomato sauce,* fry the onion in oil until glassy.
- Add the tomatoes, garlic, herbs and seasoning to taste.
- Simmer until tomato is cooked.
- Meanwhile, thickly slice the aubergines, leaving the skin on.
- Beat the egg and salt together.
- Dip each slice into seasoned flour and then into beaten egg.
- Fry in shallow oil until golden brown.
- Drain on absorbent paper and place on a shallow serving dish.
- Pour hot tomato sauce over the aubergine slices and serve.

Variation
Pour your favourite salad dressing over the cold fried aubergines and leave to marinate for 1 hour before serving as a salad.

BAKED BUTTERNUT OR PUMPKIN

Very South African, this sticky, sweet pumpkin is always a winner.

Serves 4

500 g	pumpkin or butternut, peeled and cut in large chunks
50 g	butter
45 ml (3 Tbs)	syrup
2	sticks cinnamon

▸ Preheat oven to 180 °C.
▸ Place the pumpkin or butternut in a casserole with the cinnamon.
▸ Melt the butter and syrup together and pour over the pumpkin.
▸ Bake, covered, 45 to 60 minutes.
▸ For the last 10 minutes, remove the lid to let the liquid evaporate. The pumpkin or butternut chunks will be soft and sticky.

SAVOURY SWEET POTATO

Sweet potato cooked this way is very rich, but irresistible.

Serves 6

2-3	large sweet potatoes
250 ml (1 cup)	grated cheddar cheese
250 ml (1 cup)	sour or fresh cream

▸ Preheat oven to 180 °C.
▸ Peel the sweet potatoes and boil until soft.
▸ Mash *without* adding any butter or milk.
▸ Transfer to a casserole.
▸ Sprinkle on the cheese.
▸ Spread the cream or sour cream over the cheese.
▸ Bake for about 1 hour or until the topping has set.

ROAST RATATOUILLE

By roasting instead of frying the vegetables, the individual taste of each is retained and it is less oily.

Serves 8

	olive oil
2	large aubergines, unpeeled and cubed
250 g	button mushrooms, halved
4-6	baby marrows, cubed
2	onions, diced
2	green or red peppers, diced
4	large ripe tomatoes, skinned, pipped and chopped
2	cloves garlic, chopped
15 ml (1 Tbs)	fresh basil or fresh origanum
or 5 ml (1 tsp)	dried basil or origanum
	salt and freshly ground black pepper

▸ Lightly coat the aubergine cubes, mushrooms and baby marrow in olive oil.
▸ Preheat the oven to 240 °C, then change setting to grill.
▸ Grill the aubergines, which take longer, and then the mushrooms and baby marrows, close to the element until well browned and just soft.
▸ In a pan, fry the onions and peppers in a little hot oil over high heat until just beginning to brown.
▸ Add the tomatoes, reduce the heat and cook until the tomato is soft.
▸ Add the grilled vegetables, garlic and seasoning to taste and heat through.
▸ *Do not overcook.*

IMAM BAYILDI

The priest fainted

This traditional dish of fried, baked aubergines, stuffed with tomato and onion is found all over Turkey. Serve as a starter at room temperature, or hot with a roast, grill or braai.

Serves 8

8	very small or 6 medium aubergines
80 ml (1/3 cup)	olive oil
2	large onions, thinly sliced

```
             4-6  large ripe tomatoes, skinned,
                    seeded and coarsely chopped
    15 ml (1 Tbs)  tomato paste
   125 ml (½ cup)  parsley, chopped
               4  cloves garlic, crushed
     5 ml (1 tsp)  sugar
                  salt and black pepper to taste
```

- Preheat oven to 160 °C.
- Leave the aubergines whole, but remove the leaves (calyx) at the end.
- Fry in olive oil until they are shiny, soft and browned all over. Remove from the pan.
- In the remaining oil, fry the onions very well until they are completely soft and beginning to brown.
- Add the tomatoes and tomato paste and cook until pulpy.
- Add the parsley and garlic with the sugar, and season to taste with salt and pepper.
- Slit aubergines along the length (but not through the ends) to form a large pocket. Compress the flesh with your finger to make room for the filling.
- Stuff very full with the tomato mixture.
- Place in an ovenware dish and bake for about 40 minutes.
- Serve with thick yoghurt (see *Sauces*).

FRITTERS

Fritters are made from a fruit or vegetable coated with, or mixed into, a batter. Serve as a starter with a sauce, or as part of the meal. Make them just before eating, otherwise they become oily. For potato fritters, see under *Potatoes*.

BUTTERNUT OR PUMPKIN FRITTERS

Traditional pumpkin fritters (*pampoenkoekies*) are usually very stodgy and oily, because boiled pumpkin needs lots of flour to bind it. I now make my fritters with raw pumpkin and they are soft, not so oily and have a strong pumpkin flavour.

Makes about 12 fritters

```
    500 ml (2 cups)  grated butternut or pumpkin
     125 ml (½ cup)  flour
       5 ml (1 tsp)  baking powder
       3 ml (½ tsp)  salt
       5 ml (1 tsp)  sugar
              1 ml  ground cinnamon
                 1  egg, beaten
     60 ml (4 Tbs)  milk (approximate)
                   cinnamon sugar to serve
```

- Finely grate the butternut or pumpkin.
- Mix the grated butternut and the dry ingredients in a bowl.
- Mix the beaten egg with the milk and add to the butternut mixture, adding a little extra milk if necessary.
- Mix well and fry spoonfuls slowly in a little oil over medium heat. The raw butternut/pumpkin will take a while to cook.
- When soft and brown on both sides, drain on absorbent paper and sprinkle liberally with a mixture of castor sugar and cinnamon.

GRUYERE CORN FRITTERS

Made with mealies and Gruyere cheese, these fritters are an exciting snack or addition to a meal.

Makes about 12 fritters

```
    125 ml (½ cup)  flour
       5 ml (1 tsp)  baking powder
       2 ml (½ tsp)  salt
                 1  egg, beaten in
    125 ml (½ cup)  milk
     80 ml (⅓ cup)  Gruyere
                    or mature cheddar cheese, grated
     80 ml (⅓ cup)  chopped chives
                    or spring onions
    500 ml (2 cups) cooked, fresh or blanched, frozen
                    mealie kernels
                 8  rashers rindless bacon, grilled and
                    diced (optional)
                    oil for frying fritters
```

- Mix the flour, baking powder, salt, beaten egg and milk to form a batter.
- Mix in the cheese, onions and mealie kernels (and bacon).
- Drop spoonfuls into a pan with a little hot oil and fry over a medium heat until golden on both sides.
- Drain on absorbent paper.

MARMARIS TURKISH FRITTERS

These delicious fritters from the Mediterranean coast are given a slight kick by the chilli. Serve them with yoghurt or sour cream.

Makes 12 to 16 fritters

2	medium potatoes
500 g	baby marrows
1	onion
1	chopped chilli, or *to taste*
60 ml ($^1/_4$ cup)	flour
5 ml (1 tsp)	baking powder
1	egg
	salt and pepper
	oil for frying

- Peel and coarsely grate the potatoes, baby marrows and onion.
- Salt the baby marrows and leave to drain.
- Drain the potato and dry well.
- Rinse the salt off the baby marrows and dry them on paper or in a dish cloth.
- Mix all the ingredients, adding extra flour if the mixture is too wet.
- Fry spoonfuls in oil over medium heat until well browned on both sides.
- Drain on absorbent paper.
- Place browned fritters on a baking sheet and bake in the oven at 180 °C for 15 minutes or until crisp and dry. Leave to cool.
- Serve at room temperature.

POTATOES

> The 3 main varieties of potatoes available are:
> BP1: The most commom all purpose potato
> Vanderplank: Best for chips and roast potatoes
> Up-to-Date: Best for mashing and baking

BAKED POTATOES

To get a crisp, chewy skin and a fluffy inside:

- Preheat oven to 200 °C.
- Prick potatoes in a few places to prevent them bursting.
- Bake potatoes as they are, or rub very lightly with oil and sprinkle with coarse salt.
- Bake for 1 hour. Don't remove baked potatoes from the oven until you are ready to eat. The skin loses its crispness very quickly.

ROAST POTATOES

I use one of three ways to roast potatoes, depending on my mood! However, I never roast meat in fat, so the potatoes have to be done separately.

Method 1
This method is the easiest of the three, but the potatoes end up a little leathery.

- Preheat oven to 180 °C.
- Peel the potatoes and cut them in half.
- Place in an ovenware dish big enough so the potato halves are not crowded.
- Add enough oil to cover approximately the bottom third of each potato half.
- Turn the potatoes to coat them in oil.
- Roast for the last 1 hour of the meat's roasting time.
- Remove the meat and the potatoes from the oven and turn the oven temperature up to 220 °C.
- Pour off all the oil from the potatoes (you can keep it and use it several times).
- Return the potatoes to the oven for 10 to 15 minutes or until very brown and crisp.
- Drain on roller towel.

Method 2
- Peel the potatoes and cut them in half.
- Simmer *gently* in water until the potatoes are soft.
- Drain and leave to cool.
- Roast the potatoes as in Method 1, but they need only 45 minutes in the oven at 180 °C before you pour off the oil and crisp them at 220 °C.

Hint
When you boil potatoes, do not let the water boil vigorously. If you do, the outside will cook before the centre is done, and the action of the boiling water makes the potato fall apart. Always simmer them very slowly.

Method 3
This is my favourite method but it requires constant attention.

- Prepare and boil the potatoes as in Method 2.
- Use a large, deep frying pan, big enough not to crowd the potatoes.

- Add 3 cm of oil into the pan and heat until you can feel the heat coming off the oil when you hold your hand just above it. *The oil must not be too hot.*
- Place the potatoes in the oil and cook over medium heat for about 30 minutes, turning them periodically to brown them on all sides.
- When you are ready to eat, turn up the heat and quickly crisp the potatoes. They become fluffy, with a lovely crisp outside.
- Drain them on absorbent kitchen paper.

Variations

- *Roast potatoes in their jackets* Choose large baby potatoes in their jackets. Cut in half and follow Method 3. The result is a crispy potato with a crisp, chewy skin. They are quite delicious!
- For something special, fry some chopped onion in a little butter or schmaltz until just beginning to brown. Toss this into the roasted potatoes with salt, black pepper and plenty of chopped parsley.

TWICE-FRIED POTATO CHIPS

By twice frying your chips, you can be certain of having them ready exactly when you want them. They will also stay crisp longer.

If you are cooking a large quantity of chips in a large, deep pot on a domestic stove there is not enough heat to crisp the chips before they become mushy and disintegrate. The twice-frying method avoids this problem.

- Peel the potatoes, cut into chips, and dry the potato chips well with a cloth or in a salad spinner.
- Place the chips in hot oil. The more chips you are cooking, the hotter the stove plate must be to maintain the correct oil temperature. For fewer chips, cook over a medium heat.
- Fry until the chips are just starting to brown. This should take about 15 minutes, depending on the thickness of the chips.
- Remove from the oil and drain on absorbent paper spread out on a tray. After a few minutes, remove the paper but leave the chips on the tray until you are almost ready to eat.
- Three minutes before serving, heat the oil until it is very hot. Return the chips to the oil in batches, to crisp up. This takes only a couple of minutes, so don't turn your back on them!
- Drain on absorbent paper and serve immediately.

LATKES

Potato fritters

A traditional favourite in Jewish homes.

Makes about 12

750 g	potatoes (about 6 medium)
1	small onion, grated
45 ml (3 Tbs)	flour
5 ml (1 tsp)	baking powder
5 ml (1 tsp)	sugar
3 ml ($\frac{1}{2}$ tsp)	salt
3 ml ($\frac{1}{2}$ tsp)	white pepper
1	egg, lightly beaten
	oil for frying

- Peel and coarsely grate the potatoes and leave them in a bowl of water to prevent discolouring until you are ready to fry the fritters.
- Drain off the excess water *very well.* Use a lettuce drier or place the grated potato in a clean dish cloth and squeeze out all the water. This ensures that the fritters will be very crisp.
- Mix all the ingredients into the grated potato, and drop spoonfuls into hot, shallow oil, flattening out the fritters.
- Do not crowd the pan, and fry over medium to high heat.
- Fry until you can see fritters beginning to brown underneath before turning them. Fry until both sides are well browned. If you turn them too soon, they will break.
- Drain on absorbent paper and put into a hot oven to crisp.

Hint
Serve with sour cream and apple sauce or guacamole.

BRABANT POTATOES

These Cajun or Creole roast potatoes are spicy and delicious. Serve them at your next braai or instead of roast potatoes or chips.

Serves 4

500 g	potatoes, scrubbed but not peeled
	salt
1 ml ($^1/_4$ tsp)	white pepper
3 ml ($^1/_2$ tsp)	onion salt
3 ml ($^1/_2$ tsp)	garlic salt
3 ml ($^1/_2$ tsp)	black pepper
3 ml ($^1/_2$ tsp)	cumin
1 ml ($^1/_4$ tsp)	cayenne pepper
125 ml ($^1/_2$ cup)	oil

- Preheat oven to 180 °C.
- Cut the potatoes into 3 cm cubes.
- Simmer them in salted water for about 5 minutes until just tender.
- Drain immediately and rinse in cold water.
- Combine onion and garlic salt and all the spices.
- Sprinkle evenly over the cooked potatoes. Be careful not to break up the potatoes pieces.
- Toss potatoes in oil in a shallow pan.
- Roast, uncovered, for about 30 minutes or until crisp.
- Drain and serve.

DAUPHINOIS POTATOES

This baked potato dish cooks for a long time in the oven, but once it is in, you can forget about it. And once you have tasted it, the cooking time won't worry you!

Serves 4 to 6

750 g	potatoes, peeled and very thinly sliced
2	large onions, thinly sliced
1	clove garlic, crushed
15 g	butter
125 ml ($^1/_2$ cup)	cream
125 ml ($^1/_2$ cup)	sour cream
	salt and pepper

- Sauté the onion and garlic in butter until glassy.
- Mix the cream and sour cream and toss the potatoes in this mixture.
- Layer the potato mixture and onion mixture in a casserole.
- Baked, covered, at 160 °C for 1 $^1/_2$ to 2 hours until the potatoes are cooked through.
- Remove the lid and turn oven up to 200 °C. Bake until potato is brown on top.

Hint
For lovers of blue cheese, liquidise 100 g blue cheese with the cream before pouring it over the potatoes.

QUICK DAUPHINOIS POTATOES

This is a less rich recipe with considerably fewer calories. If you like, top with grated Parmesan cheese before browning the potato dish in the oven.

Serves 4 to 6

750 g	potatoes (4-6 medium potatoes)
500 ml (2 cups)	full-cream or 2% milk
	salt and pepper to taste
1	large onion, sliced
15 ml (1 Tbs)	oil or butter
2	cloves garlic
	grated parmesan cheese (optional)

- Preheat oven to 180 °C.
- Wash but do not peel the potatoes.
- Cut potatoes into fairly thin slices and place in a pot with the milk and salt and pepper to taste.
- Simmer, uncovered, for about 10 minutes until the liquid has reduced and the potatoes are almost soft.
- Meanwhile, sauté the onions in a little oil or butter until soft and beginning to colour.
- Add the crushed garlic and carefully fold onion mixture into the potatoes.
- Transfer potatoes to an ovenware dish and bake for 30 to 45 minutes until potatoes are browning on top.
- Sprinkle a little parmesan on top before baking, if desired.

RÖSTI

Swiss potato cake

Soft inside and crisp and buttery on the outside, this traditional Swiss favourite is delicious and goes with almost everything. This recipe works wonderfully in a non-stick pan.

Serves 3 to 4

500 g potatoes
salt and pepper
25 g butter
30 ml (2 Tbs) oil

- Cook the potatoes in their jackets and chill for at least 12 hours.
- Peel cooked potatoes and very coarsely grate them. Season to taste.
- Melt half butter and add half the oil in a 20 to 23 cm frying pan.
- Press the grated potato into the pan.
- Cook over a medium heat for 15 to 20 minutes.
- Before turning the cake over, lift the edge to check that the bottom is golden brown.
- Turn the whole rösti onto a plate, add the remaining butter and oil to the pan and then gently slide the rösti back into the pan.
- Fry until the other side is golden brown. Loosen and turn out upside down on a serving plate.

Variation

Fry chopped onion and chopped bacon and carefully fold this into the grated potato before pressing it into the pan.

WENDY ROGER'S IRISH POTATO BREAD

A perfect way of using up left-over mashed potatoes. This recipe was sent to me by a *Talkabout* listener.

Serves 4

500 ml (2 cups) mashed potato
60 ml (4 Tbs) flour
salt and pepper
30 ml (2 Tbs) butter or bacon fat

- Mix all the ingredients.
- Roll the mixture out on a floured board to a thickness of about 1 cm.
- Press out circles or triangles.
- Cook through on a lightly greased griddle or in a heavy-based frying pan.

Hint

These can be made in advance and then re-fried in bacon fat or butter just before eating.

CRISPY POTATO SKINS

This is a very fashionable American snack. Use only the thick peels and keep the remainder of the potatoes for any other recipe.

Serves 4 to 6

8 medium potatoes, cut into quarters, with most of the flesh removed
1 medium onion, coarsely chopped
4 rashers rindless bacon, chopped
30 ml (1 Tbs) melted butter
30 ml (1 Tbs) oil
salt and black pepper

- Mix together butter, oil, salt and pepper.
- Toss the potato peels in butter and oil. (Use the flesh for mashed potatoes.)
- Spread on a baking tray and bake in preheated oven at 200 °C.
- Turn the skins while crisping them.
- Meanwhile, fry the onion and bacon in remaining butter and oil.
- Toss onion and bacon into crisped potato peels and check seasoning.

COOKED MAIZE MEAL

Maize meal (*mealiepap*), coarse or fine-ground, is cooked as *stywepap* (stiff porridge) or *krummelpap* (crumbly porridge) or as a thinner breakfast porridge. *Stywepap* and *krummelpap* are often eaten with a sauce at a braaivleis.

STYWEPAP

As easy as it is, I am often asked for a stywepap recipe. If you are looking for a polenta recipe, this is it!

Serves 4 to 6

1 litre (4 cups) water
7 ml (1 1/2 tsp) salt
30 ml (2 Tbs) butter (optional)
450 g (3 cups) mealie meal

- Boil the water with the salt and butter.
- Add the mealie meal.
- *Do not stir.*
- Reduce heat to a simmer and cook, covered, for 10 to 15 minutes
- Remove lid and stir the pap.
- Replace the lid and cook for 1 hour on a very low heat, stirring occasionally. *Beware of burning!* If you have a simmer plate, cook the pap on that.

KRUMMELPAP

- To make *krummelpap*, use 1 litre (4 cups) of water and 4 $^1/_2$ to 5 cups mealie meal instead of 3 cups as for *stywepap*. Follow the same recipe, but stir with a fork instead of a spoon. The pap becomes dry and crumbly.

THIN BREAKFAST PORRIDGE

- Add only 2 cups of mealie meal to 1 litre (4 cups) water and cook for 40 minutes, stirring often. Serve with milk and sugar.

RICE

Why serve plain rice when a little effort turns it into a very special part of the meal? There are many different ways of cooking rice. Stay with the one that works for you.

SIMLA RICE

This yellow rice is buttery and sweet from the onion, with the flavour of turmeric

Serves 4

250 ml (1 cup)	rice
45 g	butter
1	large onion, chopped
5 ml (1 tsp)	turmeric
	salt and pepper

- Boil rice in your usual way.
- In a frying pan, sauté the onion in butter until glassy.
- Stir in the turmeric and season to taste.
- Stir onion mixture into the cooked rice and steam for 5 minutes to blend the flavours.

AROMATIC BASMATI RICE

Basmati rice is a fragrant Indian rice with a unique flavour. It cooks very quickly and will become stodgy if overcooked. If basmati rice is unavailable, use any short-grained white rice.

Serves 4

25 g (2 Tbs)	butter or oil
8	cardamom pods
15 ml (1 Tbs)	mustard seeds
1	cinnamon stick
	salt
375 ml (1 $^1/_2$ cups)	basmati rice
500 ml (2 cups)	water
	pinch of saffron (optional)

- Crack the cardamom pods with a mallet or the handle of a knife.
- Wash the rice in a strainer under cold running water.
- Lightly fry the spices in the butter for 2 minutes.
- Add the rice and fry until beginning to brown.
- Add the water and saffron and bring to the boil.
- Simmer, covered, until rice is almost soft and water has been absorbed.
- Remove from the heat and leave to steam for 5 minutes to complete the cooking.

BASIC FRIED RICE

This is a traditional recipe for Chinese fried rice. The sesame seed oil gives it an oriental flavour.

Serves 6

375 ml (1 $^1/_2$ cups)	rice
15 ml (1 Tbs)	oil
3	eggs, beaten
1	bunch spring onions, sliced, including the green parts
2	large onions, finely chopped
4	thick slices rindless streaky bacon, cubed

250 ml (1 cup)	frozen peas
	salt
10 ml (2 tsp)	sesame seed oil (optional)

- Cook the rice in salted water until almost cooked. Place in a colander over boiling water and steam until fluffy.
- In a little oil, stir-fry sliced spring onion.
- Add the beaten eggs to the spring onion and cook, stirring constantly, until the egg is dry and crumbly.
- In a wok or large pan, fry the onion and bacon in oil until onion is glassy and bacon is cooked.
- Add the rice and fry quickly over high heat.
- Stir in the peas and egg mixture and salt to taste. Sesame seed oil can be added with the salt.

MEGADERRA

Rice and lentils

This is a modern version of Essau's favourite dish, using a mixture of lentils and rice, and served with lots of caramelised onions as a main course or a side dish.

Serves 4 as a main dish, or 8 as a side dish

250 ml (1 cup)	large green or brown lentils
500 ml (2 cups)	uncooked rice
4	onions, chopped
60 ml ($\frac{1}{4}$ cup)	olive oil
5 ml (1 tsp)	cumin
	salt and pepper
5	onions, sliced from root to shoot in strips
45 ml (3 Tbs)	olive oil

- Wash and drain the lentils.
- Parboil in water for about 15 minutes or until almost tender.
- Fry the chopped onions in oil until glassy..
- Add the onion and rice to the parboiled lentils and add enough water to cook the rice.
- Add cumin, season with salt and pepper to taste, and simmer, covered, until the rice is cooked and has absorbed all the water.
- In a separate pan, while the rice is cooking, fry the sliced onion strips in oil until golden and caramelised.
- Serve rice with a good helping of caramelised onion on top.

 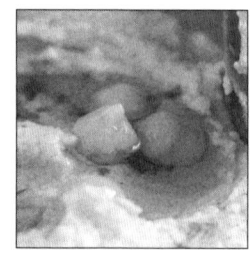 

SAVOURY SAUCES

BUTTER SAUCES

LEMON GARLIC OR LEMON BUTTER SAUCE

Lemon and melted butter will always separate when mixed together. By adding an emulsifier (in the stock powder) and a stabiliser (a small quantity of cornflour), the butter and lemon will form a creamy consistency. The addition of water will make the sauce less rich.

Serves 4 to 6

- 1/3 chicken, vegetable or onion cube, or 2 ml (1/2 tsp) vegetable stock powder
- 2 ml (1/2 tsp) cornflour
- 60 ml (1/4 cup) water
- 125 g soft butter
- fresh lemon juice
- salt and pepper to taste
- 3 cloves garlic, crushed, or to taste (optional)

▶ In a small pot, crumble the stock cube.
▶ Add the water and cornflour.
▶ Stirring continuously, boil over a high heat until it reaches a thick, syrupy consistency.
▶ Switch off the stove.
▶ Whisk in the soft butter in pieces and add the lemon juice and seasoning.
▶ Do not reboil, or else the sauce will separate.

Variation
Make a peri peri sauce using the lemon butter recipe as a base. Simply add a peri peri spice to taste. I find this peri peri has good flavour and strength, even though it does not look like the clear, red peri peri oil.

PERI PERI SAUCE

Serves 8

- 60 ml (1/4 cup) oil
- 60 ml (1/4 cup) clarified butter or ghee (available from Indian speciality shops)
- 2 cloves garlic, crushed
- 2 ml (1/2 tsp) peri peri powder
- salt to taste

▶ To clarify the butter, heat gently until melted. Then boil over medium heat for about 15 minutes until the water has boiled off, the salt scum rises to the top and the solids sink to the bottom. The butter in the middle will remain clear. Remove the scum and pour off the clear butter leaving the sediment behind.
▶ Heat all the ingredients, then leave to stand for a couple of hours before using.

BÉARNAISE SAUCE

This popular butter sauce is delicious with meat, fish and vegetables. It is also the trickiest sauce to make, because the emulsion can break very easily. The method given here is as close to flop proof as I could find. Whisking the yolks with the vinegar until they are thick and pale results in a lighter and less rich sauce and lessens the likelihood of a broken emulsion with the mixture separating.

Use the sauce *warm* or at room temperature. To reheat, place the sauce in a bowl over a pot of warm water and whisk until it has softened. Always serve it warm rather than hot.

Serves 8

125 ml ($\frac{1}{2}$ cup)	tarragon vinegar
3 ml ($\frac{1}{2}$ tsp)	tarragon
5 ml (1 tsp)	pickling spice
2	bay leaves
$\frac{1}{2}$	onion, sliced
3	egg yolks
125 g	butter
45 ml (3 Tbs)	cream *or* milk (optional)
45 ml (3 Tbs)	freshly chopped parsley

- Place the first 5 ingredients in a pot and boil until 45 ml (3 Tbs) remains.
- Strain and cool.
- Place the egg yolks and vinegar in a bowl over very hot water, but not boiling.
- Whisk until it is thick and pale.
- Melt the butter and bring it to the boil. Gradually pour into the egg yolks a little at a time, whisking continuously until thick.
- Whisk in the chopped parsley.
- Whisk in the cream or milk if the sauce is too thick.

Variation
For a different flavour, make a Hollandaise sauce. Use grape or wine vinegar or half vinegar and half lemon juice in place of the tarragon vinegar, and omit the tarragon.

Hint
If your emulsion breaks, it is fixed in the same way as for mayonnaise (see mayonnaise recipe).

GARLIC AND HERB BUTTER

Make a whole batch and leave it in a container in the fridge. It will remain slightly soft because of the oil. Use a vegetable baller and place a ball of the butter on vegetables, grilled fish or steak. Alternatively, spread thickly on a lobster tail before grilling it. It also makes wonderful garlic bread.

Makes 310 ml (1 1/4 cup); 1 to 2 garlic loaves

250 g	soft butter
30 ml (2 Tbs)	olive *or* sunflower oil
10 ml (2 tsp)	fresh lemon juice
4-6	cloves garlic, crushed, *or* to taste
5 ml (1 tsp)	dried mixed herbs
80 ml ($\frac{1}{3}$ cup)	fresh parsley, chopped
5 ml (1 tsp)	salt
3 ml ($\frac{1}{2}$ tsp)	freshly ground black pepper

- Place all the ingredients in a food processor and blend till smooth. Alternatively, cream the butter and oil with a beater and then add the remaining ingredients.
- Place on greaseproof paper and form into a sausage shape or store, chilled, in a container.
- Slice or scoop out and use as required.

Hint
To make garlic bread that is easy to serve, slice the French loaf in half and work with 2 shorter loaves. Slice the bread all the way through and then butter thickly, piling one slice on top of the other. Roll it in foil and bake in a hot oven (200 °C) for 15 minutes. The separated slices are much easier to serve.

COLD SAUCES

SAUCE TARTAR

The chopped hard-boiled eggs in this recipe make all the difference! Serve with any crumbed, battered or fried food.

125 ml (½ cup)	mayonnaise
1	gherkin, finely chopped
5	capers, finely chopped
30 ml (2 Tbs)	parsley
1	small onion, chopped
1	hard-boiled egg, finely chopped

▸ Mix the ingredients and refrigerate for 4 hours before using.

MAYONNAISE

This mayonnaise needs fewer eggs than usual and is much lighter than most home-made mayonnaise. By using a combination of different herbs, vinegars and oils you can alter the flavour without altering the texture.

1	whole egg
1	egg yolk
45 ml (3 Tbs)	vinegar, lemon juice or a mixture
3 ml (½ tsp)	castor sugar
5 ml (1 tsp)	salt
2 ml (½ tsp)	black pepper
10 ml (2 tsp)	dijon mustard, or any good prepared mustard
250 ml	sunflower oil and
125 ml	olive oil, mixed

▸ Use a liquidiser or an electric whisk (the whisk will give you more volume and a much lighter mayonnaise).
▸ Place the whole egg and yolk with the vinegar/lemon, sugar, salt, pepper and mustard in the liquidiser or bowl and whisk until it is foamy and light in colour.
▸ Continue whisking, but very gradually add the oil a teaspoon at a time for the first 15 ml (1 Tbs). Once the emulsion has been formed you can add the oil in a thin stream.
▸ The mayonnaise will become thick and creamy.
▸ Check seasoning and pour into an airtight container. It will keep for several weeks in the fridge.

Hint
If you add the oil too quickly at the beginning before you have formed an emulsion, the mayonnaise will become thin and oily. To fix this, take 2 egg yolks and whisk until they are light in colour and texture. Add a teaspoon at a time of your oily mixture, until it becomes creamy and thick. You can then add the remainder more quickly. The resulting mayonnaise will be richer and thicker.

AVOCADO SAUCE

Serve this sauce in place of sauce tartar with crumbed or battered meat, fish or vegetables. Everyone will go wild!

Serves 6 to 8

2-3	avocados
45 ml (3 Tbs)	mayonnaise
25 ml (1 ½ Tbs)	lemon juice
25 ml (1 ½ Tbs)	tarragon or cider vinegar,
1	clove garlic, crushed
	salt and pepper
1 ml (¼ tsp)	Maggi liquid seasoning

▸ Blend all the ingredients and season to taste.

MEXICAN TOPPINGS

Serve these with Mexican mince and tacos or as a dip with nachos or chips. They also go very well with any crumbed or battered meat or fish.

GUACAMOLE

2	large, ripe avocados, chopped (not mashed)
15 ml (1 Tbs)	lemon juice
15 ml (1 Tbs)	onion, finely chopped
1	ripe red tomato, skinned, seeded and chopped
1-2	fresh hot green chillies, seeded and chopped
15 ml (1 Tbs)	chopped coriander leaves
	salt and milled black pepper

▸ Mix the ingredients to a fairly coarse consistency.
▸ Do not make it too far ahead of time as it will discolour.

SALSA CRUDA

This is a Mexican fresh tomato and chilli sauce.

2-3	ripe red tomatoes, skinned, seeded and chopped
1	small onion, finely chopped
25 ml (2 Tbs)	coriander leaves
2-3	fresh hot green chillies, seeded and chopped
	salt and milled black pepper

▶ Mix all the ingredients together to make a sauce of a coarse consistency.

SAUCE AIOLI

Garlic sauce

Made from a base of mashed potatoes, this is an unusual sauce to serve with blanched vegetables or grilled fish or meat. The flavour of the olive oil, lemon and garlic is mellowed by the flavour of the potato.

Serves 4 to 6

350 g	potatoes (about 2 medium)
3-4	cloves garlic
125 ml ($^1/_2$ cup)	olive oil
45 ml (3 Tbs)	lemon juice
125 ml ($^1/_2$ cup)	chicken or vegetable stock
60 ml ($^1/_4$ cup)	chopped parsley
	salt and black pepper to taste

▶ Boil or microwave the potatoes in their jackets.
▶ Place the hot potatoes in the food processor and process, gradually adding the oil and lemon juice.
▶ Add enough stock to obtain the consistency of thick cream.
▶ Add the parsley and seasoning and serve it hot or cold. If you serve it cold, it may have to be thinned down.

COOKED YOGHURT

To prevent the yoghurt from curdling when heated, stabilise it with an egg white and cornflour. Use it in place of cream or sour cream in all your savoury recipes.

Makes 375 ml

350 ml	plain yoghurt (not drinking yoghurt)
1	egg white
5 ml (1 tsp)	salt
15 ml (1 Tbs)	cornflour

▶ Place the yoghurt in a pot.
▶ Lightly whisk egg white until foamy.
▶ Whisk into yoghurt with salt and cornflour.
▶ Bring it to the boil over medium heat, stirring constantly.
▶ Reduce the heat and simmer for 2 minutes.
▶ Remove from heat and leave to cool.
▶ Add it to any sauce in place of cream.

HOT SAUCES

Forget about your wooden spoon when making smooth sauces. Rather use a wire balloon whisk. It will give you lump-free, perfectly smooth sauces every time. If cheese is to be added to a sauce, always remove the hot, thickened sauce from the stove and then add the cheese, stirring until it has melted. Cheese cooked in the sauce will become grainy.

Roux-based sauces

The simplest sauces to make are the roux-based sauces. These are thickened with flour mixed with fat to prevent lumps from forming when added to a liquid.

▶ A white sauce is made by adding the milk to the roux as soon as the flour and fat have been mixed together.
▶ A brown sauce is made by cooking the flour in the fat until it is toasted brown before adding the liquid (see introduction to *Meat*).

BÉCHAMEL SAUCE

Basic white sauce

This is a base sauce consisting of milk, thickened with a butter and flour roux. Béchamel sauce is the French basic white sauce in which the milk is flavoured by heating it with onion, bay leaf, peppercorns and often celery or mushroom stalks and left to infuse. The milk is strained and used to make the base white sauce.

Use the following recipe as a base for cheese, mushroom, pepper and asparagus sauces.

30 g	butter
30 ml (2 Tbs)	flour
250 ml (1 cup)	milk (plain or infused)
	salt and pepper
	pinch dry mustard powder

- In a small pot, melt the butter and stir in the flour. Cook for 1 minute to cook the starch.
- Add the milk and, using a wire whisk, stir over medium heat until it thickens and comes to the boil. Simmer for 1 minute.

Variation
Add lots of finely chopped fresh parsley and seasoning to a basic béchamel sauce and pour it over cooked carrots or beetroot.

CHEESE SAUCE

This sauce is most often used on vegetables, pasta dishes and fish.

1	basic white sauce recipe
80 ml (1/3 cup)	grated cheddar cheese

- Make the basic white sauce.
- Remove the sauce from the heat and stir in the grated cheese and seasoning. Do not return the sauce to the heat once the cheese has been added.
- Pour it over the vegetables.

Variation
To make a savoury cheese crumble topping, mix 30 ml (2 Tbs) grated cheese and 30 ml (2 Tbs) fresh breadcrumbs. Sprinkle the mixture over the sauce and place under the grill until the cheese has melted and the crumbs are lightly toasted.

SPICY CHEESE SAUCE

For something special, serve this very rich sauce on hamburgers or on steak or baked potato.

Serves 4

1/2	onion, chopped
20 ml (4 tsp)	oil, or butter
22 ml (1 1/2 Tbs)	flour
125 ml (1/2 cup)	milk
250 ml (1 cup)	mature cheddar, grated
15 ml (1 Tbs)	tomato sauce
15 ml (1 Tbs)	HP sauce

- Sauté onion in oil until glassy.
- Stir in flour.
- Add milk and bring to the boil, stirring constantly.
- Remove from heat and stir in cheese until melted.
- Stir in tomato sauce and HP sauce.
- Place a spoonful of sauce on each hamburger.

CREAM AND WHITE WINE SAUCE

This sauce is perfect for mussels, grilled or poached fish, and crayfish. By adding pieces of fish and seafood, it becomes the most delicious pasta sauce.

Serves 6 to 8

1	large onion, finely chopped
30 g	butter
45 ml (3 Tbs)	flour
250 ml (1 cup)	cream
125 ml (1/2 cup)	milk or fish stock
125 ml (1/2 cup)	dry white wine
15 ml (1 Tbs)	good prepared mustard
30 ml (2 Tbs)	Old Brown sherry
80 ml (1/3 cup)	grated mild cheddar cheese
3-4	cloves of garlic, crushed
	salt and black pepper to taste
60 ml (1/4 cup)	finely chopped parsley

- In a small pot, sauté the onion until it is glassy.
- Stir in the flour and then add the cream, milk, wine, mustard and sherry.
- Bring the sauce to the boil, stirring continuously, and simmer for 3 minutes to mellow the wine and cook the flour.
- Remove from the heat and add the cheese and the garlic. Stir until the cheese has melted.
- Season to taste and stir in the parsley.

SAVOURY SAUCES

ORANGE SAUCE

Use this over boiled carrots, beetroot, butternut and, with a little extra sugar, over vanilla ice cream!

- Follow the recipe for the basic white sauce, but replace the milk with freshly squeezed orange juice.
- Add sugar and cinnamon to taste.

SIMPLE MUSHROOM SAUCE

Use over boiled beans, steak or grilled fish.

1	small onion, chopped
4-6	brown mushrooms, sliced
45 g	butter
30 ml (2 Tbs)	flour
250 ml (1 cup)	milk
	seasoning to taste

- Sauté the mushrooms and onions in the butter until soft.
- Stir in the flour.
- Add the liquid, cook for 1 minute to cook the starch and stir until it comes to the boil. Season to taste and simmer for 1 minute.

Variations
- Instead of the milk, use 125 ml ($^1/_2$ cup) milk and 125 ml ($^1/_2$ cup) chicken stock, or 175 ml chicken, mushroom or vegetable stock with 80 ml cream.
- For an easy steak sauce, add sherry, a squeeze of lemon juice, green peppercorns or plenty of black pepper and thyme or rosemary to taste. Add the sauce to the pan juices when you remove the steak and simmer to blend the flavours.

LEMON SAUCE

Serve this sauce over brussels sprouts, beans, or broccoli. It is also delicious over grilled fish, crumbed chicken breasts or pork chops.

45 g	butter
30 ml (2 Tbs)	flour
125 ml ($^1/_2$ cup)	chicken, vegetable, or onion stock
juice of	$^1/_2$ lemon, or to taste
	salt, pepper and paprika
30 ml (2 Tbs)	cream, sour cream or milk

- In a small pot, melt the butter and stir in the flour. Cook for 1 minute to cook the starch.
- Add the stock, lemon juice and seasoning and, using a wire whisk, stir over medium heat until it thickens and comes to the boil. Simmer for 1 minute.
- Stir in the cream.

BLUE CHEESE STEAK SAUCE

Use this slightly sharp sauce on steak or fried, crumbed meats.

Serves 4

1	onion, chopped
2	cloves of garlic, crushed
50 g	butter
30 ml (2 Tbs)	flour
250 ml (1 cup)	beef stock
125 ml ($^1/_2$ cup)	cream
30 ml (2 Tbs)	sweet sherry
85 g	blue cheese of your choice, crumbled or coarsely grated
	salt and pepper to taste

- In a small pot, melt the butter and sauté the onions and garlic until soft.
- Stir in the flour and cook until it turns a light golden colour.
- Add the garlic, stock and cream and bring it to the boil.
- Stir in the sherry and lemon and bring it to the boil.
- Once the steaks have been removed from the pan, pour off the excess fat and add the cooked sauce.
- Bring it back to the boil scraping all the flavour off the bottom of the pan. (This is called 'deglazing' the pan. All the bits of steak that have stuck to the pan will add a meaty flavour to the sauce.
- Just before serving, stir in the cheese.
- For a smooth sauce, stir the sauce until the cheese melts.

CREAMY BLUE CHEESE SAUCE

Very similar to the steak sauce, this sauce is lighter and creamier in texture and flavour. Use it over plain pasta, ravioli, broccoli, cauliflower or baked potato.

1	onion, finely chopped
30 ml (2 Tbs)	olive oil
1	clove garlic, crushed
20 ml (4 tsp)	flour
250 ml (1 cup)	milk
250 ml (1 cup)	cream
65 g	blue cheese, grated
	squeeze of fresh lemon juice

- Sauté the onion and garlic in olive oil until glassy.
- Stir in the flour and cook for 30 seconds.
- Stir in the milk and cream and bring it to the boil, stirring constantly.
- Remove the sauce from the heat and stir in the cheese and lemon juice.
- Stir until melted.
- Pour over the warm, cooked pasta.

MUSTARD SAUCE

Serve with pickled and cured meats, sausages or over a steak or grilled fish.

Serves 4

30 g	butter
30 ml (2 Tbs)	flour
185 ml (³⁄₄ cup)	milk
125 ml (¹⁄₂ cup)	cream
15 ml (1 Tbs)	brandy
15 ml (1 Tbs)	sherry
15 ml (1 Tbs)	whole seed mustard
10 ml (2 tsp)	strong dijon mustard
10 ml (2 tsp)	lemon juice
2 ml (¹⁄₂ tsp)	beef, chicken or vegetable stock powder
2 ml (¹⁄₂ tsp)	brown sugar
	freshly ground black pepper to taste
	salt to taste

- In a small pot, melt the butter and stir in the flour. Cook over medium heat until the flour has browned slightly.
- Add the milk and cream and, stirring well with a whisk, bring the sauce to the boil. Simmer for 1 minute.
- Add all the remaining ingredients, heat through and adjust the seasoning.

SAUCE ESPAGNOLE

This classic meat sauce, thickened with brown roux, can be made in advance and frozen. Add it to the pan juices of a roast or pan-fried meat, or just use as it is.

30 g	butter, oil, or *a mixture*
2	rashers bacon (optional)
¹⁄₂	onion, chopped
¹⁄₂	carrot, chopped
3	mushrooms, chopped
1	stick celery, chopped
45 ml (3 Tbs)	flour
250 ml (1 cup)	beef stock
2	bay leaves
3 ml (¹⁄₂ tsp)	thyme
60 ml (¹⁄₄ cup)	tomato purée
30 ml (2 Tbs)	sherry
45 ml (3 Tbs)	cream (optional)

- Sauté the bacon and vegetables in butter.
- Add the flour and cook over medium heat until the flour is well browned.
- Add the stock and herbs and simmer for 30 to 45 minutes.
- Add purée and sherry and simmer for a further 15 minutes.
- Strain and reheat.
- Stir in the cream and serve.

TOMATO MUSHROOM SAUCE

By varying the stock, this rich and creamy sauce can be made for meat, poultry or fish.

75 g	butter
2	onions, chopped
2	cloves garlic, crushed
250 g	brown mushrooms, sliced
30 ml (2 Tbs)	flour
250 ml (1 cup)	chicken, beef or vegetable stock
125 ml ($^1/_2$ cup)	sherry
30 ml (2 Tbs)	tomato paste
125 ml ($^1/_2$ cup)	cream
	salt and pepper
2	bay leaves

- Sauté the onion in butter until glassy.
- Add garlic and mushrooms and sauté until mushrooms begin to shrink.
- Sprinkle on the flour.
- Add the remaining ingredients.
- Simmer for 5 minutes.
- Check seasoning and serve.

SWEET AND SOUR SAUCE

In Chinese cooking sauces are always thickened with cornflour rather than flour. It gives the sauce a shiny texture. Serve this sauce with fried fish, fish cakes, crumbed, battered or pan-fried pork, veal or chicken.

Serves 6

30 ml (2 Tbs)	oil
1	large onion, cubed
2	small green peppers, cubed or 1 red and 1 green pepper
2	cloves garlic, crushed
440 g	tinned pineapple pieces and juice
125 ml ($^1/_2$ cup)	vinegar
125 ml ($^1/_2$ cup)	sherry
45 ml (3 Tbs)	sugar
125 ml ($^1/_2$ cup)	tomato purée
15 ml (1 Tbs)	soy sauce
30 ml (2 Tbs)	glacé ginger, chopped (optional)
10 ml (2 tsp)	cornflour

- Sauté the onion, peppers and garlic in oil.
- Add remaining ingredients except cornflour.
- Simmer for 5 minutes.
- Mix the cornflour with a little cold water and add to the sauce. Simmer for a couple of minutes until it is thick.

MONKEY GLAND SAUCE

Sweet and sour and spicy – serve it with a roast or steak, or with pap at a braai.

Serves 6 to 8

2	large onions, finely chopped
3	cloves garlic, crushed
45 ml (3 Tbs)	oil
125 ml ($^1/_2$ cup)	tomato purée
125 ml ($^1/_2$ cup)	chutney
15 ml (1 Tbs)	prepared mustard
30 ml (2 Tbs)	Worcestershire sauce
60 ml ($^1/_4$ cup)	tomato sauce
80 ml ($^1/_3$ cup)	sweet sherry
80 ml ($^1/_3$ cup)	water
45 ml (3 Tbs)	vinegar

- Sauté the onion and garlic in oil.
- Add all the ingredients and simmer for 5 minutes.

CREOLE SAUCE

Traditionally, this sauce is served with Jambalaya, chicken, rabbit, prawns or over omelettes. It is also delicious over steak or mealie pap at a braai. It is very spicy as it contains all the dry peppers, hot and sweet, as well as the traditional Creole ingredients of onion, celery, green peppers and tomato.

Seasoning mix

4 bay	leaves
5 ml (1 tsp)	origanum
5 ml (1 tsp)	salt
2 ml (½ tsp)	white pepper
2 ml (½ tsp)	cayenne pepper
3 ml (½ tsp)	paprika
2 ml (½ tsp)	black pepper
5 ml (1 tsp)	thyme
15 ml (1 Tbs)	fresh basil, chopped
or 5 ml (1 tsp)	dried basil
15 ml (1 Tbs)	sugar
80 g	butter
1	large onion, finely chopped
1	large green pepper, finely chopped
2	celery sticks, finely chopped
410 g	tinned tomatoes, chopped and drained, with juice retained
2	cloves garlic, crushed
310 ml (1 ¼ cups)	chicken stock
60 ml (¼ cup)	tomato puree
	a dash of tabasco sauce

- Mix all seasoning ingredients together.
- Sauté the onions, green peppers and celery in the butter until soft.
- Add remaining ingredients and simmer for about 20 minutes, or until the flavours have blended and the sauce has thickened and vegetables are completely soft.

SOUR CHERRY SAUCE

Usually served with poultry, especially duck, this sauce is delicious served with smoked or cured meat. Make a stock from duck giblets (without the liver), chicken giblets or cooking liquid and a stock cube.

375 ml (1 ½ cups)	stock of your choice
45 ml (3 Tbs)	fat from the roasting pan or butter
45 ml (3 Tbs)	flour
60 ml (¼ cup)	red wine
60 ml (¼ cup)	sherry
1 x 375 g	bottle sour cherries
45 ml (3 Tbs)	redcurrant jelly
	pinch of cinnamon
30 ml (2 Tbs)	kirsch or brandy
	lemon juice to taste

- Strain the cherries and use ½ the juice in the sauce. Set cherries aside.
- In a small pot, melt the butter and stir in the flour.
- Over a medium heat, stir until the flour begins to brown.
- Add the strained stock, wine, sherry, cherry juice and redcurrant jelly (apricot jam may be substituted, but only 30 ml (2 Tbs) should be used).
- Simmer to reduce the liquid (about 10 minutes).
- Add cherries, adjust the seasoning and lastly add the kirsch.

LOWER FAT VEGETABLE SAUCES

These sauces are lower in fat because they are thickened with cornflour mixed with cold water instead of roux (flour and butter). Cornflour will give a shiny, jelly-like texture. It cannot be reheated, because it will thin down. As a quick, lower fat sauce, it works perfectly.

To lower the fat in all cooking, halve the fat and sweat, rather than sauté, the onions and vegetables. Take a large piece of greaseproof paper and crumple it into a ball. Wet it through under cold water as if it were a cloth. Squeeze off the excess water and then spread it out directly on top of the onions in the pan. The moisture on the paper will stop the onions from burning and keep them moist.

CHEESE SAUCE

- 250 ml (1 cup) 2% milk
- 15 ml (1 Tbs) cornflour
- 30 ml (2 Tbs) parmesan cheese
- 5 ml (1 tsp) prepared mustard
- fresh lemon juice to taste
- salt and pepper to taste

▶ Mix the milk and cornflour with a whisk bring to the boil over a medium heat, whisking continuously.
▶ Remove from the heat and whisk in cheese and mustard.
▶ Season to taste.

ORANGE SAUCE

- 250 ml (1 cup) fresh orange juice
- 15 ml (1 Tbs) cornflour
- sugar or sweetener and cinnamon to taste

▶ Mix the orange juice and cornflour over medium heat. Bring to the boil, whisking continuously,
▶ Season to taste.

MUSHROOM SAUCE

- $1/2$ onion, chopped
- 4-6 mushrooms, chopped
- 10 ml (2 tsp) oil or butter, or a mixture
- 125 ml ($1/2$ cup) 2% milk
- 15 ml (1 Tbs) cornflour
- 125 ml ($1/2$ cup) vegetable or chicken stock
- salt and pepper and herbs to taste

▶ Over a low heat, sweat the onions and mushrooms in oil under wet greaseproof paper.
▶ When they have shrunk, remove the paper, turn the heat up and brown them slightly.
▶ Mix the cornflour with the milk and add to the mushrooms and onions with the stock.
▶ Bring to the boil, stirring constantly and season to taste.

LEMON SAUCE

- 125 ml ($1/2$ cup) 2% milk
- 15 ml (1 Tbs) cornflour
- 125 ml ($1/2$ cup) vegetable or chicken stock
- 15 ml (1 Tbs) fresh lemon juice, or to taste
- herbs, salt and pepper to taste
- cayenne pepper to taste (optional)

▶ Bring the milk, cornflour and stock to the boil and add the lemon juice.
▶ Season to taste.
▶ For extra flavour, add a touch of cayenne pepper.

DESSERTS

All pastry desserts using shortcrust, puff, phyllo and choux pastry can be found under *Pastry in Baking*, listed according to the type of pastry. This chapter offers recipes for desserts using biscuit dough or crumbles.

Most of the desserts can be made non-dairy with little change to the taste. Use a non-dairy cream, or fruit juice in place of cream and milk, and use margarine instead of butter, if you wish.

NUTTY APPLE CRUMBLE

The crumble in this recipe is very simple, using equal weights of flour, nuts, brown sugar and butter. It can be used as a topping for any fresh, stewed, dried or tinned fruit such as pears, quince, yellow cling peaches.

Serves 4

Filling

4	large green apples
30 ml (2 Tbs)	brown sugar
5 ml (1 tsp)	ground cloves (optional)

Crumble

100 g	chopped walnuts
165 ml ($^2/_3$ cup)	flour (100 g)
125 ml ($^1/_2$ cup)	brown sugar (100 g)
100 g	butter, chilled and cut into very small cubes

- Preheat oven to 180 °C.
- Peel and chop the apples. Stir in the sugar and ground cloves and place the mixture in the bottom of a greased ovenproof dish.
- Mix all the ingredients for the crumble. Do not overmix – the crumble must be fairly coarse.
- Spread the crumble in a thick layer over the apple and bake for about 45 minutes until the topping is crisp.

Hint
Replace half the flour with muesli for a more chunky crumble.

APPLE CRUMBLE

This apple crumble has a crisp biscuit dough on top and at the bottom, and can be served for tea or dessert. If left to stand for 6 to 8 hours, the crust becomes soft. Heating it in a very hot oven will crisp it up but it won't regain its original crispness. For the best results prepare it in advance and bake it just before serving.

Serves 6 to 8

Crumble

125 g	butter
200 ml (1 teacup)	castor sugar
1	egg
5 ml (1 tsp)	vanilla essence
rind of 1 lemon	
500 ml (2 cups)	flour
10 ml (2 tsp)	baking powder

Filling

1,5 kg	Granny Smith apples, peeled, cored and diced,
or 2 x 385 g	tins pie apples
7 ml (1 1/2 tsp)	ground cinnamon
1 ml (pinch)	ground cloves
30 ml (2 Tbs)	castor sugar
80 ml (1/3 cup)	seedless raisins
15 ml (1 Tbs)	lemon juice
15 ml (1 Tbs)	flour

- Preheat oven to 180 °C.
- *To make the crumble,* cream the butter and sugar together until pale and creamy. Beat in the egg and vanilla and lemon rind.
- Add half the flour and mix well, then add the remaining flour and baking powder to make a stiff dough.
- Divide the dough in half, wrap in cling wrap and place in the fridge for at least 30 minutes.
- *For the filling,* mix the apples, cinnamon, cloves, sugar, raisins, lemon juice and flour. Leave in the fridge until needed.
- Using your fingertips, press half the chilled dough in a deep tart plate, and work it all the way up the sides of the plate.
- Place the filling in the pastry, pressing it in so that it is fairly compact, especially if you are using raw apple.
- Coarsely grate the rest of the dough over the filling.
- Bake for about 40 minutes or until well browned.
- Dust with icing sugar before serving with whipped cream.

Variations

- Instead of 1 large apple crumble, make small individual crumbles in patty tins. You will need 1 1/2 times the quantity of dough for making small crumbles.
- Use other firm fruit or a combination: Apple and tinned youngberries, or add 2 sliced bananas to the apples, pears, yellow cling peaches or stewed dried fruit.

OIL APPLE CRUMBLE

This low-sugar, low-fat crumble is light and tasty, and a good choice for cholesterol watchers. The natural sweetness comes from the raisins and cooked bananas. Prepare the filling first.

Serves 4

Filling

4	large apples
2	bananas
60 ml (1/4 cup)	raisins

Crumble

125 ml (1/2 cup)	Nutty Wheat flour
125 ml (1/2 cup)	muesli
125 ml (1/2 cup)	soft brown sugar
2 ml (1/2 tsp)	salt
80 ml (1/3 cup)	oil
100 g	walnuts or pecan nuts

- Preheat oven to 180 °C.
- Dice unpeeled apples and bananas and mix them with the raisins.
- Spread apple mixture in an ovenproof dish.
- Coarsely chop the nuts.
- Combine all the crumble ingredients and spread over the filling.
- Bake for 30 to 45 minutes or until crumble is browned.
- Serve with custard.

Hint

Try using the granola in *This and that* as a crumble on any baked fruit dessert.

FRUIT SALAD CRUMBLE

This dessert has stewed dried fruit with honey as a filling for a rich winter dessert. Use any topping from the apple crumble recipes.

Serves 6 to 8

Filling

500 g	mixed dried fruit
125 ml ($^1/_2$ cup)	orange juice
80 ml ($^1/_3$ cup)	brandy
30 ml (2 Tbs)	honey
10 ml (2 tsp)	orange rind
15 ml (1 Tbs)	lemon juice
10 ml (2 tsp)	custard powder

- Soak the fruit overnight in orange juice, brandy and add just enough water to cover the fruit.
- Preheat oven to 200 °C.
- Chop the fruit coarsely and stew until soft.
- Stir in the honey, orange rind and lemon juice. Thicken with custard powder mixed with a little cold water.
- Place in a casserole and spread the crumble over the fruit.
- Bake until golden (about 40 minutes).

APPLE MUFFIN

The apples are at the bottom, covered by a layer of butter cake, and a caramel sauce is poured over. Served with cream, this makes an inexpensive, rich dessert that can be made in advance and reheated.

Serves 6

Batter

60 g	butter
125 ml ($^1/_2$ cup)	sugar
1	egg
5 ml (1 tsp)	vanilla
250 ml (1 cup)	self-raising flour
165 ml ($^2/_3$ cup)	milk

Filling

435 g	tinned pie apples
or 4	apples, sliced and stewed

Sauce

250 ml (1 cup)	cream
250 ml (1 cup)	brown sugar

- Preheat the oven to 180 °C.
- *For the batter*, cream the butter and sugar until pale and creamy.
- Add the egg and vanilla and beat very well.
- Mix in the flour and milk.
- Tip the tinned or stewed apple into a deep pie dish.
- Pour the cake batter over the apples and bake for 30 minutes.
- In a small pot bring the cream and brown sugar for the sauce to the boil.
- Pour the syrup over the cake and return it to the oven for a further 15 minutes.
- Serve with extra whipped cream.

Hints

- To make the sauce less rich, use 200 ml (1 teacup) of milk instead of the cream.
- When reheating, cover the dish with a lid or foil to keep pudding moist.

MILLER HOWE APPLE AND BERRY PIE

This is one of the fruitiest, most delicious pies I have ever tasted. It's made with a shortbread instead of a pastry crust, and when John Tovey made it, he used a combination of apples and raspberries. If raspberries are not available, add any berries fresh, frozen or tinned.

Serves 6

Shortbread crust

250 ml (1 cup)	self-raising flour
250 ml (l cup)	cake flour
250 ml (l cup)	cornflour
300 g	soft butter
185 ml ($^3/_4$ cup)	castor sugar
2	egg yolks
	grated rind of 1 lemon

Filling

6	green apples
250-500 g	raspberries or berries of your choice
80 ml (1/3 cup)	soft brown sugar

- Preheat the oven to 180 °C.
- To make the shortbread, sift the flour and cornflour into a large bowl.
- Using a very light touch, rub the butter into the dry flour mixture.
- Once the butter has been roughly absorbed, add the castor sugar, lemon rind and egg yolks and mix with a knife to form a soft dough. Do not overmix – the dough must only just come together.
- Divide the mixture in 2, wrap well and leave to rest in the fridge for several hours before using. Remove the dough from fridge 1 hour before using it.
- Using half the dough, carefully roll and line a 20 cm, loose-bottomed quiche tin. (A glass dish will not give you a crisp crust!) Roll the dough onto a large piece of greaseproof paper. Lift the paper and quickly invert it onto the tin. This is the easiest way of getting the dough into the tin without it breaking into pieces. Press the pastry back together wherever it does break. It is a tricky pastry to roll, because of the high fat content.
- Bake blind with foil or baking paper and dry beans for about 25 minutes or until the crust is golden (see introduction to *Baking*).
- Remove the beans and paper and chill the baked crust before filling.
- Peel, core and thinly slice the apples for the filling.
- Wash and dry the berries.
- Sprinkle half the sugar over the bottom of the baked crust and pile the apples and berries into the crust. Sprinkle on the remaining sugar.
- Roll out the remaining dough on a sheet of greaseproof paper and carefully place on top of the fruit. Remove the paper.
- Trim off the edges and bake at 180 °C for 20 minutes. Lower the temperature to 160 °C for a further 25 to 30 minutes. If it browns too quickly, cover loosely with foil.

TARTE TATIN

This classic French dessert uses an almond shortbread crust placed on top of caramelised apples. The crust becomes the base when the dessert is turned out. Spectacular and delicious. For this dish you need a frying pan that can also go into the oven.

Serves 8 to 10

Shortbread crust

150 g	butter
60 ml (1/4 cup)	castor sugar
3 ml (1/2 tsp)	lemon rind
1	egg yolk
1 ml	almond essence
250 ml (1 cup)	cake flour
100 g	ground almonds
or 80 ml (1/4 cup)	cornflour

Filling and caramel sauce

1,5 kg	green apples
125 ml (1/2 cup)	castor sugar
15 ml (1 Tbs)	lemon juice
30 ml (2 Tbs)	water
30 ml (2 Tbs)	brown sugar
80 g	butter
10 ml (2 tsp)	lemon rind
3 ml (1/2 tsp)	ground cinnamon

- *For the shortbread*, cream the butter, castor sugar and lemon rind until light and creamy.
- Beat in the egg yolk and almond essence.
- Add the cake flour and almonds or cornflour.
- Wrap and chill the dough while you prepare the apples.
- Preheat oven to 180 °C.
- *For the filling and sauce*, peel and core the apples with an apple corer, keeping them whole. (If you do not have a corer, cut the apples in half and remove the cores.)
- Place the castor sugar, water and lemon juice in a 20 to 22 cm 'stove-to-oven' pan.
- Cook over medium heat until the sugar has dissolved and then cook rapidly until the sugar has caramelised and has turned a golden colour.
- Add the butter and stir until it has melted.
- Place the apples in the caramel with the coring holes facing top to bottom (or if using half apples, with the rounded side down).
- Sprinkle with the remaining brown sugar, lemon rind and cinnamon.
- Cover the pan and cook over a gentle heat until the apples are almost soft.

- Remove the lid and boil away most of the liquid.
- Roll the chilled dough out onto greaseproof paper to fit the top of the pan. Turn the paper over to drop the dough on top of the apples, fitting it snugly into the top of the pan.
- Bake for about 30 minutes or until golden.
- Remove and leave to stand for 5 minutes. Place a large plate on top of the pan and quickly invert it. The apples will now be on top and the shortbread at the bottom.
- Serve with whipped cream.

APRICOT, RAISIN BREAD AND BUTTER PUDDING

The added dried fruit makes this pudding different from the usual bread and butter pudding. The apricots can be omitted for a traditional bread and butter pudding.

Serves 6

75 g ($^3/_4$ cup)	dried apricots, chopped
75 g ($^1/_2$ cup)	raisins
50 g	butter
8	slices of white bread ($^1/_2$ loaf)
	ground cinnamon
3	eggs
125 ml ($^1/_2$ cup)	castor sugar
250 ml (1 cup)	cream
375 ml (1 $^1/_2$ cups)	milk
5 ml (1 tsp)	grated orange rind

- Preheat oven to 160 °C.
- Soak apricots and raisins in boiling water for 10 minutes. Drain.
- Grease a medium-sized square ovenware dish with butter.
- Butter the slices of bread then remove the crusts and cut into triangles.
- Layer the bread, raisins and apricots in the greased dish, lightly sprinkling each layer of bread with cinnamon.
- Mix the eggs and sugar in a bowl.
- Bring the milk and cream to the boil and pour onto the egg mixture, stirring constantly.
- Stir in the orange rind and pour the mixture over the bread. Leave to stand for 5 minutes for the liquid to soak in.
- Bake for 35 or 45 minutes or until the custard has set.

OLD CAPE BRANDY PUDDING

Also known as a tipsy tart. Full of dates, nuts and brandy, it is a rich, traditional favourite.

Serves 6 to 8

250 g	dates, stoned and chopped
200 ml (1 teacup)	boiling water
5 ml (1 tsp)	bicarbonate of soda
15 ml (1 Tbs)	butter
185 ml ($^3/_4$ cup)	castor sugar
1	egg
375 ml (1 $^1/_2$ cups)	flour
15 ml (1 Tbs)	baking powder
100 g	chopped pecan nuts (optional)

Syrup

375 ml (1 $^1/_2$ cups)	sugar
250 ml (1 cup)	water
5 ml (1 tsp)	butter
5 ml (1 tsp)	vanilla essence
125 ml ($^1/_2$ cup)	brandy

- Preheat oven to 180 °C.
- Mix the chopped dates, boiling water and bicarb.
- Beat the butter and castor sugar and add the egg. Mix until creamy.
- Sift the flour and baking powder together and add with the dates to the egg and sugar mixture. Stir in the nuts.
- Pour the mixture into a greased 25 cm deep tart dish and bake for 45 minutes. Rather overbake than underbake. The syrup will make it very moist.
- Make the syrup by bringing the sugar and water to the boil.
- Add the butter and vanilla essence. Allow to cool and add the brandy.
- Remove the tart from the oven and prick it all over with a fork. Slowly drizzle the syrup onto the hot tart until all the syrup is absorbed.
- Serve hot with whipped cream.

Hint
While chopping the dates, keep dipping your scissors or a sharp knife into boiling water. This stops them from becoming sticky.

BAKED CARROT PUDDING WITH CITRUS SAUCE

This wholesome pudding is low in fat, high in fibre and delicious. Baked in muffin pans, it makes moist, long lasting carrot muffins.

Serves 8

125 ml (½ cup)	water
80 ml (⅓ cup)	oil or melted butter
125 ml (½ cup)	sultanas
125 ml (½ cup)	currants
125 g (½ block)	dates, stoned and chopped
125 ml (½ cup)	brown sugar
3 ml (½ tsp)	bicarbonate of soda
30 ml (2 Tbs)	orange juice
10 ml (2 tsp)	grated orange rind
5 ml (1 tsp)	grated lemon rind
1	egg
250 ml (1 cup)	grated raw carrot
125 ml (½ cup)	self-raising flour
125 ml (½ cup)	Nutty Wheat flour
5 ml (1 tsp)	mixed spice

Citrus sauce

4	egg yolks
80 ml (⅓ cup)	castor sugar
60 ml (¼ cup)	orange juice
30 ml (2 Tbs)	lemon juice
250 ml (1 cup)	cream

- Preheat oven to 180 °C.
- Bring the water and butter (or oil) to the boil.
- Mix sultanas, currants, dates, brown sugar and bicarb in a bowl and add to the boiling liquid. Stir and leave to cool.
- Add the orange juice, orange and lemon rind and beaten egg to the fruit mixture.
- Place the carrots, flour and mixed spice in a bowl and pour the fruit mixture onto this and mix well.
- Spoon the mixture into 6 x 250 ml greased ramekins or a 2 litre dish.
- Bake for 30 to 40 minutes.
- Serve hot with the cold citrus sauce.
- For the sauce, beat the egg yolks and castor sugar in a bowl over hot water until light and thick.
- Slowly beat in the orange and lemon juice. Leave to cool.
- Beat the cream until stiff and lightly fold it into the egg mixture. Chill until required.

MALVA PUDDING

The Boschendal wine estate in the Cape made this very rich, sweet dessert famous. We are often asked for the recipe.

Serves 6 to 8

250 ml (1 cup)	milk
15 g	butter
15 ml (1 Tbs)	smooth apricot jam
1	egg
185 ml (¾ cup)	sugar
15 ml (1 Tbs)	white vinegar
250 ml (1 cup)	flour
15 ml (1 Tbs)	baking powder

Syrup

250 ml (1 cup)	cream or evaporated milk
125 ml (½ cup)	milk
100 g	butter
125 ml (½ cup)	sugar

- Preheat oven to 160 °C.
- Place the milk, butter and jam in a pot and over a low heat, stir until the butter and jam have melted.
- Whisk the egg and sugar in a bowl over hot water until light and fluffy.
- Add the vinegar to the milk mixture.
- Fold the sifted flour and warm milk mixture into the egg mixture, then quickly fold in the baking powder last.
- Pour the mixture into a greased square 1 to 1,5 litre dish and bake for 45 minutes to 1 hour. (The cake must be brown and dry and rather overbaked than underbaked, in order to absorb the syrup.)
- Combine all the ingredients for the sauce and simmer for 3 minutes.
- Remove the dish from the oven and prick the pudding all over with a fork.
- Slowly pour on the hot syrup and return the pudding to the warm oven for 10 minutes.

Hint

If you prefer a darker coloured malva pudding, use 5 ml (1 tsp) bicarbonate of soda instead of the 15 ml (1 Tbs) baking powder.

RHUBARB WITH ORANGE SAGO CREAMS

The sago creams can be served on their own or with any fruit. The rhubarb in this recipe is cooked with caramelised sugar and orange, and is delicious on its own, with custard, or with the sago creams.

Serves 6

Sago creams

    185 ml (³/₄ cup) sago
    750 ml (3 cups) milk
    3 ml (½ tsp) finely grated orange rind
    2 ml (½ tsp) vanilla essence
    2 eggs
    2 egg yolks
    125 ml (½ cup) sugar

- Preheat oven to 160 °C.
- Soak the sago in cold water for 30 minutes. Drain well.
- Place the soaked sago and milk in a heavy-based pot and gently bring it to the boil, stirring constantly.
- Simmer until the sago is transparent. (Or microwave on 100% power for 10 minutes, then 50% power for 5 minutes, stirring often.)
- Mix the orange rind, vanilla, 2 whole eggs, egg yolks and sugar in a bowl until well blended. Do not allow to become foamy.
- Add the cooked sago mixture to the eggs and mix well. Pour into greased ramekins or bake in a casserole dish.
- Place dishes in a roasting pan and add cold water to come half-way up the side of the ramekins (Bain Marie).
- Bake for about 30 minutes.
- Remove from the oven and water and leave to cool.
- Before serving, return to the Bain Marie and heat through in the oven.
- Turn out and serve with rhubarb.

POACHED RHUBARB IN ORANGE

    2 bunches rhubarb
    1 orange, with peel for zest
    250 ml (1 cup) water
    125 ml (½ cup) castor sugar

- Scrape and trim the rhubarb and cut it into 2 cm pieces. Discard any pieces of leaf that remain.
- Peel the orange with an orange zester or peeler to remove the orange layer of zest or rind. Cut it into very thin strips. Reserve peeled orange. Place the strips in a pot with 250 ml water and boil the zest until soft (5 to 15 minutes, depending on how thin the strips are). Remove from the heat.
- Place the rhubarb in a frying pan and add the juice of the reserved peeled orange. Simmer until the rhubarb is soft. Do not stir – shake the pan and try keep the rhubarb whole.
- Meanwhile, add sugar to the orange rind and water and boil until the zest is glassy.
- Remove the zest, set aside and boil the sugar syrup until it starts to caramelise and turns a golden colour.
- Add the sugar syrup to the rhubarb and heat through to dissolve the caramel.
- Serve with sago creams or with whipped cream or custard, decorated with the caramelised zest.

CHRISTMAS PUDDING FOR FOUR

To make a larger pudding, double all the ingredients and steam it for an extra hour.

Serves 4

    250 g cake fruit
    60 ml (4 Tbs) brandy or *orange juice*
    80 g butter
    80 ml (⅓ cup) brown sugar
    1 egg
    165 ml (⅔ cup) flour
    2 ml (½ tsp) each of
        cloves
        cinnamon
        nutmeg
        ginger
        mixed spice
    2 ml (½ tsp) bicarbonate of soda
    80 ml (⅓ cup) fresh breadcrumbs
    15 ml (1 Tbs) syrup
    15 ml (1 Tbs) marmalade

- Soak the fruit in the brandy or orange juice overnight.
- Cream the butter and sugar together and beat in the egg.
- Sift the flour, spices and bicarbonate of soda over the soaked fruit and add the crumbs, syrup and marmalade.
- Add the creamed mixture to the fruit and mix well.
- Place a circle of greaseproof paper in the bottom of a greased 1 to 1,5 litre pudding bowl.
- Pour the mixture into the bowl.

- Loosely cover the top of the bowl with a double layer of greaseproof paper and a single layer of heavy foil with the shiny side facing into the bowl. Make sure that the sheet of paper is big enough to hang at least 5 cm over the edge of the bowl all round.
- Tie down the paper around the top of the bowl with a long piece of string, then tie the string across the top of the bowl to form a handle. This will make it easier to remove it from the *boiling* water.
- Place a saucer upside down in a large pot and half fill it with water. Bring the water to the boil and carefully lower the pudding into the pot to rest on the saucer. This will keep the pudding off the direct heat. The boiling water must reach $3/4$ of the way up the sides of the bowl.
- Simmer, covered, for 1 $1/2$ hours. After 1 hour check the water level. If it has dropped, top up with boiling water.
- Remove the pudding and turn out onto a serving plate.
- When you serve it, dim the lights, pour on a little brandy and quickly set it alight.
- Serve with brandy butter or apricot brandy sauce.

Brandy butter

125 g unsalted butter
125 g icing sugar
45 ml (3 Tbs) brandy

- Cream the butter and sugar very well, then gradually beat in the brandy.

Apricot brandy sauce

This sauce is wonderful served over ice cream, or instead of custard with other desserts!

250 ml (1 cup) apricot fruit juice
80 ml ($1/3$ cup) brown sugar
25 g butter
30 ml (2 Tbs) cornflour
125 ml ($1/2$ cup) cream
80 ml ($1/3$ cup) brandy

- Heat the fruit juice, sugar and butter.
- Stir the cornflour into the cream and stir the hot mixture into the cream.
- Return the mixture to the heat and bring to the boil, stirring continually.
- Remove from the heat and stir in brandy to taste.

BAKED PEARS

Pears baked in their skins are an easy and delicious dessert, plain or in a sauce. Baking the pears in their skin ensures that the taste of the pear is not overpowered by the sauce. Here are two lovely sauces to try.

Serves 6

Red wine and cinnamon sauce

6 firm pears
125 ml ($1/2$ cup) red wine or sherry
250 ml (1 cup) water
125 ml ($1/2$ cup) sugar
1 stick of cinnamon
3 slices of lemon or orange with the peel
30 g butter

- Preheat oven to 160 °C.
- Cut a deep cross in the bottom of each pear to allow the flavour to penetrate the pear. Do not peel the pears.
- Place the pears on their sides in an ovenware dish only big enough to hold all the pears.
- Add the remaining ingredients and place uncovered in the oven at 160 °C for 1 to 1 $1/2$ hours, turning a couple of times.
- The sauce will reduce and the skins of the pears become shiny and brown.
- Serve with the sauce and whipped cream.

Molasses and red wine

6 firm pears
250 ml (1 cup) water
125 ml ($1/2$ cup) red wine
100 ml (7 Tbs) molasses or treacle
30 ml (2 Tbs) honey
30 ml (2 Tbs) lemon juice
3 large pieces lemon rind

- Follow the recipe for red wine and cinnamon sauce to make this molasses sauce.

Hint

Try baking the pears plain on a baking sheet just like a potato. Quite delicious!

BAKED APPLES

Apples bake faster than pears and unless the skins are cut, they will explode while baking. Use the baked pear sauces but omit the water and use the following method.

Serves 6

    6 large green apples
    1 quantity sauce of your choice

To thicken sauce
    10 ml (2 tsp) custard powder
    30 ml (2 Tbs) cold water

- Core and cut the apples in half.
- In a small casserole, heat the sauce ingredients (not the thickening).
- Place the apples, cut side down, in the sauce and bake covered at 180 °C for about 10 minutes.
- Turn the apples over, cover again and return to the oven for a further 10 minutes or until the apples are soft.
- Transfer apples to a serving dish.
- Dissolve the custard powder in the cold water and stir it into the sauce.
- Bring the sauce to the boil to thicken, and pour over the apples.
- Serve with whipped cream.

CREME CARAMEL

Caramel made with brown sugar has a much stronger flavour than that made with white sugar, but use white sugar if you prefer. If you prefer a very rich creme caramel, replace 125 ml ($^1/_2$ cup) of the milk with 125 ml cream. The custard has to be chilled for several hours before being turned out.

Serves 6

Caramel sauce
    125 ml ($^1/_2$ cup) light brown sugar
    $^1/_2$ ml (pinch) cream of tartar
    60 ml (4 Tbs) water

Custard
    625 ml (2 $^1/_2$ cups) milk
    80 ml ($^1/_3$ cup) sugar
    3 eggs
    3 egg yolks
    5 ml (1 tsp) vanilla essence

- *Caramel sauce* Over medium heat dissolve the sugar and cream of tartar in the water. The cream of tartar will prevent the sugar from crystallising.
- Bring to the boil and boil rapidly until a little dropped in water forms a hard ball. You can see when it is thick enough to form toffee as it dries.
- Coat the bottom of 6 to 8 small warmed ramekins or 1 larger bowl with the caramel sauce, allow the sauce to run a little way up the sides. (By warming the bowls before pouring in the caramel, you will have time to coat the sides before it hardens.)
- *Custard* Preheat oven to 160 °C.
- Heat the milk and sugar to just below boiling point.
- Beat eggs and egg yolks well, but they must not be foamy.
- Gradually pour the hot milk into the beaten egg, beating continually.
- Add the vanilla essence.
- Pour the custard into the ramekins and place them in a roasting pan. Pour cold water into the roasting pan to reach half-way up the sides of the ramekins (or Bain Marie). This will keep the direct heat off the custards and prevent overcooking on the sides.
- Bake for 45 minutes or until just set.
- Remove the dishes from the roasting pan and chill for 8 hours before turning out. If you turn them out too soon, the caramel will not have dissolved completely and there will still be toffee on the sides of the dishes.

CRÈME BRULEE

Traditionally this very rich dessert is made only with cream and egg yolks. To make it less rich, I use a mixture of milk and cream and fewer egg yolks. The addition of a little starch stabilises it and gives it a smooth, velvety texture.

Serves 6

    35 ml (2 $^1/_2$ Tbs) cornflour
    330 ml (1 $^1/_3$ cups) milk
    375 ml (1 $^1/_2$ cups) cream
    80 ml ($^1/_3$ cup) sugar
    7 egg yolks
    3 ml ($^1/_2$ tsp) vanilla essence
    or 1 scraped vanilla pod
    165 ml ($^2/_3$ cup) icing sugar
      or *caramel brown sugar (for caramelising)*

- Preheat oven to 120 °C.
- Mix the cornflour with the milk, cream and sugar. Bring to the boil, stirring continually.

- Cool for 5 minutes.
- Beat the egg yolks, without making them fluffy.
- Gradually pour the hot liquid onto the yolks, beating continually.
- Add the vanilla essence.
- Pour into 6 to 8 ovenware ramekins or 1 larger dish and place in a roasting pan.
- Pour cold water into the roasting pan to come half-way up the sides of the ramekins.
- Bake in a slow oven (120 °C) for about 40 to 60 minutes, or until just set.
- Remove from the water and chill completely.
- Before serving, sift a thick layer of icing sugar on the top of the custards and place under the grill or blow torch until the sugar has melted.
- Leave to stand for 5 minutes for the sugar to harden before serving.

Hint
If using a vanilla pod, add it to the milk and cream before boiling.

Variation
For a harder caramel topping, place 165 ml (2/3 cup) brown sugar in the liquidiser and liquidise until it is fine. Use this in place of the icing sugar.

CHOCOLATE SOUFFLÉ

Light, rich and moist, this dessert should be eaten straight from the oven. Prepare the chocolate sauce in advance. Whip the egg whites, fold them in and place soufflé in the oven just before you sit down to the main course. It will be ready just in time (provided there are no speeches!).

Serves 4 to 6

60 g	butter
45 ml (3 Tbs)	flour
250 ml (1 cup)	milk
200 g	chocolate, grated
4	eggs
45 ml (3 Tbs)	castor sugar

- Preheat oven to 180 °C.
- Melt the butter in a pot and stir in the flour to form a roux.
- Add the milk and bring it to the boil, stirring constantly. It will be *very* thick. Cook over medium heat for 1 minute.
- Remove the pot from the heat and stir in the grated chocolate until it has melted. Cool slightly.
- Separate the eggs and mix the yolks into the cooled sauce.
- Whisk the egg whites to form stiff peaks. Gradually beat the castor sugar into the egg white.
- Fold the sauce into the egg whites.
- Bake in a greased soufflé dish or ramekins for 40 to 45 minutes.
- Serve immediately.

COINTREAU SOUFFLÉ

Make the chocolate soufflé with the following changes:

- Instead of the milk, use fresh orange juice and 5 ml (1 tsp) grated orange rind.
- Omit the chocolate and stir in 60 ml ($1/4$ cup) Cointreau or orange liqueur.

This recipe can be varied by using different juices, flavoured liquids and liqueurs.

CRÊPE SUZETTES

This recipe has lots of orange sauce to serve with the crêpes. Vary it by using mineola or naartjie juice, with Van der Hum.

Serves 6 to 8 (making 18 to 24 crêpes, depending on the size of the pan)

Basic crêpe batter

185 ml ($3/4$ cup)	flour
2 ml ($1/2$ tsp)	salt
30 ml (2 Tbs)	sugar (optional)
2 or 3	eggs (see Hint)
45 ml (3 Tbs)	oil
250 ml (1 cup)	milk

Sauce

15 ml (1 Tbs)	grated orange rind
juice of	2 oranges (about 250 ml)
60 ml ($1/4$ cup)	brown sugar
100 g	unsalted butter
80 ml ($1/3$ cup)	Cointreau or any orange liqueur
10 ml (2 tsp)	cornflour mixed with
30 ml (2 Tbs)	water
45 ml (3 Tbs)	brandy

- *To make the crêpes* sift the dry ingredients into a bowl. Add the eggs and oil and beat until smooth.
- Beat in the milk and leave to stand for 2 hours.
- Lightly grease the pan for the first crêpe only.
- Put the batter in a jug and pour some batter into the hot pan to cover the bottom evenly. Count to 5 and pour the excess back into the jug. This will give you a fairly thin crêpes. For a thicker crêpe, leave the mixture in longer before pouring the excess back.
- Make all the crêpes, pile them one on top of the other and cover with clingwrap until they can be filled.
- *For the sauce,* melt the butter and stir in the brown sugar and orange rind.
- Add the orange juice and simmer until the sugar has dissolved.
- Thicken slightly with the cornflour.
- Stir in the Cointreau.
- Fold each crêpe to form a triangle, arrange folded crêpes in the sauce and heat through.
- Warm the brandy slightly in a ladle and set it alight.
- Pour the burning brandy on the crêpes and serve with whipped cream.

Hint
Using 3 eggs in the crêpe batter makes the crêpes paper thin and very delicate. If you prefer a more substantial crepe use only 2 eggs.

Variation
If you prefer the pancakes to be sweet, add 30 ml (2 Tbs) sugar to the batter.

RUSSIAN CRÊPES

This is a simple dessert with a cream cheese filling. If you enjoy cheese cake, you'll love these.

Serves 6 to 8

1	quantity basic crêpes
1/2	bottle of strawberry, cherry or other jam of your choice kirsch or liqueur of your choice

Filling

250 g	cream cheese or smooth cottage cheese
60 ml (1/4 cup)	cream
30 ml (2 Tbs)	kirsch or liqueur of your choice
45 ml (3 Tbs)	castor sugar

- Stack the crêpes and set aside.
- Blend the cream cheese with a little cream, the sugar and kirsch to taste. If the cream cheese is very soft, use less cream.
- Fill each crêpe with a spoonful of the cream cheese mixture and roll them up.
- Melt the jam over low heat and stir in the liqueur.
- Serve the hot jam with the cold, filled crêpes.

Variations
Use the fruit ricotta pots or tiramisu filling in crêpes. It is light and delicious.

RICH CHOCOLATE MOUSSE

This chocolate mousse uses fewer eggs than most recipes. The whipped cream makes it light, smooth, less gooey but still very rich. Experiment with different chocolates: white, dark or milk, and for special occasions use an imported chocolate such as Toblerone.

Serves 4

300 g	dark chocolate
30 g	butter
2	eggs, separated
30 ml (2 Tbs)	sugar
45 ml (3 Tbs)	Van der Hum or Grand Marnier
250 ml (1 cup)	cream

- Break up the slab of chocolate and melt it in the liqueur in a bowl over hot water.
- Add the butter in small blocks, stirring until it has melted.
- Beat the sugar and egg yolks until pale and light. Reserve egg whites.
- Beat in the melted chocolate and butter, then leave to cool.
- Whip the egg whites to stiff peak stage. Be careful not to overbeat.
- Whip the cream until stiff.
- Fold the egg whites and cream into the chocolate mixture.
- Pour into an attractive bowl and chill for several hours before serving.

LIGHT CHOCOLATE MOUSSE

A lighter mousse made without butter and with more eggs than the rich chocolate mousse. It is not nearly as rich and is a perfect end to a rich meal. It freezes into a delicious ice cream.

Serves 8

300 g	dark chocolate
30 ml (2 Tbs)	liqueur of your choice
30 ml (2 Tbs)	sugar
4	eggs, separated
250 ml (1 cup)	cream

- Break up the slab of chocolate and melt it in the liqueur in a bowl over hot water.
- Beat the sugar and egg yolks until pale and light. Reserve egg whites.
- Beat in the melted chocolate, then leave to cool.
- Whip the egg whites to stiff peak stage. Be careful not to overbeat.
- Whip the cream until stiff.
- Fold the egg whites and cream into the chocolate mixture.
- Pour into an attractive bowl and chill for several hours before serving.

Variation
For a non-dairy chocolate mousse, follow either the rich or light chocolate mousse recipe, but replacing the 250 ml cream with 125 ml (1 sachet) Orley or Insta Whip and replace the butter with margarine.

GELATINE

Gelatine dishes will always be smooth and without strings if you apply the following method to all recipes using gelatine:

- Always soak the dry gelatine in a little *cold* water to rehydrate it. It will swell and become solid and coarse.
- Then melt the rehydrated gelatine in a bowl over boiling water, or on a low setting in the microwave oven. Alternatively, if a hot custard is part of the recipe, drop the solid mass of rehydrated gelatine into the hot custard and stir until it is completely dissolved.
- If the melted gelatine must be added to a *cold* liquid, always pour the cold liquid slowly onto the melted gelatine, stirring constantly. The temperature of the gelatine will drop slowly and it will set evenly. Pouring the hot gelatine into cold liquid will result in gelatine strings as the gelatine will set as soon as it hits the cold liquid.
- If whipped cream or beaten egg white must be added as the gelatine begins to set, ensure that the mixture sets evenly throughout. Do not put the mixture in the fridge – this would result in the outer layer cooling and setting before the middle does. Place the bowl of gelatine mixture in a larger bowl containing ice cubes and cold water. Gently stir the mixture away from the sides of the bowl. This will ensure that the temperature drops evenly throughout the mixture. As soon as it begins to thicken, remove it from the ice and quickly fold in the remaining ingredients. The dessert will set more quickly if it is worked over ice.
- If you are using egg yolks, check the heat of the custard by dipping your finger into it. If it is hot but easily bearable, it will be sufficient to cook the yolks. (Recipes often say 'until the mixture coats the back of a wooden spoon', which is difficult to judge. It simply means that the egg yolks have coagulated. I find testing the temperature with my finger much easier.)

COLD FRUIT SOUFFLÉ

Made with any fresh or tinned fruit purée, an egg custard, gelatine and whipped cream, this recipe can be adapted to suit the season and your preference.

Serves 6 to 8

15 ml (1 Tbs)	gelatine (1 envelope)
30 ml (2 Tbs)	cold water
375 ml (1 $^1/_2$ cups)	fresh fruit purée
60 ml ($^1/_4$ cup)	castor sugar
2	eggs, separated
60 ml ($^1/_4$ cup)	liqueur of your choice
250 ml (1 cup)	cream

- Soak the gelatine in the cold water.
- Place the fruit purée, sugar and egg yolks in a bowl over boiling water.
- Heat the mixture, stirring until it is just hot enough to cook the egg yolks, taking care not to let them overcook and curdle.
- Stir in the rehydrated gelatine and stir until it has completely dissolved.
- Stir in the liqueur and place the mixture in a bowl of ice.
- Whip the egg whites until stiff and whisk cream until stiff.

- Stir the fruit mixture over the ice. As it begins to thicken, carefully fold in the whipped egg whites and cream.
- Pour into a serving dish or individual glasses and place in the fridge until set completely.
- Remove from fridge 10 minutes before you serve them to allow to warm and soften slightly.
- Decorate with whipped cream and pieces of fresh fruit.

Variation

Sweetened tinned fruit can be used in place of the fresh fruit, but halve the amount of sugar used – 375 ml (1 1/2 cups) puréed tinned fruit and 30 ml (2 Tbs) castor sugar. Try using a combination of fruits such as banana and strawberries.

ALMOND CREAM

The flavour of the almonds and Amaretto liqueur make this smooth gelatine dessert perfect for a special occasion. Vary the liqueur and flavouring to suit your taste.

Serves 6 to 8

15 ml (1 Tbs)	gelatine
30 ml (2 Tbs)	cold water
2	eggs, separated
125 ml (1/2 cup)	Amaretto liqueur
60 ml (1/4 cup)	castor sugar
250 ml (1 cup)	milk
	drop of almond oil or almond essence
250 ml (1 cup)	cream

- Follow the method for the fruit cream, using milk in place of fruit pureé.
- Decorate with whipped cream and toasted almond flakes.

Variation

Try instant coffee in the milk and use Kahlua or Tia Maria liqueur.

CHOCOLATE MALTED SOUFFLÉ

If you like a double-thick chocolate malt, you will love this dessert.

Serves 6 to 8

15 ml (1 Tbs)	gelatine
30 ml (2 Tbs)	cold water
250 ml (1 cup)	milk
150 g	dark chocolate
80 ml (1/3 cup)	dry Horlicks
3	eggs, separated
250 ml (1 cup)	cream

- Break up the chocolate and melt it in the milk over boiling water, then stir in the Horlicks. Cool slightly.
- Proceed with the recipe as for the cold fruit soufflé (see page 165).
- Decorate with whipped cream and chocolate curls.

GUAVA CARAMEL SOUFFLÉ

This recipe uses only tinned and packaged ingredients one usually has in the grocery cupboard. It is rich and delicious.

Serves 8

2 x 410 g	tins guavas
1 x tin	Caramel Treat
1 packet	strawberry or cherry jelly
1 x 410 g	tin evaporated milk, well-chilled

- Drain the guavas and strain the liquid into a small pot.
- Add the jelly to the pot and dissolve it over a low heat.
- Purée the guavas and press through a strainer to remove the pips.
- Mix the Caramel Treat until smooth and mix in the guavas and jelly.
- Chill for 15 minutes or work over a bowl of ice.
- Whip the evaporated milk until it is stiff and fold into the guava mixture.
- Pour into a bowl and refrigerate until set.
- Decorate with whipped cream.

FRUIT AND NUT TRIFLE

Everyone has their own version of the simple trifle, but I receive many requests for the recipe. So here is mine. Use it as a starting point to develop your own!

Serves 6 to 8

1	packet jelly of your choice (optional)
½	trifle sponge or *any butter* or *chocolate cake*
410 g	tinned fruit cocktail or tinned fruit of your choice
30 ml (2 Tbs)	jam of your choice
60 ml (¼ cup)	sherry or brandy (optional)
2-3	bananas
100 g	pecan or walnuts

Custard

500 ml (2 cups)	milk
45 ml (3 Tbs)	custard powder
30 ml (2 Tbs)	sugar
2 ml (½ tsp)	vanilla essence
1	egg yolk
125 ml (½ cup)	cream

- Make the jelly and leave to cool but not set.
- Cut the cake into small cubes.
- Drain the tinned fruit and measure off 60 ml (¼ cup) of the liquid. Discard the rest of the liquid.
- Place the fruit liquid and jam in a pot and melt the jam over low heat. Remove from the heat and stir in the sherry.
- Place the cubes of cake in an attractive bowl and drizzle jam mixture all over them.
- Slice the bananas and coarsely (not too fine) chop the nuts.
- Fold all the fruit and nuts carefully into the soaked cake.
- *Custard* Mix the custard powder, sugar, vanilla and egg yolk with a little of the measured milk.
- Bring the remaining milk to the boil and pour it onto the custard mixture, stirring constantly.
- Return it to the stove and bring back to the boil, stirring constantly.
- Remove from the heat and cool for 10 minutes before folding in the stiffly beaten cream.
- Carefully fold the custard into the trifle while both are still warm. The cake must be coated in custard but not overmixed or it will be mushy.
- Pour on the cold jelly and chill in the fridge to set.
- Decorate with whipped cream and more nuts or grated chocolate.

TIRAMISU

This version of the classic Italian dessert called 'Lift-me-up' is as delectable but less rich than the original since it uses the more readily available ricotta cheese rather than pure cream Marscapone cheese.

Serves 10 to 12

500 g	fresh ricotta cheese
60 ml (4 Tbs)	boiling water
5 ml (1 tsp)	strong instant coffee powder
3	eggs
180 ml (¾ cup)	castor sugar
90 ml (6 Tbs)	sherry or Amaretto liqueur
250 ml (1 cup)	cream
2 packets	Boudoir biscuits or trifle sponge
125 ml (½ cup)	black coffee
	cocoa for dusting

- Mix the instant coffee powder into the boiling water.
- Beat ricotta with a whisk or electric beater and gradually add the boiling coffee, beating until it is smooth and creamy. Beat in half (3 Tbs) of the sherry or Amaretto.
- Place the eggs and sugar in a bowl over hot water and whisk until the mixture is light and fluffy.
- Whip the cream fairly stiff.
- Fold the cheese mixture, egg and cream together with a whisk or metal spoon.
- Mix the 125 ml black coffee with the remaining half of the sherry or Amaretto.
- Use a large, square shallow dish and working quickly dip the biscuits into the black coffee. Line the dish with a layer of dipped biscuit fingers.
- Spread a thin layer of the cheese mixture on top of the biscuits.
- Repeat layers of biscuits and cheese mixture, ending with a layer of cheese.
- Top with a sprinkling of cocoa and chill for at least 8 hours before serving.

Hint
This dessert freezes well and is delicious served partially frozen.

ORANGE OR MINEOLA JELLY

This is a wonderfully refreshing basic jelly that can be served with fresh fruit and cream, or fruit can be set in the jelly. Add a couple of tablespoons of Van der Hum or any citrus liqueur to make it more special. Use any pure fruit juice of your choice.

Serves 4 to 6

875 ml (3 1/2 cups)	orange or mineola juice, freshly squeezed but not strained
60 ml (1/4 cup)	sugar
30 ml (2 Tbs)	gelatine

- Mix the gelatine with 60 ml (1/4 cup) of the measured fruit juice and leave for 10 minutes.
- Dissolve the sugar in another 60 ml of the measured juice. Bring to the boil and as soon the sugar is dissolved, add the gelatine mixture and stir until the gelatine has completely dissolved.
- Add the remaining cold juice to the gelatine and sugar mixture to lower the temperature gradually. Stir well. (Do not do it the other way around, or you will get strings of gelatine.)
- Pour into a mould or individual glasses and set in the fridge.

GLAZED ORANGES

Sliced oranges marinated in a liqueur syrup are refreshing and light after a heavy meal. Allow for 8 hours chilling in the fridge.

Serves 10 to 12

8	oranges
625 ml (2 1/2 cups)	sugar
750 ml (3 cups)	water
45 ml (3 Tbs)	syrup
30 ml (2 Tbs)	lemon juice
80 ml (1/3 cup)	orange liqueur of your choice

- Remove the rind from the oranges with a sharp knife or peeler and cut into very thin strips. (The rind or zest is the dark, oily outer layer of the skin.)
- Place the strips of rind in a small pot, cover with water and boil for 10 minutes or until soft.
- Skin the oranges and remove all the pith (the white layer).
- Slice the oranges in thick slices and place them in an attractive bowl.
- Bring the sugar, water, syrup and lemon juice to the boil.
- Add the soft orange strips and boil for 10 minutes until they are transparent.
- Transfer the strips to the bowl of orange slices.
- Boil the syrup for a further 5 minutes. The syrup must be slightly thick.
- Cool for a few minutes, then add the liqueur.
- Pour the syrup over the oranges and chill for at least 8 hours.
- Serve with cream, sago creams or crème caramel (recipes in this chapter).

GLAZED NECTARINES IN ORANGE JUICE

Firm nectarines are lightly poached in an orange syrup for a fresh, light dessert. Try using any firm fruit such as cling peaches, firm white peaches or plums.

Serves 8

8	firm nectarines or peaches
2	oranges
1	lemon
375 ml (1 1/2 cups)	sugar
60 ml (1/4 cup)	orange liqueur of your choice

- Peel the nectarines and carefully cut into halves, quarters or leave them whole.
- Remove the orange rind (zest) from the 2 oranges and cut into very thin strips.
- Boil the strips in water for 10 minutes, then drain and keep the rind.
- Combine the sugar, reserved orange rind and the juice of the lemon in a small pot.
- Squeeze the oranges into a measuring jug. Add enough water to make up 500 ml of liquid.
- Add this liquid to the pot and boil until the orange rind is glassy.
- Add the prepared fruit and simmer until barely soft. This will depend on the firmness of the fruit, but about 5 minutes should be enough.
- Transfer the fruit from the syrup to an attractive bowl.
- Simmer the syrup further until it has slightly thickened.
- Pour it over the fruit and leave to cool for 30 minutes.
- Add the liqueur and chill very well before serving.

PEARS IN WINE

Try this recipe using 1 kg cherries and 500 g strawberries together in place of the pears, but be careful not to overcook the fruit.

Serves 6 to 8

330 ml (1 $1/3$ cup)	dry red wine
165 ml ($2/3$ cup)	orange juice
1	orange, sliced
$1/2$	lemon, sliced
250 ml (1 cup)	sugar
45 ml (3 Tbs)	honey
2	cinnamon sticks
	freshly grated nutmeg
1 kg	small, firm pears
15 ml (1 Tbs)	cornflour

- Place all the ingredients except the pears in a large saucepan.
- Gradually bring to the boil, dissolving the sugar before it boils.
- Peel the pears, keeping the stalks attached.
- Place in simmering liquid turning carefully to ensure equal cooking.
- Simmer for about 25 minutes until tender and thicken slightly with cornflour.
- Serve with cream or ice cream.

YOGHURT APPLE CREAM

This delicious, light dessert made with a combination of yoghurt and cream can be prepared in a minute. Use any fresh fruit in season.

Serves 4

175 ml	natural yoghurt
30 ml (2 Tbs)	honey, warmed
15 ml (1 Tbs)	lemon juice
250 ml (1 cup)	cream
15 ml (1 Tbs)	castor sugar
4	green apples
100 g	grated chocolate or granola (see This and that)

- Mix the yoghurt, honey and lemon juice.
- Whip the cream with the sugar and fold into the yoghurt mixture.
- Coarsely grate the apples with the skin on.
- Layer the yoghurt mixture, chocolate or Granola and grated apples in attractive glasses, ending with the yoghurt. Reserve a little grated chocolate for topping.
- Sprinkle with remaining chocolate and serve.

Hint

A little soft brown sugar can be sprinkled on instead of the chocolate. The sugar melts and forms a layer of caramel.

FRUIT RICOTTA POTS

Ricotta is a sweet low-fat cheese; when whipped with a little boiling water it becomes smooth and creamy. Serve it in place of cream with all your fruit desserts, if you like. The dried apricots in this recipe have to be soaked overnight.

Serves 6

60 g	dried apricots, soaked overnight in
125 ml ($1/2$ cup)	cold water
45 ml (3 Tbs)	honey or sweetener of your choice
80 ml ($1/3$ cup)	Van der Hum or liqueur of your choice
300 g	ricotta cheese
45 ml (3 Tbs)	boiling water

- Cook the apricots in the soaking water until soft.
- Purée the apricots with the honey and liqueur until smooth.
- Whip the ricotta with the boiling water until it is smooth and creamy.
- Beat in the remaining ingredients.
- Check the alcohol flavour and sweetness and adjust to your taste.
- Serve chilled in wine glasses decorated with roasted nuts and serve with biscuits.

Variation

This recipe can be modified by using any purée of fresh, tinned or stewed fruit. Add sweetness and alcohol to your taste. Pile it into a pavlova instead of a rich creamy filling.

PAVLOVAS AND MERINGUES

BASIC MERINGUE

Egg whites freeze perfectly. Accumulate them in the freezer.

You don't have to remember how many egg whites you have. Simply weigh the egg whites and then use double the weight of castor sugar.

For all meringues: Meringues are generally baked at 100 °C. If you prefer them slightly browned, take your oven temperature up by 10 °C, and shorten the baking time. Leave them in the switched-off oven to dry out completely, as for the pavlova.

This quantity is sufficient to make 36 small meringues or a pavlova.

Serves 6

120 g	egg white (3 egg whites, or about $1/2$ cup)
2 ml ($1/2$ tsp)	cream of tartar
240 g (l cup)	castor sugar
2 ml ($1/2$ tsp)	vanilla

MERINGUE SUISSE

This is the easiest and most popular method of making meringues.

- Preheat oven to 100 °C.
- Whisk egg whites until just foamy.
- Add the cream of tartar (this stabilises the egg foam).
- Whisk until the egg white forms stiff peaks when the beater is lifted.
- Add the sugar, a little at a time, beating to stiff peak stage between each addition. (Work with the sugar in 5 to 6 batches.)
- Whisk in the vanilla essence.
- Using 2 teaspoons or a piping bag, shape the meringues onto baking paper or greaseproof paper.
- Bake at 100 °C for 2 $1/2$ hours, or until dry.

MERINGUE ITALIENNE

This meringue is more brittle and dense than the Meringue Suisse. A sugar thermometer is required for perfect results.

- Add 50 g ($1/4$ cup) of castor sugar to the basic meringue ingredients. This compensates for the sugar that remains in the pot.
- Add 1 ml (pinch) cream of tartar to the sugar and water to prevent crystallisation.
- Preheat oven to 100 °C.
- Combine the sugar, 1 ml cream of tartar and 125 ml water in a pot.
- Bring to the boil and boil vigorously until the syrup reaches 130 °C on a sugar thermometer.
- Whisk egg whites and cream of tartar to form stiff peaks.
- Very gradually pour in the hot syrup while whisking continually.
- Whisk in the vanilla essence.
- Shape the meringues and bake until dry. (These meringues take a little longer to bake than Meringue Suisse.)

PAVLOVA

This elegant dessert consists of a crisp meringue encasing soft meringue, with a filing of cream and fruit. Use any filling of your choice, but fill your pavlova only just before you eat it, as it softens very quickly.

Serves 8 to 10

- Preheat oven to 110 °C.
- Follow the recipe for *Meringue Suisse*, adding all the ingredients except the last 60 ml (4 Tbs) castor sugar.
- Add 15 ml (1 Tbs) cornflour to the remaining castor sugar and mix well.
- Gently fold this into the meringue mixture, using either a balloon whisk or a metal spoon.
- Shape into 1 large or several small pavlovas using either a spoon or a piping bag.
- Bake for about 1 $1/2$ hours. Switch off the oven and leave the pavlova inside until dry.

Tropical fruit filling

  410 g tinned pitted litchis,
  310 g tinned mandarin oranges,
  115 g tinned granadillas
  or 6 fresh granadillas
  3 sliced bananas
  200 g strawberries
  or 425 g tinned cherries
125 ml (½ cup) citrus liqueur of your choice
60 ml (4 Tbs) custard powder
   whipped cream

- Drain the liquid off all the tins of fruit and mix together.
- Measure off 250 ml (1 cup) of liquid and discard the rest.
- Mix the 250 ml juice with the granadilla pulp and stir in the custard powder.
- Combine all the fruit and pour on the liqueur, then leave to stand for a few hours.
- Place the juice and custard powder in a pot and bring to the boil, stirring constantly. Simmer for 1 minute (it should be very thick).
- Strain the liqueur off the fruit and add it to the hot custard. Cool slightly.
- Pour the custard onto the fruit and *carefully* fold through.
- Pile into the pavlova and pipe with whipped cream.

Lemon curd filling

375 ml (1 ½ cups) cream
250 ml (1 cup) lemon curd
   strawberries or *other fresh fruit for decoration*

- Whip the cream and fold in the lemon curd, pile into the pavlova and decorate with strawberries or any fresh fruit.

Variation
Use the *fruit ricotta pots* (or any poached fruit) in the pavlova. Thicken the poached fruit syrup as described under *Tropical fruit filling*.

APRICOT DACQUOISE

The tart flavour of apricot goes very well with the sweetness of the meringue. This filling can also be used in a pavlova. The dried apricots have to be soaked overnight before use. Make the filling first.

Serves 8

Filling

  125 g dried apricots, soaked overnight in
  250 ml water
310 ml (1 ¼ cup) sugar
2 ml (½ tsp) lemon rind
 juice of ½ lemon
  250 ml cream
125 ml (½ cup) fresh orange juice
30 ml (2 Tbs) orange liqueur

Meringue

  150 g egg whites (about 4 eggs)
300 g (1 ½ cups) castor sugar
1 ml (pinch) cream of tartar
  1 drop almond essence
  100 g ground almonds

- Preheat oven to 140 °C.
- *Filling* Stew the apricots gently in the soaking water until soft.
- Add the sugar, lemon rind and lemon juice and stir until the sugar has dissolved.
- Purée the mixture and chill.
- *Meringue* Whisk the egg whites and cream of tartar until very stiff.
- Whisk in 125 ml (½ cup) of the castor sugar and a drop of almond essence; whisk until very thick.
- Mix the remaining castor sugar and the ground almonds and fold into the egg white mixture.
- Draw two circles (diameter 20 cm) on greaseproof paper. Spread the mixture to cover the circles and bake for 1 hour. Cool.
- Whip the cream and fold in ⅓ of the puréed apricots.
- Sandwich the two meringues together with the apricot cream.
- Decorate with sifted icing sugar, whipped cream and chocolate curls.
- Mix the remaining apricot purée with the orange juice and liqueur to form a thick pouring sauce to serve with the dessert.

Variation
For a less rich filling, use the *fruit ricotta pots*.

HAZELNUT PAVLOVA

Roasted hazelnuts, used instead of the cornflour, give this pavlova its wonderful nutty flavour.

Serves 8 to 10

    1 basic meringue recipe (see page 170)
100 g hazelnuts

Filling

2 x tins pitted black cherries
30 ml (2 Tbs) sugar
30 ml (2 Tbs) custard powder
30 ml (2 Tbs) Kirsch
    or *orange liqueur*
250 ml (1 cup) whipped cream

- Before making the meringue, roast the hazelnuts on a baking sheet in the oven at 175 °C until the skins crack and you can smell the roasted nuts. Be careful not to burn them.
- Rub the nuts in a dishcloth to remove as much of the papery skins as possible.
- Chop the nuts finely in a food processor and leave to cool.
- Make the basic meringue mixture and, with the last addition of sugar, fold in the finely chopped nuts.
- Allow oven to cool down to 140 °C.
- On baking paper, shape meringue mixture into a rectangular pavlova and bake at 140 °C for 40 minutes. Switch off the oven and leave to cool inside oven.
- *For the filling*, drain the cherries and reserve cherries and 250 ml (1 cup) liquid from the tins. Discard the rest.
- Stir the custard powder into a paste with 45 ml (3 Tbs) of the fruit juice and heat the remainder in a pot with the sugar.
- Add the hot liquid to the paste, return the mixture to the pot and bring to the boil, stirring until thick.
- Cool slightly and fold in the fruit and kirsch. Leave to cool.
- Just before serving, place the cherries on the meringue and decorate with the whipped cream.

BASIC FROZEN MOUSSE

Very few ice crystals form in a frozen mousse, due to the high fat and air content and the low water content. Unlike ordinary ice cream, a mousse therefore does not have to be churned or beaten to break down the crystals. The only disadvantage is that a frozen mousse tends to dehydrate more quickly in the deep freeze than a churned ice cream and therefore does not keep for long.

Serves 6

2 eggs, separated
250 ml (1 cup) cream
90 ml (6 Tbs) castor sugar
3 ml ($1/2$ tsp) vanilla essence

- Using 3 separate bowls, beat the egg whites until stiff. Beat in 30 ml (2 Tbs) of the sugar and beat until thick and shiny.
- In second bowl, beat the cream until it begins to thicken. Beat in another 30 ml (2 Tbs) of the sugar and beat until stiff. Do not overbeat.
- In third bowl, beat egg yolks with the remaining 30 ml (2 Tbs) sugar until thick and pale. If you beat the mixtures in this order, you will not have to wash your beaters in between bowls.
- Combine all 3 mixtures in one bowl, add the vanilla and fold together gently.
- Pour into a serving dish and freeze.

Hint
This recipe works perfectly using 1 sachet Insta Whip or Orley Whip in place of the cream.

Variations
- *Liqueur* Flavour the basic mousse or any of the variations with 30 ml (2 Tbs) of liqueur of your choice.
- *Chocolate* Melt 100 g dark chocolate and add it to the egg yolks in the basic mousse recipe. Beat the yolks, sugar and chocolate together. Continue with the basic recipe.
- *Coffee* Dissolve 10 ml (2 tsp) instant coffee in 15 ml of hot water and cool. Make up basic mousse recipe and fold in the cold coffee when combining the 3 mixtures. Add a little coffee liqueur if desired.
- *Fruit* Add 500 ml (2 cups) of any fruit purée to the basic frozen mousse. Try 125 g puréed stewed prunes or dried apricots and a little brandy. Or use fresh puréed mango, strawberries, or pawpaw.

PRALINE MOUSSE

This variation of the basic mousse has a crunchy texture.

Serves 6

1	quantity basic frozen mousse
100 g (1 packet)	flaked almonds
80 ml ($^1/_3$ cup)	castor sugar

- Roast the almond flakes in the oven at 170 °C until golden. Be careful not to burn them.
- Melt the sugar in a pot over medium heat.
- Stir until the sugar begins to turn golden, then stir in the toasted almond flakes.
- Pour into a greased tin and leave until cold, then coarsely chop in the food processor.
- Fold into the mousse mixture when combining the 3 mixtures.

FRUIT AND NUT MOUSSE

This is perfect as a frozen Christmas pudding. The fruit is soaked overnight.

Serves 6 to 8

1	quantity basic frozen mousse
125 g	glacé fruit of your choice
100 g	glacé cherries
80 ml ($^1/_3$ cup)	whisky or alcohol of your choice
100 g	flaked almonds
100 g	dark chocolate

- Chop the glacé fruit and soak fruit and cherries in the alcohol overnight.
- Roast the flaked almonds in the oven at 170 °C until they are golden.
- Coarsely chop the chocolate.
- Combine all the ingredients and fold into the basic mousse when combining the 3 mixtures.

FROZEN CHOCOLATE MERINGUE

This recipe is a combination of a chocolate meringue and a frozen chocolate banana mousse served with a mocha sauce. It is very impressive, but easy to make. Use other pavlova recipes and vary the frozen mousse and sauce to obtain spectacular results. The chocolate banana mousse can be made and served on its own as a mocha banana ice cream.

Serves 8 to 10

Meringue

165 ml ($^2/_3$ cup)	egg whites (4-5 egg whites)
2 ml ($^1/_2$ tsp)	cream of tartar
310 ml (1 $^1/_4$ cups)	castor sugar
60 ml ($^1/_4$ cup)	cocoa powder

Chocolate banana mousse

100 g	dark chocolate
15 ml (1 Tbs)	boiling water
5 ml (1 tsp)	instant coffee powder
2	ripe bananas, mashed
2	eggs, separated
45 ml (3 Tbs)	castor sugar
250 ml (1 cup)	cream

Mocha sauce

375 ml (1 $^1/_2$ cups)	sugar
250 ml (1 cup)	sour cream
30 g	butter
10 ml (2 tsp)	instant coffee powder
100 g	dark chocolate
30 ml (2 Tbs)	coffee liqueur

- Preheat oven to 120 °C.
- *Meringue* Whisk the egg whites until foamy.
- Add the cream of tartar and whisk to stiff peak stage.
- Gradually beat in 185 ml ($^3/_4$ cup) of the measured sugar in 5 to 6 batches, beating after each addition.
- Sift the remaining 100 ml sugar together with the cocoa and fold mixture into the meringue mixture.
- Draw 3 circles of 20 cm diameter on baking paper.
- Divide the meringue mixture between the 3 circles and spread to cover the circles, forming disks.
- Bake for about 2 hours or until dry.
- *Mousse* In a double boiler melt the broken chocolate in the boiling water with the coffee powder. Stir in the mashed bananas and leave to cool.
- Using 3 bowls, beat egg yolks with 15 ml (1 Tbs) sugar until pale. Then beat the egg whites until stiff. Beat in 15 ml (1 Tbs) of the remaining sugar and beat

again until stiff. Beat cream with remaining 15 ml (1 Tbs) sugar until stiff.
- Combine the cooled chocolate mixture with the contents of the 3 bowls and carefully fold together.
- Place in the deepfreeze for 2 to 3 hours till firm but not frozen.
- Divide the mixture in 2 and layer between the 3 meringue disks.
- Freeze completely before serving.
- *Mocha sauce* Place all the ingredients, except the liqueur, in a pot and gradually bring to the boil, stirring constantly.
- Simmer for 3 to 5 minutes.
- Leave to cool to room temperature and stir in the liqueur.
- Serve with the frozen meringue.

STRAWBERRY AND SOUR CREAM ICE CREAM

Yoghurt can be used instead of sour cream, if preferred. By using fruit yoghurt and varying the fruit you can conjure up a great variety of flavours.

Serves 8 to 10

500 g	strawberries
3	eggs
250 ml (1 cup)	castor sugar
250 ml (1 cup)	sour cream
250 ml (1 cup)	cream

- Wash the strawberries and purée in a blender or food processor.
- In a bowl over hot water, whisk the eggs and sugar until thick and pale.
- Stir in the puréed berries and sour cream or yoghurt.
- Place the ice cream in a large bowl and freeze overnight.
- The following day, whip cream till it forms soft peaks.
- Place the frozen ice cream in a food processor and process till smooth. Work quickly. Fold in the whipped cream.
- Refreeze completely before serving.

FRUIT SORBET

To make a light, fluffy frozen fruit sorbet is very easy, especially if you have a food processor. Made in advance, it keeps for weeks in the deepfreeze. Remember though, that as you use it and air is allowed into the container, the sorbet dehydrates and deteriorates, so don't keep it too long. Using these recipes with fruit juice and puréed fruit, you can adapt them and use any fruit or juice you want. *Makes about 1 litre (4 cups).*

STRAWBERRY SORBET

500 g	strawberries, hulled
310 ml (1 $\frac{1}{4}$ cup)	sugar
45 ml (3 Tbs)	fresh lemon juice
125 ml ($\frac{1}{2}$ cup)	fresh orange juice
5 ml (1 tsp)	gelatine
1	egg white, beaten
30 ml (2 Tbs)	orange liqueur, optional

- Heat the strawberries, sugar and juices until the sugar has dissolved.
- Rehydrate the gelatine in 30 ml (2 Tbs) cold water.
- Add to pot of hot ingredients and stir until it has dissolved.
- Liquidise the contents of the pot and cool.
- Pour into a large, flat container and freeze solid for 24 hours.
- Break it into pieces and place it in batches in the processor.
- Process until it is smooth.
- Whisk the egg white and mix it into the processed mixture, with the liqueur.
- Place in bowl and refreeze for 24 hours before using.

LEMON SORBET

250 ml (1 cup)	fresh lemon juice
125 ml ($\frac{1}{2}$ cup)	fresh orange juice
500 ml (2 cups)	water
310 ml (1 $\frac{1}{4}$ cup)	sugar
5 ml (1 tsp)	finely grated lemon zest
5 ml (1 tsp)	gelatine
1	egg white, beaten

- Follow the method for strawberry sorbet.

ICE CREAM SAUCES

Serve any of these sauces with a good vanilla ice cream.

BUTTERSCOTCH SAUCE

Serves 4 to 6

250 ml (1 cup)	brown sugar
30 ml (2 Tbs)	syrup
5 ml (1 tsp)	vinegar
45 ml (3 Tbs)	water
75 g	butter
80 ml ($^1/_3$ cup)	cream
3 ml ($^1/_2$ tsp)	vanilla essence

- Boil the sugar, syrup, vinegar, water and butter until a little dropped into water forms a soft ball (116 °C on a sugar thermometer).
- Remove from the stove plate and stir in the cream and vanilla essence.

BAR ONE SAUCE

Serves 4 to 6

3 x 100 g	Bar One chocolate bars
125 ml ($^1/_2$ cup)	milk or cream

- Cut the chocolate bars into slices and place in a pot with the milk or cream.
- Stirring constantly, over medium heat melt the chocolate and bring mixture to the boil.

ORANGE BANANA SAUCE

Serves 4 to 6

60 ml ($^1/_4$ cup)	sugar
30 ml (2 Tbs)	water
250 ml (1 cup)	fresh orange juice
15 ml (1 Tbs)	custard powder
2	bananas
30 ml (2 Tbs)	Van der Hum
	or *orange liqueur of your choice*

- Boil the sugar and water over a high heat and until the sugar turns a deep golden colour.
- Mix the orange juice with the custard powder and pour onto caramelised sugar.
- Bring the mixture to the boil.
- Thinly slice the bananas and add to the sauce. Heat through but do not overcook the bananas.
- Remove from the stove plate and add the liqueur.

CHOCOLATE CARAMEL SAUCE

Serves 8

250 ml (1 cup)	sugar
60 ml ($^1/_4$ cup)	cocoa powder
5 ml (1 tsp)	vinegar
15 ml (1 Tbs)	butter
45 ml (3 Tbs)	boiling water
15 ml (1 Tbs)	syrup
125 ml ($^1/_2$ cup)	Caramel Treat
5 ml (1 tsp)	vanilla essence

- Place all the ingredients except Caramel Treat and vanilla in a pot.
- Gradually bring to the boil, stirring continually. Make sure that the sugar is completely dissolved.
- As soon as it comes to the boil, remove from heat and stir in Caramel Treat and vanilla essence. Mix until smooth.

HOT CHRISTMAS MINCE SAUCE

Perfect over ice cream, if you don't feel like a traditional rich Christmas pudding on a hot South African Christmas day.

Serves 8 to 10

454 g	Christmas fruit mince
400 g	apple sauce
or 410 g	tinned apples, puréed
500 ml (2 cups)	cream
45 ml (3 Tbs)	custard powder
125 ml ($^1/_2$ cup)	brandy

- Stir custard powder into a little of the cream.
- Place fruit mince, apple sauce and remaining cream in a pot and bring to the boil, stirring constantly.
- Add custard mixture and bring back to the boil.
- Remove from the heat and stir in brandy to taste.
- Serve hot over ice cream.

BLACK CHERRIES FLAMBÉ

Serves 4

425 g	tinned black cherries
50 g	butter
125 ml (½ cup)	brown sugar
juice of ½	lemon
30 ml (2 Tbs)	sherry
10 ml (2 tsp)	cornflour
45 ml (3 Tbs)	Kirsch *or alcohol of your choice*

- Melt the butter and add brown sugar.
- Over a low heat, melt the sugar.
- Add the liquid from the tin of cherries.
- Simmer until all the sugar is dissolved.
- Add sherry and lemon juice to taste – thicken slightly with the cornflour, mixed with a little of the cold fruit juice or water.
- Add cherries and heat through, but do not cook the cherries.
- Warm the Kirsch in a ladle and set it alight. Pour over the cherries.
- Serve with vanilla ice cream and whipped cream.

Variations
- A peach flambé makes a simple and inexpensive, yet impressive change to the cherry flambé.
- Or use tinned pineapples and other fruit and liqueurs, following the cherry flambé recipe.
- Substitute tinned peaches in place of the cherries and use brandy instead of the Kirsch.

DOUBLE-THICK CHOCOLATE MALT

Mixed with the ice cream rather than served with it, there is nothing quite like a double-thick chocolate malt! The chocolate mixture will keep in the fridge for up to 2 weeks.

Serves 4

100 g	dark chocolate
80 ml (⅓ cup)	Horlicks or *Nestum*
125 ml (½ cup)	milk
750 ml (3 cups)	vanilla ice cream

- Place the chocolate, Horlicks and milk in a pot.
- Over low heat melt the chocolate and dissolve the Horlicks.
- Remove from heat and whisk until smooth.
- Chill overnight. It will become fairly thick.
- Using a hand beater, beat the chocolate mixture into the ice cream until smooth. (If you blend it in a food processor, be careful not to overmix, or the ice cream will break down and melt.)
- Pour into glasses and serve immediately.

THIS AND THAT

In this chapter you will find preserves, sweets, drinks and miscellaneous recipes.

BASIC JAM

Home-made jam does not involve 'cooking for 4 hours and eaten in 20 minutes!' It is easy, very satisfying and your labours can be enjoyed for months.

- Choose ripe but not over-ripe fruit.
- A few pieces of slightly greener fruit can be used to increase the pectin content of the jam.
- Add lemon juice to assist the gelling and reduce the sweetness.
- Cook firm fruit in a little water before adding the sugar. Soft fruits such as berries do not need water or extra cooking.
- Layer your soft fruit with the sugar overnight. This will draw the water from the fruit and partially dissolve the sugar.
- Gradually bring to the boil and then boil until the jam reaches gelling consistency. The temperature should be about 105 °C, but if the fruit is low in pectin, you will have to cook it to a higher temperature to increase the sugar concentration.
- Use equal quantities of fruit and sugar for the tarter fruits such as apricots and plums – in other words 1 kg fruit to 1 kg sugar.
- For sweet fruits such as the berries and grapes, use 1:75 fruit and sugar, i.e. 1 kg fruit to 750 g sugar.
- Bottle jams in sterilised jars and cover with wax or brandy to prevent mould.
- Seal and store.

Hints

- For low pectin fruits, such as strawberries, commercial pectin can be added (this is available from many pharmacies and speciality food stores).
- Mix the pectin well with equal parts of powdered glucose (this prevents it lumping when you add it to the jam).
- Sprinkle it gradually onto the boiling jam until it reaches the desired consistency. The quantity will depend on the pectin content of the jam. Start with a tablespoon at a time.

MICROWAVE JAM

- Use the same fruit to sugar proportions as above.
- Work with 500 g fruit at a time.
- Cook in a very large bowl, as it boils over easily.
- Place all the ingredients in a bowl and microwave on 100% power for 5 minutes, stirring occasionally.
- Stir well and remove any sugar crystals on the side of the bowl.
- Continue cooking on 100% power, stirring periodically, until setting consistency (about 15 minutes).

GRAPE JAM

This is an example of the basic jam recipe.

  3 kg black grapes (e.g. barlinka)
 2,5 kg sugar
 juice of 1 lemon
    large piece of bruised ginger (optional)

- Cut the grapes in half and remove pips.
- Layer the grapes, lemon juice, ginger and sugar in a heavy pot and leave to stand overnight.
- Slowly bring to the boil and simmer for about 2 hours until setting point.
- Remove scum as it appears on surface.
- Bottle in sterilised jars and pour wax or brandy over the top before sealing.

BASIC MARMALADE

Use any combination of citrus fruit that you like to vary the flavour. Using molasses will give the marmalade a darker colour.

  2,5 kg citrus fruit of your choice
 2 kg (10 cups) sugar
 45 ml (3 Tbs) molasses (optional)

- Using a strong peeler peel the rinds off all the fruit, cut into strips and place in a large bowl.
- Squeeze all the juice from the peeled fruit and pour it over the strips of rind. Leave to stand overnight.
- Cut remaining part of fruit into large chunks (i.e. all the pith and pips), place in a large pot, cover with 2 litres water and leave to stand overnight.
- Boil the ingredients in the pot for 2 hours or until the fruit is completely pulpy.
- Strain and add the liquid to the peels and fruit juice and discard the pulp. Together with the fruit juice, you should have 2 $\frac{1}{2}$ litres of liquid. Make up with extra juice or water.
- Boil peels in this liquid for about 1 hour until the peels are soft.
- Add sugar and molasses and boil for about 1 hour or until gelling point is reached. (The molasses will give the marmalade a darker colour.)
- If you are not sure, put the lid on the pot and leave to stand overnight before bottling. The next day you will be able to see whether it has gelled sufficiently. Gently heat it through again and bottle as desired.
- If it is still too runny, bring it back to the boil over gentle heat and boil for a further 15 to 20 minutes and check again.

Hint
I like to use a mixture of citrus fruit – for example 2 oranges, 2 grapefruit, 2 mineolas or naartjies and 3 lemons.

KUMQUAT MARMALADE

This is the easiest marmalade to make, because all the fruit is used. The skin of the kumquat is sweet, the thin pith is bitter and the flesh is sour – the perfect combination for marmalade.

  1 kg kumquats
  1 kg sugar
 1 $\frac{1}{2}$ litre (6 cups) water
  1 small piece of root ginger

- Slice the kumquats into thin slices and remove and discard the pips.
- Peel and thinly slice the ginger.
- Place the sliced kumquats and ginger in a medium-sized pot with the water.
- Bring it to the boil and simmer for 1 hour or until the skins are completely soft.
- Add the sugar and gradually bring the mixture to the boil, stirring to prevent the sugar from burning on the bottom.
- Boil for about 20 minutes or until the marmalade has reached gelling point (see basic marmalade recipe).
- Pour into sterilised bottles and seal.

Variation
This recipe is also delicious made with limes.

APPLE AND MINT JELLY

This recipe requires a little more effort than a simple mint sauce, but the results make it worthwhile. The base is a jelly (jam) made from apples and citrus fruit, which all have high pectin content. The fresh mint and vinegar is then added to the jelly.

THIS AND THAT

Apple jelly

500 g	sour green apples
1	orange
1	lemon
750 ml (3 cups)	sugar
1 litre (4 cups)	water

- Slice apples, oranges and lemon.
- Place in a pot with sugar and water and boil for about 45 minutes until it has gelled.
- Strain through a double thickness of muslin.
- *Do not stir the mixture* in the strainer, as this will result in a cloudy jelly.

Mint jelly

45 ml (3 Tbs)	fresh lemon juice
45 ml (3 Tbs)	apple cider vinegar
2 ml ($\frac{1}{2}$ tsp)	salt
250 ml (1 cup)	fresh mint leaves (tightly packed)
500 ml (2 cups)	apple jelly (see recipe)
1 ml ($\frac{1}{4}$ tsp)	green food colouring

- Finely chop the mint in food processor.
- Place the lemon juice, vinegar and salt in a saucepan with the apple jelly and cook rapidly until setting point (about 7 minutes).
- Remove from the heat and add the chopped mint and food colouring. Stir well.
- Pour into sterilised jars (empty herb and spice bottles are ideal for selling at fêtes).

GREEN FIG PRESERVE

Completely different to the commercially made figs, these are softer, less sweet, with the flavour of ginger and lemon.

2 kg	green figs
	syrup
2 kg	sugar
3 litres (12 cups)	water
1	large piece root ginger, peeled and sliced
45 ml (3 Tbs)	lemon juice

Soaking solution

30 ml (2 Tbs)	slaked lime per
5 litre (20 cups)	water
or 60 ml (4 Tbs)	bicarbonate of soda

- Cut a cross on the bottom of each fig (the rounded end).
- Make a solution with the bicarb or lime and water, and soak the fruit in it overnight.
- Rinse well, washing off any sediment that may have adhered to the fruit. Place in fresh water for 15 minutes.
- Prepare the syrup by dissolving the sugar in the water over a low heat.
- Add the lemon juice and the slices of root ginger and bring to the boil. For an unusual flavour, add a few star anise pods to the syrup.
- Meanwhile boil the figs in plenty of clean water for about 7 minutes, or until almost tender. If the figs are not rock hard to begin with, they will soften very quickly.
- Remove the figs with a slotted spoon and place them in the boiling syrup.
- Boil till they are tender and translucent and the syrup is thick.
- Place figs and syrup in hot sterilized jars and seal immediately.

Hint
A Talkabout listener suggests the following: Prepare the figs the same way. Scrub and cut a small cross, but instead of soaking the figs in lime, salt or bicarbonate, layer the figs in the pot with the fig leaves off the tree. Then cover them with water and bring to the boil. Simmer for 20 to 30 minutes until figs are beginning to soften. Continue as above with syrup. The leaves keep the figs very green and enhance the flavour.

Variation
Follow this recipe but use whole kumquats.

POMERANTZEN

Glacé grapefruit peel
Every time you have a grapefruit for breakfast, freeze the peel. When you have eaten enough grapefruits, use the skins to make the tastiest of all the glace fruits. It keeps well and is delicious served with coffee.

6	large grapefruit
or 2	pomelos
	or *just the frozen empty skins!*
500 ml (2 cups)	grapefruit juice
	or *orange juice*
1 litre (4 cups)	sugar
80 ml ($\frac{1}{3}$ cup)	icing sugar

- Squeeze the grapefruits (if using just the skin, use any fruit juice).
- Cut each grapefruit peel into thick wedges and carefully remove the flesh with the membrane, leaving the pith on the rind.

- Place peels in a pot and cover with water.
- Boil until skins are soft (about 30 minutes).
- Drain off water and cover with cold water.
- Allow to cool, then carefully peel off the thin yellow rind and discard. You are now left with the thick pith.
- If you want to remove more of the bitter taste, leave the pith to stand in fresh cold water overnight.
- Bring the grapefruit juice and sugar to the boil and boil the wedges of pith in the syrup until the skins are almost clear and the syrup has thickened (about 30 minutes).
- Using a slotted spoon, place the peels on a wet tray.
- Boil the syrup further until it reaches soft ball stage (116 °C on a sugar thermometer).
- Mix the remaining syrup with icing sugar to form a thin glacé icing. Dip the skins into the icing and place them on cooling racks with a drip tray underneath.
- Leave to cool.
- The pomerantzen will be wet and soft.
- For chewier results, cook the skins a little longer and take syrup up to firm ball stage (120 °C) before adding the icing sugar.

Hint
Dip them in melted chocolate for special occasions. They also make inexpensive home-made gifts.

DRINKS

MULLED WINE

Try this on a cold winter's evening to get a party warmed up! If you want it alcohol-free bring it to the boil before serving.

Makes 10 to 12 glasses

1 litre (4 cups)	dry red wine
500 ml (2 cups)	pure orange juice or apricot juice
250 ml (1 cup)	water
1	orange, sliced
1	orange, kept whole
about 25	cloves
4	cinnamon sticks
about 250 ml (1 cup)	honey
	brandy to taste, if desired

- Push the cloves into the whole orange and place it in a large pot with the remaining ingredients.
- Slowly heat through and for best results, leave to stand for several hours to infuse the spices.
- Reheat before serving.
- Just before serving, add a little brandy to taste.

SANGRIA

This Spanish drink is a lighter, sparkling version of mulled wine and is served cold.

Makes 8 to 10 glasses

750 ml (3 cups)	dry red wine
250 ml (1 cup)	apricot or orange juice
1	orange, sliced
3	cinnamon sticks
24	cloves
1	whole orange
80 ml ($1/3$ cup)	sugar
60 ml ($1/4$ cup)	brandy (optional)
500 ml (2 cups)	soda water
	blocks of ice

- Press the cloves into the whole orange.
- Place 250 ml (1 cup) wine and fruit juice in a pot with orange, cinnamon and sugar.
- Warm until the sugar is dissolved.
- Add the remainder of the wine and chill for several hours.
- Just before serving, add soda, brandy and ice cubes.

FRUIT PUNCH

This is a basic fruit punch that can be altered according to the fruit in season. Adjust the alcohol content to your taste.

Makes about 12 glasses

1	tin fruit cocktail, drained
2	bananas, sliced
125 g	strawberries
80 ml ($1/3$ cup)	vodka or alcohol of your choice
750 ml (3 cups)	dry white wine
500 ml (2 cups)	fresh fruit juice
500 ml (2 cups)	lemonade, chilled
	blocks of ice and fresh mint

- Soak the fruit in vodka for about 2 hours.
- Add the wine and fruit juice and chill.
- Add the lemonade and ice just before serving decorated with fresh mint.

Hint

If you prefer it less sweet, use soda water in place of the lemonade.

HOME-MADE LEMONADE

This is so easy to make that I almost feel embarrassed to include the recipe in the book, but it is so delicious and refreshing, it deserves a place! The secret is to use freshly squeezed lemon juice.

1 litre (4 cups)	lemonade
250 ml (1 cup)	fresh lemon juice

For garnish

Slices of orange and lemon
tinned or glacé cherries
ice cubes
few sprigs of fresh mint

- Just before serving, open the cold lemonade and mix in the fresh lemon juice.
- Pour into a long glass jug with the garnishes of your choice.
- If you find the mixture too acid, cut back a little on the lemon.

PICKLES AND CHUTNEY

Pickles are extremely easy to make and are very attractive displayed in their bottles on your kitchen shelf. They taste great too!

SALLY'S PICKLED VEGETABLES

These lightly pickled vegetables make the most attractive salad. They are at their best 2 to 3 days after being made. For the vegetables, I use coloured peppers, celery, cauliflower, carrots, cucumber, asparagus, green beans.

2 kg	firm vegetables of your choice (approximate)
425 g	green olives, with liquid
4	cloves garlic, crushed
500 ml (2 cups)	water
30 ml (2 Tbs)	salt
125 ml ($1/2$ cup)	fresh lemon juice
30 ml (2 Tbs)	oil

- Clean vegetables and cut them into chunks.
- Pour olive brine, water, garlic and salt into a pot and bring it to the boil.
- Add lemon juice and oil.
- Layer vegetables and olives in a large deep bowl or jar.
- Pour on the hot liquid and weigh down vegetables with a plastic bag full of water, a lid, or a heavy plate making sure all the vegetables are immersed in the pickle.
- Leave out of the fridge overnight.
- By the next morning, the vegetables will have shrunk so the weight can be removed.
- Refrigerate for 2 days before eating.

SALLY'S MEDITERRANEAN PICKLED CUCUMBERS

These cucumbers are quite delicious, but they must be eaten within a month of making, or else they become *very* acidic!

2 kg	gherkins or *very small firm cucumbers*
1,5 litre (6 cups)	water
60 ml ($1/4$ cup)	salt
750 ml (1 bottle)	white grape vinegar
6	bay leaves
15 ml (1 Tbs)	peppercorns
15 ml (1 Tbs)	mustard seeds
4	vine leaves (optional)
8	cloves garlic

- Wash gherkins and place in jars with a vine leaf and 2 cloves of garlic in each jar.
- Place water, salt, vinegar, bay leaves, peppercorns and mustard seeds in a pot.
- Bring to the boil, then leave to cool to room temperature.
- Pour over cucumbers and leave for 1 week before eating.

For Hint *see next page.*

Hint
If you want to bottle them for a longer period, use 125 ml (1/2 cup) salt and 250 ml (1 cup) vinegar to the 1,5 litres water. The cucumbers will take longer to pickle.

MIKI'S PICKLED AUBERGINES

Miki Ciman makes the nicest ricotta and mozzarella I have tasted. Her pickled aubergines are also something!

6-8 medium	aubergines
500 ml (2 cups)	vinegar of your choice
45 ml (3 Tbs)	salt
4-6	garlic cloves
	sprigs of fresh sweet basil
	olive oil to cover aubergines

- Wash, dry and peel the aubergines.
- Cut into thick slices.
- Bring the vinegar and salt to the boil.
- Place aubergines in vinegar and bring back to the boil.
- Remove aubergines – they should still be firm.
- Dry the aubergines well and leave in a colander overnight.
- Wash and dry basil leaves and slice garlic.
- Layer the aubergines with the garlic and basil in a jar.
- Pour on enough olive oil (or equal quantities olive and sunflower oil) to cover the aubergines.
- Seal the jars and refrigerate for several days before eating.

Hint
If you cannot get fresh basil, use bay leaves or fresh rosemary.

PEAR CHUTNEY

The flavour of the apples and pears is quite unusual in this chutney. The secret to good chutney is long, slow cooking. Be careful that as it thickens it doesn't burn on the bottom.

1,5 kg	pears, cored
2	green apples, cored
2	onions
500 g	seedless raisins
3-5 ml ($^1/_2$-1 tsp)	cayenne pepper, or to taste
1	large knob fresh ginger, peeled and finely chopped
3 ml ($^1/_2$ tsp)	nutmeg
5 ml (1 tsp)	salt
10 ml (2 tsp)	cloves
2	oranges, with juice and grated rind
625 ml (2 $^1/_2$ cups)	soft brown sugar
500 ml (2 cups)	vinegar

- Mince all the fruit and onions together.
- Bring all the ingredients to the boil, stirring occasionally.
- Simmer for about 3 hours or until thick. Bottle in preserving jars.

Variation
To make a hot chutney, add some chopped chilli to taste while you are cooking it.

SWEETS

If you are going to be adventurous and make sweets, a sugar thermometer is essential. This will equip you to make the most wonderful sugar creations. It also makes perfect frying at the correct temperature a cinch!

ECONOMICAL FUDGE

By adding a cup of flour and the vinegar while the fudge is cooking, the flour is converted into simple sugars that will stretch the recipe. It is a good recipe to make for a fête!

1,5 kg (6 cups)	sugar
250 ml (1 cup)	cake flour
125 g	butter
1 x 397 tin	condensed milk
375 ml (1 $^1/_2$ cup)	milk
30 ml (2 Tbs)	syrup
5 ml (1 tsp)	vanilla essence
10 ml (2 tsp)	vinegar

- Mix the sugar and flour together.
- Combine all the ingredients, except vanilla, in a pot.
- Bring the ingredients to the boil gradually, stirring continuously.
- Boil for about 20 to 25 minutes until a soft ball stage (116 °C).
- Add vanilla and beat for about 5 minutes or until it just begins to set. It will lose its shine and become slightly grainy.
- Pour into a greased tin just before it sets.
- Cut into squares before it cools completely.

CREAMY MICROWAVE FUDGE

By cooking the fudge in a microwave, you avoid burning it on the bottom. This is the richest and most delicious fudge I have tasted.

1 tin	full-cream condensed milk
125 g	butter
625 ml (2 ½ cups)	castor sugar
30 ml (2 Tbs)	syrup
5 ml (1 tsp)	vanilla

- Place the first 4 ingredients in a large microwave bowl.
- Microwave on 100% power for 8 minutes, stirring twice.
- Microwave on 50% power for about 8 to 13 minutes, stirring every 3 minutes.
- Add vanilla and beat with an electric hand beater for 2 minutes.
- Pour into a greased tray and cut into squares before the fudge sets.

Hint

Microwave ovens vary enormously. Judge the cooking time by the colour. It should be a dark caramel colour. Once you have it perfect, write down the time it took to cook on your recipe. You will then be able to get it perfect every time.

CHOCOLATE FUDGE

Using the creamy microwave fudge recipe:

- Add 125 ml (½ cup) sifted cocoa to the first 4 ingredients.
- Microwave on 50% power for an extra 1 to 3 minutes.

CARAMEL POPCORN

Even though this recipe makes lots of popcorn, you will soon realise that you should perhaps have made double once the family starts eating it!

250 g	popcorn
250 g	butter
500 ml (2 cups)	brown sugar
125 ml (½ cup)	syrup
3 ml (½ tsp)	baking powder
5 ml (1 tsp)	vanilla

- Pop the corn and set aside.
- Place the butter, sugar and syrup in a pot and boil for 5 minutes.
- Add the vanilla and baking powder and pour over the popped corn.
- Stir to coat corn evenly.
- Spread corn on baking sheet and bake in oven at 160 °C for 30 to 40 minutes until caramel is golden.
- Stir periodically.
- Cool and store in an airtight container.

TOFFEE APPLES

This recipe works every time, but until you know it well, it is essential to have a sugar thermometer. To prevent the toffee from sliding off the apples, don't wash the apples before coating them. The syrup is so hot that they will be sterilised as you dip them.

Makes 10 to 12 apples

625 ml (2 ½ cups)	sugar
165 ml (⅔ cup)	powdered glucose (100 g)
5 ml (1 tsp)	vinegar
125 ml (½ cup)	water
60 g	butter
	red colouring
10-12	small, firm apples
	wooden skewers, cut in half

- Place the sugar, glucose, vinegar and water in a pot.
- Stir over medium heat until the sugar has dissolved.
- Boil rapidly, without stirring, until the mixture reaches 154 °C to 160 °C (hard crack stage).
- Push the sticks into the stalk end of each apple.
- Beat in the red colouring and butter very well. Make sure the butter is completely mixed, otherwise the toffee will slip off the apples. It takes plenty colouring to get deep red apples.
- Place the pot of toffee in a larger pot of boiling water to keep toffee hot and to give you enough time to coat all the apples.
- Dip the apples into the toffee and twist them until they are completely coated.
- Leave to cool on a greased tray.

Hint

Toffee apples become sticky within 24 hours. As soon as they are cold, wrap them and keep them in a cool, dry place.

HONEY NOUGAT

This firm, sticky nougat has a strong flavour of honey and roasted nuts. By using glacé fruit instead of cherries, this recipe makes better nougat than you can buy. The only disadvantage is the sticky pot to be washed!

125 ml ($1/2$ cup)	honey
310 ml ($1 \, 1/4$ cup)	sugar
80 ml ($1/3$ cup)	powdered glucose (50 g)
60 ml ($1/4$ cup)	water
80 ml ($1/3$ cup)	egg whites (about 2 eggs)
200 g	toasted almonds, hazelnuts, or *a combination, roasted*
150 g	mixed glacé fruit or *coloured cherries*
3 ml ($1/2$ tsp)	vanilla
	rice paper

- Use a 23 cm square, or equivalent rectangular tin.
- In a small pot, place the honey, sugar, powdered glucose and water.
- Gradually bring the mixture to the boil, stirring until the sugar has dissolved.
- Place the egg whites in a large heat-resistant bowl and beat until they form stiff peaks.
- Boil the syrup rapidly until it reaches 155 °C to 160 °C on a sugar thermometer, or hard crack stage.
- Remove the syrup from the stove and pour it slowly into the egg whites, beating continuously, preferably with a small electric beater. Add the vanilla and beat until it is smooth.
- In a pot big enough to hold the glass bowl to form a double boiler, bring 500 ml (2 cups) water to the boil.
- Place the bowl over the continuously simmering water and cook, stirring periodically, for 20 to 30 minutes. It will become slightly dry and very sticky.
- Place the fruit and nuts in the oven to warm or warm them in the microwave.
- Mix the fruit and nuts into the mixture.
- Line the tin with rice paper. Spread the mixture onto this and cover with rice paper.
- Place a chopping board or another tin the same size on top of the rice paper and weight it down with a pot full of water (or anything heavy). Leave until completely cold.
- Cut into squares and wrap in cellophane paper.

Hint
To prevent the knife sticking as you cut, keep dipping the knife into boiling water and wipe it dry with roller towel.

GRANOLA BARS

This combination of granola and peanut brittle requires a little effort, but the satisfaction you have makes it well worth it.

80 ml ($1/3$ cup)	sesame seeds
250 ml (1 cup)	oats
125 ml ($1/2$ cup)	wholewheat flour
100 ml (7 Tbs)	coconut
100 ml (7 Tbs)	wheatgerm
100 ml (7 Tbs)	sunflower seeds
125 ml ($1/2$ cup)	All Bran flakes
100 g	chopped almonds
100 g	chopped hazelnuts
80 ml ($1/3$ cup)	sunflower oil
125 ml ($1/2$ cup)	honey
250 ml (1 cup)	brown sugar
5 ml (1 tsp)	vanilla essence
8 ml ($1 \, 1/2$ tsp)	baking powder

- Mix the first 9 ingredients and spread them on a baking sheet.
- Toast in the oven at 180 °C for about 15 minutes, stirring periodically.
- Place the oil, honey and sugar in pot and bring it to the boil.
- Boil to 121 °C (hard ball stage).
- Stir in the vanilla and baking powder and stir into the hot dry ingredients.
- Press into a greased baking tin of about 20 cm x 20 cm.
- Cut into squares with a serrated knife before they set completely.

ODDS AND ENDS

SPICED NUTS

Roasted nuts are delicious and add spice to any cocktail party. Instead of using tree nuts, try using unsalted peanuts.

300 g	mixed tree nuts of your choice
45 ml (3 Tbs)	oil
45 ml (3 Tbs)	coarse salt
30 ml (2 Tbs)	cumin
1 ml ($1/4$ tsp)	cayenne pepper

- Coat the nuts with the oil and spread them on a baking sheet.

- Bake at 175 °C for 15 minutes, stirring occasionally or until slightly browned.
- Mix salt, cumin and cayenne pepper.
- Drain the nuts well on absorbent paper and coat with spices.
- Leave to cool. They are best eaten while still warm.

Hint
If you prefer the nuts plain roasted, omit the cumin and cayenne pepper.

MUESLI

250 ml (1 cup)	sunflower seeds
500 ml (2 cups)	oats
250 ml (1 cup)	bran
100 g	sprinkle-nuts, or chopped nuts of your choice
500 ml (2 cups)	wheatgerm
125 ml (½ cup)	raisins
250 ml (1 cup)	coconut
45 ml (3 Tbs)	oil
45 ml (3 Tbs)	honey

- Mix all the ingredients, except the honey, and roast on a baking sheet at 140 °C for 20 minutes, taking care not to burn it.
- Mix in the honey while still warm and store in an airtight container.

Hint
Add any chopped dried fruit to the basic recipe.

GRANOLA CRUNCH

Much richer than the plain muesli. Eaten with fruit and yoghurt, you will want breakfast three times a day!

Makes lots!

500 ml (2 cups)	oats
185 ml (¾ cup)	wholewheat flour
250 ml (1 cup)	coconut
250 ml (1 cup)	sunflower seeds
250 ml (1 cup)	wheatgerm or bran
250 ml (1 cup)	All Bran flakes
100 g	almonds or hazelnuts, chopped,
or 200 g	sprinkle-nuts
185 ml (¾ cup)	oil
250 ml (1 cup)	honey
15 ml (1 Tbs)	vanilla essence

- Place all the dry ingredients in a large mixing bowl and mix.
- Heat the oil, honey and vanilla essence together.
- Add it to the dry ingredients and stir for 4 to 5 minutes to combine the ingredients well.
- Spread onto 1 or 2 roasting pans and bake at 140 °C for 25 to 30 minutes until golden brown.
- Allow to cool, crumble and store in an airtight container.

SCHMALTZ

Mock chicken fat
This vegetable fat can be used in any savoury dish in place of butter or oil. It is fairly soft.

4	large carrots
3	large onions
310 ml (1 ¼ cup)	oil
250 g	hard white margarine

- Chop the carrots and onions, but not too small.
- Place all the ingredients in a pot and bring to the boil.
- Simmer over medium heat until the onions and carrots have browned. This takes about 30 minutes or more, if it simmers slowly.
- Strain off the liquid through a fine strainer and pour it into a container.
- Cool and place in the fridge, where it will keep indefinitely.

Hints
- To make the schmaltz a harder consistency for spreading, use only 250 ml (1 cup) oil in place of 310 ml (1 ¼ cups).
- The browned onions and carrots that are left over are delicious on bread.

GREEK YOGHURT

This rich Greek yoghurt is perfect for making cacik (see *Starters*), or just to eat. It is much richer than commercial yoghurt, because it is made with full-cream milk and full-cream milk powder.

1 litre (4 cups) full-cream milk
80 ml (1/3 cup) full-cream milk powder
175 ml (1 container) natural yoghurt

- Stir the powdered milk into the milk in a pot.
- Bring it to the boil, stirring to prevent catching on the bottom.
- Remove from the heat and leave to cool to just above body temperature (about 40 °C).
- Stir in the yoghurt, cover well and leave in a warm place for 24 hours. (I place mine in a bowl, in a cooler box and stuff newspaper around the bowl to keep the heat in.)
- Remove from the cooler box and place it in the fridge until needed.

Hints

- For very thick yoghurt, leave it standing out of the fridge for 24 hours, then pour the yoghurt into muslin and hang it in the fridge, over a bowl, for a further 24 hours. The consistency will now be like cream cheese.
- To cut back on the fat content, use skim milk powder in place of the full-cream milk powder.

BAKING MYTHS EXPOSED

Of all the cooking queries I have received over the years, the most common are those concerning metric measuring and altitude problems. I hope you will find your answers here.

Altitude

Q *I have moved from Johannesburg to the coast and my cakes are just not working. (or from the coast to Johannesburg)*

A ▸ At high altitudes, for example Johannesburg, the atmospheric pressure, which prevents your cake from rising, is less than at the coast. You will therefore need less baking powder to make your cake rise. The opposite is true at the coast.

▸ At higher altitudes water boils at a lower temperature than at the coast, so more liquid in your cake will have evaporated by the time it is baked. You must therefore add more water at high altitude to end up with the same moisture content.

▸ The effect of the sugar at different altitudes is quite complicated, so just trust me: At higher altitudes, decrease your sugar content.

▸ At higher altitudes you may have to increase your baking temperature by 5 °C to 10 °C. Temperatures vary from oven to oven in any case, and the best way, short of buying an oven thermometer, is to experiment in your oven. Once you get the cake perfect, *write down on the recipe* what temperature you have used.

The above is a general guide. Some cakes need more changes than others and many may not need any changes at all. You will simply have to experiment with your recipes.

I have personally tested all the cake and baked pudding recipes in this book, both at the coast and at high altitude in Johannesburg. I have given the appropriate quantities for both conditions where altitude had effected the recipe. Please use the correct measurements for your conditions.

The performance of ovens, even two similar ovens, varies considerably. Try recipes in your own oven and make a note of the best temperature and baking time to use. You may find that you need a temperature ±10 o higher or lower, and a cooking time that differs to that recommended in this book.

Measuring problems

Q *Why do recipes, nowadays, give measurements for solids such as flour in millilitres?*

A Ingredients can be measured by weight or by volume. To measure by weight, you need a very accurate scale. Mea-suring by volume can be done in cups, spoons or in millilitres.

Note Cup and spoon measurements in all South African recipes refer to:
a standard metric cup of 250 ml
a standard tablespoon of 15 ml, and
a teaspoon of 5 ml.

I recommend having measuring cups in both millilitres and cups. If you have both sets (250 ml, 100 ml, 50 ml, 25 ml and then 1 cup, $\frac{1}{2}$ cup, $\frac{1}{3}$ cup and $\frac{1}{4}$ cup), you can measure very easily according to the recipe. They are inexpensive and they will make your measuring very easy. An accurate scale makes a big difference.

Q *Are measurements rounded or level?*

A Measurements are always exactly level – your 'rounded or heaped' is bound to be different to mine. Use only standard measuring spoons and cups – a standard cup that you drink tea from (not a mug) is usually only 200 ml not 250 ml.

Q *At what stage do I measure the flour?*

A Always measure flour before sifting it.

Q *Is 250 ml the same as 250 g?*

A Only 250 ml of water weighs 250 g. Be very careful when reading a recipe, making sure that you measure in the correct units. Flour, sugar and butter seem to cause the most confusion.

1 x 250 ml cup will contain 150 g of flour
1 x 250 ml cup will contain 200 g of sugar
1 x 250 ml cup will contain 210 g of castor sugar (because it is finer than sugar)

Fats are almost the same as water, and in baking you can work on volume and weight as being the same

1 x 250 ml cup of butter, oil or margarine contains 230 g

Please refer to the metric conversion table at the beginning of the book for a list of all the other ingredients.

General baking problems

Q *What exactly does it mean to 'cream butter and sugar'?*

A The soft (not melted) butter and sugar (preferably castor sugar) are beaten either with an electric beater or a wooden spoon (and a little elbow grease), until the sugar has dissolved in the butter and the butter has become light in colour and fluffy in texture. It needs considerable beating. If the butter and sugar are not well creamed, the cake will have a coarser and heavier texture from the sugar and the lack of air which should have been beaten into the butter.

Q *Bicarb, baking powder, cream of tartar – what is the difference?*

A Baking powder and bicarbonate of soda are both used as raising agents in baking. Cream of tartar is purely an acid used with the raising agent. This is how the food chemistry works:

Bicarbonate of soda, in contact with liquid and heat, gives off carbon dioxide gas, which makes your cake rise. The bicarb now becomes sodium carbonate which, I hate to tell you, is washing soda. That accounts for the bitter taste and dark colour you get in your ginger bread. In most cakes you don't want the bitter taste, which is a strong alkaline, so you need to add some acid to neutralise it. Any acid will do – cream of tartar and yoghurt are the two most often used, but you can also use vinegar, lemon or buttermilk. Be careful of tartaric acid, it is 5 times more acidic than cream of tartar!

By not completely neutralising the alkali, you can get a dark colour in your baked product and still get rid of the bitter taste. This is the reason why we use yoghurt in soda breads!

The easiest way of completely neutralising the washing soda is to add double the quantity of cream of tartar to bicarb. For every 1 teaspoon of bicarb, use 2 teaspoons of cream of tartar. This takes the guesswork out of neutralising the alkali.

Cream of tartar or any other acid can also be used when beating egg whites, as it makes them more stable.

Baking powder is a commercially made mixture of bicarbonate of soda, a completely neutralising acid and a little starch filler to keep the powder loose.

To make 15 ml (1 Tbs) of baking powder, mix 5 ml (1 tsp) bicarb with 10 ml (2 tsp) cream of tartar. It is not as good as the commercially made baking powders, but in an emergency you can make it yourself.

Q *I have run out of self-raising flour. How do I make my own?*

A Add 8 ml (1 $\frac{1}{2}$ tsp) of baking powder to every 250 ml (1 cup or 150 g) cake flour.

Q *I never know how stiff to beat my egg whites. Can I overbeat them?*

A Egg whites can very easily be overbeaten. This will result in a cake or soufflé that collapses. For meringues, beat your eggs to *stiff peak stage*. This means when you lift the beater the whites stand up in sharp points. For *everything else*, only beat to soft peak stage. When you lift the beater up, the egg white will form little peaks that fall over. Overbeaten egg white looks lumpy and loses its sheen.

Q *What size eggs do I use for baking?*

A I use extra large eggs in most of my baking. In sponge cakes, chiffon cakes and soufflés, part of the raising agent is the air in the stiffly beaten egg whites. In these I use jumbo eggs, which contain the most egg white. When in doubt, and unless otherwise stated in a specific recipe, use extra large eggs.

The standard sizes for eggs are

South African size	English size	Mass
Jumbo	1	66 g plus
Extra Large	2 and 3	61-66 g
Large	4 and 5	51-61 g
Medium	6	43-51 g
Small	7	35-43 g

Q *Whenever I add eggs to creamed butter and sugar the mixture curdles.*

A What actually happens is that the butter fat and the water in the egg white will not mix easily. When you mix fat and water it separates. The egg yolk contains a substance that will emulsify the butter and egg white if beaten well enough. Once you have creamed the butter and sugar very well, add the eggs one at a time and beat vigorously until the mixture has become smooth and creamy. By beating in one egg at a time, you will form a smooth emulsion. Now you can continue adding the sifted dry ingredients and liquid. Adding a little flour will hide the broken emulsion, but it will not fix it.

Q *I have been told I must never overmix a cake.*

A Overmixing can occur only when adding flour to a mixture, baking powder to a warm mixture, or folding in egg whites. Overmixing occurs very easily at any stage while using a food processor, because the blades move so fast.

Q *What is the best way of preparing the tin when baking?*

A The simplest is the best. Using greaseproof or baking paper (never use wax wrap!), cut out the exact shape of the bottom of the pan. No greasing is needed, as the steam between the paper and the cake makes it easy to peel off.

Two exceptions are:
- Chiffon cakes: Either leave the tin ungreased, or lightly spray only the bottom with Spray and Cook.
- Roulades and Swiss rolls: Because these contain almost no fat, I either use Spray and Cook, or lightly oil the paper.

Q *What is the best way of keeping baked products?*

A *Not in the fridge!!* Baked products very quickly become stale in the fridge. The best is to keep them covered at room temperature.

You can freeze your baked products (whether iced or not), but once they have come to room temperature, eat them as soon as possible, otherwise they will become stale very quickly.

QUICK-MIX BAKING

Made in a jiffy, quick-mix baking is easy and fun, but because of the low fat content of most of these recipes, they become stale very quickly and should be eaten the day they are made.

WHOLEWHEAT BRAN MUFFINS

The unbaked mixture will keep for days in the fridge. Bake as you need them.

Makes 12 large muffins

250 ml (1 cup) flour
250 ml (1 cup) wholewheat flour
250 ml (1 cup) digestive bran
45 ml (3 Tbs) brown sugar
1 ml (pinch) salt
20 ml (4 tsp) baking powder
330 ml (1 $\frac{1}{3}$ cup) buttermilk
1 jumbo egg
80 ml ($\frac{1}{3}$ cup) oil or melted butter

- Preheat oven to 200 °C.
- Place all the dry ingredients in a bowl.
- Beat the buttermilk, egg and oil together.
- Add the liquid ingredients to the dry ingredients and mix with a knife only until the liquid is incorporated.

- *Do not overmix.*
- Bake in greased muffin tins for about 20 minutes.

Hint

If you want the muffins to be very dark, add 5 ml gravy browning. This is a brown liquid colouring and *not* a gravy flavoured powder. For *Raisin Muffins* add 62 ml (1/4 cup) raisins to the dry ingredients.

DATE AND BRAN MUFFINS

Makes 12 large muffins

250 g (1 block)	dates, finely chopped
250 ml (1 cup)	boiling water
5 ml (1 tsp)	bicarbonate of soda
500 ml (2 cups)	cake flour
250 ml (1 cup)	bran
60 ml ($^1/_4$ cup)	brown sugar
5 ml (1 tsp)	bicarbonate of soda
100 g	walnuts or pecan nuts, chopped (optional)
65 g	butter, melted
250 ml (1 cup)	buttermilk
2 ml ($^1/_2$ tsp)	vanilla
1	egg

- Preheat oven to 200 °C.
- Mix the dates, boiling water and bicarbonate of soda and allow to cool.
- Place all the dry ingredients in a bowl.
- Beat the buttermilk, egg and melted butter together with the cooled date mixture.
- Add the liquid ingredients to the dry ingredients and mix with a knife only until the liquid is incorporated.
- *Do not overmix.*
- Bake in greased muffin tins at 200 °C for about 20 minutes.

CHOC-CHIP MUFFINS

These will give you an instant chocolate fix!

Makes 12 large or 16 small

500 ml (2 cups)	cake flour
100 ml (7 Tbs)	castor sugar
20 ml (4 tsp)	baking powder
250 g	packet chocolate chips
100 g	walnuts, chopped (optional)
1	egg
80 g	butter, melted
185 ml ($^3/_4$ cup)	buttermilk
2 ml ($^1/_2$ tsp)	vanilla

- Preheat the oven to 200 °C.
- Place all the dry ingredients, including the chocolate and the nuts, in a bowl.
- Beat the buttermilk, egg and melted butter together.
- Add the liquid ingredients to the dry ingredients and mix with a knife only until the liquid is incorporated.
- *Do not overmix.*
- Bake in greased muffin tins for about 20 minutes.

SAVOURY MUFFINS

Served as a savoury with drinks, or even at tea time, there won't be any left to go stale!

250 ml (1 cup)	flour
250 ml (1 cup)	finely grated cheddar cheese
15 ml (1 Tbs)	baking powder
2 ml ($^1/_2$ tsp)	salt
2 ml ($^1/_2$ tsp)	mustard
	pinch of paprika
	pinch of cayenne pepper
1	egg, mixed with enough milk to make a total of 250 ml (1 cup)

- Preheat oven to 180 °C.
- Place all the dry ingredients in a bowl.
- Beat egg and milk together.
- Add the liquid ingredients to the dry ingredients and mix with a knife only until the liquid is incorporated.
- *Do not overmix.*
- Pour into a greased 20 cm to 22 cm tart plate or muffin tins.
- Bake for 20 minutes (about 15 minutes for muffins).

Topping

100 g	butter, melted
7 ml (1 $^1/_2$ tsp)	Marmite
250 ml (1 cup)	cheese, grated

- Mix melted butter and Marmite.
- As soon as the muffin is baked, prick holes all over and gradually pour on the butter/Marmite mixture.
- Sprinkle on grated cheese and return to the oven for further 10 minutes.
- Serve warm.

CRUMPETS FOR TEA!

Or breakfast on Sundays! In America, they are called pancakes and in England flapjacks, but wherever, whenever they are simple to make and delicious.

Makes about 12

```
375 ml (1 1/2 cups)  cake flour
 30 ml (2 Tbs)       sugar
 10 ml (2 tsp)       baking powder
 45 ml (3 Tbs)       oil or melted butter
              2      eggs
125 ml (1/2 cup)     buttermilk
185 ml (3/4 cup)     milk
```

- Place all the dry ingredients in a bowl.
- Beat the eggs with the butter, buttermilk and milk.
- Add the liquid ingredients to the dry ingredients and mix with a knife only until the liquid is incorporated.
- *Do not overmix*. Mixture should still look a little lumpy.
- Preferably leave to stand for one hour before using.
- Drop spoonfuls onto a lightly greased, fairly hot pan and turn when the bubbles on the top have burst. Work on a low to medium heat.
- Serve hot or cold with butter jam and cream.

AMERICAN CORN PANCAKES

Slightly coarser than our crumpets because of the mealie meal, these are much less doughy and lighter. To keep it traditional, make them larger and serve with butter, maple syrup and cream.

- Use crumpet recipe, but in place of 375 ml flour use 185 ml (3/4 cup) of flour and 185 ml (3/4 cup) of mealie meal.
- Follow the recipe as above.

YEAST CRUMPETS

These are slightly bread-like and faintly yeasty. Use the crumpet recipe, but leave out the baking powder and use half cake flour and half self-raising flour, i.e. 185 ml of each (3/4 cup).

```
 5 ml (1 tsp)  instant yeast
 5 ml (1 tsp)  sugar
50 ml (3 Tbs)  warm water
```

- Mix yeast, sugar and water together.
- Add to the eggs, milk, buttermilk and butter.
- Add the liquid ingredients to the dry ingredients and mix with a knife only until the liquid is incorporated.
- *Do not overmix*. Mixture should still look a little lumpy.
- Leave, covered, in a warm place until the mixture has doubled its size.
- Cook in the same way as plain crumpets or waffles.

WAFFLES

- Use the crumpet recipe, but separate the eggs and use only the yolks in the batter.
- Whip the egg whites until they are stiff.
- Fold into the batter and drop spoonfuls onto a hot, greased waffle iron.

YORKSHIRE PUDDING

Popovers

Makes 12

```
185 ml (3/4 cup)    cake flour
  2 ml (1/2 tsp)    salt
             3      eggs
 30 ml (2 Tbs)      butter, melted
200 ml (1 teacup)   milk
```

- Preheat oven to 190 °C.
- Sift flour and salt into a bowl. Stir in the beaten eggs and melted butter.
- Using a whisk or a wooden spoon, mix in the milk until it is just smooth. *Do not overmix.*
- In the hot roasting pan, pour the batter into the fat from your roast. To make individual puddings, place 5 ml oil or roasting fat in each muffin tin and place it in the oven until the oil is very hot.
- Remove the pan from the oven and immediately divide the mixture between the 12 muffin tins.
- Bake for 40 to 50 minutes.

To serve as popovers

- Preheat oven to 190 °C.
- Lightly grease the muffin tins.
- Pour the mixture into the muffin tins.
- Bake for 50 minutes.
- Make a slit in each popover to allow the steam to escape and leave in the oven for a further 10 minutes.
- Serve hot with butter.

For Hint *see next page.*

Hint
If you prefer your Yorkshire pudding a little less 'eggy', use only 2 eggs.

BASIC SCONE DOUGH

I am frequently asked for the recipe for my scones. A good scone is not in the recipe, but rather in the way you make it. I have tried many different recipes with buttermilk and other liquids, but I get the best results with water. The secret is to handle the mixture as little and as lightly as possible. Because of the small amount of fat and sugar, the gluten in the flour develops *very* quickly when you mix it. (Refer to the information on gluten under *Yeast*.) To prevent the gluten from forming, cut the liquid in with a knife, rather than mixing it with a spoon. Turn it out onto a *lightly* floured surface. Very gently pat down to a thickness of about 4 cm and cut with a cookie cutter. Before each scone is cut, dip the cookie cutter in flour. The wetter the mixture, the lighter the scones. Never use a rolling pin!

Makes 6 to 8 scones

500 ml (2 cups)	flour
80 g	butter
17 ml (3 $\frac{1}{2}$ tsp)	baking powder
30 ml (2 Tbs)	sugar
1	egg plus enough water to make a total of 185 ml ($\frac{3}{4}$ cup) liquid

- Preheat oven to 200 °C.
- Sift the dry ingredients into a bowl.
- Cut the butter into small pieces and rub it into the dry ingredients using your fingertips.
- Place the egg in a measuring cup and add the water to the 185 ml mark.
- Add the liquid ingredients to the dry ingredients and mix with a knife only until the liquid is incorporated. *Do not overmix*. The dough should be soft and only just manageable.
- Add the liquid carefully. The mixture may need a little more or less, depending on the dryness of the flour.
- Pat out gently on a *lightly* floured board and cut with cookie cutters.
- Place the scones close together on a greased baking sheet and brush with a little milk if you want them glazed. I like them rough and earthy, so I don't glaze them.
- Bake at 200 °C for 15 to 20 minutes.
- Break apart and allow to cool on cooling rack.

High altitude changes
Use only 15 ml (3 tsp) baking powder in place of the 17 ml (3 $\frac{1}{2}$ tsp).

CHEESE SCONES

Use basic scone recipe, but omit sugar and add:

60 g	butter in place of 80 g
	pinch of cayenne pepper
2 ml ($\frac{1}{2}$ tsp)	dry mustard
125 ml ($\frac{1}{2}$ cup)	grated cheese, added to rubbed-in mixture

WHOLEWHEAT SCONES

Use the basic scone recipe. In place of 500 ml (2 cups) cake flour, use:

250 ml (1 cup)	flour
250 ml (1 cup)	wholewheat or brown flour

OAT SCONES

These are very crumbly, but delicious. Use the basic scone recipe. In place of 500 ml (2 cups) of cake flour, use

250 ml (1 cup)	flour
125 ml ($\frac{1}{2}$ cup)	Nutty Wheat
125 ml ($\frac{1}{2}$ cup)	oats

Fruit scones
Use the basic scone recipe. Add 50 ml (4 Tbs) of any fruit to dry ingredients e.g. currants, raisins or finely chopped dates.

Bacon scones
Use basic cheese scone recipe and add 50 ml (4 Tbs) crumbled grilled bacon to the dry ingredients.

BAKING: Pirozhki page 230.

BAKING: Tarte au citron page 226.

DESSERTS: Rhubarb with orange sago creams page 160.

MY WAY WITH FOOD

BAKING: Cheese rough puff pastry steps

Step 1: Butter and flour mixing.

Step 2: Adding water.

Step 3: Rolling out.

Cheese rough puff pastry pie with filling, pages 221 – 222.

THIS AND THAT: Toffee apples page 183.

PROBLEM FREE YEAST BAKING: Kitke, page 240

PROBLEM FREE YEAST BAKING: plaiting kitke page 240.

Kneeding kitke.

Plaiting step 1.

Plaiting step 2.

Plaiting step 3.

BAKING: Assorted biscuits pages 212 – 220.

BUTTER CAKES

Butter cakes are rich, slightly heavy, with a high proportion of butter. They are always made in the same way: Butter and sugar creamed together, eggs added one at a time and beaten thoroughly to get rid of the 'curdled' effect. The sifted dry ingredients and liquid are then added in 2 or 3 batches and mixed to make a smooth batter. Because the fat content is so high, butter cakes are not easily overmixed and rewarding results are easier to achieve.

Butter cakes are not as light as a hot milk sponge or a chiffon cake, but they are richer and stay fresh much longer.

The basic recipe is very versatile and can be made in chocolate, coffee, orange, lemon, granadilla, fruit or cherry flavours, lammington squares and fairy cakes. Use your imagination and add any flavour you want to the basic butter cake recipe.

FOUR-EGG BUTTER CAKE

250 g	butter
375 ml (1 $\frac{1}{2}$ cups)	castor sugar
4	X-large or jumbo eggs
5 ml (1 tsp)	vanilla essence
625 ml (2 $\frac{1}{2}$ cups)	cake flour
20 ml (4 tsp)	baking powder
125 ml ($\frac{1}{2}$ cup)	milk
125 ml ($\frac{1}{2}$ cup)	water

High altitude changes

310 ml (1 $\frac{1}{4}$ cup)	castor sugar
280 ml (1 cup + 2 Tbs)	water and milk combined
18 ml (3 $\frac{1}{2}$ tsp)	baking powder

- Preheat oven to 180 °C.
- Cream the butter and sugar until light and fluffy.
- Beat in the eggs one at a time. Beat very well after each egg to get rid of 'curdled' effect. Extensive beating at this stage will give you a very creamy texture and a beautiful light cake.
- Beat in vanilla.
- Sift the dry ingredients and mix into the creamed mixture, together with the liquids in 3 or 4 batches. Mix to make a smooth batter.
- Bake in ungreased but paper-lined tins: two deep tins (23 cm), one large tube tin, a 23 cm square tin, or three loaf tins or muffin tins – at 180 °C for about 30 minutes. If you bake it in one large tin, lower the temperature to 160 °C and bake for about 50 to 60 minutes. At high altitude, leave the temperature at 180 °C.

Chocolate cake
- Use 560 ml (2 $\frac{1}{4}$ cups) flour and add 125 ml ($\frac{1}{2}$ cup) cocoa.

Marble cake
- Complete the four-egg butter cake mixture and divide it in half.
- Sift 60 ml ($\frac{1}{4}$ cup) cocoa onto one half of the mixture and mix it in.
- Place large spoonfuls of alternating colours in a large papered chiffon or tube tin.
- Bake at 160 °C for about 50 minutes, or until baked through. At high altitude, bake at 180 °C.

Coffee cake
- Heat the water in the recipe.
- Dissolve 15 ml (1 Tbs) good strong instant coffee in it and allow to cool.
- Proceed with recipe.

Orange or lemon cake
- Add 10 to 15 ml (2 to 3 tsp) finely grated citrus rind of your choice to the butter and sugar for creaming.
- Use some fresh fruit juice in place of the required milk and water.

Granadilla cake
- Add the pulp of 3 to 4 granadillas or the equivalent in canned pulp to your measuring jug before you measure the liquid.
- Top up with the liquid to the required quantity.

BASIC BUTTER ICING

This quantity is enough for the top and middle of the cake. Make 1 $\frac{1}{2}$ to 2 times the recipe if you want to ice the sides and decorate with a piping bag as well.

80 g	soft butter
375 ml (1 $\frac{1}{2}$ cups)	icing sugar, sifted
	liquid, e.g. orange juice, coffee, milk
15 ml (1 Tbs)	boiling water

- Cream together the butter and half the icing sugar.
- Gradually add the remaining sugar with a little liquid to end up with a creamy, spreading consistency. If your icing is too dry it will break the surface of the cake.
- Add cocoa or coffee, or any other desired flavouring.
- Just before spreading it on the cake, beat in the boiling water. This will result in a creamy icing that will set slightly on the cake.

THREE-EGG BUTTER CAKE

This size butter cake makes a standard 20 cm sandwich cake. It is usually baked in two *deep* cake tins (20 cm) and then sandwiched together and iced with a butter icing of your choice.

- 190 g butter
- 250 ml (1 cup) castor sugar
- 3 eggs
- 3 ml (½ tsp) vanilla essence
- 500 ml (2 cups) cake flour
- 18 ml (3 ½ tsp) baking powder
- 185 ml (¾ cup) milk and water mixed

High altitude changes
- 185 ml (¾ cup) castor sugar
- 200 ml (1 teacup) liquid
- 15 ml (3 tsp) baking powder

- Preheat the oven to 180 °C.
- Cream the butter and sugar until light and fluffy.
- Beat in the eggs one at a time. Beat very well after each egg to get rid of 'curdled' effect. Extensive beating at this stage will give you a very creamy texture and a beautifully light cake.
- Beat in the vanilla essence.
- Sift the dry ingredients and mix into the creamed mixture, together with the liquids, in 3 or 4 batches. Mix to make a smooth batter.
- Bake in two 20 cm, ungreased but paper-lined tins for about 30 minutes.
- Cool for 5 minutes, turn out and, when cooled, ice together.

Variations
For a chocolate cake, use 435 ml (1 3/4 cup) flour and 80 ml (1/3 cup) cocoa.

Cup cakes
Makes 36

- Place the paper cups in muffin tins to keep their shape.
- Spoon the mixture into the paper cases.
- Bake at 190 °C for about 12 to 15 minutes.

LAMMINGTON SQUARES

This three-egg butter cake is slightly heavier than the basic recipe, so that when the squares are rolled in the chocolate sauce they do not crumble or become soggy.

Makes about 36

- 190 g butter
- 250 ml (1 cup) castor sugar
- 3 eggs
- 3 ml (½ tsp) vanilla essence
- 500 ml (2 cups) cake flour
- 15 ml (3 tsp) baking powder
- 125 ml (½ cup) milk

High altitude changes
- 185 ml (¾ cup) castor sugar
- 165 ml (⅔ cup) milk
- 12 ml (2 ½ tsp) baking powder

- Preheat the oven to 180 °C.
- Cream the butter and sugar until light and fluffy.
- Beat in the eggs one at a time. Beat very well after each egg to get rid of 'curdled' effect. Extensive beating at this stage will give you a very creamy texture and a beautifully light cake.
- Beat in vanilla essence.
- Sift the dry ingredients and mix into the creamed mixture, together with the liquids, in 3 or 4 batches. Mix to make a smooth batter.
- Pour into an ungreased but papered 25 cm square tin or the equivalent size in a rectangle tin.
- Bake for 25 minutes.
- Turn onto cooling rack.
- When cool, cut into about 36 squares.
- Ice only once cake is completely cold.

Hot chocolate sauce
- 430 ml (1 ¾ cups) boiling water
- 125 g butter
- 750 ml (3 cups) icing sugar
- 80 ml (⅓ cup) cocoa
- 10 ml (2 tsp) vanilla essence
- 375 ml (1 ½ cup) coconut (approximate)

- Bring all ingredients (except coconut) to the boil, stirring constantly.
- Quickly coat squares with hot chocolate sauce, then coconut.
- Leave to cool and dry on cooling rack.

ORANGE FRUIT RING OR CHERRY CAKE

When making a light fruit or cherry cake the fruit often sinks to the bottom. I have heard all sorts of remedies for this problem, such as coat the fruit with flour, wash the fruit before you use it. It all boils down to one thing: If the fruit is too heavy for the cake batter to keep it up, it will sink to the bottom. To make the cake dense enough to hold the fruit, use slightly less liquid (about 100 ml). The resulting cake will not be quite as light, but the fruit will stay suspended in the batter. I prefer to have a lovely light cake even if the fruit is at the bottom. This recipe is dense enough to keep the fruit suspended. Alternatively, use the madeira cake as your basic mixture. It is a much richer, heavier cake in the first place. If you are using the madeira cake (which is a bigger mixture), double the fruit quantity and make 2 cakes. They freeze very well.

Orange fruit ring

190 g	butter
250 ml (1 cup)	castor sugar
10 ml (2 tsp)	orange rind
3	eggs
500 ml (2 cups)	cake flour
15 ml (1 Tbs)	baking powder
165 ml ($^2/_3$ cup)	buttermilk
250 g	mixed cake fruit
100 g	pecan or walnuts, chopped

High altitude changes

185 ml ($^3/_4$ cup)	castor sugar
185 ml ($^3/_4$ cup)	buttermilk
12 ml (2 $^1/_2$ tsp)	baking powder

- Preheat the oven to 160 °C.
- Cream butter and sugar and orange rind.
- Beat in eggs one at a time.
- Fold in sifted dry ingredients with buttermilk.
- Lastly fold in fruit and nuts.
- Bake in an ungreased but paper-lined, 23 cm tube tin or large loaf tin for 50 to 60 minutes.
- Remove from tin and, while on a cake rack, dribble on the hot syrup. Place the cake under the grill until it browns.

Syrup

80 ml ($^1/_3$ cup)	orange juice
80 ml ($^1/_3$ cup)	sugar
10 ml (2 tsp)	orange rind

- Boil together for 3 minutes.

Variations

Cherry cake

Use 150 g glacé cherries in place of the 250 g fruit and omit the nuts and orange rind. The syrup poured on afterwards is delicious with the cherries.

Poppy seed cake

- Take 80 ml ($^1/_3$ cup) poppy seeds and simmer it in water for 2 hours. Pour through a strainer and rinse under cold water. This softens and swells the seeds and the flavour becomes stronger and sweeter.
- Using the basic cake recipe, omit the fruit and nuts and use only 5 ml (1 tsp) orange rind in place of 10 ml. You can still pour on the syrup after the cake is baked if you want. It gives the cake a sticky, crispy top.

ORANGE CHRISTMAS RING

This is a fruitier, darker and richer version of the light fruit cake. Because bicarbonate of soda is used as a raising agent, the cake has a much darker colour.

Syrup

250 ml (1 cup)	orange juice
250 ml (1 cup)	sugar
30 ml (2 Tbs)	orange rind
125 ml ($^1/_2$ cup)	brandy

- Boil first three ingredients together for 5 minutes – add brandy and chill.

Cake

250 g	butter
250 ml (1 cup)	sugar
15 ml (1 Tbs)	orange rind
2	eggs
500 ml (2 cups)	flour
5 ml (1 tsp)	bicarbonate of soda
185 ml ($^3/_4$ cup)	milk
15 ml (1 Tbs)	vinegar
500 g (3 cups)	mixed cake fruit
250 g	dates, chopped
100 g	cherries, halved
100 g	walnuts, chopped

- Preheat the oven to 160 °C.
- Cream the butter, sugar and orange rind until light and fluffy.

- Beat in the eggs one at a time. Beat very well after each egg to get rid of 'curdled' effect.
- Sift the dry ingredients and mix into the creamed mixture, together with the liquids, in 3 or 4 batches. Mix to make a smooth batter.
- Mix in fruit and nuts.
- Pour into a large ring and bake for about 1 hour.
- Pour the cold syrup over the hot cake.

MADEIRA CAKE

This cake is ideal for novelty birthday cakes, because it is not fragile and can be cut, shaped and iced easily.

250 g (1 cup)	butter
435 ml (1 3/4 cup)	castor sugar
10 ml (2 tsp)	lemon rind
5	X-large or jumbo eggs
625 ml (2 1/2 cups)	flour
10 ml (2 tsp)	baking powder
60 ml (1/4 cup)	milk (approximate)
125 ml (1/2 cup)	mixed peel, optional

- Preheat the oven to 160 °C.
- Cream the butter, sugar and lemon rind until light and fluffy.
- Beat in the eggs one at a time. Beat very well after each egg to get rid of 'curdled' effect.
- Sift the dry ingredients and mix into the creamed mixture, together with the liquid, in 3 or 4 batches. Mix to make a smooth batter. A little more or less liquid may be needed, depending on the size of the eggs.
- Pour into a deep, paper-lined, 23 cm cake tin or a large loaf tin.
- Sprinkle on mixed peel.
- Bake for 1–1 1/2 hours.

Variations

Coconut madeira
Add 250 ml (1 cup) medium coconut to the dry ingredients. It makes the cake more moist and *quite* delicious!

Chocolate madeira
This makes a good base for a novelty birthday cake, but I prefer the texture of the butter chocolate cakes.
In place of the 625 ml (2 1/2 cups) flour use 500 ml (2 cups) flour and 125 ml (1/2 cup) cocoa.

Hint
Partially freeze the cake before cutting and shaping it for a birthday cake. It is also delicious as the base for a rich, slightly heavy fruit or cherry cake.

RICH FRUIT CAKE

This fruit cake can be made with any combination of cake fruit and glacé fruit of your choice. I use the *Sugar Bird Special Mix* which is very wet and sticky. If you use a dry mix, you may need to add a little extra liquid. If you intend to keep the cake for longer than a month, use almonds rather than walnuts which tend to go rancid.

Bake-in-the-box method
Baking a fruit cake in a corrugated cardboard box without a top provides good insulation to the outside of the cake. The common practice of putting layers of paper on the inside of the cake tin to prevent burning is not as effective as the thick layer of cardboard.

Preparing the tin
- Line the bottom and sides of the cake tin with a single layer of greaseproof paper (*not wax paper*), using tiny dabs of butter to secure it.
- Find a corrugated cardboard carton that will hold the tin, or make up a box to fit, cutting a larger one down to size and tying it with string. The box can be re-used. A round tin in a square box is fine!
- The cake can be baked in a box without the tin. Line the box with heavy foil, shiny side facing out and then line again with a single layer of greaseproof paper.

Conventional method
- Use a slightly larger tin because the paper takes up 'cake space'.
- Line the inside of the tin with 3 layers of newspaper, one layer of brown paper and end with a layer of greaseproof paper.

1 kg	special cake mix (see Hint)
250 g	mixed cake fruit
125 g	dates, chopped
125 g	cherries
or 1,5 kg	mixed fruit of your choice
100 g	walnuts or almonds
150 g	butter
250 ml (1 cup)	brown sugar
3	eggs
5 ml (1 tsp)	gravy browning liquid (optional)

625 ml (2 ½ cups) cake flour
30 ml (2 Tbs) cocoa
8 ml (1 ½ tsp) bicarbonate of soda
3 ml (½ tsp) ground ginger
5 ml (1 tsp) ground cinnamon
3 ml (½ tsp) ground nutmeg
7 ml (1 ½ tsp) mixed spice
250 ml (1 cup) orange juice or water (approximate)

Brandy syrup

For a better flavour, add the brandy syrup onto the cake after baking rather than using brandy in the mixture.

120 ml (½ cup) orange juice
60 ml (4 Tbs) sugar
125 ml (½ cup) brandy

- Bring the juice and sugar to the boil.
- Boil for 1 minute.
- Cool and then add the brandy.
- Pour syrup over the hot cake while it is still in the tin.

Easy creaming method

- Preheat the oven to 160 °C.
- Line the bottom of a 20 cm to 25 cm square tin with a single layer of greaseproof paper.
- Cream butter and sugar very well.
- Add the eggs one at a time and beat very well. Add the gravy browning. Although this mixture always 'curdles' it does not affect the texture of such a heavy cake.
- Combine all the fruit in a large bowl. Sift the dry ingredients onto the fruit and stir it in or mix with your hand, breaking up the lumps.
- Add the creamed mixture and enough orange juice to make a thick, wet batter. The quantity will be determined by the moisture content of the fruit.
- Mix with a wooden spoon or with your hands. (Using your hands to mix is messy, but it is the best tool for the job.)
- Spoon the mixture into the papered tin, place the tin in a cardboard box and bake for 1 hour.
- Reduce to 140 °C for about 4 to 5 hours. The baking time varies according to the size of the tin and the thickness of the insulation. Remove the cake from the oven and pour on the brandy syrup.
- Without the box, bake only at 140 °C for about 4 hours. Do not start it off in an oven of 160 °C. The slower the cake bakes, the better the results.

Hint

- Gravy browning is a liquid food colouring made from caramelised sugar and it has no taste. It is *not* a gravy powder. It is used to make the fruit cake darker in colour.
- To prevent the middle of the cake from sinking, cover the top of the tin with foil, shiny side towards the cake. Pierce a few holes in the foil to allow the steam to escape. Remove for the last 30 minutes of baking time (for both creaming and boiling method).

Easier boiled method

The texture of this cake is slightly drier and more 'chewy' than the creaming method.

- Preheat the oven to 160 °C.
- Prepare the tin in the same way as for the creaming method.
- In a large pot, place all the fruit, butter, sugar and orange juice.
- Bring the mixture to the boil and remove it from the heat.
- Stir in the gravy browning.
- Sift the dry ingredients over fruit and mix well.
- Beat the eggs, add and mix well.
- Pour the mixture into the prepared tin and bake, in a box, for about 2 ½ hours. Or bake, without a box, for about 2 hours. This method bakes much quicker, because the mixture is already hot.
- Check if the cake is ready by inserting a skewer. If it is clean, the cake is ready.

Easiest microwave method

- In a large bowl, place all the fruit, butter and sugar and orange juice.
- Microwave on high for 5 minutes.
- Stir in the gravy browning.
- Sift the dry ingredients over the fruit and mix well.
- Beat eggs, add and mix well.
- Pour into papered microwave ring mould (with a central funnel), about 24 cm in diameter.
- Microwave on medium high (70% power) for 28 to 30 minutes.
- Leave to cool for 15 minutes before pouring on brandy syrup.

Hint

To make a ring mould, use a plain container and place a heat resistant glass in the middle.

HOT MILK SPONGE METHOD

The sponge cake method of whisking the sugar and eggs, preferably over hot water, is used in Swiss rolls and sponge cakes. They have a high proportion of egg and sugar and a low proportion of fat. This results in a very light and sweet, but dry cake which stales very quickly.

The hot milk sponge uses the best of the butter cake and the sponge cake and puts them together. By using the whisking method, the result is a very light cake. By adding melted butter to the liquid, the cake is richer and longer lasting. This recipe has more butter than most hot milk sponges, but it works perfectly.

125 g	butter
60 ml ($^1/_4$ cup)	water, combined with
60 ml ($^1/_4$ cup)	milk
3	eggs
250 ml (1 cup)	castor sugar
5 ml (1 tsp)	vanilla essence
375 ml (1 $^1/_2$ cup)	cake flour
15 ml (1 Tbs)	baking powder
1 ml (pinch)	salt
2 ml ($^1/_2$ tsp)	lemon rind

High altitude changes
Increase the liquid to 75 ml + 75 ml = 150 ml ($^1/_2$ cup + 2 Tbs).

Decrease the sugar content to 200 ml (1 teacup) Decrease the baking powder to 13 ml (2 $^1/_2$ tsp).

- Preheat the oven to 180 °C.
- Heat the milk and butter over a low heat until the butter has melted. Do not boil.
- Whisk the eggs and sugar until very thick and pale. Place the bowl over a pot of hot water while you are whisking. It helps to dissolve the sugar and makes the whisking quicker. (The water must not boil.)
- Sift the dry ingredients, but *not the baking powder*. Add the dry ingredients and the hot liquid in 3 batches to the whisked eggs. Fold in gently with a whisk or metal spoon. Be careful not to overmix, or you will lose all the air you have incorporated into the eggs.
- Fold in the baking powder last. The heat from the milk activates the baking powder. In a hot mixture it must always be added last and then be put straight into the oven.
- Bake in two papered, ungreased tins (22 cm) for 25 minutes.
- Remove the cakes from the tins while still warm and cool on a cooling rack.
- Ice with butter icing (see *Four-egg butter cake*)

CHOCOLATE CAKE

Use the basic hot milk sponge recipe, but in place of the 375 ml (1 $^1/_2$ cup) flour use:

330 ml (1 $^1/_3$ cup)	cake flour
45 ml (3 Tbs)	cocoa
	omit the lemon rind

Variation
This basic hot milk sponge cake can be made in different flavours by using orange rind and orange juice, granadilla juice, or even coffee as the liquid. Refer to the butter cake variations.

CHIFFON CAKE

Many chiffon cakes use extra egg whites, resulting in an extremely high, light and springy cake, but lacking in flavour. This recipe is not quite as light, but it is full of flavour.

Orange

250 ml (1 cup)	flour
2 ml ($^1/_2$ tsp)	salt
250 ml (1 cup)	castor sugar
15 ml (3 tsp)	baking powder
80 ml ($^1/_3$ cup)	oil
4	eggs, separated
80 ml ($^1/_3$ cup)	orange juice
10 ml (2 tsp)	orange rind
2 ml ($^1/_2$ tsp)	cream of tartar

High altitude changes
Increase the orange juice to 100 ml.

- Sift the dry ingredients into a bowl.
- Add oil, yolks, liquid and rind and beat well.
- Whip the egg whites and cream of tartar to soft peak stage and fold into the batter. Do not overbeat your whites, as the cake will collapse.
- Bake in a large chiffon tin at 160 °C for about 40 to 45 minutes.
- Hang the tin upside down until cool.
- Remove the cake from the tin.
- Sprinkle with icing sugar or icing, as desired.

Use the basic orange chiffon recipe with the following adjustments:

Lemon
- Use lemon rind in place of the orange rind.
- Use boiling water in place of the orange juice.

Chocolate
- Add 45 ml (3 Tbs) cocoa to the dry ingredients.
- Leave out the orange rind and use boiling water in place of the orange juice.
- Add 5 ml (1 tsp) vanilla essence.

Coffee
- Use boiling water in place of orange juice, with about 30 ml (2 Tbs) instant coffee dissolved in it.
- Omit the orange rind.

Spice
- Omit the orange rind.
- Add 5 ml (1 tsp) cinnamon, 1 ml ($^1/_4$ tsp) nutmeg, 3 ml ($^1/_2$ tsp) mixed spice and 3 ml ($^1/_2$ tsp) cloves to the dry ingredients.
- This cake is delicious iced with the chocolate glaze from the sachertorte recipe.

CARROT CAKE

This is a variation on a chiffon cake. The grated carrot provide the liquid in the mixture, so rather have too much than too little grated carrot. It is iced with a butter icing made with a little cream or cottage cheese to give it a slightly acidic, cheesy flavour.

There are no changes to the recipe for high altitude because it is a fairly heavy, moist cake. Make sure that the cups of grated carrot are fairly tightly packed!

```
             4  jumbo eggs
310 ml (1 1/4 cup)  castor sugar
310 ml (1 1/4 cup)  oil
       5 ml (1 tsp)  vanilla essence
625 ml (2 1/2 cups)  flour
      10 ml (2 tsp)  bicarbonate of soda
       5 ml (1 tsp)  baking powder
      10 ml (2 tsp)  cinnamon
625 ml (2 1/2 cups)  carrot, grated
            100 g  pecan nuts, chopped
```

- Preheat the oven to 160 °C.
- Beat the eggs and sugar until light and fluffy.
- Sift the dry ingredients together.
- Add the oil and the vanilla essence to the egg mixture.
- Add the dry ingredients, nuts and grated carrots to the egg mixture in 3 batches and mix gently.
- Bake for 45 minutes in a large, square glass dish or in two 23 cm to 25 cm round tins.
- Ice when cold.

Icing

```
            90 g  butter
500 ml (2 cups)  icing sugar
   3 ml (1/2 tsp)  vanilla essence
           125 g  cream cheese (approximate)
```

- Rub the butter into the icing sugar; there is not enough butter to cream it.
- Mix the vanilla into the cheese.
- Add about 45 ml (3 Tbs) cottage or cream cheese – just enough to cream sugar and butter. Mix with a wooden spoon until *just* smooth. If you overmix, the icing will become runny.
- Carefully stir in as much as possible without making icing watery.
- Spread it over the cake.

Hint
The thicker the cheese, the more you will be able to use and the better the flavour will be. When I remember, I hang the cheese in the fridge overnight, wrapped in a clean Daily Wipe or a piece of muslin, to get rid of the excess liquid.

Variation
Serve this cake as a pudding with a caramel cream sauce:

Caramel sauce

```
         1 tin  Caramel Treat
250 ml (1 cup)  cream
  1/2 ml (2 drops)  caramel essence
```

- Beat the ingredients together and serve it with the cake.

MELTING METHOD

The melting method used in baking is the easiest and quickest method of cake making. The butter, sugar and syrup are heated in a pot and then added to the dry ingredients. The only raising agent is the baking powder. There is no creaming or whisking to incorporate air. The high sugar, syrup and butter content results in an extremely wet, sticky texture.

STICKY GINGERBREAD SQUARES

This is a really sticky ginger bread! I bake it in a large, rectangular pan and then cut them into squares. You can bake it in two loaf tins if you prefer. If you bake it in one large loaf tin it may collapse, because it is very wet. These squares are delicious as they are or they can be served with apple sauce and cream.

250 g	butter
125 ml ($1/2$ cup)	syrup
125 ml ($1/2$ cup)	treacle
250 ml (1 cup)	brown sugar
200 ml (1 teacup)	buttermilk
2	X-large or jumbo eggs
500 ml (2 cups)	flour
30 ml (2 Tbs)	ground ginger
8 ml (1 $1/2$ tsp)	bicarbonate of soda

High altitude changes
Decrease the brown sugar to 200 ml (1 teacup).
Decrease the bicarb to 5 ml (1 tsp).
Increase the buttermilk to 225 ml ($3/4$ cup + 3 Tbs).

- Preheat the oven to 160 °C.
- In a pot, place the butter, syrup, treacle, brown sugar and half the buttermilk.
- Over medium heat, melt the butter and dissolve the sugar. Do not boil.
- Beat the eggs with remaining half of the buttermilk.
- Sift dry ingredients.
- Add egg and buttermilk mixture and gradually beat in enough hot mixture to form a stiff, smooth batter.
- Add remaining hot mixture and mix well.
- Pour into a papered or greased, deep square tin (an oven roaster is fine), or in a four-litre rectangular glass dish. The tin should be about 35 cm x 25 cm and it should bake for about 20 minutes.
- Cool and cut into squares.

CHOCOLATE FUDGE BROWNIES

The texture of the gingerbread reminds me of fudge brownies I had in New York. By working with the basic gingerbread recipe I ended up with these very moist brownies. Divided into two 23 cm cake tins, it makes a delicious layer cake.

250 g	butter
200 ml (1 teacup)	syrup
100 g	dark chocolate
60 ml ($1/4$ cup)	cocoa
200 ml (1 teacup)	brown sugar
200 ml (1 teacup)	buttermilk
2	eggs
500 ml (2 cups)	flour
8 ml (1 $1/2$ tsp)	bicarbonate of soda
100 g	walnuts (optional)

High altitude changes
Decrease sugar to 185 ml ($3/4$ cup).
Increase buttermilk to 225 ml ($3/4$ cup + 3 Tbs).
Decrease bicarbonate of soda to 5 ml (1 tsp).

- Preheat the oven to 160 °C.
- In a pot, place the butter, syrup, chocolate, cocoa brown sugar and half the buttermilk.
- Over medium heat, melt the butter and dissolve the sugar. Do not boil.
- Beat eggs with remaining half of the buttermilk.
- Sift dry ingredients.
- Add egg and buttermilk mixture and gradually beat in enough hot mixture to form a stiff, smooth batter.
- Add remaining hot mixture and mix well.
- Mix in nuts.
- Pour into papered or well-greased roasting pan, or a large square glass dish (about 4 litres as you would for the gingerbread), or pour it into two 23 cm deep cake tins.
- Bake for 25 to 30 minutes, or for 40 minutes in a large tin.
- Spread the topping on while the cake is still warm.

Hot chocolate fudge topping

100 g	butter
45 ml (3 Tbs)	syrup
225 g (small tin)	condensed milk
30 ml (2 Tbs)	cocoa
100 g	dark chocolate
500 ml (2 cups)	icing sugar
5 ml (1 tsp)	vanilla essence

- Place the first 5 ingredients in a pot and melt over a low heat.

- Gradually bring to the boil, stirring continuously to prevent burning.
- Boil for 1 minute, stirring constantly.
- Beat in sifted icing sugar and vanilla.
- Spread onto the warm cake and leave to cool completely.
- Cut into squares.

Hint
This fudge sauce is wonderful over ice cream. Use 1/2 the amount of icing sugar.

CHEESE CAKES

There is nothing quite like a baked cheese cake. The following three recipes are my favourites.

LIGHT CHEESE CAKE

This cake uses a thin layer of butter cake as the base. This goes very well with the light texture of the filling. A pastry base or biscuit crumb base can also be used with the filling.

Batter base

60 g	butter
60 ml ($^1/_4$ cup)	sugar
1	egg
200 ml (1 teacup)	flour
5 ml (1 tsp)	baking powder
80 ml ($^1/_3$ cup)	milk

- Cream the butter and sugar until fluffy.
- Beat in the egg.
- Mix in the sifted ingredients and the milk.
- Grease a large square, 2-litre ovenware dish, or two round, 20 cm foil plates.
- Spread the batter as evenly as possible over the bottom and sides of the dish, using a plastic spatula.
- Pour in the filling.

Filling

500 g	smooth cottage cheese of your choice
125 ml ($^1/_2$ cup)	sour cream
2 eggs,	separated
125 ml ($^1/_2$ cup)	sugar
15 ml (1 Tbs)	self-raising flour

- Preheat the oven to 200 °C.
- Whisk the egg whites until stiff.
- Blend all the other ingredients together.
- Fold in egg whites.
- Pour the mixture into the crust and bake for 15 minutes.
- Bake at 100 °C until just set (±1 hour).
- Switch off the oven and open the oven door fractionally. Leave it to cool in the oven.

'SERIOUS' CHEESE CAKE

This is a heavy, rich cake and should not be taken lightly! It is not for the calorie conscious, but what a way to go!

1	x quantity sweet, rich shortcrust pastry (see Pastry)
	or batter base for light cheese cake

- Line a deep spring-form tin (about 23 cm) with the pastry.
- Bake blind for about 15 minutes at 200 °C, or until just beginning to brown (see introduction to Pastry).

Filling

1 kg	low fat cream cheese
250 ml (1 cup)	cream
or 125 ml	cream plus 125 ml yoghurt
185 ml ($^3/_4$ cup)	sugar
45 ml (3 Tbs)	flour
5 ml (1 tsp)	lemon rind
45 ml (3 Tbs)	lemon juice
3	whole eggs
3	egg yolks (extra)

- Preheat the oven to 200 °C.
- Place the cheese in a bowl with the remaining ingredients and mix until smooth.
- Pour into the baked pastry and bake for 10 minutes.
- Switch oven to 100 °C and leave the cake there until it is just set (±1 hour).
- Switch off the oven and leave to cool in the oven with the oven door open slightly.

Variation
For a change, soak a handful of seedless raisins in warm water for a couple of hours. Drain and dry them before adding to the filling.

POPPY SEED CHEESE CAKE

Mon
And now for something extraordinary and well worth the effort …

    1   quantity sweet, rich shortcrust pastry (see Pastry)

- Line a deep spring-form tin (about 23 cm) with the pastry.
- Bake blind for about 15 minutes at 200 °C, or until just beginning to brown (see introduction to *Pastry*).

Poppy seed filling

125 g	poppy seeds
30 g	butter
1	small green apple
2	egg yolks
45 ml (3 Tbs)	honey, or to taste
30 ml (2 Tbs)	custard powder
60 ml (¼ cup)	sour cream (approximate)
60 ml (¼ cup)	sultanas

- Boil the poppy seeds in water for two hours.
- Rinse very well under running water.
- Place the poppy seeds in a food processor or liquidiser with remaining filling ingredients, except sultanas, and blend until smooth.
- Place the mixture in a pot with the sultanas. Bring the mixture to the boil and cook for 1 minute, stirring continuously.
- Cool the mixture and pour into blind-baked pastry.

Cheese filling

3 x 250 g	smooth cottage cheese or cream cheese
125 ml (½ cup)	sour cream
165 ml (⅔ cup)	sugar
30 ml (2 Tbs)	flour
5 ml (1 tsp)	lemon rind
45 ml (3 Tbs)	lemon juice
2	whole eggs
2	egg yolks

- Preheat the oven to 200 °C.
- Place the cheese in a bowl with remaining ingredients and mix well until smooth.
- Pour into the pastry on top of the poppy seed filling.
- Bake for 15 minutes at 200 °C.
- Switch oven to 100 °C and bake until just set.

Variation
For a change, add 8 ml (1 1/2 tsp) grated lemon rind to the dry ingredients of the pastry.

Note You need 250 ml sour cream in all: 125 ml for the cheese, a little in the pastry and the rest in the poppy seed filling.

GATEAUX AND OTHER SPECIAL TREATS

A fancy name for fancy cakes! Baking them is not difficult, but these recipes will take a little more time and effort to complete. I promise that the compliments will make the extra effort worthwhile!

GATEAU AU CHOCOLAT

This cake, made with trifle sponge crumbs and ground almonds, plenty of eggs and oil rather than butter, gives you a slightly dry, almost pliable cake, which is excellent for pouring syrups on, or for using very rich icings such as butter cream or cream.

5	eggs, separated plus 1 whole egg
185 ml (¾ cup)	castor sugar
15 ml (1 Tbs)	hot water
15 ml (1 Tbs)	oil
5 ml (1 tsp)	vanilla
60 ml (¼ cup)	flour
60 ml (¼ cup)	cocoa
185 ml (¾ cup)	trifle sponge cake crumbs
50 g (½ packet)	ground almonds

Syrup

60 ml (¼ cup)	water
60 ml (¼ cup)	sugar
15 ml (1 Tbs)	whisky, brandy, rum, or alcohol of your choice, or to taste

- Preheat the oven to 160 °C.
- Add the whole egg to the 5 yolks.
- Beat yolks well, gradually adding sugar.
- Beat in the hot water, oil and vanilla.
- Sift the flour and cocoa.
- Add the crumbs, ground almonds and the sifted dry ingredients to the mixture.

- Beat egg whites until stiff but not dry.
- Fold in the stiffly beaten egg whites.
- Bake in two lined, 20 cm tins for 25 minutes. Cool and either leave as two layers, or cut each half in two to form four layers.
- For the syrup, bring sugar and water to the boil for 1 minute. Cool and add the alcohol.
- Dribble onto the cakes.

CHOCOLATE BUTTER CREAM

Two-layer cake

Butter cream is fairly tricky and it should be made with a sugar thermometer. The texture of butter cream is absolutely smooth and creamy and much richer than normal butter icing. I would definitely not recommend using margarine in this recipe.

```
200 ml (1 teacup)   sugar
 80 ml (1/3 cup)    water
              3     egg yolks
          165 g     butter
          100 g     melted dark chocolate
250 ml (1 cup)      cream, whipped (optional)
```

- Boil the sugar and water to thread stage (112 °C).
- Beat the yolks and gradually beat in the syrup to form a mousse. Beat in melted chocolate and cool.
- Cream the butter until fluffy and light in colour.
- Gradually beat in the mousse.
- Chill for several hours if not firm enough to pipe.
- Layer the cakes with whipped cream and butter cream on alternating layers, or use only butter cream. You will then need double the butter cream recipe.
- Ice the top and sides with butter cream and decorate with chocolate – either chocolate caraque made by peeling a slab of dark chocolate with a cheese slicer or vegetable peeler, or coarsely grated plain or mint chocolate, or use a Flake.

SACHERTORTE

This rich, heavy Viennese chocolate cake needs a good cup of coffee and an absolute addiction to chocolate.

```
         250 g    dark chocolate (not cooking
                  chocolate)
         125 g    butter
185 ml (3/4 cup)  castor sugar
              6   X-large or jumbo eggs, separated
  2 ml (1/2 tsp)  vanilla
185 ml (3/4 cup)  cake flour
  15 ml (1 Tbs)   cocoa
  1 ml (1/4 tsp)  bicarbonate of soda
  1 ml (1/4 tsp)  cream of tartar
```

- Preheat the oven to 160 °C.
- Line a deep cake tin (20 cm to 23 cm) with paper.
- Melt the chocolate in a small bowl over hot water, or in the microwave oven on low.
- Cream the butter and sugar together very well.
- Beat in 5 of the egg yolks, vanilla and melted chocolate. Keep the remaining egg yolk for the chocolate glaze.
- Sift the flour, cocoa and bicarb together and mix into the chocolate mixture.
- Beat the egg whites with the cream of tartar until they form soft peaks. They must be stiff but not dry.
- Fold them into the chocolate mixture.
- Pour the mixture into the tin and bake for 60 to 70 minutes.
- Cool for 10 minutes then remove from tin.
- Make the chocolate glaze and pour it hot over the warm cake.
- Allow the chocolate to set before cutting the cake.

Glossy chocolate glaze

```
         150 g    dark chocolate (not cooking
                  chocolate)
              1   egg yolk
185 ml (3/4 cup)  sugar
 60 ml (1/4 cup)  water
       1 ml (pinch) creme of tartar
  30 ml (2 Tbs)   brandy
```

- Place the chocolate in a bowl over hot water until it has melted.
- Beat in the egg yolk.
- In a separate pot, bring the sugar, water and creme of tartar to the boil. Boil vigorously for 1 minute or until it reaches 110 °C on a sugar thermometer.
- Beat the hot syrup into the chocolate.
- Beat in the brandy and immediately pour over the cake.

Hints

- If you do not want to use brandy, add 30 ml (2 Tbs) extra water to the sugar syrup once it has reached 110 °C.
- To make the icing process easier, place the cake on an upturned bowl slightly smaller than the cake. Place the cake and bowl on a plate to catch the run off. Pour on all the glaze at once. The excess will run smoothly off onto the plate. Smooth the sides quickly with a palette knife. As soon as it starts to set it can no longer be worked!

BOCCONOTTI

Amsterdammetjies

Something very special ... rich butter cakes filled with a soft chocolate filling. I am not sure whether this is the correct name for these shortbread-like, chocolaty dreams. At an Italian wedding where these little cakes were served, the lady who had made them said the recipe was a secret known only by the women from her little village in Abruzzi and she would not give it to me. Well, this is as close as I could get!

Makes 24

250 g	unsalted butter
125 ml (½ cup)	castor sugar
2 ml (½ tsp)	almond essence
1	egg
375 ml (1 ½ cup)	cake flour
100 g	ground almonds
10 ml (2 tsp)	baking powder
60 ml (¼ cup)	milk

Chocolate filling

100 g	dark chocolate
45 ml (3 Tbs)	cream

- First make the chocolate filling.
- Melt the chocolate and cream and beat until it is smooth.
- Leave it to cool.
- Preheat the oven to 180 °C.
- *To make the cakes,* cream the butter and the sugar well.
- Beat in the essence and egg and beat well.
- Sift the flour and the baking powder, and add almonds, then beat into the creamed mixture with the milk.
- Chill for 30 minutes before using.
- Take 15 ml (1 Tbs) of the cake mixture. Using floured hands, roll it into a ball and then flatten into a disc.
- Place the disc in the bottom of a greased patty pan.
- Drop a small amount of chocolate into the centre.
- Make another disc and cover the chocolate filling with it.
- Bake for about 15 minutes.
- Leave to cool slightly before removing and placing on a cooling rack.
- Dust with icing sugar before serving.
- Once these are baked, *hide them away. They are decadent!*

Variation

Without the chocolate filling, spoon the mixture into greased muffin pans and bake a little longer. They are then called *Amsterdammetjies.*

BISCUITS

I find the use of baking or greaseproof paper (not wax wrap) invaluable in baking biscuits. Cut papers the size of your baking sheets and place the unbaked biscuits on the paper rather than directly onto the baking sheet. This saves time by allowing you to have the next batch ready to slip onto the baking sheet as soon as the first batch comes out. It also avoids washing the trays between batches.

CHEDDAR SNAPS

These savoury biscuits are quick and easy to make. Serve them with drinks.

Makes about 50

250 g	mature cheddar cheese, grated
125 g	butter
250 ml (1 cup)	flour
5 ml (1 tsp)	salt
1 ml (¼ tsp)	cayenne pepper
2 ml (½ tsp)	paprika
2 ml (½ tsp)	dry mustard

- Preheat the oven to 180 °C.
- Blend all the ingredients to form a dough.
- Roll into marbles, place on baking paper and flatten with a fork, or roll out on a floured surface and cut into strips to make cheese straws.
- Bake for about 15 minutes or until slightly brown.
- Cool on cooling rack.

CHOC-CHIP BISCUITS

These delicious, rich biscuits are known in America as *Tollhouse cookies.* And where would America be without the chocolate chip?

Makes about 48 biscuits

250 ml (1 cup)	sugar
125 g	butter
1	egg
375 ml (1 ½ cup)	cake flour
12 ml (2 ½ tsp)	baking powder
250 g	chocolate chips
100 g	pecan or *walnuts, roughly chopped*

- Preheat the oven to 180 °C.
- Cream the butter and sugar together until light.
- Beat in the egg.
- Sift the dry ingredients, add and mix well into the creamed mixture.
- Mix in the chocolate and nuts by hand to avoid crushing them.
- Place spoonfuls on baking paper and flatten them with the heel your hand.
- Bake for 12 to 15 minutes.
- Place on a cooling rack to cool.
- Store in airtight container.

CRUNCHIES

These are the good, old-fashioned, quick biscuits that kids always love.

Makes about 40

130 g	butter
250 ml (1 cup)	brown sugar
15 ml (1 Tbs)	syrup
5 ml (1 tsp)	bicarbonate of soda
250 ml (1 cup)	oats
250 ml (1 cup)	flour
250 ml (1 cup)	coconut

- Preheat the oven to 180 °C.
- Heat the butter, brown sugar and syrup in a pot.
- Add the bicarb to the hot ingredients.
- Place the dry ingredients in a bowl and pour on the hot mixture.
- Mix well.
- Press into a small rectangular baking tray (about 24 cm x 34 cm).
- Bake for about 15 minutes or until golden.
- Cut while hot, but leave to cool in the tray.

CZECHOSLOVAKIAN BISCUITS

These are a cross between shortbread and the Greek almond biscuits. Sprinkling nuts instead of almonds makes it more economical.

Makes about 60

250 g	butter
125 ml ($^1/_2$ cup)	castor sugar
500 ml (2 cups)	flour
125 ml ($^1/_2$ cup)	cornflour
150 g	sprinkle nuts
	or *nibbed almonds*
2 ml ($^1/_2$ tsp)	almond essence
15 ml (1 Tbs)	milk
	icing sugar for rolling the biscuits in

- Preheat the oven to 180 °C.
- Cream the butter and castor sugar very well.
- Add the remaining ingredients and mix to a soft dough, adding a little milk if the mixture is too dry.
- Roll into balls the size of large marbles and flatten with a fork onto baking paper.
- Bake for about 12 minutes or until starting to brown.
- Working with a few at a time and keeping the biscuits warm in the oven until you coat them, roll them in sifted icing sugar, coating them completely.
- Cool on a drying rack.

DEE'S ONE-IS-ENOUGH BISCUIT

Make these big and one is almost enough. They are full of crunchy things.

Makes between 48 and 60, depending on size

250 g	butter
500 ml (2 cups)	sugar
2	eggs
15 ml (1 Tbs)	vinegar
500 ml (2 cups)	cornflakes
500 ml (2 cups)	oats
500 ml (2 cups)	coconut
500 ml (2 cups)	flour
250 ml (1 cup)	sprinkle nuts
125 ml ($^1/_2$ cup)	currants
	or *raisins*
1 ml	nutmeg
10 ml (2 tsp)	baking powder
10 ml (2 tsp)	bicarbonate of soda

- Preheat the oven to 180 °C.
- Cream the butter and sugar well.
- Beat in the eggs and vinegar.
- Mix in all the dry ingredients by hand.
- Shape into balls the size of large marbles (goons). The mixture is fairly dry and you have to work them into balls because of all the solid ingredients in the mixture.
- Flatten them with a fork and place on baking paper, leaving room for spreading.
- Bake for about 15 minutes or until golden.

MRS JOUBERT'S VERSATILE BIKKIES

Mrs Joubert gave me this recipe a few years ago. They have become a firm favourite with everyone who has tasted them.

Makes about 80

500 ml (2 cups)	sugar
250 g	butter
2	eggs
500 g (1 packet)	self-raising flour
5 ml (1 tsp)	bicarbonate of soda
250 ml (1 cup)	coconut

- Preheat the oven to 180 °C.
- Cream the butter and sugar well.
- Beat in the eggs.
- Sift the flour and bicarb together and add to the creamed mixture with the coconut. Mix well.
- Shape with a cookie press, or roll into balls and flatten with a fork.
- Place on baking paper. Leave room for spreading.
- Decorate with cherries, choc chips or nuts.
- Bake at 180 °C for 12 to 15 minutes or until golden.

GINGER SPICE BISCUITS

These spicy biscuits must be stored separate from other biscuits. Their strong flavour is absorbed by any other biscuit in a container. (They won't be in the container for long anyway.)

Makes about 48

125 g	butter
250 ml (1 cup)	treacle brown sugar
1	egg yolk
60 ml ($^1/_4$ cup)	molasses
375 ml (1 $^1/_2$ cups)	cake flour
6 ml (1 $^1/_4$ tsp)	bicarbonate of soda
8 ml (1 $^1/_2$ tsp)	allspice
10 ml (2 tsp)	ginger
	caramel brown sugar for sprinkling on top

- Preheat the oven to 180 °C.
- Cream the butter and sugar. Add molasses and egg and beat well.
- Sift the dry ingredients and mix into the creamed mixture to form a soft dough.
- Roll into a long sausage, wrap in greaseproof paper and chill for a few hours.
- Cut the sausage into 7 mm slices and place on baking paper.
- Sprinkle the top with extra brown sugar and flatten slightly with a fork or two fingers.
- Bake for 12 to 18 minutes. Cool on a cooling rack.

COCONUT MACAROONS

These are so easy to make, even children can do it.

Makes about 24

2	eggs
5 ml (1 tsp)	vanilla
625 ml (2 $^1/_2$ cups)	coconut
250 ml (1 cup)	castor sugar
	glace cherries

- Preheat the oven to 180 °C.
- Lightly beat the eggs and vanilla.
- Place the coconut and sugar in a bowl and add the beaten eggs.
- Mix well with a wooden spoon.
- Place heaped teaspoonful on baking paper and place a $^1/_4$ cherry on top of each biscuit. Slightly press the cherries in, otherwise they fall off.
- Bake for about 15 minutes or until golden.
- Remove from paper once they are cool.

MUESLI WALNUT SQUARES

I enjoy making biscuits that are cut into squares after baking, rather than shaping them individually, as it goes much quicker. These squares are wholesome and delicious.

Makes about 40

500 ml (2 cups)	muesli
125 ml ($^1/_2$ cup)	coconut
80 ml ($^1/_3$ cup)	raisins
100 g	walnuts
125 ml ($^1/_2$ cup)	self-raising flour
2 ml ($^1/_2$ tsp)	cinnamon
125 g	butter
50 ml (3 Tbs)	honey
125 ml ($^1/_2$ cup)	brown sugar

1	egg
5 ml (1 tsp)	vanilla
100 g	chocolate, melted

- Preheat the oven to 180 °C.
- Combine muesli, coconut, raisins, walnuts, self-raising flour and cinnamon.
- Melt the butter honey and sugar.
- Add to the dry ingredients, together with the egg and vanilla. Mix well and press into a square or rectangular baking tin (about 23 cm).
- Bake for 20 minutes.
- When cool, spread on the melted chocolate, leave to set and then cut into squares.

SHORTBREAD

Shortbread is made with a lot of butter. Use unsalted butter to avoid a salty taste. Using baking powder is cheating a little. Shortbread does not traditionally have baking powder, but I like the slightly lighter texture achieved by adding a small amount of baking powder.

Makes about 48

250 g	unsalted butter
125 ml (1/2 cup)	castor sugar
500 ml (2 cups)	flour
125 ml (1/2 cup)	cornflour
5 ml (1 tsp)	baking powder (optional)
1 ml (1/4 tsp)	almond essence (optional)
	castor sugar for sprinkling on top

- Preheat the oven to 160 °C.
- Cream the butter and castor sugar very well.
- Add remaining ingredients and mix to a soft dough.
- Press into a square tin (about 23 cm) and prick well with a fork. This enables the heat to penetrate, the steam to escape and the centre to cook.
- Bake for about 40 minutes or until just starting to brown.
- Remove from oven and immediately sprinkle liberally with castor sugar.
- Cut into squares or fingers before the mixture cools completely.
- Carefully remove from the tin and cool on a cooling rack.

Variations
Add 10 ml (2 tsp) orange rind in place of the almond essence. The biscuits can also be dipped into melted chocolate for something special.

Hint
To make individual biscuits, press mixture through a cookie press, or roll mixture in balls and press flat with a fork. Bake at 180 °C for 15 to 20 minutes. Sprinkle liberally with castor sugar as soon as they come out. Shaped and baked separately these biscuits become very light and fluffy.

JAM OR CHRISTMAS MINCE SQUARES

This basic crispy apple crumble topping makes the most delicious biscuits with fruit or jam fillings.

Makes about 48

125 g	butter
200 ml (1 teacup)	castor sugar
rind of	1 lemon
1	egg
5 ml (1 tsp)	vanilla essence
500 ml (2 cups)	flour
10 ml (2 tsp)	baking powder
	jam of your choice
	or *Christmas wheel filling*
	(see Pastry)

- Preheat the oven to 180 °C.
- Cream the butter, sugar and lemon rind until light. Add the egg and vanilla, and beat well.
- Sift the flour and baking powder together.
- Add half the flour and mix well.
- Add the rest of the flour and mix well.
- Divide dough in half, wrap it in cling wrap and place in the fridge for at least 30 minutes.
- Press one half of the dough into a square tin (about 23 cm).
- Spread on a layer of jam or Christmas mince filling.
- Grate the rest of the dough over the filling.
- Bake for about 20 minutes, or until the top is well browned.
- Cut into squares while hot, but leave in tin to cool.
- Remove and place on cooling rack.

Hint
Because of the moisture in the filling, these do not stay crisp for very long, but even when soft, they are still delicious.

ITALIAN COFFEE BISCUITS

Italian coffee biscuits are usually served with good coffee or espresso. The ingredients are expensive, but they are special occasion rather than school box biscuits. Even the names make one's mouth water!

BRUTTI MA BUONI

Ugly but good
These are chewy and tangy and a change from the ordinary.

Makes about 24

200 g	ground almonds
330 ml (1 1/3 cup)	icing sugar
2 ml (1/2 tsp)	vanilla essence
2 ml (1/2 tsp)	almond essence
1	egg white
100 g	walnuts, coarsely chopped
24	dried apricots, finely chopped

- Preheat the oven to 180 °C.
- Combine the ground almonds and icing sugar. Add vanilla, almond essence and egg white and mix well.
- Add the walnuts and apricots.
- Roll into balls, flatten and pinch into irregular shapes.
- Bake for about 15 minutes until golden.

PALLOTTOLE AL BUTTO

Butterballs
Italian shortbread with the flavour of honey and Brazil nuts.

Makes about 24

125 g	butter
60 ml (1/4 cup)	sugar
30 ml (2 Tbs)	honey
30 ml (2 Tbs)	rum
250 ml (1 cup)	flour
3 ml (1/2 tsp)	baking powder
100 g	brazil nuts, coarsely chopped
	icing sugar

- Preheat the oven to 180 °C.
- Cream the butter and sugar. Add the honey and rum.
- Add the flour and baking powder and mix in the nuts.
- Roll into balls and flatten slightly to form discs.
- Bake for about 15 minutes. Remove from oven and sift icing sugar over biscuits while still hot.

FLORENTINES

With a texture similar to brandy snaps, these fruit and chocolate biscuits are for grown-up children.

Makes 18 to 24

125 g	butter
185 ml (3/4 cup)	sugar, white or brown
45 ml (3 Tbs)	syrup
125 ml (1/2 cup)	flour
100 g	slivered almonds
50 g	flaked almonds
125 g	mixed peel
125 g	chopped cherries
100 g	dark cooking chocolate

- Preheat the oven to 160 °C.
- Melt the butter, sugar and syrup. Bring the mixture to the boil.
- Switch off the heat, but still working on the stove stir the flour, fruit and nuts into the pot.
- Place spoonfuls on a sheet of baking paper, leaving room for spreading.
- Bake for about 10 to 12 minutes. While hot, pull edges in with cookie cutter to form circles.
- When cool, coat the bottom with melted cooking chocolate.

BISCOTTI DI REGINA

Queen's biscuits
These orange-flavoured, sesame-coated biscuits are definitely good enough for royalty.

Makes about 24

165 ml (²/₃ cup) castor sugar
100 g butter
375 ml (1 ½ cup) flour
3 ml (½ tsp) baking powder
5 ml (1 tsp) orange rind
1 egg
5 ml (1 tsp) vanilla
250 ml (1 cup) sesame seeds (approximate)

- Preheat the oven to 180 °C.
- Cream the butter and sugar well.
- Sift the dry ingredients.
- Add the remaining ingredients and mix well.
- Roll into thin ropes and cut into 5 cm pieces.
- Roll each rope in sesame seeds and bake for about 15 minutes.

MIKI'S ITALIAN ALMOND RUSKS

These sweet rusks are reminiscent of Italian nougat without the stickiness.

Makes about 50

250 ml (1 cup) egg whites (about 6)
250 ml (1 cup) castor sugar
330 ml (1 ⅓ cup) flour
5 ml (1 tsp) vanilla
200 g almonds with the skins

- Preheat the oven to 160 °C.
- Beat the egg whites until they are stiff but not dry.
- Gradually beat in the sugar and then the vanilla essence.
- Fold in the sifted flour and, lastly, the nuts.
- Line the base of a loaf tin with baking paper and grease the sides.
- Pour the mixture into the loaf tin and bake for about 45 minutes or until a skewer comes out clean and the loaf is lightly browned.
- Remove from the tin and, when cool, wrap in cling wrap and leave in the fridge for 2 days.
- Cut the loaf into thin slices. Then cut each slice in half. Place on cooling racks or baking trays in a cool oven (about 110 °C) for 45 minutes to 1 hour, or until rusks are lightly browned and dry.
- Store in an airtight container.

BRANDY SNAPS

Filled with cream, brandy snaps can be served as a tea-time treat, or for dessert.

Makes about 16

100 g butter
125 ml (½ cup) castor sugar
60 ml (¼ cup) golden syrup
165 ml (²/₃ cup) cake flour
5 ml (1 tsp) ground ginger

- Preheat the oven to 160 °C to 170 °C.
- Place the butter, sugar and syrup in a small saucepan and melt over gentle heat.
- *Do not allow to boil.*
- Stir in the flour and ginger to make a smooth batter.
- Place the bowl of mixture in a larger bowl of hot water to keep it warm.
- Drop small spoonfuls of mixture onto baking paper and place the paper on a baking sheet. Drop only 2 to 3 spoonfuls on each tray to allow space between them for spreading.
- Bake for 7 to 10 minutes, or until golden brown.
- Remove the tray and leave to cool slightly for 10 to 15 seconds.
- Lift a biscuit from the tray using a spatula and as it begins to firm , wrap it around the handle of a wooden spoon or dowel stick. If the stick is long enough, leave the brandy snaps on the stick until almost cold. They keep their shape much better.

Hint
To form them into little dishes to use for dessert, drape them over a small orange or place in a muffin tin while they are still warm.

CIGARETTES RUSSE

These delicate, crispy biscuits, shaped like brandy snaps, can be served as part of an elaborate dessert or on their own with good coffee.

Makes about 36

125 ml (½ cup)	egg whites (about 4)
125 g	butter, melted
185 ml (¾ cup)	icing sugar
125 ml (½ cup)	flour
3 ml (½ tsp)	vanilla essence

- Preheat the oven to 180 °C.
- Beat the egg whites until foamy.
- Add all the remaining ingredients and mix well.
- Place the bowl of ingredients in a larger bowl of warm water to keep the mixture warm.
- Working on baking paper, spread 10 ml (2 tsp) of the mixture in a circle, as if you were thinly buttering bread.
- Bake for about 10 minutes.
- Lift them immediately with a palette knife and roll up tightly into a scroll.

Hint
If you want to fill the cigarettes, roll them around a wooden spoon handle. To use as a container for a dessert, remove the hot biscuits from the paper and drape them over an orange, a small bowl or in a muffin tin.

BRAN MOLASSES RUSKS

500 ml (2 cups)	Nutty Wheat
500 ml (2 cups)	cake flour
250 ml (1 cup)	bran
125 ml (½ cup)	oat bran
5 ml (1 tsp)	salt
125 ml (½ cup)	brown sugar
30 ml (2 Tbs)	baking powder
250 g	butter
30 ml (2 Tbs)	caraway or anise seeds (optional)
250 ml (1 cup)	currants
2	eggs
30 ml (2 Tbs)	molasses
330 ml (1 ⅓ cup)	buttermilk (approximate)

- Preheat the oven to 160 °C.
- Place the first 7 ingredients (dry) in a large bowl.
- Cut the butter into small blocks and rub it into the dry ingredients.
- Add the caraway seeds and currants.
- Mix the eggs, molasses and buttermilk and add to the mixture.
- Mix with a knife or metal spoon to a soft dough. *Do not overmix.*
- Roll dough into egg-shaped balls and pack loosely into two large, greased loaf tins or a small roasting pan.
- Bake for about 45 minutes, or until baked through. It will take less time in two pans.
- Break the rusks apart and dry them out, preferably on cooling racks in the oven, or on baking sheets at 75 °C for 4 to 5 hours or until well-dried.
- Store in an airtight container.

Variation
For muesli rusks, omit the wholewheat flour and add the same quantity muesli of your choice.

Hint
If the mixture is a little too soft while shaping them, dust your hands with wholewheat flour. The softer the dough, the lighter your rusks will be.

UNBEATABLE BROWNIES

These are chewy, full of chocolate and have the distinctive brownie crust on top.

Makes about 24

200 g	dark chocolate
125 g	butter
4	X-large or *jumbo* eggs
375 ml (1 1/2 cups)	castor sugar
5 ml (1 tsp)	vanilla essence
250 ml (1 cup)	flour
30 ml (2 Tbs)	cocoa
3 ml (1/2 tsp)	baking powder
100 g	walnuts or *pecan nuts, optional*

- Preheat the oven to 180 °C.
- Melt the chocolate in a bowl over hot water, or in the microwave.
- Beat in the softened butter and leave it to cool slightly.
- Beat the eggs and sugar until very light and fluffy (whisking over hot water speeds up this process).
- Add vanilla.
- Sift dry ingredients.
- Fold the dry ingredients, the chocolate and the nuts into the egg mixture. *Do not overmix.*
- Pour into a greased baking dish (about 270 mm x 320 mm). Most oven roasters are fine.
- Bake for about 20 minutes.
- Leave to cool in the tin before cutting into squares.

BUTTERMILK RUSKS

1 kg	self-raising flour
7 ml (1 1/2 tsp)	salt
10 ml (2 tsp)	baking powder
375 g	butter
250 ml (1 cup)	sugar
2	eggs
330 ml (1 1/3 cup)	buttermilk (approximate)

- Preheat the oven to 180 °C.
- Sift the flour, salt and baking powder.
- Rub the butter into the dry ingredients.
- Add the sugar.
- Beat the buttermilk with the eggs and stir into the flour.
- Knead well to make a soft, pliable dough.
- Roll into balls and arrange next to each other in a deep, greased baking tin, or in two loaf tins.
- Bake for 50 to 60 minutes.
- Cool and break apart with a fork.
- Dry out in a cool oven (100 °C) for 3 to 4 hours.

KICHEL

These traditional Jewish biscuits are eaten with chopped herring (see *Fish*). I love them as they are with tea.

Makes lots!

6	egg yolks
4	egg whites
30 ml (2 Tbs)	oil
2 ml (1/2 tsp)	salt
5 ml (1 tsp)	sugar
750 ml (3 cups)	flour
or 500 ml (2 cups)	cake meal (matzo)

- Preheat the oven to 240 °C.
- Place dry ingredients in a food processor.
- Add oil.
- Switch on the processor and add eggs one at a time through the funnel, until the mixture forms large, wet crumbles.
- When pressed together with your fingers, it should form a dry dough. (A little extra flour or a drop of water may be needed, depending on the size of the eggs and the dryness of the flour.)
- Roll the dough out until paper thin. *A pasta machine is perfect for the job!*
- Cut into diamond shapes. Prick well and sprinkle with sugar.
- Bake for about 7 minutes.
- Store in air tight container.

Hint
If you do not have a food processor place the flour in a large bowl. Make a well in the centre and pour in the beaten eggs and oil. Gradually incorporate the flour to form a stiff dough.

HONEY TEIGLACH

Another traditional Jewish biscuit, teiglach has a fairly dry, egg-like texture with a hard, chewy toffee coating. Most recipes use syrup. The honey gives this recipe a distinctive flavour.

These are quite tricky and messy to make and definitely not for the faint-hearted!

Makes about 48

- 5 *whole eggs*
- 2 *egg yolks (extra)*
- 10 ml (2 tsp) *dry ginger*
- 45 ml (3 Tbs) *oil*
- 750 ml (3 cups) *cake flour (approximate)*

Syrup
- 250 ml (1 cup) *syrup*
- 250 ml (1 cup) *honey or extra syrup*
- 250 ml (1 cup) *sugar*
- 435 ml (1 ¾ cup) *water*
- 15 ml (1 Tbs) *ginger*
- 125 ml (½ cup) *black coffee or boiling water (approximate)*

- Mix the eggs, oil, and ginger.
- Add enough cake flour to make a firm but still sticky dough.
- Very roughly roll into small goon-sized balls. The surface must be rough and full of cracks.
- Place syrup ingredients (except coffee) in a large pot and bring it to the boil.
- Quickly drop the teiglach into the boiling syrup.
- Cover with a tight-fitting lid and boil on high for 20 minutes without opening the lid, but shaking the pot every now and then.
- Open the lid and carefully stir with a metal spoon.
- Turn the stove to medium and replace the lid.
- Cook for a further 20 to 40 minutes, stirring periodically to prevent burning
- Remove the lid and continue cooking, stirring almost continuously until teiglach are the right colour. The timing varies enormously depending on the type of pot you use. Judge when they are ready by the colour rather than the cooking time.
- Remove from the stove and pour on boiling coffee or water to loosen teiglach. This will prevent a hard, tooth-breaking toffee from forming around the teiglach.
- Quickly remove with a slotted spoon and place on a tray covered with sugar or coconut.
- Sprinkle with more sugar or coconut and leave to cool.

Hint
If they collapse (heaven forbid!), put the lid back on and bring back to the boil for 5 to 10 minutes. They will puff up again.

For stuffed teiglach
- 125 g (½ block) *dates, chopped*
- 45 ml (3 Tbs) *boiling water*
- 125 ml (½ cup) *raisins, roughly chopped*

- Mix the dates with boiling water until mushy.
- Mix in the raisins and leave to cool.
- When shaping, place a very small quantity in the middle before rolling each piece into a ball.

PASTRY, TARTS AND QUICHES SWEET AND SAVOURY

In this chapter you will find anything, sweet or savoury, wrapped up or sitting in a pastry of any kind.

The sweet pastries can be used for teas or desserts and the savoury recipes for starters, main courses or snacks.

Rolling pastry
- When you roll pastry, keep loosening it with a long palette knife to make sure it is not sticking to the surface and stretching.
- To lift the pastry onto the tart plate, hold the rolling pin stationary with your thumb and roll the pastry back onto the rolling pin. You can now lift the rolling pin with the pastry and carefully lower the pastry onto the dish without putting your fingers through it. The thinner the pastry is rolled out, the better it is. This comes with practice.
- Pastry always shrinks when it bakes. Make sure that when you line a tart plate, the pastry is loose and not stretched in the plate.

Baking blind
Baking blind is baking the pastry before you put in the filling. It is more trouble, but will give you a much crispier crust.

I find two methods equally successful:

Method 1
- Once you have lined the tart with pastry, take a large piece of *heavy* foil and apply Spray and Cook on the *shiny* side.
- Carefully place the foil over the pastry, flattening it out on the bottom and up the sides. The ends must then be folded over the top of the tin. Bake at 200 °C for 15 minutes and then *very* carefully loosen the foil from the pastry and remove it. Return the pastry to the oven until it is just starting to brown on the bottom. It is now ready for the filling.

Method 2
- Line the pastry with a round piece of greaseproof or baking paper (not wax wrap). Pour a packet of dry beans into the paper to weigh it down. Bake as in method 1.
- I keep my packet of 'blind' beans and use them only for baking. You can cook them if you have used them only once, but not if you have baked blind with them several times.

Hint
When baking a deep pastry blind, to prevent the sides from falling in, use a long strip of foil folded over the rim of the tin and covering the top edge of the pastry.

PUFF, FLAKY AND ROUGH PUFF PASTRY

All three, puff, flaky and rough puff pastry contain the same proportion of fat to flour. The difference between the three is the method of incorporating the fat into the pastry. Most often butter is used.

I have tried many different recipes for puff, flaky and rough puff pastry. I have not found one to compare with this cheese rough puff pastry.

```
      300 g            butter
500 ml (2 cups)        flour (300 g)
      250 g            smooth cottage
                       or cream cheese (approximate)
 30 ml (2 Tbs)         iced water (approximate)
```

- Cut the butter into very small blocks and freeze it.
- Place the butter and flour in a food processor bowl or a mixing bowl and pulse or mix just to coat butter with flour. Do not rub the butter into the flour completely.
- Add cottage cheese and mix to form a dough. You may need a little extra iced water. The dough will have lumps of butter in it.
- Roll the pastry into a long rectangle.
- Find the middle and bring the two ends into the middle and then fold in half where the two ends meet. This will give you 4 layers.
- Turn the pastry so the folds are on your left and right (180° turn).
- Repeat the rolling and folding three more times.
- Leave in the fridge, covered, before using, preferably for 12 hours. This pastry freezes perfectly.

Variation
If you prefer a pastry that is less rich, omit the cheese in the pastry and use a total of about 150 ml to 175 ml iced water, to which you have added a squeeze of lemon juice.

CUSTARD SLICE

1 quantity rough puff pastry

- Roll out the pastry into a rectangle about 40 cm x 24 cm and 1,5 cm thick.
- Cut a *very* thin strip off each side to leave a cut edge for rising.
- Prick the pastry all over with a fork. This allows the steam to escape and the pastry will cook more evenly through the layers.
- Place on an ungreased baking sheet and bake at 220 °C for about 30 minutes or until the pastry is very well browned and cooked through. Rather slightly overbake than underbake.
- Place on a cooling rack and leave to cool until needed.

Custard filling
```
500 ml (2 cups)        milk
100 ml (7 Tbs)         sugar
              2        egg yolks
 50 ml (3 1/2 Tbs)     custard powder
 25 ml (5 tsp)         gelatine
  5 ml (1 tsp)         vanilla essence
125 ml (1/2 cup)       cream
```

- Heat 400 ml milk with the sugar. Mix until the sugar has dissolved.
- Stir the custard powder into the remaining 100 ml cold milk and 2 egg yolks.
- Add the hot milk to the cold mixture and return to the stove. Bring to the boil, stirring continuously.

- Soak the gelatine in 50 ml (3 to 4 Tbs) cold water. It will go solid and grainy.
- Drop the lump of gelatine into the hot custard and stir until it is completely dissolved.
- Allow the custard to come to room temperature, then place the bowl in a larger bowl containing a few blocks of ice and iced water. Stir the custard until it begins to thicken.
- Whip the cream and fold into the custard before it sets completely.
- Slice the cold pastry into two layers. Spread the setting custard on the bottom layer and place the top layer on the custard.
- Make glacé icing by mixing icing sugar and enough boiling water to form a spreading consistency. Spread on the top.
- Leave in the fridge for a few hours and then slice very carefully, using a bread knife with a sawing action. Do not put pressure on the knife or the custard will squeeze out.

CHRISTMAS MINCE WHEEL

This filling is delicious any time of the year, so why wait until Christmas? The filling is cooked and is much firmer than a mince pie filling. You can use it in little mince pies if you prefer, but you will need double the quantity of pastry.

1 quantity rough puff pastry

Filling

500 ml (2 cups)	green apple, with skin, grated
60 g	butter
60 ml (1/4 cup)	flour
454 g (1 bottle)	Christmas mince
3	egg yolks
45 ml (3 Tbs)	brandy

- Drain grated apple well. (The juice is good to drink!)
- Fry the apple in butter to remove excess moisture.
- Stir in the flour and cook for 1 minute.
- Stir in the remaining ingredients and bring to the boil over a low heat.
- Remove from the pot, cool and use in pastry.
- To shape, roll out the pastry to a thickness of 5 mm. Cut out a 35 cm circle.
- Roll out the remaining pastry and cut out a 30 cm circle.
- Place the smaller circle on a baking sheet and brush it with egg white.
- Spread the cooled mince filling on, leaving a 10 mm border of pastry all around.
- Brush the other circle of pastry with egg white and place, egg-side down, on top of the filling. Press the pastry together around border.
- Brush the top with egg white and sprinkle liberally with sugar.
- Using the point of a sharp knife, cut slashes almost through top pastry to resemble the spokes of a wheel.
- Bake at 200 °C for about 60 minutes, or until pastry is well browned all the way to the centre of the wheel.
- Allow to cool for 30 minutes before cutting into slices with a serrated knife.

Variation

Use any combination of glacé or mixed cake fruit in place of the Christmas mince and add 125 ml (1/2 cup) fruit juice to replace the moisture in the Christmas mince.

SAVOURY PIES

BOUREKAS

These small pies are found all over Eastern Europe and the Middle-East. They are made from a variety of pastries such as puff, shortcrust and phyllo. All kinds of fillings such as meat, spinach, potato, different combinations of cheese, and vegetables are used.

To make about 18 small pies, make double the rough puff pastry recipe (4 cups flour; *or* a single recipe quantity of the hot water pastry recipe for perogen in this chapter.

- Roll the pastry out fairly thin and cut out 12 cm circles.
- Brush the circles with beaten egg.
- Place a teaspoonful of filling in the middle and fold over to form a half moon.
- Pinch the edges together and decorate the closed edge with a fork.
- Brush the pies with a beaten egg and sprinkle liberally with sesame seeds.
- Bake at 220 °C for about 20 to 30 minutes, or until well browned.
- Cool for 5 to 10 minutes before serving, to allow the cheese to set.

Cheese filling

250 g		cream cheese
		or ricotta
90 g (³/₄ cup)		Tussers
		or cheddar cheese, grated
90 g (³/₄ cup)		feta cheese, grated
2		egg yolks
30 ml (2 Tbs)		flour
3 ml (½ tsp)		dried dill
or 1 Tbs		fresh dill
		pepper to taste

▶ Mix all ingredients.

Potato filling

500 g (about 3 large) potatoes, boiled and mashed
1 large onion, finely chopped
45 ml (3 Tbs) butter
60 ml (¼ cup) plain yoghurt
250 ml (1 cup) feta cheese, grated
250 ml (1 cup) Tussers
  or mild cheddar cheese, grated
2 egg yolks
45 ml (3 Tbs) fresh parsley, chopped
3 ml (½ tsp) nutmeg
  pepper to taste

▶ Fry onion in butter and add to mashed potatoes with the yoghurt. Leave to cool.
▶ Add remaining ingredients and mix well.

Spinach filling

Use the filling given for *Spanakopita* in this chapter.

OLLIE'S CHICKEN AND MUSHROOM PIE

Olive Heuvel was famous in the staff canteen for her delicious chicken pie. The recipe is in her head, so I watched, wrote it down and here it is – simple and delicious. It is a large recipe, but make one and freeze one.

Serves 10 to 12

125 ml (½ cup) sago
15 ml (1 Tbs) whole coriander
5 ml (1 tsp) cloves
7 ml (1 ½ tsp) black peppercorns
2 whole chickens
4 bay leaves
2 medium onions, cut in chunks
3 litres chicken stock
2 x quantities rough puff pastry, made and chilled
or 2 x packets frozen pastry

Filling

3 medium onions, diced
60 g butter
250 g brown mushrooms, diced
85 ml (⅓ cup) flour
1 packet mushroom soup
1 litre (4 cups) strained cooking liquid
  diced chicken

▶ Soak the sago in a bowl with 375 ml (1 ½ cup) cold water for 30 minutes.
▶ Bruise the coriander, cloves and peppercorns by hitting them with a hammer, the bottom of a heavy based pot, or in a pestle and mortar.
▶ Place chicken, bay leaves, onions, spices and chicken stock in a large pot.
▶ Simmer until the chicken is just cooked (about 30 minutes).
▶ Remove the chickens from the pot and leave to cool.
▶ Debone, skin and dice the chickens into 3 cm pieces.
▶ Strain the cooking liquid and discard the solids.
▶ *To make the filling*, sauté onions in butter until soft and glassy.
▶ Add the mushrooms and cook for 3 minutes.
▶ Sprinkle the flour onto the onion mixture and cook for 3 minutes.
▶ Add stock, strained sago and mushroom soup powder.
▶ Add chicken and simmer for about 10 minutes.
▶ Season with black pepper.
▶ Cool completely.
▶ Using ⅓ of the pastry, roll out and line one large or two small, deep ovenware dishes.
▶ Pour the cold filling into the pastry shell.
▶ Cover with the pastry, brush with beaten egg and bake at 200 °C for 30 minutes, or until pastry is crispy and brown.

FISH IN PASTRY

Use any fish available and vary your vegetables for different flavours.

Serves 4 to 6

1	quantity rough puff pastry, made and chilled
15 ml (1 Tbs)	cornflour

Filling

750 g	hake or fresh line fish fillets
	seasoned flour
60 g	butter
125 ml ($^1/_2$ cup)	onion, chopped
125 g	brown mushrooms, sliced
3 ml ($^1/_2$ tsp)	dried dill
125 ml ($^1/_2$ cup)	celery, chopped
125 ml ($^1/_2$ cup)	carrots, grated
15 ml (1 Tbs)	lemon juice
60 ml ($^1/_4$ cup)	parsley, chopped
5 ml (1 tsp)	sugar
1 tin	smoked mussels (optional)
	salt and pepper to taste
1	egg, beaten

- Roll $^1/_3$ of the pastry into a large rectangle.
- Prick pastry and bake at 220 °C for 10 to 15 minutes and leave to cool.
- Coat fish with seasoned flour and brown well in butter. Remove from pan.
- In remaining butter, gently fry vegetables until they have softened.
- Add lemon juice, chopped parsley and seasoning.
- Dust the baked pastry with cornflour and place the fish on top.
- Arrange the smoked mussels on top of the fish and then spread on the vegetables.
- Roll out the remaining pastry and cover fish and vegetables with it. Tuck the ends in under the baked pastry.
- Score the pastry in diamond shapes to puff up while baking.
- Brush with beaten egg trying to avoid the cut edges.
- Bake at 220 °C for 15 minutes, then reduce to 190 °C for 15 to 20 minutes or until well browned.

Hint
If it is in season, use 60 ml (1/4 cup) fennel root, chopped or 7 ml (1 1/2 tsp) fresh fennel, dill or tarragon leaves in place of the dried dill in the recipe.

SHORTCRUST PASTRY

Shortcrust pastry generally has half the fat content of puff pastry. That means the fat to flour content is 1 to 2. To make it a rich shortcrust pastry, add an egg yolk per cup of flour, or a little extra butter. A sweet shortcrust pastry is usually a rich shortcrust pastry with sugar added. As more sugar is added to the pastry, it becomes more like a biscuit and more difficult to roll.

Rich shortcrust pastry and sweet shortcrust pastry can be used raw or baked blind (baked before being filled), for any tart.

RICH SHORTCRUST PASTRY

This quantity is a little more than you need for a 21 cm to 26 cm tart, but by having that little extra, it is much easier to roll and line the tart plate or dish. With the bits left over, you can make jam tarts or coconut tarts (recipe elsewhere in this chapter). If you find rolling out pastry easy, then 250 ml (1 cup) flour is *just* enough. Use 80 g butter but still 1 egg yolk.

375 ml (1 $^1/_2$ cup)	cake flour
125 g	butter
1	egg yolk
60 ml ($^1/_4$ cup)	iced water (approximate)

- Cut the butter up into very small blocks and chill well.
- Rub butter into flour until almost all the butter has disappeared. By leaving a little of the butter visible you will end up with a slightly flaky, light pastry. The easiest way of rubbing it in is to use the food processor, but then the butter must be very cold.
- Mix the egg yolk and cold water and add enough to form a stiff dough.

Hint
Chill pastry for several hours before baking. This will diminish the shrinking of the pastry when baking.

SWEET SHORTCRUST PASTRY

To the basic rich shortcrust pastry, add 60 ml (4 Tbs) castor sugar to rubbed in mixture, before adding the liquid.

SIMNEL TART

This tart is based on the simnel light fruit cake made with marzipan in the middle and traditionally served at Easter.

1 quantity sweet shortcrust pastry, rolled out

Filling

- 250 g marzipan
- 125 g cherries
- 100 g blanched almonds
- 125 g dates, chopped
- 310 ml (1 $\frac{1}{4}$ cup) mixed cake fruit
- 60 ml ($\frac{1}{4}$ cup) brandy or orange juice
- 165 ml ($\frac{2}{3}$ cup) cake flour
- 2 ml ($\frac{1}{2}$ tsp) baking powder
- 60 g butter
- 60 ml (4 Tbs) sugar
- 2 eggs

▸ Preheat the oven to 200 °C.
▸ Line a 20 cm loose-bottomed pan or tart pan with the pastry.
▸ Slice the marzipan and place a layer on top of the pastry.
▸ Reserve 4 cherries and 12 almonds and chop those remaining.
▸ Combine the fruit, nuts and brandy in a bowl.
▸ Sift the flour and baking powder over the fruit and mix to coat fruit.
▸ Cream the butter and sugar.
▸ Add eggs and mix well.
▸ Add to the fruit and dry ingredients and mix well.
▸ Pour the mixture into the pastry, over the marzipan.
▸ Arrange the whole almonds and cherries on top of the filling.
▸ Bake for 15 minutes. Lower oven setting to 180 °C for a further 20 minutes.

Hint
This tart is best if stored for several days before eating.

NORMANDY APPLE TART

This is an apple tart with a difference. It has thinly sliced apples in an almond cream frangipane filling and is brushed with jam. It can be served as dessert or for tea.

1 quantity rich shortcrust pastry

Filling

- 4 apples (approximate, depending on size)

Frangipane

- 100 g butter
- 125 ml ($\frac{1}{2}$ cup) castor sugar
- 1 whole egg
- 1 egg yolk
- 15 ml (1 Tbs) Kirsch or brandy
- 15 ml (1 Tbs) flour
- 100 g ground almonds
- melted apricot jam to finish

▸ Roll out the pastry and line a tart tin or loose-bottomed pan (about 22 cm to 24 cm) – preferably not glass.
▸ Peel and core the apples and cut in half. Slice apples thickly and dip in water with a little lemon juice. Do not leave in the water as they absorb water and become mushy.
▸ For the frangipane, cream the butter and sugar.
▸ Beat in the egg and egg yolk and beat until creamy..
▸ Add remaining ingredients and mix until smooth.
▸ Pour the frangipane into the pastry and spread it evenly.
▸ Arrange apple slices on top, pushing edges into frangipane mixture.
▸ Bake at 200 °C for 10 to 15 minutes.
▸ Turn down oven to 170 °C and continue to bake until frangipane is golden (about 30 minutes).
▸ Allow to cool partially. Melt 60 ml ($\frac{1}{4}$ cup) smooth apricot jam with 10 ml (2 tsp) water and carefully brush onto baked tart.

Hint
This tart is best eaten the day it is made.

PECAN PIE

1 quantity sweet shortcrust pastry

Filling

3	eggs
15 ml (1 Tbs)	milk
250 ml (1 cup)	moist brown sugar
125 ml (½ cup)	maple or golden syrup
50 g	butter
2 ml (½ tsp)	vanilla essence
200 g	pecan nuts

- Roll out the pastry and line a 23 cm tart plate.
- Whisk eggs and milk.
- Dissolve sugar in the syrup, then boil for 3 minutes.
- Stir in butter and vanilla.
- Slowly whisk syrup mixture into eggs and milk.
- Arrange the halved nuts in the pastry case.
- Carefully pour in the filling and bake at 200 °C for 10 minutes, then lower the temperature to 160 °C and bake for a further 40 minutes or until filling is set.

Hint

If the pastry is baked blind before adding the filling, bake the pie at 160 °C for about 45 minutes.

SPECIAL LEMON MERINGUE PIE

This is a *real* lemon meringue pie. It contains no condensed milk!

1 quantity sweet shortcrust pastry

- Roll out and line a deep, 23 cm tart plate with the pastry.
- Bake the pastry blind at 200 °C for 15 minutes (see introduction to this chapter).

Filling

330 ml (1 ⅓ cup)	sugar
125 ml (½ cup)	cornflour
2 ml (½ tsp)	salt
375 ml (1 ½ cup)	water
4	eggs, separated
45 ml (3 Tbs)	butter
15 ml (1 Tbs)	grated lemon rind
125 ml (½ cup)	lemon juice

- Mix the sugar, cornflour and salt in a saucepan.
- Add the water and whisk over medium heat until the mixture is thick. Cook for 1 minute.
- Separate the eggs.
- Pour the hot mixture onto beaten yolks, whisking continuously.
- Stir in the butter.
- Return the mixture to the pot and whisk over low heat for 1 to 2 minutes.
- Add lemon juice and lemon rind and pour into baked pie shell.

Meringue

4	egg whites
2 ml (½ tsp)	creme of tartar
250 ml (1 cup)	castor sugar

- Whisk the egg whites until stiff. Beat in the sugar and pile it on top of the lemon filling.
- Bake at 160 °C for about 20 minutes until meringue is golden. Cool completely before cutting.

Hint

This tart is at its best for the first 24 hours. This kind of filling and meringue will always weep on standing.

TARTE AU CITRON

This French lemon tart is rich and tart and makes the most delicious end to a meal. It is almost like a lemon cream caramel in a crust.

1 quantity rich shortcrust pastry

- Roll out and line a 23 cm spring-form tin.
- Bake pastry blind at 200 °C for 15 minutes (see introduction to this chapter).
- Cool.

Filling

4	whole eggs
1	egg yolk (extra)
375 ml (1 ½ cups)	sugar
15 ml (1 Tbs)	lemon rind
125 ml (½ cup)	fresh lemon juice
250 ml (1 cup)	cream

- Mix the sugar and eggs well without making it foamy.
- Add remaining ingredients and mix well.

- Chill until required.
- Pour lemon mixture into the cooled, baked crust and bake at 150 °C for 45 to 60 minutes, or until set.
- Cool before cutting.

Variation

This mixture can be baked in ramekins as for cream caramel, cooled and turned out. Serve with whipped cream and Cigarette russe (see *Biscuits*), or finger biscuits.

MELKTERT

1 quantity rich shortcrust pastry
or $1/4$ quantity rough puff pastry

- Roll out and line a 1 to 1,5 litre tart plate.
- Bake blind at 200 °C for about 15 minutes until golden.

Filling

750 ml (3 cups) milk
2 sticks cinnamon
80 g butter
80 ml ($1/3$ cup) sugar
60 ml ($1/4$ cup) cornflour
45 ml (3 Tbs) flour
3 eggs
1 ml almond essence (optional)
ground cinnamon

- *Infuse the milk* by heating it with the cinnamon to just under boiling, then leave to stand for a few hours while making the pastry.
- Mix the sugar, cornflour and flour thoroughly.
- Separate the eggs and beat the whites to a soft peak.
- Bring milk and butter to the boil and strain onto sugar and cornflour mixture, mixing well with a whisk.
- Add milk mixture to egg yolks.
- Add almond essence.
- Working over a medium heat and gently using a whisk, cook until the mixture is thick.
- Fold in the egg whites.
- Pour into the baked pastry shell and sprinkle with cinnamon.
- Bake at 180 °C for 20 minutes. If using rough puff pastry, bake at 220 °C for 10 minutes, then lower the oven setting to 160 °C for 10 to 15 minutes.
- Cool before cutting.

COCONUT TARTS

These little tarts are easy to make and they are a good way to use up leftover pastry. And the filling is a great way of using up egg whites! You can always halve the filling quantities.

Makes about 36 little tarts

1 quantity rich shortcrust pastry
4 egg whites
250 ml (1 cup) coconut
250 ml (1 cup) castor sugar
apricot jam

- Roll out the pastry and cut into circles to fit into patty tins. Cut circles slightly too large, to allow for shrinkage.
- Whip egg whites until only foamy. *Do not overwhip.*
- Mix in coconut and castor sugar.
- Place a dot of apricot jam in each patty tin, spoon the coconut mixture on top and bake at 200 °C for 15 to 20 minutes.

Variation

Use the melktert or cheese cake filling in place of the coconut.

QUICHES

Often the 'quiche' of life at any cocktail party, light meal or brunch! A quiche is made up of a pastry base, a layer of grated cheese, a filling of your choice and an egg custard topping. The choice of fillings is almost unlimited. Use this basic formula and your own inventiveness to create original quiches.

CHEESE PASTRY BASE

This pastry is a rich shortcrust pastry with added cheese. The little bit of baking powder is a cheat – it helps keep the pastry light, as the cheese can make it heavy.

55 g butter
250 ml (1 cup) flour
2 ml ($1/2$ tsp) salt
3 ml ($1/2$ tsp) baking powder
50 g ($1/2$ cup) cheddar cheese, grated
1 egg yolk
45 ml (3 Tbs) iced water (approximate)

- Rub the butter into the dry ingredients.
- Cut in grated cheese.
- Mix the egg yolk and water and add to the dry ingredients. Mix to form a pastry.
- Roll out and line a 20 cm to 23 cm quiche tin.

Variations

For a plain pastry base, use the rich shortcrust pastry recipe. For a wholewheat pastry base, use the pastry from the spinach and mushroom quiche in this chapter.

Cheese layer

250 ml (1 cup, 100 g) cheddar cheese, grated (approximate)

- Sprinkle the grated cheese onto the pastry base

Filling

- Use one of the following quiche fillings or create your own.
- Loosely spread the filling onto the grated cheese.

Topping

2 X-large eggs
250 ml (1 cup) cream
pinch salt, pepper, cayenne pepper and mustard

- Whisk the topping ingredients and pour over filling.
- Bake at 200 °C for 10 minutes, then reduce to 180 °C for 30 minutes or until topping has turned a golden colour.
- Cool before cutting.

Variation

For a change, use 250 ml sour cream, or 250 ml evaporated milk in place of the cream. For a less rich quiche, use 125 ml ($1/_2$ cup) cream and 100 ml ($1/_3$ cup + 1 Tbs) milk in place of the 250 ml cream. Because the milk is thinner, less is used.

QUICHE FILLINGS

Asparagus filling

410 g tinned asparagus salad cuts
1 onion, coarsely chopped
30 g butter

- Sauté onion in butter and mix with asparagus cuts.
- Spread over cheese.

Leek or onion filling

4 leeks or 2 large onions, washed and cut into rings
50 g butter
2 ml ($1/_2$ tsp) nutmeg
45 ml (3 Tbs) fresh parsley, chopped

- Sauté the leeks or onions in butter until soft. Add nutmeg and parsley.
- Spread over cheese.

Variation

For caper lovers, add 15 ml of capers to the filling.

Spinach filling

1 bunch spinach, washed and steamed
1 onion, chopped
30 g butter
2 ml ($1/_2$ tsp) nutmeg
salt and black pepper

- Chop the steamed spinach.
- Sauté the onion in butter and add the spinach and seasoning.
- Spread over cheese.

Quiche Lorraine filling

1 onion, chopped
125 g bacon, chopped
30 ml (2 Tbs) parmesan cheese

- Sauté onion and bacon in a little butter and spread over grated cheese.
- Pour on the topping and sprinkle with parmesan.

Mushroom filling

250 g mushrooms, brown or white
1 large onion, sliced
50 g (2 Tbs) butter
1 ml ($1/_4$ tsp) mixed herbs
15 ml (1 Tbs) flour

- Sauté onions in butter. Add mushrooms and season with salt, pepper and mixed herbs.
- Sprinkle on the flour and cook until almost dry.
- Spread over grated cheese.

WHOLEWHEAT SPINACH AND MUSHROOM QUICHE

This very substantial quiche is more pie than quiche! It makes a delicious vegetarian main course.

Pastry
This pastry is heavy and nutty.

60 g	butter
250 ml (1 cup)	Nutty Wheat flour
2 ml ($\frac{1}{2}$ tsp)	salt
1 ml ($\frac{1}{4}$ tsp)	mustard
3 ml ($\frac{1}{2}$ tsp)	baking powder
125 ml ($\frac{1}{2}$ cup)	cheddar cheese, grated
1	egg yolk
45 ml (3 Tbs)	water (approximate)
125 ml ($\frac{1}{2}$ cup)	extra grated cheese

- Rub the butter into the dry ingredients.
- Cut in the cheese.
- Mix the egg yolk with water and add it to the dry ingredients to form a pastry.
- Roll out the pastry, or simply press into deep quiche or shallow ovenware dish.
- Sprinkle the 125 ml grated cheese onto the pastry.

Filling

1	large onion, chopped
45 ml (2 Tbs)	olive oil
2	cloves garlic, crushed
250 g	brown mushrooms, sliced
1	bunch spinach, chopped

- Sauté the onion in oil until glassy.
- Add mushrooms and crushed garlic, and continue cooking.
- Add spinach, cover and steam until cooked.
- Remove the lid and boil until the water has evaporated.
- Season with salt and pepper.
- Spread on top of grated cheese

Topping

250 ml	sour cream
250 g	chunky cottage cheese
80 ml ($\frac{1}{3}$ cup)	rigatello
	or *any strong cheese, grated*
3	eggs
	salt and pepper to taste
$\frac{1}{2}$ cup	black olives, pitted

- Mix all the ingredients except olives.
- Spread onto the spinach layer.
- Dot with olives.
- Bake at 200 °C for about 30 minutes, or until starting to brown.

Hint
Use 45 ml (3 Tbs) Parmesan as a substitute for the rigatello cheese for the topping.

HOT WATER PASTRY

Hot water pastry is the simplest and quickest pastry to make. You can use it for all the different kinds of pies, replacing puff, flaky and rough puff pastry. It has half the fat content of these pastries. The pastry is soft and warm and it takes a little practice to work with. The two recipes using this pastry are variations on the same theme, both originating in Eastern Europe.

PEROGEN

This small pie is traditionally served with chicken soup in Jewish homes. Originally the filling was made from lung. Nowadays chopped beef is used. It is shaped like a cornish pastie.

Schmaltz is rendered chicken fat. Nowadays a mock schmaltz made from vegetable fats, carrots and onions is available. To make your own, see *This and that*. Butter or hard white margarine can be used in place of the schmaltz.

Pastry

200 ml (1 teacup)	water
185 ml ($\frac{3}{4}$ cup)	oil
100 ml (7 Tbs)	schmaltz
4 x 250 ml (4 cups)	flour (600 g)
8 ml (1 $\frac{1}{2}$ tsp)	salt
2	egg yolks

- Bring the water, oil and schmaltz to the boil.
- Place the dry ingredients in a food processor or in a bowl and pour on the hot liquid.
- Mix for a few minutes to cool slightly before adding the yolks.
- Mix to form a soft pastry and knead until smooth.
- Work with the pastry while it is still warm.

Filling

500 g	chuck, off the bone
	schmaltz or oil
3	medium onions, chopped
410 g	tinned tomatoes, with juice, chopped
125 ml ($^1/_2$ cup)	strong beef stock
3	hard-boiled eggs, chopped
60 ml (4 Tbs)	freshly chopped parsley
	salt and pepper to taste

- Cut the chuck into tiny cubes.
- Brown the meat well in a little oil or schmaltz. Remove from the pan.
- Sauté onions in remaining oil until glassy and just starting to brown.
- Return meat and add tomatoes and stock.
- Simmer until the meat is very soft.
- Remove the lid and simmer until almost all the liquid has evaporated. The stew should be fairly dry.
- Stir in the eggs and parsley and check seasoning.
- Allow the filling to cool before making into pies.
- To shape, roll out pastry and cut into circles about 15 cm in diameter.
- Brush circles with beaten egg.
- Place a spoonful of the filling in the middle and bring the edges up to meet on the top of the filling.
- Seal well with fingers to have a wavy effect.
- Place on greased baking sheet and brush with beaten egg. For something special, sprinkle with sesame seeds.
- Bake at 220 °C for about 20 minutes, or until well browned. Keep bowl of pastry covered with a cloth while you are working. This will keep the heat in.

PIROZHKI

Small Russian meat pies

1	quantity hot water pastry, (made with butter or hard white margarine instead of schmaltz) or double quantity rough puff pastry

Filling
To the perogen filling, add the following when adding the stock and tomatoes to the pot:

1	large potato, finely grated
125 ml ($^1/_2$ cup)	sour cream
5 ml (1 tsp)	dried dill

- Make and shape the pirozhki following the perogen method.
- Before baking, brush with beaten egg and sprinkle liberally with sesame seeds.

PHYLLO PASTRY

This is one pastry that I buy ready-made. It is easily available, the quality is good and it is very easy to use. Make sure that it is covered while you are using it, to prevent it drying out and becoming brittle. I use a large plastic bag to cover it while I work. Also use plenty of butter while you are layering the sheets. The pastry is made from flour and water only and you have to add the fat in the form of melted butter or oil.

PHYLLO APPLE STRUDEL

4-6	sheets phyllo pastry
200 g	butter, melted (approximate)

Filling

60 g	butter, melted
325 ml (1 $^1/_2$ cups)	fresh white bread- or cake crumbs (approximate)
125 ml ($^1/_2$ cup)	sugar
2 ml ($^1/_2$ tsp)	cinnamon
1 ml ($^1/_4$ tsp)	allspice
1 ml	cloves
45 ml (3 Tbs)	brandy
5 ml (1 tsp)	lemon rind

100 g blanched almonds,
          toasted and coarsely chopped
60 g raisins
1 x 785 g tin pie apples

- Brush each sheet of phyllo pastry liberally with butter and lay them on top of each other.
- Mix all the filling ingredients.
- Pile the filling along one edge of the pastry, turn in the side edges and roll it up.
- Place the strudel on a greased baking sheet.
- Brush with melted butter.
- Bake in oven preheated to 200 °C for 30 to 45 minutes, or until golden and crisp.
- Sprinkle with icing sugar and serve warm with whipped cream.

Savoury phyllo

Phyllo is the most versatile of all the pastries, because it is thin and does not overpower the dish.

SPANAKOPITA

This popular Greek dish can be made as a large pie or in individual triangular pastries.

12 sheets phyllo pastry
    butter, melted

Filling

2 large bunches fresh spinach,
    steamed, chopped and cooled
1 onion, finely chopped
45 ml (3 Tbs) olive oil
80 ml (1/3 cup) fresh parsley, chopped
5 ml (1 tsp) dry dill
or 15 ml (3 tsp) fresh dill
2 ml nutmeg (1/2 tsp)
250 ml (1 cup) feta cheese, crumbled
30 ml (2 Tbs) parmesan cheese
2 eggs, beaten
30 ml (2 Tbs) flour
    salt and black pepper

- Sauté onion in olive oil and leave to cool.
- Combine all the filling ingredients.
- Place 4 sheets of the phyllo on base of an ovenware dish, brushing butter liberally in between each layer.
- Place the filling on the pastry and layer remaining 8 sheets of phyllo on top of each other, again brushing liberally with butter in between each layer.

- Brush the top with butter and score through the top layers with a sharp knife into diamond shapes.
- Bake at 200 °C to 220 °C for about 30 minutes until golden brown.
- Allow to cool partially before serving.

Variations

- To make individual pastries, cut pastry in 6 cm strips. Place a spoonful of the filling in one corner and fold into a triangle, or roll the pastry up in cigar shapes.
- For cheese or potato pastries, use the cheese or potato fillings from the boreka and follow the directions for Spanakopita.

KINGKLIP, CHICKEN, LAMB OR FILLET IN PHYLLO

These recipes will give you an idea of how to use phyllo with fish, chicken and meat portions. Then use your imagination and put different toppings on before you wrap the food up in the pastry.

Serves 6

12 sheets phyllo pastry
125 g melted butter

Filling

750 g kingklip, cut into 6 portions
or 6 lamb chops
or 6 slices of beef fillet
or 6 chicken breast fillets
60 g butter
250 g button mushrooms
2 bunches spinach,
    washed and sliced
    salt and pepper to taste
15 ml (1 Tbs) flour
    lemon juice to taste
250 g feta cheese

- In a hot pan, brown meat quickly on each side in a little butter. To brown the fish lightly, coat it in flour before you brown it.
- Melt 60 g butter in a frying pan, sauté mushrooms and spinach until just wilted.
- Add lemon juice, salt and pepper to taste and thicken with flour.
- Place 2 sheets of phyllo on top of each other, brushing liberally with the melted butter – between them, as well as on top.

- Cut the pastry in half lengthways.
- At one end of the pastry, place about 45 ml (3 Tbs) mushrooms and spinach mixture, topped with crumbled feta cheese. Place the browned fish or meat on top of the vegetables. Pile on more vegetables and cheese.
- Tuck in the edges and roll it up into a parcel.
- Brush the surface of the parcel with melted butter.
- Place on a baking tray and bake at 200 °C for 25 to 35 minutes or until brown and crispy.

CHOUX PASTRY

This versatile pastry can be made sweet or change it to savoury by adding grated mature Cheddar cheese.

CUSTARD PUFFS

Round éclairs

The easiest way of shaping the choux paste is using two teaspoons and forming them into small balls. I prefer the confectioners' custard filling to plain cream. To make eclairs, pipe the mixture into sausage shapes and, once baked, fill them with whipped cream. Using baking powder is cheating, but it makes a firmer crust that will not collapse.

Makes about 30

Choux paste

250 ml (1 cup)	water
125 ml (½ cup)	butter or oil
250 ml (1 cup)	flour
4	X-large eggs
10 ml (2 tsp)	baking powder

- Melt the butter in a pot, with the water, over a low heat.
- Bring the water and melted butter to the boil. It is essential that the water comes to a rolling boil.
- Switch off the stove.
- Add all the flour to the pot at once and stir well until all the flour has been mixed in.
- Empty the contents of the pot into a mixing bowl or large food processor bowl.
- Add the eggs one at a time, beating well after each addition.
- Add the baking powder and beat until the mixture is smooth and shiny.
- Using two teaspoons or a piping bag, shape the puffs onto baking paper or a greased baking sheet.
- Bake at 200 °C for 10 minutes.
- Lower the temperature to 180 °C for a further 40 to 50 minutes.
- Bake until dark golden brown – rather overbake than underbake!
- Cool on a cooling rack.

Custard filling

100 ml (7 Tbs)	sugar
60 ml (¼ cup)	custard
15 ml (1 Tbs)	gelatine
2	egg yolks
500 ml (2 cups)	milk
15 ml (1 Tbs)	butter
2 ml (½ tsp)	vanilla
250 ml (1 cup)	cream

- Mix the sugar and custard powder.
- Mix the gelatine with 45 ml (3 Tbs) cold water.
- Beat the yolks with 60 ml (¼ cup) of the milk and blend with custard powder.
- Bring the remaining milk and butter to the boil.
- Pour the boiling milk onto the egg mixture and blend well.
- Return to the stove and bring to the boil over medium heat, stirring constantly. Be careful not to burn it on the bottom!
- Cook for 1 minute to get rid of the starchy taste.
- Add the solid lump of gelatine and stir until it has dissolved. Add the vanilla and leave to cool.
- Whip the cream and fold it into the cooled custard. Chill before using.

Topping

100 g	dark chocolate
45 ml (3 Tbs)	cocoa
375 ml (1 ½ cup)	icing sugar (approximate)
80 ml (⅓ cup)	boiling water
30 g	butter

- Place the chocolate and the boiling water in a pot and melt the chocolate over a low heat.
- Add the remaining ingredients and blend to form a thick, creamy consistency.
- Spread the warm topping on the puffs.

Hint

The custard can be made very easily in the microwave oven with no possibility of burning on the bottom.

 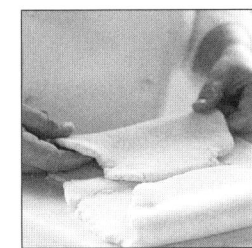 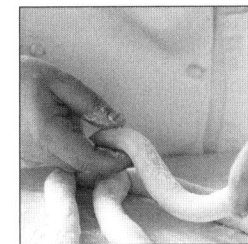

PROBLEM-FREE YEAST BAKING

The best thing about baking with yeast is that the quantities of the ingredients are not as critical as in other baking. You can experiment at will (within reason!) without worrying about the proportions. If you add extra flour or sugar or water, the yeast will just work a little harder but your dough will still rise perfectly. Altitude does not affect it either, except that at high altitude it will rise somewhat quicker.

Two types of yeast are available in South Africa

- *fresh yeast*, available from bakeries and some supermarkets
- *instant granular yeast* in a shiny sachet with the word 'instant' on it.

The two types are interchangeable in all recipes

25 g fresh = 1 sachet (15 ml) instant

The fresh yeast must be a pale grey colour with no black spots. If you mix it with a little sugar, it becomes liquid and can then be added to the other ingredients. If you are mixing by hand, it is easier to dissolve the yeast with the sugar before adding. I simply throw the whole block of yeast into the Kenwood Chef bowl with the other ingredients and knead it with the dough hook. Fresh yeast freezes very well, but take it out of the fridge 1 hour before you use it.

The instant yeast is simply added to the dry ingredients and away you go! It is easy and much quicker to use than the other yeasts, but the shelf life is shorter.

Hint
When using instant yeast in high sugar or fat recipes, mix with a little liquid before adding to the other ingredients. The yeast is incorporated more evenly.

These are the questions that I am most often asked:

Q *What does kneading do and what does 'knocking down' mean?*

A The protein in the flour is called gluten. In its natural state in the wheat it is in 2 parts. When the 2 parts are manipulated in the presence of water they join together and become a rubbery, elastic substance. This is what gives bread its elastic texture. In cake and scone making you do not want that elastic texture but rather a soft, almost crumbly texture. That is why you must never overmix a cake once you have added the flour.

As you knead and the gluten is developed, water is taken up by the gluten. Always start off kneading when the dough is a little too wet, to allow for the water to be taken up by the developing gluten. Knead until the dough has a smooth texture on the surface like a blown up balloon and when you push your finger a little into the dough you can feel that it is springy.

Leave the dough to rise in a warm place, covered with cling wrap or a damp cloth, leaving room under the cover for the dough to rise double in size. Covering it prevents the surface from drying out. The elastic gluten traps the carbon dioxide as it is given off by the yeast and the dough rises.

Once it is double its size, the dough is knocked down and shaped. This does not mean kneading it again – you will then knock out all the air! The air bubbles in the dough after the first rising are not very even, so knocking down is just a way of distributing the air more evenly. Knocking down is shaping and moulding the dough.

Q *Help, my dough is not rising!*

A Mix $1/2$ a block of fresh, or 1 teaspoon of instant yeast with a little sugar and water and add it to the unrisen dough. Add a little warm water and knead it all together again until smooth and wetter than it was. It is quite a messy business, but persevere and you will save your bread.

Q *Why did the dough not rise?*

A The most common reason is that the dough is too dry. While kneading, the flour absorbs water to form the gluten. If the resulting dough is too dry, it will not rise. Your yeast dough must always be a little too wet rather than too dry when kneading. Work on about 100 ml (7 Tbs) liquid for every 250 ml (1 cup) flour.

The rate at which your dough will rise is determined by the yeast content, water content, temperature and ingredients like sugar and fat. I have found the most common problem is the moisture content. Rich, sweet doughs will need a little more yeast and more time to rise.

Q *What is a warm place for the dough to rise in?*

A Many people wrap the bowl in a blanket, on a hot tray or in a warming oven. The trouble with a hot tray and warming oven is the heat from the bottom kills the yeast and you end up with a dense layer. For the dough to rise I turn my *oven*, not warming oven, onto the lowest possible temperature. (Just where the light comes on and well below 100 °C). When the light goes off, feel the oven rack. It should be warm to the touch. Now place your covered bowl in the oven to rise. The thermostat will maintain that warm temperature. A plastic bowl is fine, because the oven is only warm.

WHOLEWHEAT BREAD

The joy of this recipe is its versatility. This bread is made using the batter method, which is the easiest way of making yeast bread. The wet batter is not kneaded, but simply mixed with your hands or a wooden spoon.

You must have 5 x 250 ml (5 cups, approximately 750 g) dry ingredients of your choice:

750 g (5 cups)	wholewheat flour

or

750 ml (3 cups)	wholewheat (450 g)
250 ml (1 cup)	bran (50 g)
250 ml (1 cup)	crushed wheat (180 g) (very moist and heavy)

or

625 ml (2 $1/2$ cups)	wholewheat (375 g)
375 ml (1 $1/2$ cup)	cake flour (225 g)
250 ml (1 cup)	crushed wheat (180 g) (lighter)

and add

250 ml (1 cup)	seeds (sunflower, sesame, linseed, aniseed and/or *poppy seeds*)

or

add nuts, raisins, herbs, grated cheese, chopped celery or *parsley*.

Roast the sunflower and sesame seeds. Use 125 ml ($1/2$ cup) *stampkoring*, which has been soaked overnight in boiling water. Use brown sugar, honey or, if desired, a little molasses or treacle. Bake in a tin, a potjie or an earthenware flowerpot. The variations are endless …

1	packet instant yeast
or 25 g	fresh yeast
15 ml (1 Tbs)	brown sugar
5 x 250 ml (5 cups)	combination flour of your choice (about 750 g)
15 ml (1 Tbs)	salt
30 ml (2 Tbs)	oil
5 ml (1 tsp)	vinegar
625 ml (2 $1/2$ cups)	warm water (approximate)

- Place all the dry ingredients in a mixing bowl.
- Add yeast according to type (see introduction).
- Add enough warm water to make a moist mixture. The mixture should fall off the spoon easily. Rather have the mixture too wet than too dry.
- Mix with a wooden spoon, or your hands to make a batter.
- Pour into a well-greased, 1 kg tin.
- Cover with a damp cloth or cling wrap and leave to rise to double its size in a warm place (about 45 to 60 minutes).
- If you like, sprinkle the top with seeds of your choice, or crushed wheat before baking.
- Bake at 200 °C for 1 hour.
- Remove from the tin immediately to prevent the crust from becoming soggy.

Variation
This recipe can be made in 12 little mini-loaf tins:
- Fill each tin half full and leave, covered, to rise to double its size.
- Bake at 220 °C for about 25 minutes or until brown.
- Remove from tins immediately.

Hint
I only recently discovered how delicious aniseed and raisins are together in this bread. Eat it with mild cheddar cheese – it is quite mouth-watering!

WHITE BREAD

This is a standard recipe for kneaded yeast bread. The texture of a kneaded bread is much finer and more elastic than the wet, coarse texture of a batter bread. This dough can also be used for making bread rolls.

Makes 2 loaves

1 packet	*instant yeast,*
or 25 g	*fresh yeast*
30 ml (2 Tbs)	*sugar*
6 x 250 ml (6 cups, 900 g)	*cake flour*
15 ml (1 Tbs)	*salt*
30 ml (2 Tbs)	*olive oil*
	or *vegetable oil of your choice*
	or *soft butter*
625 ml (2 ½ cups)	*warm water (approximate)*

- Sift all the dry ingredients into a mixing bowl.
- Add yeast according to type (see introduction).
- Add the remaining ingredients to the bowl and enough liquid to form a soft dough. Mix well, adding a little extra flour if the dough is too wet or a little extra liquid if the dough is too dry.
- Turn it out onto a well-floured surface and knead until the dough is smooth and elastic.
- Place the dough in a large bowl, cover it with a damp cloth or cling wrap and leave in a warm place to rise to double its size.
- After it has risen, return the dough to the floured surface knock down, shape it into a loaf and gently place in a greased loaf tin.
- Cover it loosely and leave it in a warm place to rise until double its size.
- The top can be glazed with milk, egg or sprinkled with flour.
- For an attractive effect, make diagonal slash on the top with a sharp blade or snip a row of shallow V cuts with a scissors.
- Bake at 180 °C to 200 °C for about 50 minutes.
- For a crusty top, brush with oil or melted butter as the bread comes out of the oven and return it to the oven for 5 minutes.
- For bread rolls, bake at 180 °C for 10 to 15 minutes.

Variations
- Try adding two large boiled, mashed potatoes to the dough before you start kneading for a very special flavour and a wonderful moist texture.
- For kneaded wholewheat bread, use the white bread recipe, but in place of 900 g (6 cups) of cake flour use 450 g (3 cups) cake flour and 450 g (3 cups) wholewheat flour.
- To shape into rolls, if you have a pasta machine, roll balls out flat, then roll up into rolls. They then end up in a lovely shape.

Hints
- Baking at 200 °C to 220 °C will give you a thicker, harder crust and baking at 180 °C to 200 °C, a softer thinner crust.
- For a delicious flavour and a softer texture, use half water and half yoghurt. Use boiling water, which will warm the cold yoghurt when mixed together.
- Use iced water, make the dough at night and leave in a cool place, not the fridge, overnight to rise. Shape and bake in the morning for fresh bread for breakfast.

DARK RYE BREAD

Most rye breads are made using a mixture of rye and wheat flour. Rye flour contains very little gluten, which causes the dough to be very heavy or to collapse easily during baking. This recipe contains cake flour to overcome this problem. This bread can be made using all rye flour. It is moist and a little heavier.

Although not traditional, I prefer to bake rye bread in a loaf tin. The dough can be a little wetter because the tin will keep it in shape. This results in a lighter, moist bread with a longer shelf life.

Whole grain rye flour is available from health shops and some supermarkets. If you do not want a coarse rye, substitute rye flour for the whole grain rye. Make sure you use gravy browning and not gravy powder. Gravy browning is a liquid colouring made from caramelised sugar.

Makes 1 large loaf

1	packet instant yeast,
or 25 g	fresh yeast
15 ml (1 Tbs)	brown sugar
750 ml (3 cups)	rye flour
250 ml (1 cup)	whole grain rye
250 ml (1 cup)	cake flour
15 ml (1 Tbs)	salt
45 ml (3 Tbs)	caraway seeds (optional)
30 ml (2 Tbs)	vinegar
15 ml (1 Tbs)	oil
30 ml (2 Tbs)	molasses
375 ml (1 $\frac{1}{2}$ cup)	beer or water, warmed (approximate)
2 ml ($\frac{1}{2}$ tsp)	gravy browning, liquid, not powder (optional)

- Sift all the dry ingredients into a mixing bowl.
- Add yeast according to type (see introduction).
- Add the remaining ingredients to the bowl and enough liquid to form a soft dough. Mix well adding a little extra flour if the dough is too wet or a little extra liquid if the dough is too dry.
- Turn it out onto a well floured surface and knead until the dough is smooth and elastic. It will remain sticky.
- Place the dough in a large bowl, cover it with a damp cloth or cling wrap and leave in a warm place to rise to double its size.
- After it has risen, return the dough to the floured surface knock down, shape it into a loaf and gently place in a tin.
- Cover it loosely and leave it in a warm place to rise until double its size.
- Sprinkle with rye flour.
- Bake at 200 °C for 15 minutes, then lower the temperature to 180 °C for 35 minutes.

PITA BREADS AND PIZZAS

The use of olive oil gives the bread a distinctly Mediterranean flavour, but the method for making the dough is exactly the same as for the white bread. There are many different types of pita bread in the Middle East. In South Africa, pocket breads have become popular. To achieve the pocket the breads are baked at an extremely high temperature.

Turkish pita has become my favourite! To get the best results, use a dry, heavy-based frying pan with the lid on. The bread is chewy and has a very distinctive flavour.

Makes 12 pita breads or 6 pizza bases

1	packet instant yeast,
or 25 g	fresh yeast
15 ml (1 Tbs)	sugar
4 x 250 ml (4 cups)	cake flour (600 g)
10 ml (2 tsp)	salt
30 ml (2 Tbs)	olive oil
400-450 ml (1 $\frac{3}{4}$ cup)	warm water (approximate)

- Sift all the dry ingredients into a mixing bowl.
- Add yeast according to type (see introduction).
- Add the remaining ingredients to the bowl and enough liquid to form a soft dough. Mix well, adding a little extra flour if the dough is too wet or a little extra liquid if the dough is too dry.
- Turn it out onto a well-floured surface and knead until the dough is smooth and elastic.
- Place the dough in a large bowl, cover it with a damp cloth or cling wrap and leave in a warm place to rise to double it's size.
- After it has risen, return the dough to the floured surface.
- Roll out to a thickness of about 3 mm and cut into circles about 12 cm in diameter using a pot lid or circular cutter.
- Place circles on baking paper and cover loosely with cling wrap.
- Leave to rise for a further 10 minutes.

To make pocket pita breads
- Preheat oven to maximum (240 °C to 250 °C).
- On lowest rack, or on the bottom of the oven between the elements, place a deep roasting pan full of hot water.
- Place the pita breads on the paper on a cooling rack.
- Place the cooling rack in the oven and bake for 3 to 5 minutes.
- The pita are cooked when they have puffed up. They should be removed from the oven before they turn brown.
- Place in a small table cloth to keep them soft while they are cooling down.
- These pita freeze well and can be heated in the toaster or in a hot oven.

Variation
For wholewheat pita, use half cake flour and half wholewheat flour.

To make Turkish pita breads
- Using a very sharp knife, cut diagonal slashes across the surface of the pitas.
- Using a heavy-based pan with a lid, heat on high.
- Place pita in the dry pan, turn heat to medium and cook, covered, for about 5 minutes or until lightly browned.
- Turn and cook until second side is browned.

ITALIAN PIZZAS

To get the best results from a domestic oven, bake the base on its own, without any topping, for 5 minutes. This will ensure a crispy base. Fried onion and tomato makes the pizza very rich. I prefer the traditional use of plain tomatoes.

The basic pizza dough will make enough pizza for 6 to 8 people, if you roll the dough out fairly thin.

- Make pita dough according to the recipe.
- After it has risen, roll out the dough to a thickness of about 3 mm and cut it into 6 large circles.
- Prick the circles all over with a fork and bake the bases at 240 °C for 5 minutes.
- Proceed with the topping.

Topping
Used on all pizzas

	olive oil
2 x 410 g	tins tomatoes
1 x 65 g	tin tomato paste
	salt, black pepper
	origanum
250 g	grated mozzarella cheese

On to the basic topping, any combination of your choice may be added such as: garlic, onions, olives, capers, anchovies, salami, ham or bacon, asparagus, mushrooms, artichoke hearts, tuna …

To make up
- Brush the partially baked base with olive oil.
- Drain liquid off tomatoes, chop finely and mix in tomato paste and seasoning.
- Spread over dough leaving a border of dough of about 2,5 cm all the way around.
- Salt, pepper and sprinkle with origanum.
- Sprinkle on grated cheese.
- Extras of your choice are then placed on top of the cheese.
- Sprinkle with origanum and olive oil.
- Bake on hot tray at 240 °C for about 15 minutes.

Hints
- For very crispy pizzas, omit the oil and make the dough as wet as possible, but still manageable.
- Buy a large, unglazed floor tile and place it in the oven to preheat. Using a flat baking sheet, slide the pizza onto the hot tile.

PIZZA RUSTICA

This is a most delicious closed pizza filled with ricotta cheese and all sorts of pizza goodies. Serve it in place of a quiche next time and see the reaction!

Serves 6 to 8

- Use half a quantity of the pita dough recipe.
- After the dough has risen to double its size, divide the dough in 2 and roll each piece into a large circle about 30 cm in diameter, or the size of your pizza pan.
- Place one circle on the pan and pile on the filling leaving a 3 cm border all the way round.
- Place the second circle of dough on top of the filling

and seal by rolling the 2 layers together towards the centre of the circle.
- Cut deep slashes to allow steam to escape.
- Brush with milk and sprinkle with sesame seeds.
- Bake at 220 °C for about 20 minutes.
- Switch off and leave to cool in the oven.

Filling

3	eggs
500 g	ricotta
10 ml (2 tsp)	cornflour
90 g	ham, chopped and
90 g	salami, chopped
	or *1 x tin tuna and 1 tin anchovies*
200 g	mozzarella, cut into blocks
50 g	rigatello, piccorino, grated,
	or *any strong cheese, grated*
20	black olives, stoned, halved and dried (approximate)
20 ml (4 tsp)	whole capers
5 ml (1 tsp)	dried origanum
	salt and black pepper
	sesame seeds

- Mix ricotta cheese, eggs and cornflour.
- Fold in other ingredients.

AMERICAN DEEP CORN PIZZAS

This is a slightly coarse-textured deep pizza with lots of vegetables as a filling. It is more like an open pie than an Italian pizza.

Makes about 12 small pizzas

Crust

500 ml (2 cups)	cake flour
250 ml (1 cup)	mealie meal
15 ml (1 Tbs)	olive oil
10 ml (2 tsp)	salt
15 ml (1 Tbs)	sugar
1	packet instant yeast
or 25 g	fresh yeast
250 ml (1 cup)	warm water (approximate)

- Place all the dry ingredients and the yeast in a bowl and add enough warm water to form a soft dough.
- Knead until the dough is soft and elastic.
- Leave in a warm place to rise to double its size.
- Roll out and either line two shallow cake tins (20 cm), or 12 deep muffin tins or pie tins.
- Spoon in filling, sprinkle on extra cheese and place olives on top.
- Bake at 220 °C for about 15 minutes or until well-browned.

Hint
Yellow mealie meal gives the crust a golden colour.

Filling

2	aubergines, diced
250 g	mushrooms, diced
2	onions, diced
45 ml (3 Tbs)	olive oil
410 g	tinned tomatoes, chopped
60 ml ($^{1}/_{4}$ cup)	tomato purée
2	cloves garlic, crushed
15 ml (1 Tbs)	fresh sweet basil, chopped
or 5 ml (1 tsp)	dried origanum
	salt and black pepper to taste
250 g	*Tussers* or *mozzarella cheese* (approximate)
1	packet black olives, stones removed

- Sauté the onions, mushrooms and brinjals in the olive oil.
- Add the remaining filling ingredients (except the cheese and olives) and simmer until soft.
- Allow to cool.
- Grate 50 g of the cheese and the rest cut into small blocks.
- Mix the blocks of cheese into the cold filling and spoon into dough.
- Use grated cheese to sprinkle on the top and then the olives.

MUSTARD BREAD

I tasted the most delicious mustard seed bread at the Labia Museum Coffee Shop in St James, Cape Town. Subsequently, I had several requests for a recipe for this bread. This is my version. White mustard seed are usually easy to find. Black mustard seeds are available at spice shops.

Makes 1 large loaf

80 ml ($^{1}/_{3}$ cup)	white mustard seeds
80 ml ($^{1}/_{3}$ cup)	black mustard seeds
375 ml (1 $^{1}/_{2}$ cups)	boiling water
375 ml (1 $^{1}/_{2}$ cups)	chopped onion (about 2 small)
45 g	butter
1	packet instant yeast
or 25 g	fresh yeast

30 ml (2 Tbs) sugar
4 x 250 ml (4 cups) flour (600 g)
125 ml (1/2 cup) buttermilk or milk
150 g (1 1/2 cup) mature cheddar cheese, grated

- Pour the boiling water over the mustard seeds and leave to stand overnight, or boil for one minute and then leave to cool. Rinse well in a strainer.
- Sauté onions in butter and cool.
- Sift all the dry ingredients into a mixing bowl.
- Add yeast according to type (see introduction).
- Add all the ingredients except the cheese to the bowl and enough liquid to form a soft dough. Mix well, adding a little extra flour if the dough is too wet, or a little extra liquid if the dough is too dry.
- Turn it out onto a well-floured surface and knead until the dough is smooth and elastic.
- Place the dough in a large bowl, cover it with a damp cloth or cling wrap and leave in a warm place to rise to double its size.
- After it has risen, return the dough to the floured surface.
- Knock down and lightly knead the cheese into dough.
- Shape into 1 large or 2 smaller loaves and place in loaf tins.
- Cover and leave to rise until double its size.
- Bake at 200 °C for about 40 minutes or until brown.
- Remove from tin and cool on a cooling rack.

SEED BREAD

Yeast baking allows you to be creative. With a basic dough and a little imagination, original recipes can easily be developed. From the wholewheat bread came the roast seed bread. Then from the mustard bread and the roast seed bread, here is a white seed bread.

Makes 1 loaf

125 ml (1/2 cup) crushed wheat
45 ml (3 Tbs) sesame seeds
60 ml (1/4 cup) sunflower seeds
30 ml (2 Tbs) linseed
30 ml (2 Tbs) poppy seeds
375 ml (1 1/2 cup) boiling water
1 packet instant yeast,
or 25 g fresh yeast
30 ml (2 Tbs) sugar
4 x 250 ml (4 cups) cake flour
10 ml (2 tsp) salt
45 g soft butter
125 ml (1/2 cup) buttermilk or milk

- Toast the sesame seeds in a dry frying pan over medium heat. Shake the pan to prevent burning.
- Sift all the dry ingredients into a mixing bowl.
- Add yeast according to type (see introduction).
- Add all the ingredients to the bowl and enough liquid to form a soft dough. Mix well, adding a little extra flour if the dough is too wet, or a little extra liquid if the dough is too dry.
- Turn it out onto a well-floured surface and knead until the dough is smooth and elastic.
- Place the dough in a large bowl, cover it with a damp cloth or cling wrap and leave in a warm place to rise to double its size.
- After it has risen, return the dough to the floured surface.
- Knock down and shape into 1 large, or 2 smaller loaves and place in loaf tins.
- Cover and leave to rise until double its size.
- Bake at 200 °C for about 40 minutes or until brown.
- Cool on a cooling rack.

OLIVE BREAD

Try this recipe for an interesting, tasty variation on the bread theme.

Makes 1 loaf

- Make half the basic white bread dough, omitting the oil and using the full yeast quantity.
- Place the dough in a large bowl, cover it with a damp cloth or cling wrap and leave in a warm place to rise to double its size.
- Make the filling (recipe follows) and leave to cool.
- After the dough has risen, return it to the floured surface. Knead in the cooled filling, adding an extra 125 ml flour.
- While you are kneading the olive mixture into the dough, it becomes very oily and messy. Just add a little extra flour if necessary and keep going; it does knead in and it is definitely worth the effort!
- Shape into a large ball and place on a greased baking sheet.
- Sprinkle liberally with flour, cover loosely with cling wrap or a dish cloth and leave to rise to double its size.
- Using a sharp knife, make diagonal slashes across the bread.
- Bake at 200 °C for 40 to 50 minutes.

Filling

250 ml (1 cup)	chopped onions
45 ml (3 Tbs)	olive oil
5 ml (1 tsp)	salt
165 ml (2/3 cup)	black olives, pitted and quartered
30 ml (2 Tbs)	origanum
125 ml (1/2 cup)	flour (approximate)

- Sauté onions in olive oil until glassy.
- Mix in salt, olives and origanum and leave to cool.

KITKE

Soft milk bread

This is the traditional Jewish bread eaten on the Sabbath, at weddings and over high holidays. The high egg and fat content gives it a soft cake-like texture. In a Jewish home, where it may be eaten with meat dishes, milk and butter are omitted and oil or margarine and water used.

This recipe makes 2 plaited (or round) loaves; 12 small plaited loaves; 2 x 750 g loaf tins; 12-18 soft hamburger rolls

1 packet	instant yeast
or 25 g	fresh yeast
45 ml (3 Tbs)	sugar
5 x 250 ml (5 cups)	cake flour (750 g)
15 ml (1 Tbs)	salt
3	eggs, lightly beaten
60 g (1/4 cup)	soft butter, margarine or oil
310 ml (1 1/4 cup)	warm water or milk (approximate)

- Sift all the dry ingredients into a mixing bowl.
- Add yeast according to type (see introduction).
- Turn it out onto a well-floured surface and knead until the dough is smooth and elastic.
- Place the dough in a large bowl, cover it with a damp cloth or cling wrap and leave in a warm place to rise to double its size.
- After the dough has risen, return it to the floured surface. Make one large loaf or divide into 2 halves.
- Divide each half into 4 or 5 and roll each piece into a long sausage.
- Plait as per the diagram.
- Cover and again leave to rise to double its size.
- Brush with beaten egg and sprinkle with poppy or sesame seeds.
- Bake at 180 °C for about 30 minutes or until golden.

Hint

If you have a pasta machine to shape, roll each piece out flat and then roll into a sausage. This will ensure a very definite plait after baking.

Polish four-strand plait

The plaiting sequence is as follows:

Refer to page 200 for step by step photographs

- Start from the top where the strands are fastened together.
- The numbering of the strands is 1 to 4 from left to right and renumber from left to right after each move.
- 2 over 3
- 4 over 2
- 1 over 3

Repeat this sequence until the plait is finished.

Five-strand plait

The plaiting sequence is as follows:

- Start from the top where the strands are fastened together.
- The numbering of the strands is 1 to 5 from left to right and renumber from left to right after each move.
- 2 over 3
- 5 over 2
- 1 over 3

Repeat this sequence until the plait is finished.

BEIGELS

There is nothing quite like the dense, chewy, faintly sweet taste of beigels. The secret of making a good beigel is not to let them rise very much before you drop them in the boiling water.

Makes about 18

1 packet	instant yeast,
or 25 g	fresh yeast
15 ml (1 Tbs)	sugar
4 x 250 ml (4 cups)	cake flour (600 g)
15 ml (1 Tbs)	oil
2	eggs
15 ml (1 Tbs)	salt
310 ml (1 1/4 cup)	warm water (approximate)

- Sift all the dry ingredients into a mixing bowl.
- Add yeast according to type (see introduction).
- Add all the ingredients to the bowl and enough liquid to form a soft dough. Mix well, adding a little extra flour if the dough is too wet or a little extra liquid if the dough is too dry.
- Turn it out onto a well-floured surface and knead until the dough is smooth and elastic.
- Place the dough in a large bowl, cover it with a damp cloth or cling wrap and leave in a warm place to rise to double its size.
- After the dough has risen, return it to the floured surface.
- Shape into sausages, joining the ends with a little beaten egg. An alternative method of shaping is to use cookie cutters for the outer and inner circles.
- Leave to stand for no longer than 10 minutes. If they rise too much before you put them into the water, they will collapse as you take them out of the water.
- While the dough is rising, bring a pot of water to the boil. Add 15 ml salt and 15 ml sugar.
- Drop the beigels into the boiling water for about 1 minute until they rise to the top.
- Remove from the water and place on a greased baking sheet.
- Brush with beaten egg and bake either plain or sprinkled with sesame, poppy or caraway seeds, or with coarse salt.
- Bake at 220 °C until golden brown (about 15 minutes).

SOUR DOUGH BREAD

A lot of interest in sour dough bread was aroused following one of my radio programmes with Leslie McKenzie. In the cities where a large variety of bread is easily available, sour dough bread-baking has become a dying skill, but it is still alive and doing well in the rural areas. The unique flavour of this bread is well worth the effort.

Makes 1 large or 2 small loaves

Sour dough

1	large potato
500 ml (2 cups)	cake flour
15 ml (1 Tbs)	salt
15 ml (1 Tbs)	sugar
325 ml (1 $\frac{1}{3}$ cups)	warm water
5 ml	instant yeast
or 10 g	fresh yeast

- Boil the potato in its jacket. Peel and mash.
- Place potato, with all above ingredients, in a bowl and beat well.
- Cover bowl with cling wrap and place in a larger bowl of hot water.
- Cover both bowls in a thick towel or blanket to keep it warm. Change the water twice a day to keep the dough warm.
- Repeat this for 3 to 4 days until dough has a strong sour smell.
- Continue making the bread as follows:

Bread

1	quantity sour dough
4 x 250 ml (4 cups)	cake flour (600 g)
1	packet instant yeast,
or 25 g	fresh yeast
45 g (3 Tbs)	soft butter or oil

- Place all ingredients in a bowl and mix to form into a soft dough, adding a little warm water or milk if needed.
- Knead well until smooth and elastic.
- Leave covered in a warm place to rise to double its size.
- Divide into two and shape into loaves. Place in loaf tins and again cover and leave to rise to double its size.
- Bake at 200 °C for about 50 minutes or until golden.

Hint
You can keep back 1/4 of the dough before shaping the loaves, to make your next sour dough starter. Keep the dough in a sealed container in the fridge. Twenty-four hours before making your next loaf, add 250 ml (1 cup) flour, 15 ml (1 Tbs) sugar, 15 ml (1 Tbs) salt and enough liquid to make a wet mixture. Leave in a warm place to ferment for 24 to 36 hours. This will give you one quantity of sour dough for your next loaf.

Variation
For sour rye bread, make the starter using rye flour in place of cake flour and beer in place of the water. Use this with the rye bread recipe in this chapter, but omit the liquid.

SWEET AND UNUSUAL RECIPES

LAVASH

Middle-Eastern cracker bread

These are crispy and delicious. They keep very well in an airtight container for several weeks. This recipe was developed in answer to requests for a 'Provita-type' recipe. Well, it is nothing like that, but it is a delicious flat cracker bread.

```
625 ml (2 1/2 cups)   cake flour
      10 ml (2 tsp)   instant yeast
         or 15 g      fresh yeast
       15 ml (1 Tbs)  sugar
        8 ml (1 1/2 tsp) salt
                      pinch of cayenne pepper
       60 ml (4 Tbs)  sesame seeds
       250 ml (1 cup) warm water
```

- Lightly toast sesame seeds in a dry frying pan over a medium heat. Stir them to prevent burning.
- Place all dry ingredients in a bowl.
- Add enough water to form a firm dough.
- Knead the dough until it is smooth and elastic.
- Chill for 2 hours before using.
- Using a rolling pin or pasta machine, roll out the dough into very thin (about 8 cm wide) strips.
- Prick all over with a fork and cut into pieces the size of cream crackers.
- Place on floured baking sheets and bake at 200 °C for about 12 minutes or until golden.
- Store in an airtight container.

Variation

For wholewheat crackers, follow the same recipe as for Lavash, but in place of 625 ml (2 1/2 cups) of cake flour, use:

```
250 ml (1 cup)    cake flour
250 ml (1 cup)    wholewheat flour
125 ml (1/2 cup)  3 wheat
```

BASIC BUN DOUGH

This is a moist, delicious basic foundation dough that can be used for any kind of bun or doughnut.

Makes about 18

```
4 x 250 ml (4 cups)   cake flour (600 g)
  125 ml (1/2 cup)    sugar
     5 ml (1 tsp)     salt
                  2   packets instant yeast
       or 2 x 25 g    blocks fresh yeast
           90 g       soft butter
              2       eggs beaten
  200 ml (1 teacup)   buttermilk (approximate)
```

- Place all the dry ingredients in a mixing bowl.
- Add yeast according to type (see introduction).
- Add soft butter and beaten eggs.
- Add enough buttermilk to form a soft dough. Mix well, adding a little extra flour if the dough is too wet or a little extra liquid if the dough is too dry.
- Turn it out onto a well-floured surface and knead until the dough is smooth and elastic.
- Cover and leave in a warm place to rise to double its size or in a cool place (not the fridge) to rise overnight.
- Roll out and shape as desired.
- Place on baking paper or grease proof paper on a baking sheet, cover very loosely with cling wrap or a dishcloth and leave to rise to double its size (about 30 minutes).
- Bake at 180 °C for about 20 minutes.

Hint

This dough takes longer to rise because the ingredients are cool and there is a high proportion of sugar and fat.

CINNAMON BUNS

Boolkes

Boolkes are buns with a cinnamon and raisin filling and a streusel topping. There are many different ways of shaping them, but this shape holds the most cinnamon butter!

```
1   quantity basic bun dough
```

Cinnamon butter

125 g		butter
200 ml (1 teacup)		castor sugar
53 ml (3 1/2 Tbs)		flour
53 ml (3 1/2 Tbs)		cinnamon
125 ml (1/2 cup)		raisins

- Cream butter and sugar.
- Beat in cinnamon and flour.

Variation

For a slightly custardy taste, use 30 ml (2 Tbs) of custard powder in place of the flour.

Streusel topping

45 ml (3 Tbs)		cake flour
2 ml (1/2 tsp)		baking powder
45 g		butter
45 ml (3 Tbs)		sugar
10 ml (2 tsp)		cinnamon

- Rub butter into dry ingredients to form a crumble.
- Chill until needed.
- Roll out risen dough into a rectangle of about 50 cm x 35 cm.
- Spread the cinnamon butter evenly over half the dough along the length.
- Sprinkle with raisins and fold dough in half (the plain dough over the cinnamon butter).
- Cut the rectangle into 16 to 18 slices.
- *To shape the boolkes,* twist the slice gently into a loose rope.
- Tie the rope into a loose knot and place on baking paper, cover loosely with cling wrap and leave to rise to double its size in a warm place.
- Beat an egg with a pinch of salt and very carefully brush the buns. Sprinkle on streusel topping and bake at 180 °C for 20 to 25 minutes.

CINNAMON LOAF

Babke

Makes 2 to 3 loaves

- Make one quantity of the basic bun dough.
- Make the cinnamon butter and the streusel topping from the cinnamon bun recipe.
- Roll the dough into 2 or 3 rectangles, depending on how large you want the loaves to be. Spread the cinnamon butter over the entire rectangle and roll up like a Swiss roll. Place in a greased loaf tin to rise to double its size. Brush with egg and sprinkle with streusel topping. Bake at 180 °C for 20 to 30 minutes, depending on the size of the loaf.

COPENHAGENS

These are made and shaped in the same way as the cinnamon buns. The differences are:

- Use the custard powder in the cinnamon butter.
- Use mixed cake fruit in place of the raisins.
- Do not use the streusel topping and do not brush with egg. As they come out of the oven, brush with jam glaze (recipe follows) and once they are almost cool, mix 185 ml (3/4 cup) icing sugar with a little boiling water to make runny glacé icing. Drizzle this over the glazed copenhagens.

Glaze

45 ml (3 Tbs)		smooth apricot jam
45 ml (3 Tbs)		sugar
45 ml (3 Tbs)		water

- Place the ingredients in a pot and, over high heat, stir until dissolved.
- Boil for 1 minute until syrupy.

RAISIN BREAD

Makes 2 loaves

- Make one basic bun dough recipe and leave covered to rise to double its size.
- Lightly knead 250 g raisins into the risen dough.
- Shape into two loaves and place in two loaf tins.
- Leave covered in a warm place to rise to double in size.
- Bake at 180 °C for 35 to 40 minutes.
- Glaze with copenhagen jam glaze.

CHELSEA BUNS

        1 quantity basic bun dough
250 ml (1 cup) mixed cake fruit
25 ml (5 tsp) cinnamon sugar
       50 g butter

- Roll out one quantity risen basic bun dough into a rectangle of about 50 cm x 20 cm.
- Spread with butter, and sprinkle on fruit and cinnamon.
- Roll up as for a Swiss roll. Cut into 16 to 18 slices and place on baking sheet and leave to rise as described for the copenhagens.
- Bake at 180 °C for about 20 minutes.
- Remove from oven and immediately brush with copenhagen jam glaze.
- Once they are almost cool drizzle with glace icing. (see *Copenhagens*)

HOT CROSS BUNS

Using basic bun dough recipe, add the following to the dry ingredients:

10 ml (2 tsp) cinnamon
10 ml (2 tsp) mixed spice
3 ml ($^1/_2$ tsp) cloves
375 ml (1 $^1/_2$ cup) mixed cake fruit

- Use about 250 ml (1 cup) buttermilk instead of 200 ml; the dough must be very soft.
- When the dough has risen to double its size, divide it into 18 pieces and shape them into round buns. Place on a greased baking sheet. Cover and leave to rise in a warm place until double their size.
- Very carefully brush with beaten egg and put on the pastry crosses.
- Bake at 180 °C for 20 to 25 minutes and glaze as they come out of the oven with the copenhagen jam glaze.

Hints

- The dough will take longer to rise because of the spices in the recipe.
- The dough should be much wetter than normal because the dried fruit will absorb moisture while it is rising.

Pastry for the crosses

40 g butter
125 ml ($^1/_2$ cup) flour
       iced water

- Rub butter into flour.
- Add water to form pastry.
- Roll out thin and cut into strips to form crosses.

CHOC-PECAN WHEELS

Make one basic bun dough recipe and leave it to rise.

Filling

160 g soft butter
250 ml (1 cup) sieved icing sugar
125 ml ($^1/_2$ cup) sieved cocoa
200 g pecan nuts, chopped

- Cream butter, sugar and cocoa together until light and creamy.
- Roll out the risen basic dough recipe into a rectangle of about 50 cm x 20 cm.
- Spread the creamed mixture over rectangle.
- Sprinkle on the nuts.
- Roll up as for a Swiss roll and slice into 2,5 cm slices.
- Place slices in a 23 cm cake tin, cover with cling wrap and leave to rise to double in size in a warm place.
- Bake at 180 °C for about 35 to 40 minutes, or until well browned.
- Turn out as a cake, keeping buns attached to each other.
- Brush with copenhagen jam glaze and ice with glacé icing.

DOUGHNUTS

Makes about 24

- Make one basic bun dough recipe and leave it to rise covered in a warm place to double its size.
- Roll out the dough until it is about 2 to 3 cm thick.
- Cut into circles with a cookie cutter. For American doughnuts, cut out the centre with a small cookie cutter or a sherry glass.
- Cover loosely with cling wrap and leave to rise to double their size (about 20 minutes).

- Fry in fairly hot, deep oil (150 °C) until golden (about 10 minutes). If the oil is too hot, the doughnuts will brown on the outside too quickly, preventing the inside from rising and making them doughy and heavy.
- Drain on absorbent paper and coat with sugar or pour on glacé icing once they are cool.
- For filled doughnuts, use an icing bag and plain nozzle to force the jam or whipped cream into the centre.

KOEKSISTERS

Make the syrup at least a day in advance. Chill.

Syrup

750 ml (3 cups)	water
1,5 litres (6 cups)	sugar
30 ml (2 Tbs)	lemon juice
45 ml (3 Tbs)	syrup
15 ml (1 Tbs)	glycerine (optional)
rind of 1	lemon, in strips
1	piece of crushed ginger
4	pieces cinnamon or cassia

- Dissolve sugar in water.
- Add remaining ingredients and boil for 5 minutes.
- Chill overnight.
- Make one basic bun dough recipe and leave it to rise to double its size.
- Roll out the dough on a floured surface until it is 1 cm thick.
- Cut into small rectangles (about 3 cm x 6 cm). Cut each rectangle into 3 strips and *very loosely* plait the strips joining the ends with a little beaten egg.
- Cover loosely with cling wrap and leave to rise for 30 minutes.
- Fry in deep oil over medium heat (150 °C) until golden.
- Immerse in the ice cold syrup as you remove it from the oil.
- Drain on cooling racks.

Hint
The glycerine will keep the koeksisters shiny longer.

OLIEBOLLEN

The Dutch version of koeksisters or doughnuts is full of apple and raisins and not as sweet. Quite delicious!

625 ml (2 1/2 cup)	flour
1	packet instant yeast
or 25 g	fresh yeast
15 ml (1 Tbs)	salt
25 ml (5 tsp)	sugar
1	egg
250 ml (1 cup)	lukewarm milk
185 ml (3/4 cup)	currants
185 ml (3/4 cup)	sultanas
2	tart cooking apples, peeled and grated
	oil for deep frying
	icing sugar

- Measure the flour, salt, sugar and yeast into a mixing bowl.
- Beat the egg and milk and add it to the dry ingredients to form a thick batter.
- Mix well with a wooden spoon or with a beater until it is stringy and elastic.
- Add currants, grated apple and sultanas. Mix well.
- Leave the batter covered in a warm place to rise to double its size.
- Heat a pot of deep oil.
- Using 2 spoons, shape a spoonful of batter into a ball and drop it into the hot oil (oil must not be too hot!). Dip the spoons in the oil to prevent the dough from sticking to them.
- Fry for about 8 minutes or until golden.
- Drain on absorbent paper and dredge with icing sugar while they are still hot.

INDEX

A

Abalone (perlemoen) 47
Almond cream 166
Almond stir-fried chicken 111
American corn pancakes 191
American deep corn pizzas 238
Amsterdammetjies
   (*see* Bocconotti) 212
Apples
   Baked 162
   Crumble 155
   in avocado salad 28
   in pea soup 33
   in yoghurt cream 169
   jelly 179
   mint jelly 178
   muffin 156
   strudel in phyllo 230
   tart, Normandy 225
   with Cheddar filling for
      omelettes 118
Apricot, raisin bread & butter
   pudding 158
Apricot brandy sauce for Christmas
   pudding 161
Apricot dacquoise 171
Aromatic Basmati rice 142
Arrabiata 128
Asparagus quiche filling 228
Aubergines
   in tomato 135
   in yoghurt 31
   in tomato sauce for pasta 124
   Imam Bayildi 136
   pate 7
   Pickled 181
   rolls with basil cheese 13
Avocado
   and bacon filling for omelettes 118
   and apple salad 28
   and pawpaw salad 28
   Sauce 146

B

Babke (*see* cinnamon loaf) 243
Baby beans with red pepper 132
Baby marrow and Ricotta stuffing for
   chicken breasts 110
Bacon
   and avocado filling for
      omelettes 118
   and cabbage salad with caraway 27
   and chicken liver sauce for
      pasta 124
   and mushroom sauce for chicken
      casseroles 112
   scones 192
Baked
   apples 162
   bean salad 30
   carrot pudding with citrus
      sauce 159
   fish au gratin 51
   line fish en papilotte 51
   pears 161
   potatoes 138
Baking
   altitude changes for 187
   baking blind 220
   general problems in 188
   measuring problems in 187
Banana chocolate mousse 173
Banana orange sauce for ice
   cream 175
Bar one sauce for ice cream 175
Brabant potatoes 140
Basic fried rice 142
Basmati rice 142
Basting sauces for chicken
   Lemon, honey & mustard basting
      sauce 87
   Peri peri sauce for chicken 87
   Simple lemon & rosemary basting
      sauce 87
   Spicy soy sauce 87
Batters, various 45
Bean soup augier 38
Beans, with samp 115
Bearnaise sauce 145

Béchamel sauce
   for fish lasagne 127
   for lasagne 81
   for tuna cannelloni 128
Beef
   basic mince sauce 81
   basic pot roast 72
   Bitkis (meat patties in tomato) 83
   Bobotie 82
   Brisket flaumen tzimmes 74
   Brown stew 75
   Carbonade of 76
   Fillet in phyllo pastry 231
   Hamburgers 71
   Hungarian goulash 76
   Lasagne 81
   mince sauce for lasagne 81
   Moussaka 82
   Oxtail stew 80
   Perogen (small pies) 229
   Pirozhki (small pies) 230
   Rare roast fillet 64
   Rendang (curry) 76
   Rosemary roast beef 64
   Sizzling steak 69
   Spicy chilli mince 83
   Steak and kidney 79
   Steak in red wine 78
   Steak with pepper sauce 68
   Stroganoff 69
   Stuffed cabbage leaves 84
   Stuffed smothered 72
Beer coleslaw 28
Beetroot salad 27
Beetroot, sweet and sour soup
   (*see* Borscht) 37
Beigels 240
Bigarade sauce
   for chicken casseroles 112
Biscuits
   Biscotti di regina 216
   Bran molasses rusks 218
   Brandy snaps 217
   Brutti ma buoni 216
   Butterballs 216
   Buttermilk rusks 219
   Cheddar snaps 212
   Choc-chip biscuits 212

Christmas mince squares 215
Cigarettes russe 218
Coconut macaroons 214
Crunchies 213
Czechoslovakian biscuits 213
Dee's one-is-enough biscuit 213
Florentines 216
Ginger spice biscuits 214
Honey teiglach 220
Italian coffee biscuits 216
Jam squares 215
Kichel 219
Miki's Italian almond rusks 217
Mrs Joubert's versatile bikkies 214
Muesli walnut squares 214
Pallottole al butto 216
Queen's biscuits 216
Shortbread 215
Unbeatable brownies 218

Bitkis 83
Black roux 41
Black cherries flambé 176
Blintzes, cheese and other 16
Blue cheese potatoes 140
Blue cheese salad dressing 19
Blue cheese steak sauce 149
Bobotie 82
Bocconotti 212
Boolkes (see cinnamon buns) 242
Borscht 37
Boston baked beans 113
Bouillabaisse 40
Bourekas 222
Bran molasses rusks 218
Brandy butter for Christmas
    pudding 161
Brandy snaps 217
Brandy pudding 158
Bread and butter pudding 158
Brie and courgette soup 33
Brinjals (see aubergines)
Brisket flaumen tzimmes 74
Broccoli, curried cream of 33
Broccoli Roman style 133
Brown rice and lentil salad 26
Brownies 208
Brutti ma buoni 216
Butter icing 201
Butterballs 216
Butterbean salad 30
Buttermilk and mayonnaise salad
    dressing 20
Buttermilk rusks 219

Butternut
    Baked 136
    Fritters 137
    in sour cream 135
    salad 30
    soup 33

C

Cabbage
    and tomato casserole 133
    stuffed 84
    red with East Indian peas 133
    salad with caraway and bacon 27
Cacik 10
Cakes
    cherry cake 203
    Chiffon cakes with variations 206
    chocolate cake 201, 206
    coffee cake 201
    cup cakes 202
    four-egg butter cake 201
    granadilla cake 201
    Lamington squares 202
    lemon cake 201
    marble cake 201
    orange cake 201
    poppy seed cake 203
    three-egg butter cake 202
Caesar salad 21
Calamari in tomato sauce 54
Calamari, pickled 57
Caramel popcorn 183
Carbonade of beef 76
Carrot and orange soup 34
Carrot cake 207
Carrot pudding with citrus sauce 159
Carrots, green beans and salami 132
Cauliflower and mushroom soup 34
Cauliflower and walnut salad 28
Celery soup 34
Cheddar snaps 212
Cheese cakes 209
    light cheese cake 209
    poppy seed cheese cake 210
    'serious' cheese cake 209
Cheese
    and sausage salad 23
    baby marrow and Ricotta stuffing
        for chicken breasts 110
    blintzes 16
    blue cheese salad dressing 19

blue cheese steak sauce 149
cheddar and apple filling for
    omelettes 118
cheddar snaps 212
creamy blue cheese sauce 150
floating cheese islands 18
fruit Ricotta pots 169
Gruyere corn fritters 137
herb marinated Mozzarella 25
onion and tomato filling for
    omelettes 118
pastry base for quiche 227
sauce for vegetarian casserole 114
sauce for baked fish au gratin 51
sauce, basic and spicy 148
sauce, low-fat 153
scones 192
soufflé, basic 17
Chelsea buns 244
Cherry cake 203
Chicken
    a' la King 107
    and mushroom pie 223
    and seafood jambalaya 121
    and smoked sausage gumbo 41
    Bonne femme 103
    Casserole with herbs 103
    Casserole with parsley
        dumplings 106
    Coq au vin 102
    curried salad 23
    Dhansak – with vegetables and
        lentils 106
    Hong Kong chicken wings 101
    Lemon and garlic 104
    liver pate 9
    liver pilaff 120
    Marengo 105
    Mexican 107
    Paprika 104
    Polynesian 102
    Pot roast in ginger ale 97
    Rabies chicken curry 105
    Soup 35
    Spicy southern fried 101
    Stock 41
    Stuffed in orange caramel sauce 97
    Turkish stuffed 88
Chicken Breasts
    casseroles and sauces 111
    Chop suey 110
    Chow mein 110
    cooking methods 108
    in phyllo pastry 231

marinades for 108
preparation of 108
Stir fried with almonds 111
stuffed under the skin 109
stuffing for 109
Chiffon cakes with variations 206
Chinese barbecued spare ribs 67
Choc-chip biscuits 212
Choc-chip muffins 190
Choc-pecan wheels 244
Chocolate
   banana mousse for meringue 173
   butter cream 211
   cake 201, 206
   caramel sauce for ice cream 175
   chiffon cake 206
   choc-chip biscuits 212
   choc-chip muffins 190
   choc-pecan wheels 244
   Four-egg butter cake 201
   fudge 208
   fudge brownies 208
   gateau 210
   light chocolate mousse 165
   Madeira 204
   malt, double-thick 176
   malted soufflé 166
   pareve mousse 165
   rich chocolate mousse 164
   soufflé 163
Chopped liver 9
Chopped herring 58
Choux pastry 232
Christmas mince pies 215
Christmas mince squares 215
Christmas mince wheel 222
Christmas pudding for four 160
Chutney and pickles 181
Chutney, pear 182
Cigarettes russe 218
Cinnamon buns 242
Cinnamon loaf 243
Coconut macaroons 214
Coconut Madeira 204
Coconut tarts 227
Coffee chiffon cake 207
Coffee cake 201
Cointreau soufflé 163
Cold ratatouille salad 29
Coleslaw with beer 28
Cooked yoghurt 147
Copenhagens 243
Coq au vin 102

Courgettes
   and Brie soup 33
   and feta filling for crepes 15
   omelette 118
   roulade with cream cheese and smoked salmon 17
Court bouillon (stock) 40
Couscous salad 25
Cracked wheat salad 27
Cream and white wine sauce 148
Cream of tomato soup 34
Cream of vegetable soup 33
Creamy blue cheese sauce 150
Crème brulee 162
Crème caramel 162
Creole sauce 152
Crepes
   basic crepe batter 14
   cheese blintzes 16
   courgette and feta filling for 15
   peppered mackerel filling for 16
   Russian 164
   seafood filling with Hollandaise sauce for 15
   suzettes 163
   wholewheat sesame crepes 15
Crispy potatoe skins 141
Croutons 21
Crumbed vegetables 14
Crumpets 191
   American corn pancakes 191
   Waffles 191
   yeast crumpets 191
Crunchies 213
Cucumbers, pickled 181
Cup cakes 202
Curried
   chicken salad 23
   cream of broccoli 33
   cream of peas 33
   potato salad 24
   rice salad 24
Curry dressing 20
Custard puffs 232
Custard slice 221
Czechoslovakian biscuits 213

D

Dafna's hot jumped mushroom salad 22
Danish herring 59

Date and bran muffins 190
Dauphinois potatoes 140
Dee's one-is-enough biscuit 213
Desserts (see also Ice-cream)
   almond cream 166
   apple crumble 155
   apple muffin 156
   apricot dacquoise 171
   apricot, raisin bread and butter pudding 158
   baked apples 162
   baked carrot pudding with citrus sauce 159
   baked pears 161
   black cherries flambé 176
   chocolate malted soufflé 166
   chocolate soufflé 163
   Christmas pudding for four 160
   Cointreau soufflé 163
   cold fruit soufflé 165
   crème brulee 162
   crème caramel 162
   crepe suzettes 163
   double-thick chocolate malt 176
   frozen chocolate meringue 173
   frozen mousse, basic method 172
   fruit and nut mousse 173
   fruit and nut trifle 167
   fruit Ricotta pots 169
   fruit salad crumble 156
   glazed nectarines in orange juice 168
   glazed oranges 168
   guava caramel soufflé 166
   hazelnut pavlova 172
   hot Christmas mince sauce 175
   lemon creams 226
   light chocolate mousse 165
   malva pudding 159
   meringue, basic method 170
   meringue Italienne 170
   meringue Suisse 170
   Miler Howe apple and berry pie 156
   nutty apple crumble 154
   oil apple crumble 155
   old Cape brandy pudding 158
   orange or mineola jelly 168
   pareve desserts 164, 165, 172
   pavlova 170
   pears in wine 169
   praline mousse 173
   rhubarb with orange sago creams 160
   rich chocolate mousse 164

Russian crepes 164
Tarte tatin 157
Tiramisu 167
Yoghurt apple cream 169
Devilled marinade for chicken breasts 109
Dhansak-chicken with vegetables and lentils 106
Doner kebab 67
Double-thick chocolate malt 176
Doughnuts 244
Drinks
    fruit punch 180
    home-made lemonade 181
    mulled wine 180
    sangaria 180
Duck, roasted 99
Dumplings 79, 106

E

East Indian peas and red cabbage 133
Easter lamb andros 66
Egg and cheese dishes
    apple and Cheddar filling for omelettes 118
    avocado and bacon filling for omelettes 118
    cheese, onion and tomato filling for omelettes 118
    flat courgette omelette 118
    fondue a la beer 118
    fried eggs 117
    omelette 117
    vegetable frittata 118
Eggplant (*see* aubergines)
Eggs, fried 117

F

Falafel 12
Farfel 36
Feta and courgette filling for crepes 15
Feta and spinach stuffing for chicken breasts 109
Fillet in phyllo pastry 231
Fish
    bake with sour cream or yoghurt 53
    bake, basic 52

baked line fish en papilotte 51
baked fish au gratin 51
basics of cooking 43
basting for 46
braaiing of 45
cakes 46
casserole, basic (*see* bake, basic) 52
crisp batter for fried fish 45
crumb coating for fried fish 45
filleting 44
frying 44
gefilte fish 56
ginger pineapple yellowtail 55
Greek flavour fish bake 52
Grilling 44
herbed fillets 53
hints 43
Israeli crispy fried fish 50
Jeans fish bake 53
Kabeljou biryani 55
kingklip sesame gujons 49
marinades 48, 49, 57
Milanese 48
pan-fried line fish with julienne vegetables 48
pickled 56
poached line fish with lemon sauce 54
poaching 45
roast line fish 50
seasoned flour for fried fish 44
smoked fish Shanghai 57
soft batter for fried fish 44
spicy red fish 48
stock 45
sweet and sour baste 46
thin batter coating for fried fish 44
types of 43
yellowtail biryani 55
Flaky pastry 221
Floating cheese islands 18
Florentines 216
Fondue a la beer 119
Foolproof kneidlach 36
Four-egg butter cake 201
French onion soup 37
Fried rice, basic method 142
Frozen chocolate meringue 173
Frozen mousse, basic method 172
Fruit
    and nut mousse 173
    and nut trifle 167
    cake (rich) 204

    poached 169
    punch 180
    Ricotta pots 169
    salad crumble 156
    scones 192
    sorbet 174
    soufflé, cold 165
Fudge
    Chocolate 183
    creamy microwave 183
    economical 182

G

Gammon, glazed 75
Garlic and herb butter 145
Garlic sauce 145
Gateau au chocolate 210
Gateaux
    Amsterdammetjies (*see* Bocconotti) 212
    Bocconotti 212
    chocolate butter cream 211
    gateau au chocolate 210
    sachertone 211
Gefilte fish 56
Gelatine 165
Ginger, orange and honey sauce for chicken casseroles 112
Ginger pineapple yellowtail 55
Ginger spice biscuits 214
Gingerbread, sticky squares 208
Giouvetsi 73
Glace grapefruit peel 179
Glazed nectarines in orange juice 168
Glazed oranges 168
Gnocchi, potato or spinach 129
Goulash soup 38
Granadilla cake 201
Granola bars 184
Granola crunch 185
Grape jam 178
Greek pot-roasted lamb with orzo (*see* Giouvetsi) 73
Greek tzatzikki 10
Greek yoghurt 186
Green beans, carrots and salami 132
Green fig preserve 179
Green pepper dolma 116
Gruyere com fritters 137
Guacamole 146
Guava caramel soufflé 166

H

Haddock and spring onion soufflé 17
Haddock and spinach bake 127
Ham and mushroom sauce for pasta 123
Hamburgers 71
Hazelnut pavlova 172
Herb dumplings for steak and kidney with vegetables 79
Herb marinated Mozzarella and tomato 25
Herbed fish fillets 53
Herrings
    chopped herring 58
    Danish herring 59
    Pickled 58
    pineapple herring 59
Hollandaise sauce 145
Homemade lemonade 181
Honey
    and lemon sauce for chicken casseroles 112
    and mustard salad dressing 19
    nougat 184
    orange and ginger sauce for chicken casseroles 112
    teiglach 220
Hong Kong chicken wings 101
Hot and sour soup 45
Hot Christmas mince sauce 175
Hot cross buns 244
Hot raw beetroot 32
Hot tomato relish 10
Hot water pastry 229
Hummus 9
Hungarian goulash 76

I

Ice cream
    Bar one sauce for 175
    butterscotch sauce for 175
    chocolate caramel sauce for 175
    chocolate fudge sauce for 208
    Christmas mince sauce for 175
    frozen chocolate meringue 173
    fruit sorbet 174
    lemon sorbet 174
    orange banana sauce for 175
    strawberry sorbet 174
    strawberry and sour cream 174

Imam Bayildi 136
Indian vegetable curry 114
Israeli crispy fried fish 50
Italian
    almond rusks 217
    coffee biscuits 216
    pizzas 237

J

Jams
    apple jelly 179
    apple and mint jelly 178
    basic method 177
    glace grapefruit peel 179
    grape jam 178
    green fig preserve 179
    kumquat marmalade 178
    kumquat preserve 179
    lime marmalade 178
    marmalade 178
    microwave method 177
    mint jelly 179
    pomerantzen 179
Jams Californian vegetables 131
Jam squares 215
Jeans fish bake 53
Julienne carrots and turnips 133

K

Kabeljou biryani 55
Kassler bigarade 74
Kichel 219
Kingklip in phyllo pastry 231
Kingklip sesame gujons 49
Kitke 240
Kneidlach 36
Koeksisters 245
Kreplach 36
Kumquat marmalade 178
Kumquat preserve 179

L

Labaneh 11
Lamb
    Bobotie 82
    cabbage bredie 77
    Easter lamb andros 66
    Giouvetsi 73
    in phyllo pastry 231
    Lasagne 81
    lemon honey, roasted or braaied 65
    mince sauce for lasagne 81
    Moussaka 82
    Navarin of 77
    Raan roasted 66
    roasted with rosemary 64
    Schwarma 67
    spiced with spinach and yoghurt 80
    tomato bredie 77
Lammington squares 202
Lavash 242
Leek quiche filling 228
Leeks in tomato 31
Lemon
    and garlic chicken 104
    and honey sauce for chicken casseroles 112
    butter sauce 144
    cake 144
    chiffon cake 206
    creams 226
    curd filling for pavlova 171
    garlic sauce 144
    honey and mustard basting sauce for chicken 87
    honey lamb, roasted or braaied 65
    meringue pie 226
    sauce 149
    sauce (low fat) 153
    sorbet 174
Lemonade 181
Lentils
    and brown rice salad 26
    and rice 143
    and spinach salad 29
    in mild curry sauce 135
    spiced, with vegetables 115
    with Dhansak chicken and vegetables 106
Lettuce soup 34
Light cheese cake 209
Light chocolate mousse 165
Lime marmalade 178
Line fish
    pan-friend with vegetables 48
    poached with lemon sauce 54
    roast 50
Liver and onions in orange 71

Lokshen 36
Lower fat vegetable sauces
    Cheese 153
    Lemon 153
    Mushroom 153
    Orange 153
Low-oil salad dressings 20

M

Macaroni cheese 125
Mackerel, peppered filling for crepes 16
Mackerel, pepper salad 24
Madeira cake 204
Maize meal 141
Malva pudding 159
Marble cake 201
Marinated vegetable dressing 22
Marmalade 178
Marmaris Turkish fritters 138
Mayonnaise 146
Mayonnaise and buttermilk dressing 20
Meat
    (see also Beef, Lamb, Pork and Veal)
    Basic marinade for 63
    Braaing 62
    Casseroles and stews 62
    Cooking methods for 61
    Cuts of 60
    Dry roasting 61
    Dry roasting timetable 61
    Frying 62
    Grilling 62
    Pot roasting 62
    Simple gravies for 63
Meat patties in tomato sauce 83
Meat pies, small Russian 229
Mediterranean braaied vegetables 134
Mediterranean pickled cucumbers 181
Megaderra 143
Melba toast 8
Melktert 227
Meringues, basic method 170
    Suisse 170
    Italienne 170
Mexican chicken with fruit 107
Mezze table 9–14

Middle-Eastern salads
    aubergine in yoghurt 31
    butterbean salad 30
    leeks in tomato 31
Middle-Eastern cracker bread 242
Middle-Eastern starters 9–12
Mild and spicy Indonesian curried beef 76
Miller Howe apple and berry pie 156
Mince, spiced chilli 83
Mince sauce, basic 81
Mineola jelly 168
Minestrone 35
Mint jelly 179
Misto di mare with pasta 126
Mixed salad 12, 21
Mocha sauce for meringue 173
Mock chicken fat (schmaltz) 185
Monkey gland sauce 151
Moussaka 82
Mrs Joubert's versatile bikkies 214
Muesli 185
Muesli walnut squares 214
Muffins 185
    choc-chip 190
    date and bran 190
    raisin 190
    wholewheat bran 189
Mulled wine 180
Mushrooms
    and bacon sauce for chicken casseroles 112
    and cauliflower soup 34
    and chicken pie 223
    and ham sauce for pasta 123
    and oyster stuffing for poultry 86
    and spinach quiche 228
    and tomato sauce 151
    Dafna's hot jumped salad 22
    Pate 8
    quiche filling 228
    sauce, low-fat 153
    sauce, simple 149
    soup 34
Mussels in tomato sauce 47
Mustard and honey salad dressing 19
Mustard bread 238
Mustard salad dressing 20
Mustard sauce 150

N

Navarin of lamb 77
Nectarines, glazed in orange juice 168
Normandy apple tart 225
Nuts, roasted or spiced 184
Nutty apple crumble 154

O

Oat scones 192
Oil apple crumble 155
Old Cape brandy pudding 158
Oliebollen 245
Olive bread 239
Omelette with fillings 118
Onion soup, French 37
Onions and liver in orange 71
Orange
    and carrot soup 34
    banana sauce for ice-cream 175
    cake 201
    chiffon cake 206
    Christmas ring 203
    fruit ring 203
    ginger and honey sauce for chicken casseroles 112
    jelly 168
    juice for glazed nectarines 168
    sago creams with rhubarb 160
    sauce 149
    sauce, low-fat 153
Oranges, glazed 168
Osso bucco 78
Oxtail stew 80

P

Pallottole al butto 216
Pan-fried line fish with julienne vegetables 48
Paprika chicken 104
Pareve desserts 164, 165, 172
Parsley, chilli and garlic sauce 128
Parsley dressing 19
Pasta
    Arrabiata 128
    aubergine and tomato sauce for 124

avocado and garlic 122
chicken liver and bacon sauce
  for 124
Elaine's quick macaroni cheese 127
fish lasagne 127
haddock and spinach bake 127
ham and mushroom sauce for 123
home-made 122
macaroni cheese 125
Miki's salmon sauce for 122
Misto di mare with 126
pesto sauce for 129
Puttanesca 123
quick spinach and tuna pasta
  sauce 125
quick tuna noodle bake 125
spaghetti Siciliana 126
spinach gnocchi 129
tomato sauce for 123
tuna cannelloni 128

Pastry and tarts
(see also Phyllo pastry and Quiches)
  baking blind 220
  bourekas 222
  choux pastry 232
  Christmas mince wheel 222
  coconut tarts 227
  custard puffs 232
  custard slice 221
  fish in pastry 224
  hot water pastry 229
  melktert 227
  Normandy apple tart 225
  Ollie's chicken and mushroom
    pie 223
  pecan pie 226
  perogen 229
  pirozhki 230
  puff, flaky and rough puff
    pastry 221
  rich shortcrust pastry 224
  rolling pastry 220
  savoury pies 222
  shortcrust pastry 224
  simnel tart 225
  small Russian meat pies 229
  special lemon meringue pie 226
  sweet shortcrust pastry 225
  tarte au citron 226

Pates and dips
  Aubergine 7
  Cacik 10
  chicken liver 9
  chopped liver 9

Greek tzatzikki 10
hot tomato relish 10
hummus 9
labaneh 11
Mushroom 8
smoked aubergine 10
snoek 8
taramasalata 11
tuna mousse 12
Turkish tzatzikki 10
yoghurt cheese 11
za'atar 11

Pavlovas and meringues
  apricot dacquoise 171
  basic method 170
  hazelnut pavlova 172
  lemon curd filling for pavlova 171
  Meringue Italienne 170
  Meringue Suisse 170
  tropical fruit filling for pavlova 171

Pawpaw and avocado salad 28
Pea soup with apple and cumin 33
Pears
  Baked 161
  in chutney 182
  in wine 169
Peas, East Indian and red cabbage 133
Peas, curried cream of 33
Pecan pie 226
Pepper mackerel salad 24
Peppered mackerel filling 16
Pepsi's potato salad 24
Pepsi's tomato marinade for chicken
  breasts 109
Peri peri sauce 144
Perlemoen (abalone) 47
Perogen 229
Pesto sauce 129
Phyllo pastry
  chicken in phyllo 231
  fillet in phyllo 231
  kingklip in phyllo 231
  lamb in phyllo 231
  phyllo apple strudel 230
  savoury phyllo 231
  spanakopita 231
Pickled
  aubergines 181
  calamari 57
  cucumbers 181
  fish 56
  herring 58
  vegetables 181
Pilaf, chicken liver 120

Pineapple herring 59
Pirozhki 230
Pita breads and pizzas 236
Pizza, Italian 237
Pizza rustica 237
Poached line fish with lemon sauce 54
Polynesian chicken 102
Pomerantzen 179
Popovers 119
Poppy seed cake 203
Poppy seed cheese cake 210
Pork
  Chinese barbecued spare ribs 67
  Glazed gammon 75
  Kassler bigarade 74
  Sweet and sour 70
Pot-roast chicken in ginger ale 97
Pot-roast turkey in orange 99
Potage bonne femme 34
Potato gnocchi 129
Potatoes
  Baked 138
  Brabant potatoes 140
  crispy potato skins 141
  curried potato salad 24
  Dauphinois potatoes 130
  Fritters 139
  Latkes 139
  Quick Dauphinois potatoes 140
  Roasted 138
  Rosti 140
  Russian potato salad 26
  Salad 24
  Swiss potato cake 140
  twice-fried potato chips 139
  Vichyssoise 33
  Wendy Roger's Irish potato
    bread 141
Poultry
  Whole birds 85
  Trussing of 85
  Butterflying 86
  Cooking times 86
  Flavouring 86
  Gravy for 86
  Stuffing's for 86
  Dry roasting 88
  Pot roasting 97
Poultry Portions
  Dry heat cooking 100
  Frying 100
  Grilling 100
  Roasting 87
  Stews and Casseroles 102

Praline mousse 173
Prune and sweet potato stuffing for poultry 86
Puff pastry 221
Pumpkin
　Baked 136
　Fritters 137
　Soup 33

Q

Queen's biscuits 216
Quiches
　asparagus filling for 228
　cheese pastry base 227
　leek filling for 228
　mushroom filling for 227
　onion filling for 228
　quiche lorraine filling 228
　spinach filling for 228
　wholewheat spinach and mushroom 229
Quick tuna noodle bake 125

R

Raan roasted lamb 66
Rabie's chicken curry 105
Raisin bread 243
Raisin bread, apricot and butter pudding 158
Rare roast fillet 64
Ratatouille 136
Ratatouille, cold salad 29
Rendang 76
Rhubarb with orange sago creams 160
Rhubarb, poached, in orange 160
Rice
　and lentils 143
　aromatic basmati rice 142
　basic Italian risotto 120
　chicken and seafood jambalaya 121
　chicken liver pilaf 120
　curried salad 24
　fried rice 142
　megaderra 143
　simla rice 142
　vegetarian rice mould 119
Rich brown stew 75
Rich chocolate mousse 164

Rich fruit cake 204
Rich shortcrust pastry 225
Ricotta and baby marrow stuffing for chicken breasts 110
Ricotta fruit pots 169
Risotto, basic Italian 120
Roast duck 99
Roast lamb with rosemary 64
Roast turkey 98
Rosemary roast beef 64
Rough puff pastry 221
Rouille sauce 40
Roulade 17
Roux, black 41
Roux-based sauces 147
Rusks
　bran molasses rusks 218
　buttermilk rusks 219
　Miki's Italian almond rusks 217
Russian cabbage soup 39
Russian crepes 164
Russian potato salad 26
Rye bread, dark 236

S

Sachertorte 211
Sago creams 160
Salad dressings
　blue cheese 19
　curry 20
　honey and mustard 19
　low-oil 20
　marinated vegetable 22
　mayonnaise and buttermilk 20
　mustard 20
　parsley 19
　sweet basil 19
　yoghurt 20
Salads
　apple and avocado 28
　aubergine in yoghurt 31
　baked bean salad 30
　beer coleslaw 28
　beetroot 27
　brown rice and lentil 26
　butterbean salad 30
　butternut salad 30
　cabbage with caraway and bacon 27
　Caesar 21
　cauliflower and walnut 28

　cold ratatouille 29
　couscous 25
　cracked wheat 27
　curried chicken 23
　curried potato 24
　curried rice 24
　Dafna's hot jumped mushroom 22
　herb marinated Mozzarella and tomato 25
　hints for perfect 18
　leeks in tomato 31
　lentil and spinach 29
　mixed 21
　pawpaw and avocado 28
　pepper mackerel 24
　Pepsi's potato 24
　Russian potato 26
　sausage and cheese 23
　Tabbouleh 27
　three bean salad 30
　tossed 22
　Waldorf 23
Salami stuffing for poultry 86
Salami with green beans and carrots 132
Sally's pickled vegetables 181
Salmon sauce for pasta 122
Salsa cruda 147
Samp and beans 115
Sangria 180
Sauces for pasta
　Alfredo 123
　Arrabiata 128
　pesto 129
　salami and chilli 123
Sauces (various)
　Aioli 147
　Apricot Brandy 161
　Arrabiata 128
　Aubergine and tomato 124
　Avocado 146
　Avocado and garlic 122
　Bacon and chicken livor 124
　Bacon and mushroom 112
　Bar one 175
　Béarnaise 145
　Béchamel 148
　Bigarade 112
　Blue cheese 149
　Brandy butter 161
　Brown butter 49
　Butterscotch 175
　Casserole sauces 112
　Cheese sauce 148

Chocolate caramel 175
Chocolate fudge 208
Cooked yoghurt 147
Cream and white wine 148
Creamy blue cheese 150
Creole 152
Espagnole 150
For pasta 128, 129
Garlic and herb 145
Guacamole 146
Hollandaise 145
Hot Christmas 175
Lemon 149
Lemon butter 144
Lemon garlic 144
Low fat cheese 153
Low fat lemon 153
Low fat mushroom 153
Low fat orange 153
Mayonnaise 146
Monkey gland 151
Mushroom 149
Mushroom and ham 123
Mustard 150
Orange 149
Orange Banana 175
Pepper 68
Peri Peri 144
Pesto 129
Puttanesca 123
Salmon 122
Salsa cruda 147
Sour cherry 142
Spicy cheese 148
Spinach and tuna 124
Sweet and Sour 151
Tartar 146
Tomato (basic) 123
Tomato mushroom 151
White (basic) 148
Sausage, smoked gumbo with chicken 41
Sausage and cheese salad 23
Savoury muffin 190
Savoury phyllo 231
Savoury pies 222
Savoury sweet potato 136
Schmaltz 185
Schwarma 67
Scones
  bacon scones 192
  basic method 192
  cheese scones 192
  fruit scones 192

oat scones 192
wholewheat scones 192
Seafood
  abalone (perlemoen) 47
  and chicken jambalaya 121
  basics of 47
  calamari 47
  calamari in tomato sauce 54
  crayfish (South African rock-lobster) 47
  filling with Hollandaise sauce for crepes 15
  mussels 47
  mussels in tomato sauce 47
  perlemoen (abalone) 47
  pickled calamari 57
  prawns 47
  sauce for pasta 126
  sesame fried prawns 49
Seed bread 239
Serious cheese cake 209
Shortbread 215
Shortcrust pastry 224
Simla rice 142
Simnel tart 225
Smoked aubergine pate 10
Smoked fish Shanghai 57
Snoek pate 8
Soft milk bread 240
Sorbets 174
Soufflés
  basic cheese 17
  courgette roulade with cream cheese and smoked salmon 17
  floating cheese islands 18
  haddock and spring onions 17
Soups
  bean soup augier 38
  Borscht 37
  Bouillabaisse 40
  butternut 33
  carrot and orange 34
  cauliflower and mushroom 34
  celery 34
  chicken 35
  chicken and smoked sausage gumbo 41
  courgette and Brie 33
  court bouillon (stock) 40
  cream of tomato 34
  cream of vegetable 33
  curried cream of broccoli 33
  curried cream of peas 33
  French onion 37

  Goulash 38
  Hints for 32
  hot and sour soup 42
  kneidlach in 36
  lettuce 34
  lokshen, farfel and kreplach in 36
  miinestra 35
  minestrone 35
  pea soup with apple and cumin 33
  potage bonne femme 34
  pumpkin 33
  rouille sauce 40
  Russian cabbage 39
  special cream of mushroom soup 34
  stock cubes, use of 32
  sweet and sour beetroot 37
  Vichyssoise 33
  Waterblommetjie 34
Sour cherry sauce 152
Sour dough bread 241
Spaghetti Siciliana 126
Spanakopita 231
Spice chiffon cake 207
Spiced lamb with spinach and yoghurt 80
Spiced lentils with vegetables and yoghurt 115
Spiced nuts 185
Spicy chilli mince 83
Spicy red fish 48
Spicy Southern fried chicken 101
Spicy soy sauce for chicken 87
Spicy yoghurt marinade for chicken breasts 109
Spicy yoghurt sauce 52
Spinach
  and feta cheese stuffing for chicken breasts 109
  and haddock bake 127
  and lentil salad 29
  and mushroom quiche 228
  and tuna pasta sauce 124
  gnocchi 129
  Spanakopita 231
  quiche filling 228
Spring chicken casserole with parsley dumplings 106
Starters
  aubergine rolls with basil cheese 13
  aubergine pate 7
  basic cheese soufflé 17
  cacik 10
  cheese blintzes 16

chicken liver pate 9
chopped liver 9
courgette and feta crepe filling 15
courgette roulade with cream
    cheese and smoked salmon 17
crumbed vegetables 14
falafel 12
floating cheese islands 18
Greek tzatzikki 10
haddock and spring onion
    soufflé 17
hot tomato relish 10
hummus 9
labaneh 11
mixed salad 12
mushroom pate 8
pawpaw, avocado and chicken 28
peppered mackerel crepe filling 16
quick tuna noodle bake 125
seafood crepe filling with
    Hollandaise sauce 15
smoked aubergine pate 10
snoek pate 8
stuffed mushrooms and
    Hollandaise sauce 13
taramasalata 11
tehina salad dressing 13
tomato sauce 14
tuna mousse 12
Turkish salad 10
Turkish tzatzikki 10
wholewheat sesame crepes 15
yoghurt cheese 11
za'atar 11
Steak and kidney with vegetables and
    herb dumplings 79
Steak in red wine 78
Steak with pepper sauce 68
Sticky gingerbread squares 208
Stir-fried chicken with almonds 111
Strawberry and sour cream
    ice-cream 174
Strawberry sorbet 174
Stuffed
    chicken in orange caramel sauce 97
    green peppers 116
    smothered beef 72
    mushrooms and Hollandaise
        sauce 13
    vegetables 13, 84, 116
Sweet
    and sour beetroot soup 37
    and sour pork 70
    and sour sauce 151

    and sour stuffed cabbage 84
    shortcrust pastry 225
    potato and prune stuffing for
        poultry 86
    potato, savoury 136
Sweets
    caramel popcorn 183
    chocolate fudge 183
    creamy microwave fudge 183
    economical fudge 182
    granola bars 184
    honey nougat 184
    toffee apples 183

T

Tabbouleh 27
Taramasalata 11
Tarte au citron 226
Tarte tatin 157
Tarts (see Pastry)
Tehina salad dressing 13
Teiglach, honey 220
Three-bean salad 30
Three-egg butter cake 202
Tiramisu 167
Toffee apples 183
Tomato
    and aubergine sauce for pasta 124
    and cabbage casserole 133
    and herb marinated Mozzarella 25
    bredie 77
    cheese and onion filling for
        omelettes 118
    leeks in 31
    marinade for chicken breasts 109
    mushroom sauce 151
    sauce for bitkis 83
    sauce for calamari 54
    sauce for mussels 47
    sauce for pasta 123
    sauce for tuna cannelloni 128
    sauce with aubergines 14
    soup 34
Tossed salad 22
Tropical fruit filling for pavlova 171
Tuna
    and spinach pasta sauce 125
    cannelloni 128
    mousse 12
    noodle bake 125

Turkish
    salad 10
    stuffed chicken 88
    tzatzikki 10
Turkey
    pot-roast in orange 99
    roast 98
Turnips and julienne carrots 133
Two-day oxtail stew 80
Tzatzikki 10

V

Veal
    Marsala 68
    Osso Bucco 70
    Wiener schnitzel 78
Vegetable frittata 118
Vegetable side dishes
(also see Potatoes)
    aubergines in tomato 135
    baby beans with red pepper 132
    baked butternut 136
    baked pumpkin 136
    broccoli Roman style 133
    butternut fritters 137
    butternut in sour cream 135
    cabbage and tomato casserole 133
    casserole 114
    chunky vegetable stir-fry 131
    East Indian peas and red
        cabbage 133
    green beans, carrots and
        salami 132
    Gruyere corn fritters 137
    hot raw beetroot or baby
        marrows 132
    Imam bayildi 136
    Jams Californian vegetables 131
    julienne carrots and turnips 133
    lentils in mild curry sauce 135
    marmaris Turkish fritters 138
    Mediterranean braaied
        vegetables 134
    Pickled 181
    Potjie 134
    pumpkin fritters 137
    roast ratatouille 136
    savoury sweet potato 136
    serving of 130
    stir-fried 130
    with sauce aioli 132

Vegetable soup, cream of 33
Vegetable potjie 134
Vegetarian main courses
    Casserole 114
    green pepper dolma 116
    Indian vegetable curry 114
    rice mould 119
    samp and beans 115
    spiced lentils with vegetables and yoghurt 115
    stuffed cabbage leaves 116
    stuffed green peppers 116
Vichyssoise 33

W

Waffles 191
Waldorf salad 23
Walnut muesli squares 214
Waterblommetjie soup 24
White bread 235
White sauce, basic method 148
White wine and cream sauce 148
Wholewheat
    bran muffins 189
    bread 234
    scones 192
    sesame crepes 15
    spinach and mushroom quiche 229
Wiener schnitzel 70

Y

Yeast baking
    American deep corn pizzas 238
    Babke (cinnamon loaf) 243
    Beigels 240
    Boolkes (cinnamon buns) 242
    bun dough, basic method 242
    Chelsea buns 244
    choc-pecan wheels 244
    Copenhagens 243
    Crumpets 191
    dark rye bread 236
    doughnuts 244
    general hints 233
    hot cross buns 244
    Italian pizzas 237
    Kitke 240
    Koeksisters 245
    Lavash 242
    Methods 232
    Middle-Eastern cracker bread 242
    mustard bread 238
    oliebollen 245
    olive bread 239
    pita bread and pizzas 236
    pizza rustica 237
    raisin bread 243
    seed bread 239
    soft milk bread 240
    sour dough bread 241
    white bread 235
    wholewheat bread 234
Yellowtail biryani 55
Yoghurt
    apple cream 169
    cheese 11
    cooked for spiced lentils 115
    dressing 20
    Greek 186
    spicy sauce 52
Yorkshire pudding 191

Z

Za'atar 11